1971

W9-DDD-210

This book may be kept

FOURTEEN DAYS

A fine will be charged for each day the book is kept overtime.

AP 13 '72			
AP 27 72			
MY 11 '72	*fr. pd.*		
GAYLORD 142			PRINTED IN U.S.A.

Peace in Their Time

PEACE IN THEIR TIME

Men Who Led Us In and Out of War, 1914-1945

BY

EMERY KELEN

DRAWINGS BY DERSO & KELEN

19  63

New York : Alfred·A·Knopf

L. C. catalog card number: 63–9152

THIS IS A BORZOI BOOK,

PUBLISHED BY ALFRED A. KNOPF, INC.

FIRST EDITION

TO

Derso, my shipmate

"I like to think of caricature as no more nor less than the attempt to read inner characteristics into outward appearances. . . . The process has had as much to do with serious portraiture as with comic entertainment. . . . An obsession with personality is necessary for true caricature."

DRAPER HILL

Contents

I	*Death of an Archduke*	3
II	*My Personal Revolution*	24
III	*In and Out of the Red*	42
IV	*Schellingstrasse, 41*	62
V	*Peace Motions*	87
VI	*The Courting Years*	123
VII	*Locarno Idyll*	152
VIII	*The League Around the League*	178
IX	*Prelude to Pearl Harbor*	202
X	*I Must Reduce Myself to Zero*	239
	INTERMEZZO	277
XI	*Summer in Venice*	283
XII	*Désarroi de l'Esprit*	312
XIII	*The Umbrella Age*	325
XIV	*Early Pioneering Days*	355
XV	*The Home of the Brave*	373
XVI	*Revival in the San Francisco Opera House*	400
	INDEX	*follows* 444

Peace in Their Time

*The author wishes to express his thanks
to E. B. Stone for editorial assistance*

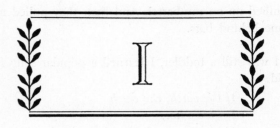

Death of
An Archduke

WHEN the stork dropped me down the chimney into my mother's lap, she did not suspect that she was faced with the rearing of a caricaturist; and neither did I. God made me good, but the capsized values of our time, a world war, and a salvo of revolutions made a jester out of me.

I was a little boy who told my mother that if ever there was a war I'd climb on a barrel and shout: "Enemy! I want to make peace with you!" Whenever guests came, I got up on a parlor chair and went into my act, drawing cries of praise for my peace-loving tendencies. But in 1914, I marched into the army like everyone else, and fought for three and a half years before I finally climbed up on my barrel. And then they pulled me down and put me behind bars.

When I was still a toddler, I learned a popular song from our rustic maid:

> If the earth, the earth
> Is God's hat,
> Our fatherland, our fatherland
> Is the bouquet on it.

In this way I learned very young that it was an honor and a privilege to have been born a Hungarian, and I loved my land, where there were clouds of geese to chase, so white across the flowery fields, and a river where I caught minnows with a bent pin; I snuffed up the scent of wild camomile, and collected the pollen of jasmine on the tip of my nose. By and by I was taught to extend this primitive attachment to the nest to other peoples: Slovaks, Wends, Carpatho-Russians, Rumanians, Saxons, Swabians, Serbs, Croats, Sokacs, Bunyevacs, all who lived within the boundaries of thousand-year-old Hungary and shared with me the right to call themselves Hungarians.

In school I learned that we had bought our beautiful land rather cheap from a Slavic king named Szvatopluk for a loaf of bread, a hunk of salt, and a white horse. My head was crammed with dates of battles we had won, peace treaties we hadn't kept, the exact duration of the reigns of Kings Bela the First, Second, Third, and Fourth, who were not considerate enough to live consecutively, but came sandwiched between Louis's and Andrews, to the confusion of future generations. And there were martyrs, such as St. Gellert, who brought Christianity to our pagan forefathers and for his efforts was stuffed in a barrel lined with nails and rolled down a mountain into the Danube; and heroes, such as Paul Kinizsi, who, after a battle, held one dead Turk between his teeth and one in either hand and danced while knocking the heads together; and scoundrels, such as Gyorgy Dozsa, who in

1514 led a peasant revolt against the feudal landlords. The landlords caught him, sat him on a flaming throne, topped him with
a red-hot crown, and roasted him to a turn, so that his followers—
who had been provided with pincers—could be made to dine on
him piecemeal.

With no adult Westerns and gangster films to corrupt my
young mind, a careful study of my country's history made me a
better patriot and a better man. I swore not to become a pagan
—or a saint—never to lead a revolt against landlords, but for my
country's sake to become a hero like Paul Kinizsi and have a
street—or better still, something to eat—named for me. We Hungarians have a delicious way of honoring the names of our great
men. For Janos Hunyadi, a gallant general of the Turkish wars,
we named a mineral water the laxative effect of which was recognized by the entire civilized world—the French call it *eau de Janos*.
For his son, Matthias Corvinus Rex, we christened a *Bierkeller* in
Budapest where from 10 a.m. to 4 p.m. you could have marvelous
smoked pigs' knuckles and short ribs with horse-radish sauce to
the glory of that monarch who, judging by the menu, fully deserved his cognomen, the Just. We flushed down these blessings
of our land with dark beer from a bottle that bore the image of
our first Apostolic King St. Stefan, crown, sceptre, and all.

Thus was old history planted in my heart and guts.

Once a gypsy at a fair said to his son: "Sit on that horse and
ride it around. I want to look at it." The son asked: "Shall I ride
it for selling or for buying?"

History is like that. You can write it for selling or for buying,
depending upon what you leave out or keep in, and how you in-
terpret the sequences of events. Hitler vowed in *Mein Kampf*
to rewrite the history of Europe on a racial basis. The Communists have already rewritten the history of Hungary, placing
Gyorgy Dozsa among the good guys. The history books of my
childhood were written along nationalistic and patriotic lines.

And the history I am now about to write is that of a caricaturist.
It will not deal so much with dates, or with the economic causes

of war, or with texts of treaties. It will try to sketch for you the
character of these years I have lived, and that so many others have
lived by the skin of their teeth. I'll do it as a caricaturist must—
through people's faces I have drawn, and what I've seen in them;
and odd events and observations which in some heavenly script
conference it was decided should be noted by caricaturists alone.

And yet I swear that this caricaturist's history book is no more
crooked than the rest!

I spent my childhood and youth in an amiable world such as
no crop of children have seen since: where war was only possible
in far-off places between boisterous Englishmen and savages; or
among the incorrigibly unstable people of the Balkans; but impossible to conceive among really civilized people like the Hungarians.

The doings of our politicians were ordered and stately as a
gavotte. None were called upon to face the nation, still less to
answer the awkward questions of youth wanting to know. In my
teens I opened my newspaper at the back to read the sports page,
and while I knew the tongue-twisting English names of center
halves who played for the Woolwich Arsenal and Manchester
United soccer teams, I couldn't have told you the name of my
country's prime minister. Sometimes I'd browse as far as the middle section, where I'd learn that a former member of the Hungarian parliament had been bitten by a mad dog; or that, in a
remote village, pigs had devoured a "Witness of the Glorious
Time"—which was what we called the surviving veterans of the
Kossuth Revolution. When the police apprehended a shipping
agent for attempting to induce the peasantry to emigrate to
America by telling them whopping lies about America being a
better land than ours, that was news. *Extra Hungariam non est
vita; si est vita, non est ita:* Beyond Hungary there's no life; and if
there's life, it's not like our life. This was a phrase well understood even by the dullest boys in our class.

Now and again we'd read that the maneuvers of the Austro-

Hungarian army had ended in total success. It was heart-warming to know that we won all our maneuvers. If we lost the world war, it is no doubt because our enemies did not take part in our maneuvers.

**THE AUTHOR AS A SCHOOLBOY
BY HENRY MAJOR**

We had goulash and gypsy music, rosy girls and golden wines, salami, soccer, and garden restaurants with red-checked tablecloths where pussycats slept in the sun. Certainly it was a bizarre idea for a Bosnian student named Gavrilo Princip to go to Sarajevo and shoot the heir to the Austrian throne!

Still, murder is murder and it's got to be punished. The night

war was declared on Serbia the streets were decked with flowers
and flags, and I and my friends carried Japanese lanterns and
rushed about shouting at the top of our lungs: "Down with the
swineherds," and we sang:

Wait, just wait, you dog-faced Serbia,
Never, but never, will you get Bosnia!

How could we know that behind all the halleluiahs lurked the
competition of Serbian pigs with Hungarian pigs on the world
market? Or the Pan-Slavic dreams of Serb jingo societies? Or the
Kaiser's ambitions in North Africa? Or Alsace, and Poincaré's
revenge? We just followed the brass band, picked up the hurrahs
where we found them, cheered and jeered, shouted and shrieked,
and did what youngsters do, demonstrated without knowing, because it is fun to be noisy in crowds. Only at night in bed I curled
myself up in fright, and wondered what would happen next.

What happened next was that troop trains began to roll, and a
staff sergeant was billeted on us who occupied my bed. I looked
with awe and envy at his brand-new Zeiss field glasses, and
thought that so long as we had such armament the Serbs would
never get Bosnia.

But they did. And after the troop trains had rolled out, hospital
trains rolled back, and our staff sergeant too came back to pay us
a visit—minus his field glasses and one leg.

Still, we didn't worry. We had the assurance of Kaiser Wilhelm
II, Emperor of Germany, that when the leaves fell from the trees,
our soldiers would come home victorious, and on every street
corner there was a poster showing our good old Apostolic King
Franz Josef I, in general's uniform, praying, his wise, bald head
bowed over his folded hands: "I have deliberated, and examined
everything."

One day another poster appeared next to that of the king, telling
me that I was wanted in the army. My father was an office hermit,
seldom seen on the street. But that day, for some reason, as I was
coming home from school I bumped into him.

"Father," I said, "I've just seen the poster. I have to go into the army."

He was so surprised that he answered me in German. *"Du bist verrückt!* You're crazy. They don't take children in the army!" Then he turned his back to me and said: "Go and do your duty." I stared at his back as he walked away, and it was the last time I saw him in the awesome guise of a father. The next time, he was a man whose son I was.

Mid-May 1915, the day Italy declared war on the Hapsburg Empire, found me in the dungeons of a seventeenth-century fortress on the Danube, where I had what is now called "basic training." This is a process of depersonalization which begins with dressing you up in a uniform that doesn't fit. Then they place you in the power of a wart-hog-faced sergeant who, by barking at you, forces you to make motions you would never perform in civilian clothes. The process continues until you realize that you are a worm. Then that same sergeant builds you up again into a soldier, teaching you how to pierce a straw man with a bayonet, extract it, run, and pierce another straw man until you fall down exhausted. He induces new conditioned reflexes in you so that you stiffen whenever you meet an officer, and pant with patriotic fervor whenever you hear someone beating with a couple of pieces of wood upon an ass's skin.

When I had become an expert straight man to my straw men, I was sent to an officers' training school to learn the higher arts of warfare. I was taught how to build a bridge where there was none, and how to blow up a bridge where there was one. And there, among my fellow cadets, I made a discovery: my beloved nest of Slovaks, Rumanians, Swabians, Poles, Ruthenians, Saxons, Serbs, Croats, and all the rest, was really a vipers' nest; none of them wanted to belong to thousand-year-old Hungary or gave a fig for calling themselves Hungarians. In fact, they considered that we were barbarians from the Asiatic steppes and that the friendliest thing we could do would be to go back where we came from. In retaliation, I came to understand that all Slovaks had stinking feet, that all Poles cheated at cards, that all Croats were traitors and all Ruthenians sissies. I learned never to pronounce the word Swabian without the adjective dumb, and, as for the Rumanians, it was necessary, if one shook hands with them, to count one's fingers afterwards to make sure none was missing. Tribalism ran as high as in the Congo. The famous Hapsburg melting pot had a few cracks in it.

I was on the threshold of a promising military career when a confounded German invented a sort of stovepipe that, with the help of compressed air, tossed winged mines at the enemy. The device had one minor flaw: sometimes the winged mine got stuck in the pipe and exploded. Once a group of eighteen Turks who had come all the way from Anatolia to study the instrument were blown to bits in such a mishap—including their commander, Sammy Effendi.

With two stovepipes and a detachment of Hungarians under my command, I was sent to South Tyrol to spread havoc among the Italians.

South Tyrol in April is a beautiful country. The sky is royal blue, the rocks pomegranate red, the snow melts in white patches, and from beneath the snow countless tender crocuses poke their blue noses. On God's majestic heights the prayer of singing birds sounds nearer and louder than anywhere else. Go there—but in peace! Alas, I was there in war, attached to an Austrian regiment waiting to go into action. One evening the order came to get ready to march, and dawn found us on the move, destination unknown.

After three hours' march we descended into a sweet valley, and there in a clearing of the woods we were lined up and told to stand, and we stood. For two solid hours and more we stood, when suddenly a bugle sounded, scaring the hell out of us and out of the entire choral society of warblers, finches, and yellow-bellied sapsuckers. At the edge of the forest a group of high-ranking officers oozed into sight. They were not bespectacled, cherry-nosed, potbellied homey Austrian generals, but sparkling, spick-and-span young men in impeccable uniforms, chatting, chirping, and winding through the trees as nonchalantly as if they were in a ballroom at the Hofburg. In the center of the group was a young cavalry officer whom I recognized, in a breath-taking second, as Charles I, Emperor of Austria and (as Charles IV) Apostolic King of Hungary, called "the Sudden," because he had popped on to the throne quite unexpectedly on the death of his uncle, Franz Josef I (the one who had examined everything). Husband of handsome Zita of Bourbon and Parma, father of Otto von Hapsburg, His Majesty was a pleasant-looking young man with weak, downward-slanting blue eyes and a small chin, and he sported a jaundice-struck mustache over a fleshy Hapsburg lip.

We had been galvanized to attention. Our commander stepped forward with an electric salute and in a voice that brooked no contradiction reported that we were twelve officers, six horses, and three hundred men.

Thereafter I witnessed the most embarrassing spectacle known to principalities and powers: a royal inspection. His Majesty stepped before the first officer and asked him in German: "How long have you been serving in this regiment, Major?"

"Twenty-four months, Your Imperial Majesty."

"Where did you earn your decorations?"

"In Volhynia, Serbia, and the Doberdo, Your Imperial Majesty."

"Very good, very good," replied the king, and saluted. He stepped before the next officer.

"How long have you been serving in this regiment, Captain?"

"Eighteen months, Your Imperial Majesty."

"Where did you earn your decorations?"

"In the South Tyrol, at Doberdo, and Lemberg, Your Imperial Majesty."

"Very good, very good," said the king, saluting again, and proceeding down the line.

This crawling horror was coming toward me. Twelve times, in precisely the same words, the stereotyped conversation was repeated—before every officer in the company—with the spanking-new officers bird-dogging behind. Then my king stood before me and my stovepipes at the end of the line.

The weather was sharp in the mountains, and I was wearing a windbreaker that partly covered my insignia of rank.

"How long have you been serving in this regiment, Lieutenant?" asked the king.

"I'm not a lieutenant, I'm only a cadet-aspirant," said I.

The effect was instantaneous. All the king's men turned into pillars of salt. His Majesty, uncued, fluffed his lines, lost the power of speech, and stood there looking right and left, an emperor with egg on his face. Then my stovepipes came to his rescue.

"What's that?" he asked, pointing.

"A mine-thrower, Your Imperial Majesty."

"Load it."

I motioned to the sergeant, who lifted one of the winged monsters out of its wooden casket and began to stuff it into a stovepipe. But the wretched thing wouldn't fit. The sergeant squeezed, pushed, screwed, sweated, and groaned—all in vain—and at the sight of his efforts the thought slunk into my mind that these winged monsters were wont to blow up, and if they did, my king and I, my men and his, would all join Sammy Effendi in Paradise. But I didn't say a word. I had caused enough trouble already.

After long minutes of fruitless exertion, the sergeant looked at me and said in Hungarian: "The wings are bent, sir."

"Never mind then," snapped King Charles, also in Hungarian, and turning to me he continued, in German: "*Auf Wiedersehen,* Herr Cadet-Aspirant, or whatever you are." And off he went, leaving me standing there like ten cents' worth of cheese strudel, ordered and then forgotten.

That evening I was called before my commandant. I stood at his door, cap under my arm, clicked my heels, and said with superb correctness: "Cadet-Aspirant Kelen humbly reports that he has entered the room." The commandant then delivered a speech in which he quoted generously from the Guidebook of the New York

Zoological Society, Jackass Edition. Oxen, apes, and insolent pups romped through his discourse, and he wound up by saying: "If the king calls you a lieutenant, you are a lieutenant; and if I call you an idiot, you are an idiot!"

A résumé of all this was placed in my personal file and for a long time it kept me from becoming an officer.

I have since tried to figure out what on earth inspired me to this singular behavior. Perhaps it was just dumb honesty that objected to being addressed by a higher rank than I deserved; or the boorishness of an introvert youngster faced with an oppressive situation; and perhaps it was something more than that. Perhaps in me there had already sprung to birth that seed of scorn for established authority that germinates in young hearts during every war and, after war, flourishes with uneasy names: Dada, Fauves, existentialists, beatniks, Balillas, Spartacists, yes, and rock-and-rollers; cracking with vehement life the firmest foundations of art, music, literature, the social order, and Empire itself.

Whatever rebellious impulse made me fling words back at a king, it was certainly a suicidal wish that led Herr Cadet-Aspirant Kelen, a son of the gentle *Puszta*, who had never before seen a mountain close up, to dig out some skis from the back of a log cabin and put them on. They fished me out of a brook with a broken ankle, and I had a blessed sojourn in the hospital before they sent me back to a town near Vienna to give lessons in—shall I tell you, or can you guess?—the care and handling of air-operated stovepipes.

There was in my new barracks a fragile, weedy staff sergeant. Whenever a recruit turned left instead of right, or whenever the staff sergeant noted trifles like a dirty button or a speck on a rifle butt, he would sigh deeply and with *Weltschmerz* all over his face mourn: "This is a misery." One night an enormous ammunition dump exploded half a mile from our barracks, a tower of fire raised the roof of the sky, and hundreds of missiles were catapulted into the air and pounded our camp, exploding as they hit the dirt. I did what three thousand others did: ran for my life in a nightshirt. In the demoniacal light we looked like ghosts fleeing a burning cemetery. The next day the camp was flat, dead bodies littered the litter. I met our staff sergeant on crutches, his foot bandaged, and he said to me: "This is a misery!"

And for once it was a misery. The mine-throwing operations of the Austro-Hungarian army, stovepipes and all, were wiped out. The Powers that ruled my destiny had to think of something else to do with me. For a while they just let me be, a sorry sight: an expert without the tools of his *expertise*. Finally, in kindness, someone promoted me to the rank of lieutenant and sent me off to the front to have another crack at the Italians.

In those days the Austro-Hungarian army had the habit of shipping men to the battlefront like sacks of potatoes from freight yard to freight yard. I was transferred from one command to another. I traveled on muleback, atop ammunition boxes, and on foot, never knowing where I would end up. All this was to confuse the enemy, who was presumably watching and listening.

But the enemy would have had to be deaf, dumb, and blind not to have noticed that hundreds of troop trains, full to bursting with Germans, had been converging in the direction of Tolmein, a little village on the Isonzo River. This was the first time German soldiers had appeared on the Italian front.

The Italians had entered the war in May 1915, exactly when I had. All this time they had been thrusting almost their entire force against the bridgehead of Gorizia, just down the river. In two and a half years, after eleven offensives, they had succeeded in occupying three mountains. On October 20, 1917, we were to launch an offensive—with the help of the Germans, who said we wouldn't have gotten anywhere without them—that would break through the front at Tolmein. In one night we would capture everything the Italians had gained, and more. We called this victory the Tolmein Breakthrough.

On the night of my arrival I hadn't a notion where I was. Twenty-one years later I found out. In 1938, en route to the

United States on board the SS *Champlain*, I met a young journalist named Martha Gellhorn, with whom I discussed Ernest Hemingway's autobiographical novel, *A Farewell to Arms*. I had heard of this novel, of course, but I hadn't read it; I even knew that the *mise en scène* was the battle of Caporetto, but I couldn't remember any such battle. It was Martha Gellhorn (later Mrs. Ernest Hemingway) who told me that what we called the Tolmein Breakthrough (after the village on our side of the Isonzo) was called, by the Allies, Caporetto (after the village on their side of the river). In war, the battle line separates not only two worlds but two nomenclatures.

So in 1917, I, a sack of potatoes with the rank of lieutenant, had come to fight the battle of Caporetto and to face, besides Hemingway, a military bandleader named Arturo Toscanini; Philip Noel-Baker, Nobel Prize winner; a bemustached sergeant in the medical corps, Angelo Giuseppe Roncalli, later Pope John XXIII; and doubtless thousands of others to whom it would have been far better to say: "Enemy! I want to make peace with you."

Six weeks before the battle began, I was attached to a Czech engineering battalion tucked away in a forest back of Tolmein. By night we sneaked to the front line to build barbed-wire fences. By day we slept in our log cabins. Now and again Hemingway and Company plastered our crossroads with an artillery barrage; otherwise life in the Tolmein forest could not have been improved upon: the autumn foliage was radiant.

Just one point in the landscape smoldered, smoked, and rumbled night and day under heavy shelling; but it was in the distance and no concern of ours.

This good life couldn't last. One night we were hauled out and marched off, destination unknown but darkly suspected as we dragged on in the melancholy October mist, the ominous rumble becoming louder at every step. Out of the amethyst dawn a snub-nosed outline emerged: Monte San Gabriele, the last position of the bridgehead at Gorizia. Its big brother, Monte San Michele, camel-back-shaped Monte Sabotino, and pyramidal Monte Santo, dark and heavy, were in Italian hands, and all held ghastly vigil over little San Gabriele. When a mouse burped on it, howitzers roared back.

How shall I bring to the mind's phantom life that mountain, which month after month had been churned by artillery fire? From a distance it looked like one of those gray coffin-shaped heaps of rubble one sees piled at the side of a road. Close up it was like Bald Mountain on Halloween, not a tree, not a blade of grass, but its crevasses were alive with men as gray as rocks, in macabre mimicry.

Half of the mountain was already in enemy hands; but a Hungarian *Honved* brigade held the other half. The pivot of our defense was a natural cavern that held three hundred men. This was the position the Italians had to take at any price.

The first night I was sent up Monte San Gabriele through a *Laufgraben*, a runway carved in the rocks, to knit a maze of barbed wire around the toothpicks that had once been a proud pine forest. The second night I was sent a bit closer to the cavern to do the same job. And so on, night after night, up San Gabriele, where there wasn't a trench, foxhole, or any kind of cover. Men lay in the open pretending to be rocks, and such was the confusion that one night I crashed into our own trembling sentinel, his gun going clickety-clack against the stone. If I hadn't hissed in Hungarian, I would now be smelling violets from the wrong end.

Still I was better off than the wretches in the cavern. At daybreak I could return to our camp, which was snuggled safe in a canyon, and snooze.

Then the ax fell. The Italians, unable to take the cavern, were undermining it in order to blow it up. An officer was urgently needed to build countermines. I was the officer.

Ever since I had joined the army a dark presentiment had festered in me that I would perish in the war. Now I had a full afternoon to trace how fate, in the last six weeks, step by step, had plotted my perdition. First I was safe in the forest of Tolmein, then on that damned *Laufgraben*, and now headed into a cavern which was to be blown to bits. For hours I lay in my tent in agony. A man who is involved in a sudden accident often sees his entire life pass before his eyes in a split second. I saw mine in slow motion that afternoon.

At sundown I set out with my orderly in the direction of the cavern. Our first visit was to the regimental command, to join others with the same black destiny. Then we had to wait for the right moment to sneak through the Italian artillery barrage. For artillery barrages have their rhythm, like the song of the cuckoo, and after listening a while, you can figure out the intervals when it is safe to make a dash. While I waited I was offered a mess kit full of black coffee, and I sat and studied the life around me.

The regimental headquarters was a cozy little place deep underground, with heating and electric lights. Compared to our soldiers' quarters, it was the Isonzo-Hilton. Field telephones buzzed, a telegraph went *tetee-tetee*, muddy messengers scuttled through the corridors. It was the nerve center of round-the-clock war-making.

A macaque-faced, redheaded artillery lieutenant with pansy-light steps sashayed along the corridor, back and forth, back and forth. "Lucky dog!" thought I. "Soon I'll be dead, but he'll be here, nice and warm, shaving, washing the mold out of his ears. Lucky dog!" His image scored my brain.

The fury of the artillery pounding subsided and we got the signal to dash up the road to the cavern—before the next barrage started. War flourishes at night. By day that road was deserted, but now it was coursing with life. Huddled shadows passed by; heavily loaded mules tiptoed alongside; shivering, cursing wounded were being carried from the cavern on stretchers. I stumbled over objects, fell into rain-filled bomb craters, my feet snarled in barbed wire. In the dark I couldn't know what I would hit or miss next. Then suddenly from the top of Monte Santo a blinding searchlight, a devil's eye, snapped on, turning night into day. A short *hoho!* stopped the mules; stretcher bearers dropped their loads and flung themselves to the ground. Life quick-froze on the road. For a while there was dead silence, then the pounding began. I lay on my belly, hugging the earth my mother, my head hidden up to my neck under the steel helmet. I heard the crack of guns, followed the squeal of the shells in the air, and shuddered as they hit, splitting trees, whacking up rock, tearing men and beasts to pieces with a thundering fracas. I lay there dumb under the haven of my steel helmet, my body with all its miracles vulnerable; yet that sardine can over my brain case lent me safety and confidence. It all goes to show that Darwin was wrong: man is really descended from the ostrich.

The fireworks took their bloody toll, the huge searchlight was turned off, just as you turn off a bathroom light; but for us it meant being born again. Like prairie dogs we tumbled out of our burrows, and with busy steps staggered in the dark toward the cavern.

The cavern had two entrances. At each was a machine gun on the ready, flanked by a phalanx of troglodytes with hand grenades in their fists. I climbed in. The horrible stench of a human stable seized me by the throat. In the flickering light a gray mass of damned souls was wallowing in the slough, like Doré's illustrations to the *Inferno*. Here and there one would drag himself to the entrance, and surrounded as we were, not daring to step out, the damned soul would let his trousers down, sit on one of the ammunition boxes, and under martial protection satisfy his urgent need.

The cavern was a natural formation in the rocks with a ninety-meter entranceway that crossed a general gallery at the back. The Italians sat thirty feet above the entrance—the height, perhaps, of your house. At sundown and at sunset they tried to break into the cavern. Our storm troopers received them with a shower of hand grenades, the machine guns rattled, and amid the pandemonium someone would shoot up a red rocket; and then our own artillery would open up on the entrance to the cavern until the Italians were chased off. This was routine, twice a day, fourteen times a week, sixty times a month. After the battle we shoved the dead out of the cavern, carried the wounded inside, and at the crosspath where the corridors met, a medical student with the rank of

corporal did what he could in the queasy candlelight. On rainy
days a large red puddle collected at the heart of the cross; and
around it, on stretchers, the wounded shivered and quaked, waiting
for nightfall, when they would be carried down San Gabriele.
Many bled to death on the shores of this crucible of blood.

After weeks of trying and failing to take the cavern, the Italians
were now intent on blowing us up. Once before, they had played
this trick, blowing up a whole mountain top they had failed to take
by ordinary attack. When I arrived, I heard them hammering on
the rocks and singing, because Italians can't even blow up a cavern
with three hundred men in it without making an operatic production out of it. Now and again, as they hammered, unseen cracks
must have opened in the rocks, because new cold drafts would
blow upon us and the singing sounded louder and nearer.

I made a survey of the situation and decided to wall in the en-
dangered areas. In case they should accidentally hammer through,
I built a machine-gun post in each wall, and asked also for flame
throwers so that we could receive the visitors *con brio*. I mined the
entrance, to blow the cavern up if we were forced to evacuate.

To build walls I needed rocks, cement, and water. Rocks we had
in plenty; cement was sent up by muleback and arrived, unless the
mules were shot to mincemeat on the way up. As for water, on
rainy days it ran down the walls, and if it didn't rain for a couple
of days I could always find water in the puddles at the crosspath
where the medical student cared for the wounded and where boys
like me were bleeding white. Muddy and bloody the water was,
but we were racing those hammers, and so I mixed cement with
my comrades' blood.

During those days our lives depended on the telephone line that
linked us to regimental headquarters at the Isonzo-Hilton down
below. The wire ran down the hillside between the rocks, and
under the heavy bombardment it got snapped several times a day.
A telephone linesman had to climb out, whether it was night or
day, follow the telephone wire, find the break, and mend it. He
was a shrimp-sized Hungarian peasant with a big Armenoid nose,

the legacy probably of Turkish ancestors, and a walrus mustache: one of those little men who usually marries a huge Queen Bee and to compensate for his size manufactures children. The telephone wire was his recurrent Calvary. As he crawled, time and again, out of the cavern, he would send up a whispered cry: "My God, my sweet God, when will this end?" But he crawled out, night and day.

The first couple of days in the cavern I spent in terror, ready to be blown up, but finally I tamed my heart, and I suppose I was no more agitated than when I sit in a New York taxi. All day long —or was it night?—we played poker. Unsure of an hour's life, we worried when we lost a year's pay in advance. When the Italians attacked, and the air pressure from the first hand grenade blew out the candle that stood in a bottle between us, we ran to the entrance to help defend the cavern. Those who came back, and not everyone did, picked up the cards and asked: "Who's dealing?"

And never believe that rats are not pleasant companions. They played gleeful tag over our feet, and in their love games twittered like swallows. If you look at rats as you would look at squirrels without bushy tails, you'll see them as friendly, intelligent, personable, well-disposed fellow creatures. Of course, our rats were not those neurasthenic big-city rats who sometimes take a desperate bite out of a baby; they were well-groomed, upper-income rats who fed on our dead.

How bizarre! In the South Tyrol and in the Tolmein forest, when war had a jolly face, I hated it; but now it had turned to me its hideous ass, it seemed as friendly as a brother. We endure so much and no more physical and mental stress; then come to a threshold of the mind beyond which indifference, if not insanity, changes compassion into hatred, fear into heroism. On this paranoid plane, the cavern on the San Gabriele was my alma mater, safe and good, and to make it perfect the sodality consisted of Hungarians. For don't suppose that our Austrian commanders sent Austrians to our cavern, any more than I, in their place, would have sent Hungarians. This college was strictly for the neighbors' kids. So in addition to Czechs, around me were my own folk, speak-

ing the tongue of tongues, and I was one of the pack and dwelt
in a mood that was a mad mixture of tribal solidarity, individual
sacrifice, collective self-defense, extended suicide, vengeance, and
the will to live. I knew the organic, baboonish oneness which
keeps wars going; it is heroism without patriotism, because in wartime patriotism shrinks back to the home front.

As nobly united as we were, in the very gorge of death, we
bickered among ourselves as baboons do. Full of lice, I lay on my
cot and scratched myself. A comrade-in-arms next to me said I was
scratching too loud and ordered me to stop. We worked ourselves
into a shouting argument, but this was the army, and he was a
first lieutenant and I was only a second, so in the end I was obliged
to let my lice have their way with me.

One day a staff sergeant came to the cavern. He said he was to
relieve me.

I climbed out, saw daylight again; but all was green—sky, ground,
my hands in front of my face—and not until hours later did my
eyes accept the spectrum. I was given permission to go to the adjacent town for a delousing ceremony, and as my foot touched the
warm bath water I heard myself saying aloud: "Thank you, Lord,
that I lived to see this day!"

The same night I was back again, this time atop San Gabriele,
to the left of the cavern. A harvest moon shone on a landscape
where there was no harvest. The night was quiet, but to the south,
in the valley that lay toward the Adriatic Sea, red and green rock-
ets arched through the sky, and a dull rumbling and a thousand
flickering fireflies on the ground told us that something was afoot.
Then to the north of us, in the mountain range near Tolmein, a
huge bonfire burst, painting the sky orange and violet, and then
another tower of fire, and another, five, six, seven at a time, and as
one sunk to cinders, new ones flared. The villages were burning,
munitions depots were bursting into flaming fury. The battle of
Caporetto was on, and row upon row of hell fire marked the fiery
footsteps of the racing war.

Well, we beat the Italians into *spumoni*, *gelati*, and *tortoni*. They ran for 150 miles, leaving 600,000 men behind. The morning after found me on my cot, feverish, sweating hot and cold. My orderly asked permission to search for loot in the Italian dugouts, and he brought me back the most precious gift, something I hadn't seen since the outbreak of war, my only glorious, golden wartime booty—a lemon—and I gobbled it up.

My high temperature persisted, and I was advised to go to the hospital, but I refused. I had lived through the misery; now I felt like visiting sunny Italy. First Monte San Gabriele by light of day. If there is a road to hell, it must look like the road to the cavern. For months the dead had not been buried. Corpses of Italians, Czechs, Hungarians in tattered uniforms of all colors lay scattered amid carcasses of mules, soup tureens, cement sacks, and barbed wire. One Italian soldier lay on his belly, with outstretched hands, the white bones sticking out of his fingertips. Somebody must have kicked his head off but had had the piety to place it nicely on his back, still in its steel helmet, staring to heaven. And farther on, in a puddle of mud, I found my little walrus-mustached telephone linesman, his chest torn wide open, his sweet God having answered him at last. Not long after me, Emperor Charles visited the place, and he wept, with good reason.

Now by daylight I saw Monte Santo, from which that devil's eye of a searchlight had directed death on us. Years later I learned that Arturo Toscanini had been on that mountain, leading a military band in the midst of bloody battle, and that he had been decorated for it.

In war one sees many dead men, but there is always one never to be forgotten. Passing the cavern on the Italian side of the road leading to Gorizia, I noticed a young man, not more than nineteen, lying on the mountainside. His head was gently tilted; his hand rested on his chest like that of a saint. No wound showed, no tear in his clothes, only his butter-colored complexion told me he was dead. His lips were gently open, showing a set of healthy teeth, and his face had the classic beauty Italy produces in remote

villages. I stood and mourned him because he was my age and
might just as well have been alive, as I was. When you can feel
such pity at the age of nineteen, then something in you has been
torn in two.

Because life is shaped like a corkscrew, the macaque-faced redheaded artillery officer whose pretty promenade I had so admired at
the Isonzo-Hilton crossed my path three times after the war. The
third time, in 1936, I met him at a cocktail party in Budapest. As
we shook hands I said to him: "In October 1917 you were an artillery officer at Monte San Gabriele. In June 1921 at eleven o'clock
in the morning you crossed the Theatiner Strasse in Munich. In
1928 you traversed the Jardin du Louvre in Paris in the company
of a young lady."

His jaw fell, his eyes popped, he stared at me as if I were a
necromancer. "B . . . but how . . . ? Do you know me?"

"Not at all. But once I wanted to be in your skin."

After my intimacy with rats I landed in an epidemics hospital
in Croatia with typhus, and lay for days watching my belly cave in
between the curved ranges of my iliac. At the edge of the hospital
grounds the crematorium worked incessantly.

By Christmas 1917 I was home with mamma, who with love,
care, and smoked pork built me up again. For the New Year,
Charles the Sudden awarded me the Cross of Military Merit,
Third Class. At about the same time my first drawing was published in a magazine called *Donkey*.

I've long since lost both medal and drawing. But what came
after the drawing is threaded to what went before the medal.

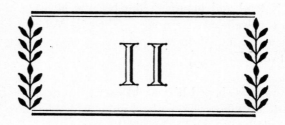

My Personal
Revolution

THE GREAT Russian physiologist, Anton Pavlov, wrote that the
dumbest animal, put in a cage, would try to get out.

My personal revolution began six months before the people of
the Hapsburg Empire began theirs.

The last months of the war were wretched ones for Hungary.
Ours had been a country where the minister of agriculture, water-
tank-sized Count Janos Hadik, could say: "The turkey is the sil-
liest bird! For one man it's too much, for two it's not enough";
and where there was a popular saying that "the river Theiss has
more fish than water." Now people had to stand in line all night
in order to buy a horse knuckle in the morning. In the barracks

we ate spinach made out of boiled nettles, and stale lumps of crumbly cornbread which we carried in our kepis. Meat had disappeared altogether, and once a week, on Friday, we got salted fish; but we smelled it coming on Wednesday.

In Budapest, deserters outnumbered stray cats, and our tough little General Baron Geza von Lukasich rounded them up and shot them like stray cats.

Once more I was ordered to the Italian front. After the horrors of San Gabriele this was bitter news, and I said so to a cartoonist colleague of mine, Tibor Polya.

"Why don't you do what my brother did?" he said. "He piled up all the straw mattresses in the barracks and set fire to them. They clapped him in the loony bin, and in six weeks he was a free man."

I dismissed this fantastic story with a smile.

I was dispatched to northern Italy by the usual potato-sack route. I don't know exactly where I arrived, but it must have been at the source of the Brenta River, for I washed my feet in a muddy torrent of that name. There was a village called Nemci. In front of the railroad station two huge shell craters copulated, and the village lay in the shadow of an angry blue mountain with low-flying white clouds cascading over the high peak. Behind the mountain I heard the bubbling bombardment of the war. It was April weather. Sudden showers drenched the village, and yellow mud sucked the feet of men and mules dragging themselves toward the battle line.

Then a munitions dump blew up, killing a boy I had known all my life. He was the son of our pork butcher, who used to come to our house every year to kill the pigs and do up the sausages.

I felt the war choking me again: the rats, the telephone man, the dead man with his head on his back, the corpses impaled on the barbed wire, the beautiful Italian boy. Deep inside me my feelings were coiled like snakes—fear, self-pity, self-defense, defiance, the conviction that the Kaiser didn't love me. All of this added up to tears of anger, and I remember standing there under the metal sky, shaking my fist in the air. Beyond the helpless confusion was an ardent wish to run away and be alone.

It was time to go mad or play mad. To this day I don't know how it was with me. I remember clearly every face, every setting, and what I did, but I can't recall having a clear thought.

I began by telling my orderly to burn down the house where we were billeted. He guffawed in my face, but froze as I grabbed him by the throat and told him that I was going to see the doctor and that when I came back the house had better not be there.

In front of the doctor's door, with its Red Cross flag, I stuck my walking stick into the ground and began to pace around it in circles like a horse threshing. I was dizzy and sick when the doctor examined me. "Walk straight," he said. I staggered. I asked him to assign me a separate room because the officer who shared my attic quarters had the air going in and out of his nostrils all night, and I had lain awake for three nights on account of this.

The doctor promised me a separate room. An ambulance was called, and I was dispatched to Trentino, guarded by two male nurses. It was hot and dark in the ambulance, and the roads were bumpy; I was shaken to a pitch of anger. I tore Emperor Charles's golden rosette from my cap, ripped off my officer's star and my decoration. I stomped on them, ground them under my feet. One of the male nurses made a sniggling sound: "Khee . . . khee."

In Trentino they put me in the fortress hospital in a solitary cell with bars. There common sense came seeping back into me. I was like a child who realizes he has misbehaved and is full of shame. The nature of the crime also dawned on me: I was guilty of *lèse majesté*, as well as rebellion and mutiny on the battlefront, actions that called for court martial, hard labor, and possibly the firing squad.

I was at a point of no return. From that time on I would be either mad or dead.

In a week I had grown a beard like Rasputin's. I told one of the doctors I hated my cell because the door had eyes, they were watching me, and this was an intrusion on my privacy. The good

little doctor was sympathetic, and one morning he showed up
flanked by six giant male nurses holding a strait jacket.

"We are going to send you to Innsbruck," said the doctor, "but
we will give you a little injection to make you comfortable on the
road."

"Don't you dare!" I growled, jumping out of bed and taking a
Neanderthal stance in the corner of the room. I must have been
an intimidating sight: big and hard, with a face half-hawk, half-
ape, covered with hair and snarling in my nightshirt. I saw the strait
jacket tremble in the hands of the male nurses.

"Let him have it!" commanded the little doctor. But they just
trembled.

"Don't come near me!" I yelled. "I'll go! I'll be glad to get out
of here!"

Somehow I talked them out of the injection and the strait
jacket. I don't know why I objected to them. After all, I was trying my best to be a lunatic, and the strait jacket was a sort of
bouquet for a successful performance. But my dignity rebelled
against it, and I'd rather they had broken every bone in my body
than have it on.

In the garrison hospital at Innsbruck I was shoved into a cellar
full of maniacs. My bed was separated from the others by a cage
made out of ropes. A chicken dinner was offered to me, and although I was ravenous, in order to make a good impression on the
doctor I threw it against the ropes, saying: "I don't eat pelican
meat."

The next day I was let out of my cage to make friends with the
neighbors. A childlike adult slithered up to me dressed in a striped
hospital robe and thrust under my nose a color print showing
Christ carrying the cross on His way to Golgotha. He whispered
with awe: "Jesus beard . . . I beard; Jesus robe . . . I robe. Seven
angels . . ." and he held his fist to his lips and went: "Toot . . .
tooot!" It was a simple and touching enunciation of faith. The
next moment an athlete in a nightshirt and a brown bowler descended upon him, tore the picture out of his hand, and ran, chased

by a crowd of howling dervishes. The tackle came to an end in the men's room, where the athlete installed the picture on a toilet seat and yodeled silly psalms to it amid the squawling, cursing, mocking congregation. "I pray . . . I good. You pray . . . you good," said my companion. Then he tooted again.

The faces of the insane fascinated me. I paid a guard to get me some grubby paper and a pencil and began to draw. My tooting

friend with his seven angels had a mildly rounded, egg-shaped head with a shining brow and no brow ridge. His bloodless lips, half open, were framed by sparse fuzz, and he had a wispy, two-pointed beard. His cold, blue watery eyes widened in amazement as if he were seeing a faraway vision. I have seen this mask of transfiguration on the face of many a saint in a museum. But the frail body of my friend had collapsed under the stress of ecstasy, and instead of a museum he had landed in a military asylum.

When I finished the portrait, I asked for his autograph, and he wrote a scraggly psalm, ending with *Amen*.

After Innsbruck, Salzburg. I was chaperoned en route by a rose-nosed Czech lieutenant. At each station he would leave the train and come back redder and redder in the nose. By the time we got to Salzburg it looked like sealing wax and he couldn't stand up.

I helped him to the hospital and pushed him ahead of me toward the doctor at the desk, but he was tongue-tied, unable to utter a word. "Beg to report, sir," I said. "I'm insane, and he is delivering me." I could have explained things the other way around, but I wasn't that crazy.

And so on, through Linz and Vienna, *Am Wege der Spitäler*— by the hospital route. I arrived in Budapest, Garrison Hospital 16, Closed Section. Here my case was to be thoroughly examined.

I found myself in some really choice company. There was a sinister Rumanian priest accused of high treason; a ruddy Swabian lieutenant accused of raping and shooting two women in Volhynia; a supply major who had run away with the regimental cash register; and a flock of minor criminals, all under psychiatric observation, teetering, as I was, between the firing squad and the madhouse. All day long we played cards. A poker party with a traitor, a rapist, and an embezzler, all with a few buttons loose, is not relaxing. The games always ended with wild accusations, shrieks, fights, near-murder. The priest had the reputation of being the worst cheat. "Blanket!" someone would shout, and we'd grab a blanket, wrap it around the priest's head, and paddle him. The guards would come and beat us back and remove the broken chairs.

The poker game was interrupted whenever a female visitor crossed the hospital grounds. My partners would jump to the windows, press their faces between the bars, and ululate, yowl, caterwaul. At first I held aloof from this undignified fun, but there's something contagious about a cockledoodledoo, and soon I was joining in with full throat, savoring the horror of those poor skittering women.

I was just beginning to feel that I had joined an excellent fraternity, and that if I hoed my onions properly I might be considered fit to be released in the custody of my parents, when a plug-ugly master sergeant penetrated our room, holding in his hand my cap, from which I had ripped His Majesty's rosette.

"Lieutenant," said he, pointing to the kepi, "where is your rosette?"

"The Italians shot it off," I stammered.

"We shall see," he said ominously and, with a sharp turnabout, left, snapping the iron bars shut behind him.

I was terrified. Had they seen through my little game? Was it possible that they were fooling me and not I fooling them? The very thought sent me out of my wits. I began to cry. For days I was lost in agony; I played no more poker; I slunk around in corners, couldn't eat or sleep for imagining the faceless, unfriendly Powers now coldly conferring, plotting my end.

Then the master sergeant came to see me again. He handed me my kepi with a brand-new rosette sewn on, and my golden star of rank resplendent on the purple velvet collar. He told me to pack and be ready to leave the following day. He had hardly closed the door when the rapist, the traitor, and the embezzler fell upon me, accusing me of influence peddling, treachery, double-dealing, and slipping bribes to the doctors. They thought I was to be set free, and were ready to kill me for it. I didn't sleep a minute that night. I wasn't sure what was to happen to me: would I be released or was I being dressed up chic and dandy to face a military tribunal?

The next morning I followed the master sergeant through the corridors of the hospital. We wound up at the front entrance, where an officer, dressed for traveling, my papers in hand, was waiting for me. He told me I was being moved to another hospital, in a little town in Slovakia. On the train he was very friendly, talked to me like an uncle, won my good will, calmed me down. But when we arrived at the new hospital, he handed me over to the doctor coldly, like any package safely delivered.

That little town in Slovakia, like other towns where national minorities live, had three names: Tyrnau for the Germans, Trnava for the Slovaks, and Nagyszombat for the Hungarians. The hospital where I had been deposited turned out to be merely a rest home for people with light nervous disorders. When I began to suspect that I had been promoted from the snake pit, I took fright and thrashed about wildly. "This is a madhouse," I screamed. "Get me out of here!"

"What makes you think this is a madhouse?" asked the doctor.

"There are bars on the window. Wherever there are bars on a window, it's a madhouse."

"Where do you want to go?"

"I want to go home to mamma."

Finally the doctor called two male nurses and sent me off with them. We walked back to the railroad station, but we didn't stop there. I asked one of the nurses: "Where are you taking me?"

"Home to mamma," he said.

He took me, in fact, to the other side of town, where we entered the Klosterka, the dual monarchy's most ancient military madhouse. Here was home indeed, my last stop.

The Klosterka was an eighteenth-century monastery, yellow and decrepit, with a moat crossed by a bridge, and high walls surrounding a garden centuries old. Nothing had been changed. Only a double-headed eagle was affixed over the door, and presto! the cloister became a military asylum. In cells where once monks had said their prayers, madmen now howled to the moon, and malingering Italian officers, prisoners of war, asked God to arrange for them to be sent home in exchange for Hungarian prisoners malingering in Italian asylums.

I was assigned a cell whose gray walls were covered with erotic scrawls and sex symbols with "Long live the Fatherland!" written over them. Some of these drawings must have been a hundred years old, since the walls hadn't been washed for at least that long.

There were two beds in the room, and so I had a roommate. When I arrived, it was an electric little Rumanian whose black whiskers, contrasting with his pale face, gave him the look of Mme Tussaud's model of Landru, the French butcher of women. For a while he seemed an ideal cellmate, a cheerful man who liked to play chess. But when the nights of the full moon came round and threw barred shadows on the floor, my roommate tossed for hours and couldn't sleep. One night around midnight he jumped up and, in his long nightgown that touched the floor, went to the window and with his two hands stretched above his head clutched the bars, pressing his face tightly between them like a wolf in a zoo, and looked intently at the moon. From under my covers I watched him. With eyes wide open, he stared fixedly for a while, tapping his feet; then he began to speak, at first softly, then louder, until he was howling: "I was always true to you . . . loved you truly . . . you loved me too. I swear I was faithful . . . maybe just a few times, just in my thoughts . . . but you . . . naughty little girl . . . but you ran away, you left me . . . why did you leave me? Come back! I beg you, come!"

By this time I was thoroughly frightened. You can never tell what a lovesick Rumanian will do even when sane. If he thought the moon was his ladylove, he might easily take a notion that I was her seducer. I got out of bed and ran from the room, and at my going he shouted: "Go! Go! You too!"

I went into the next room, where the Italian officers were wide awake, listening. "You're still alive? He hasn't choked you?" they exclaimed.

Hours later the Rumanian quieted down and I crept back. He was lying on his back on the bed, his arms folded under his head, and he looked at me with stricken eyes. "You spoke beautifully," I stammered. He didn't answer.

The following day he was taken to a solitary cell. He put up a struggle with the nurse, and a knife fell out of the nurse's pocket. The Rumanian pounced on it and knifed the nurse.

My next roommate was a drug addict with the face of an ant-eater, a physician who came equipped with syringes and a hidden supply of morphine. One by one the syringes were found and confiscated. He ended by swallowing the morphine, and when his last bottle of the drug was discovered—in my trunk!—the poor doctor went berserk and broke every piece of furniture in the place. He, too, was taken away.

In the Klosterka, for the first time in months, I was able to have coherent conversations with the malingering Italian officers. One of them had taken advantage of having been born in Assisi to pretend to be St. Francis. Another, a stocky lieutenant by the name of Maurice Saracco, had his chest covered with decorations cut out of paper and brightly colored with crayon. He insisted upon being addressed as "General," and if anyone dared to call him "Lieutenant," he staged a ruckus, screaming:

"Nix lieutenant! *General* Saracco!"

These elegant Italian officers, some wearing monocles, strolled along the corridors of the madhouse as if it were the Galleria in Milan. They walked with a theatrical swagger as if hundreds of feminine eyes were upon them. And just as strolling in the Galleria is contagious in Milan, so it was contagious in the Klosterka. Everyone strolled up and down the corridors, and soon I was doing the same. My black-bearded Rumanian roommate zigzagged through

the crowd with a chess board under his arm, begging someone for God's sake to sit down and play a little chess with him. Now and then we crashed into a miserable human skeleton who had sneaked up from the common soldiers' quarters; with tears in his eyes he begged the resplendent Italian officers for a furlough. He needed it desperately, for he had been in the Klosterka for fifteen years.

The highest-ranking officer in our midst was Kasimir von Kiss de Hunfalva, colonel of the Hussars. He came to us because his brains had finally dissolved in alcohol. Tall as an oak and proud as a Hungarian nobleman, he had a lordly face and a stiff mustache like a tomcat's in the mating season; but his nose was like a kosher pickle, and his porcine eyes were swollen.

When he arrived at the Klosterka, he was as furious as a pocket gopher. He immediately tore off his clothes and had to be placed in a solitary cell, where he sat, naked, by the window, cursing and singing obscene ditties or, in a voice shaking with sobs, that grand old Hungarian song:

> *In the pond of Tata*
> *A carp swims sideways,*
> *He swims in, he swims out,*
> *He swims out, he swims in,*
> *And makes my heart weep.*

But all good things must come to an end, and one day the colonel joined us on the Galleria, attired in spangled Hussar uniform, brass collar, spurred boots, and all.

My friendship with Colonel von Kiss began when I was permitted to join him in a daily stroll in the city, discreetly followed by a male nurse. Nagyszombat is an old city, nicknamed Little Rome because of its many churches. We walked through splendid arcades of chestnut trees, like lanterns against the summer sun, the colonel strutting like a conquering hero, with the clang of his spurs providing martial music. Only a slight vacillation of his step gave rise to the suspicion that he was a bit loose at his moorings. Still, he wasn't as crazy as he might have been. In the city he bought three boxes of matches for five kreutzers and sold them to the Italian officers for two kreutzers apiece, thus making a handy profit of one kreutzer. "Do you want to buy eggs?" he whispered to me. Only one reply is possible when a Hussar colonel asks you a question, and that is: "Yes, sir." It seemed that, because of his rank, the colonel was entitled to two hard-boiled eggs for breakfast, and he sold them to me for five kreutzers apiece. He explained these financial finaglings to me: "I want to put away a little capital for my old age."

Colonel von Kiss inspired a question in my mind that I haven't answered yet: How long, in a hierarchy, does it take to discover that one of the top brass is mad as a hoot owl? How long can a great man, protected by a habit of discipline and unquestioning obedience, get away with insanity? In a democracy, two psychiatrists can put a politician in a madhouse, and it takes one good lawyer to get him out. But in any pyramidal structure, whether it be the army or a totalitarian state, millions might have to die before it becomes clear that a general, or a fuehrer, or a duce should have been locked up a long time ago.

How far education and conditioned reflexes can turn one's values upside down is proved by me. I knew that Colonel von Kiss was mad as a hatter. I knew that we were being shadowed by a muscular male nurse. Yet I was proud to be seen strolling down the avenues of Nagyszombat with a high-ranking officer in a brass collar all agleam with stars.

POSPISCHIL

As you might imagine, the craziest man among us was one of the chief doctors, Herr Oberstabsarzt Pospischil, a puffed-up greasy Austro-Hungarian Czech, popeyed and apoplectic blue, who wore a wooden smile of benevolence. His military blouse was rank with soup stains, and, like the walls, he had not been washed for a hundred years. He had fenced in part of the garden, where he grew pumpkins, stringbeans, and tomatoes; he also lived in the garden, sleeping among his beloved vegetables, on a rough board, fully dressed in his sloppy uniform, his black Franz Josef officer's cap on his head. He had just enough sense to take shelter in the cellar when it rained.

Sometimes a wretched kleptomaniac would sneak into the doctor's garden and steal a tomato. Then the otherwise kindly doctor would leap out of the foliage like an outraged tomato-djin and, with the cane he kept handy for the purpose, chase the thief through the monastery garden and beat him like a rug.

As for me, I spent my time drawing. The Klosterka was a peace-time asylum too, and there were faces there as old as the walls. Pencil in hand, I ventured into the common soldiers' quarters to draw portraits. I sketched an old man who had been in the Klosterka since he was a cadet, and I asked him to sign his name, Josef Roth. *Jo . . .* he wrote, then *Ro . . .*; each word ended in an illegible squiggle. He threw down the pencil and ran away.

In front of a window protected by iron mesh, I found a Croat huddled like a vulture, a hunted expression in his eyes; with gestures of despair and frustration he complained over and over to his wispy reflection in the pane: *"Nema chleba, nema chleba"*— no bread, no bread. A young homosexual with a turban fashioned out of a dirty towel, and lips rubbed with red rose petals stolen from the garden, danced around me, pulling his robe tightly around his buttocks. And, of course, my old friend from the Galleria followed me, begging pathetically for a furlough.

The best models were the catatonic schizophrenics who stood straight and still as fakirs in odd positions, never budging. There was one, stiff as a poker, who stood on one leg, his arm twisted, his fingers cramped, and thus he stood petrified day after day. When night came, the male nurses had to lift him like a statue and carry him to bed.

An elderly man in a nightshirt loomed before me like a ghost, looked deep into my eyes, and began to talk; and talked and talked and talked, as if he had lost his brakes. As I walked away, he followed, still talking, and a long way past the gate I heard him shouting in the distance.

There was a man with a long neck and a long beak who like a stork cautiously walked around the courtyard, nose to the ground; and if he noticed a fallen acacia leaf, a used match, a thread, a cigarette butt, or a piece of paper, he carefully picked it up between two fingers, holding his little finger elegantly in the air, and put the bit of trash in his pocket. By the end of the afternoon his coat pockets were stuffed. The male nurses then descended upon him like barracudas, pulling, pushing, cursing, and emptied his pockets —for the day only, because in the morning he started all over again. He wrote his name on my drawing with great accuracy: Sigmund Reisz, Soda-Water Factory, Košice; complete with street address and house number.

A stern man held three fingers before his face and talked to them very seriously. I took his fingers one by one and drew little faces on them. He looked at me with gratitude and resumed his argument.

There was a woman in the Klosterka—God knows how she had come. She was a Dalmatian, young, golden-haired, beautiful, and she spent her days at her solitary cell window, weeping incessantly, in a soft moan, her eyes down-slanting. I drew her over and over, *Mater Dolorosa.*

These unfortunate, half-naked, dirty ragtails crowded the court-yard, pressed in the dust between moldy walls. Some of them sat in the gutter like apes, sunning themselves. Now and then one of them would shout, shriek, or gobble like a turkey. At mealtimes they lay in ambush for the soup caldron, plunged their heads into the boiling soup and lapped it like beasts, while the cooks with kicks, soupspoons, and fists beat them back, forcing them into line.

In the corner of the courtyard was an isolated little shack that tickled my curiosity. One day, in passing, I hoisted myself up and looked through the window. I saw several naked cadavers lying on the wet pavement like macaroni, while workmen sprayed them with a black rubber hose. Some of them were wide open from bladder to larynx, others had already been sewn up crudely like stuffed turkeys.

Who was interested in how these creatures looked from the inside after death? Nobody cared how they looked from the outside, while alive.

The Klosterka was my academy of caricature. There I got my first inkling of the extraordinary unity that exists between mind and body. For on the faces and bodies of the insane a state of mind is expressed in most striking form. A melancholic is a melancholic all over, a paranoid a paranoid not only in mind but in face, posture, gait, and voice.

Beyond the walls of the Klosterka, among people we call "normal," the same unity exists. I was to recognize, in the face of Rudolf Hess, the Croat soldier with the expression of a hunted beast. How often have I seen among civil servants those bird-faced bureaucrats, picking up little pieces of paper and filing them, numbering them, signing them, with the same meticulous care as the soda-water manufacturer from Košice; how often listened to marathon speeches of statesmen who talk for seven or eight hours, like the man who couldn't stop talking.

Statue-men aren't seen on the street, except perhaps in India; but we all know stiff men with ramrod backs whose joints have an overdose of starch and whose ideas are stiffer than their knees. They have the negativism and stereotyped demeanor of their catatonic brothers who are locked up.

Watch those executives who are forever calling meetings so that they can preside over them, and remember my friend with the three fingers. He was grateful when I drew faces on them, but when they were faceless, he talked to them all the same.

No hard and fast line separates the normal from the abnormal. Insane behavior is but a caricature of the sane. That's what made Bedlam and Bicêtre the greatest shows on earth, where good bourgeois parents took their families for a Sunday afternoon's hilarious entertainment.

Sane or insane, a man's outside is a continuum of what goes on inside him. Many years later I was to learn what psychiatrists know about this; but with what an explicit hand Nature writes her messages, I learned in the Klosterka, from the faces of the insane.

When Dr. Pospischil found that I was a well-behaved madman, he allowed me to go for a stroll in the city every afternoon, without a guard and without Colonel von Kiss. Naturally I made straight for the fair girls of the locality, without, however, mentioning my home address to them.

It was October, and Nagyszombat—trees and churches and parks—was poured over with gold. There was a Slovakian girl who showed every sign of wanting to walk through the park with me, and in her honor I paid a visit to the barbershop to be steamed, cleaned, pressed, and polished. A masterpiece of the barber's art, I stepped out into the street just as three soldiers approached, surrounded by a cohort of noisy, dirty-faced street urchins.

"Excuse me, Lieutenant," said the leader. "The revolution has come. There are no more officers. Permit me . . ." and with a penknife he slashed my stars from my collar. The barefoot boys whooped for joy, and they all moved off, leaving me standing in front of the barbershop, pulling at the golden threads that hung from my collar. This was my second degradation. The first, self-inflicted, had been elevating; but this one humiliated me.

My Slovakian girl didn't mind the loss of my stars. We walked hand in hand through the golden arcades and kissed, while the purple night hesitated behind the bushes, and the stars descended to earth. Gradually a light, clear night enfolded us. We sat silently on a bench. Then from the center of the town a black pillar of smoke rose to the sky, followed by tall flames. A round of shots sounded—then cries, dull blows, the clatter of frightened horses. The revolution had reached Nagyszombat, and whoever wasn't lame was running to the main street to take part in the looting.

My girl and I made our way with the crowd, some of whom were pushing carts and wheelbarrows. The Slovaks looted Hungarian stores, the Hungarians looted Slovak stores, the Germans were neutral and looted both, and all went for the Jewish stores. Long live the revolution! A stone smashed a delicatessen window; they were dragging sacks of flour into the street—and rice, sugar, all terribly scarce—and pouring it everywhere, rolling in it, tossing it into the air and all around. Furniture, rugs, bedding came hurtling through windows. Urchins of five or six toddled about, clutching bedspreads and alarm clocks. A young man proudly wore a beautiful new toilet seat around his neck. A drunken soldier had pulled a pair of lace-trimmed panties over his trousers.

"Lieutenant," said a passer-by. "You had better go home. They are shooting officers on sight down the street."

I hurriedly kissed my girl goodbye, hid my officer's cap under my arm, and ran through dark alleys back to the Klosterka—the sanest place in town.

During the night, all the male nurses and the entire staff, headed by Dr. Pospischil, ran away. We madmen awoke to find ourselves alone, and everyone who had enough sense fled.

At the railroad station I met Maurice Saracco. The paper decorations had disappeared from his chest. He greeted me with a shout.

"Nix general!" he yelled. "LIEUTENANT Saracco!"

And so we stood there laughing and slapping each other on the back, two enemies who had managed to avoid killing each other.

In and Out of
the Red

WHILE we lunatics, real and near real, dwelt sedately in the Klosterka, all around us sane people were going mad, kicking the bottom out of thousand-year-old Hungary. The Czechs overran Slovakia; the Rumanians, Transylvania; and the Serbs moved into the Banat. Soldiers at the front shot their officers and headed home.

In this travail the Karolyi Revolution had burst into being, and the new government promptly did what I would have done at the age of three. They climbed on a barrel and shouted to the enemy: "I want to make peace with you."

Hungary became a republic without knowing what a republic was. Homecoming soldiers stuck chrysanthemums in the muzzles of their guns and shouted: "Long live the Royal Hungarian Republic!" The peasants thought the republic meant free looting and quickly went to work on the castles of the landowners. When one of them was asked how he liked the republic, he replied: "The first two days were all right, but then the sheriff came and took everything back."

The muddle reached even the highest echelons of the revolutionary government, who began by swearing allegiance to Emperor Charles the Sudden. Then they had to call him on the telephone and get him to absolve them of their oath before they could chase him out of the country. Archduke Josef of Hapsburg, on the other hand, was very much on the democratic ball. He offered to swear allegiance to the new regime, he even said he would change his name from Hapsburg to Alcsuti (after a locality in which he had huge properties); but he abandoned this plan when someone observed that the name Alcsuti sounded Jewish.

On the whole, ours was a sort of light-opera revolution. There was not even a militia to spoil the fun. The minister of defense, General Bela Linder, made a speech from a balcony, declaring: "I don't want to see any more soldiers!" Since the soldiers didn't want to see any more generals either, the army melted like cotton candy, and for a while in Budapest you could not have mustered a chorus line of Hussars.

Perhaps the most engaging aspect of our brief dance with democracy was its leading man, who gave his name to it, Count Michael Karolyi.

In my young days the very word *Count* rang like a gold coin upon a marble table. From such titles hung gorgeous names, Eszterhazy, Szechenyi, Fesztetich; names that sparkled and flared through every phase of our country's history, like gems embroidered on a cloak of medieval splendor, and in the very depths of which burned sinister semantical suggestions: "divine right," "*jus primae noctis,*" "power of life and death." Our aristocrats in no way resembled those cozy English lords who scrape through Eton, get sent down from Oxford, and bumble around the House of Lords in tweeds. Their young were raised like the Lord Buddha in splendid isolation, moated from reality. When one of them took a public examination, it was the professor, not the student, who sweated. The soul of a Hungarian nobleman was a fruitcake of Savile Row urbanity, Dark Age omnipotence, ancestral pride and rust, Viennese caprice, Asiatic stubbornness, and modern maggots.

We middle-class children fed on the true legends that surrounded the lovely names. When Prince Miklos Jozsef Eszterhazy gave a dinner for five hundred, the guests ate with golden forks from golden plates, and the music was provided by his household musician, Joseph Haydn. When Prince Paul Eszterhazy wished to buy a stallion in London and was warned that he might find the price too high, he paid £10,000 for it, then shot it on the spot. One Hungarian aristocrat abroad ordered a bucketful of well-chilled French champagne and told the waiter to chill a bottle of Hungarian wine in it. Another bet an English lord that he had more shepherds than the Englishman had sheep, and won; then he bet all his sheep and shepherds on one card, and lost.

Still, none of these beauties had done anything half so incredible as to head a republican revolution.

Count Karolyi's holdings consisted of 62,000 acres of arable land, forests, mines, towns, villages, and a famous spa, Parad, whose foul-smelling waters alone were worth a fortune. His income was so huge that he could neither spend it nor throw it away nor gamble it away, though he tried. On one occasion a party at the Magnates' Casino ended so late the next morning that Count Karolyi dreaded to face his countess; so he stopped downtown and bought her a sumptuous sixteenth-century painting by Sebastiano del Piombo. The countess gave him a peppery reception: "Where have you been? Is this a time to come home? Naturally you've been gambling, and naturally you've been losing."

"No, Katus, I was winning. Look at the beautiful painting I've brought you."

The countess took the painting and flung it through the window, and del Piombo, like another Sebastian, was transfixed on the branches of an acacia tree.

In addition to gambling and hunting, Count Karolyi had another aristocratic duty: politics. And here he really went to the bad. For Karolyi had a harelip. As a child no doubt he had suffered the agonies reserved for children with a defect. His father, who had a primitive horror of this lip, had wished to hide him away in the

backlands as a gentleman horsebreeder. Karolyi, for all his exalted rank, was born on the side of the scorned; and he became contaminated with democratic ideas.

An admirer of French and English culture, he hated the fate that shuffled Hungary along with a pack of iron-breeched Germans. Throughout the war he had agitated for a separate peace. Thus, when in October 1918 that same fractious madness that had seized me seized the entire nation, it was this gentle, cultivated count who found himself bobbing to the surface of events.

He was one of those horse-faced men like Woodrow Wilson

and Lord Halifax: dedicated, idealistic, and inflexible. He made many excellent speeches through his nose, but he did not have the foggiest notion how to make a revolution succeed. A revolution, to gain respect, must have two hands: one to throw bombs, another to shake hands. We had only a hand to shake hands, and it belonged to Count Karolyi.

It is inherent in the nature of war that when the shooting dies down, and the real trouble—that of peacemaking—begins, the mood of the victor is incompatible with the mood of the vanquished. When the Hungarian nation laid down its arms after years of fighting a war for which we had no heart, we wholly believed in the Fourteen Points of Woodrow Wilson, in self-determination, in the free association of nations, in international law; we were ripe for democracy. In this mood, which was shared by the entire nation, Count Karolyi, with his colleagues, went to Belgrade to see Louis Félix Marie François Franchet d'Esperey, Marshal of France and Commander of the Allied Forces in the Balkans. He went to receive armistice terms. He had to face the tragic clash of moods between victor and vanquished.

The little, golfball-shaped, Charlemagne-mustached Frenchman received our delegation with the words: *"Messieurs, vous êtes vaincus."*—Gentlemen, you're beaten. He didn't shake hands or offer them a seat. When General Linder presented himself as the representative not of the army but of the soldiers' council, the marshal remarked with a sneer: *"Vous êtes tombés si bas?"*—Have you sunk so low?

Two ugly phrases called the tune, whipped up a spirit of humiliation and despair in Hungary that found expression first in Bela Kun and then in Horthy. It was such a spirit that prepared Hitler's path in Germany. Trampled enemies and discontented allies set the stage for World War II.

Up to the time of the Karolyi Revolution, our peasants had lived in medieval huggermugger and the sparse middle class had no cohesion. The only politically schooled bodies in the country

were the Social Democratic labor unions. A new contagious disease swept the country: *unionitis.* Overnight, everyone became
class conscious. The maid organized against my mother, the gar-
bage collector against my father, and those who refused to organized were organized by a poke in the nose.

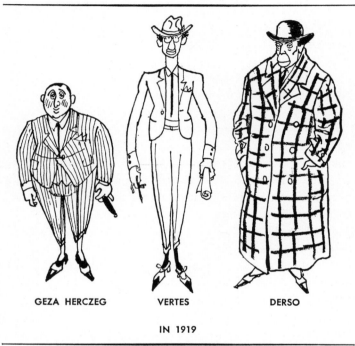

GEZA HERCZEG   VERTES   DERSO

IN 1919

Naturally there was a cartoonists' union and a writers' union.
But it was not Marcel Vertès or Alois Derso who organized the
cartoonists; nor Ferenc Molnar who organized the writers. Squig-
glers and scribblers took charge. For the first time I saw in action
the efficient and expeditive man, the pusher, the doer, the man
who says "leave it to me." Such men have since been beatified, and
God help us, they are running our lives!

Ever since 1917, when my first drawing had been accepted by
Donkey, even as I went in and out of insane asylums I continued

to contribute to magazines and newspapers in Budapest. In pre-Karolyi days sometimes only a blank square was published, and under it: "Drawing by Kelen." By this the publisher wanted his readers to understand that I had drawn an anti-militaristic cartoon and that the censor had wiped it out.

During the Karolyi Revolution I became connected with a little magazine called *Sensation* for which I covered topical events. This was before the time when newspapers and magazines could reproduce photographs on newsprint, and it fell to us artists to attend any important or gruesome event and report it in graphic detail, as much in the manner of Daumier as possible. This was our art school, and a good one too. Today young artists have to get their training drawing bosoms and bottles for advertising agencies.

One day a murder was committed on the outskirts of the city. A peasant girl butchered her mistress with a pickax. The editor of *Sensation* dispatched me to the scene of the crime to sketch the surviving members of the family.

I arrived at the small apartment just as the dead woman was being removed from the cozy, everyday, middle-class surroundings in which she had lived out her life. There was left for me to draw only a poor old man, weeping, devastated. He beseeched me, sobbing, not to draw him in such a pit of misery. I stood there with pencil shaking, eyes smarting, and in another minute I would have burst into tears, so I fled. "I couldn't do it," I told my editor. "All right," he said. "Then go to the morgue and make a drawing of the body."

I went to the morgue and found that the autopsy was being performed. I knocked on the door of the laboratory. It opened just a crack and the head of a bearded, bespectacled professor appeared, with a black satin cap on it. Through the slit of the door, just behind him, I saw the body with a number of rubber hoses protruding from it. I explained what I wanted. The professor snapped: "Go to hell!" and slammed the door in my face.

Since I had to deliver a drawing, any drawing, I drew the professor's head disagreeably peering out of the door.

A warm home, a weeping old husband, a cold body bristling with rubber hoses, all within one hour's time, smote me with the full force of tragedy, and I perceived that I was not cut out to be a crime reporter—at least not a reporter of little crimes.

About this time, Bela Kun and his shock troop of agitators arrived from Moscow with a new religion in their minds and Russian rubles in their pockets. The name Bela Kun was as unknown in Hungary as the backside of the moon, but he proceeded to preach the new faith on street corners and in factories. In the wake of these sermons violence flared up, a few policemen were hurt, and avenging cops beat up Bela Kun so thoroughly that he was taken to a hospital, where he hovered between life and death for days. The editor of *Sensation* sent me to draw his portrait.

I was eager to see this man who had gained such a reputation as a troublemaker, and with great expectations, in the company of other journalists, I tiptoed into his hospital room. There, in bed, lay Bela Kun, but what I saw on the pillow was a large bundle of gauze with a cherry on top, which I took to be his nose. That's what I saw, and that's what I drew for *Sensation:* a snowman with a cherry for a nose. It was my first portrait of a major historical figure, but I did not experience an ineffable feeling that I was face to face with my destiny.

No one in Hungary, except a *Stammtisch*-ful of longhairs, had ever heard of Communism. The people, including me, didn't know whether it was eaten with a spoon or with a fork. Little groups were beginning to form on street corners to discuss it. The story of the day had one worker explaining Communism to another worker.

"It's simple," he said. "If I have two houses, one belongs to you. If I have two cows, one belongs to you."

"And if you have two pigs, does one belong to me?"

"No."

"Why not?"

"Because I have two pigs."

The particular thorn in our sides in those days was the loss of pieces of thousand-year-old Hungary, particularly Slovakia (the Czechs had moved in), Transylvania (the Rumanians had picked it out of our pockets), and the Banat, which had been presented to the Serbs by the Allies, as a reward, I suppose, for having started World War I.

The war had wrung the patriotism out of me; yet the roots of nationalism are deep. I didn't see why Slovaks should have to be Hungarians; still, I felt with most of my countrymen that Hungarians shouldn't have to be Slovaks either. It meant something to me then that historic places with good old names like Pozsony should now be called Bratislava; that Komarom, where my mother was born, should be part of a foreign land. During the Karolyi Revolution we trusted to Wilson's Fourteen Points to put matters straight and save by plebiscite those territories peculiarly Hungarian.

Franchet d'Esperey's crude treatment of Karolyi was a warning of what was in store for us; and by the time Clemenceau the Tiger had finished chewing up Wilson's fourteen lambs, even the bones were no more. The day Clemenceau notified Karolyi that the occupation of Slovakia, Transylvania, and the Banat were permanent and that there would be no plebiscite, 30,000 steelworkers joined the Communist Party, and we woke up Red.

Count Karolyi fled into the mountains of Buda. He had finally succeeded in relieving himself of his fabulous riches, and only a skinny cow was left to provide milk for his children, Adam and Eve. He ended his days in Paris, where often I kibitzed at his chess game, which he played in the evening at the Café du Dôme with a Hungarian painter named Lajos Tihanyi. The painter was deaf and dumb, the count had his harelip, and they barked at each other over the chessboard.

When Tihanyi died, a small colony of Hungarian artists attended his cremation. Count Karolyi delivered the funeral oration, the most touching funeral oration I have ever heard. We couldn't understand a word he said, but he cried, and we all cried, and not just for Tihanyi.

"If we can't get justice from the West, we'll get it from the East" sounds like a new cry, but to my ears it is old: I first heard it in my native tongue. Communism in Hungary sprang out of a patriotic desire to get rid of our pushy friends, the Czechs and Rumanians. Singing the national anthem under the Red flag, and the *Internationale* under our own red, white, and green flag, the Red Army marched to reconquer our lost territories. They were joined by many good patriots, but not by me.

At home we soon discovered that Communism was not just a minor matter of justice and glory. The Soviets grabbed the bank deposits. Beautiful new money appeared with pictures of Marx, Engels, and Lassalle on it. However, nobody wanted it. Peasants refused to sell food to the city in return for this money; merchandise disappeared from the stores; and there was nothing to eat in Budapest except sauerkraut for breakfast, lunch, and dinner. A story went the rounds about a certain gentleman who caught his puppy about to misbehave on the carpet. Promptly he pushed a thousand-kronen bill under the pup, enveloped the product in it, and threw it into the street. During the night somebody stole the dog-dirt and left the money behind.

Still, I'll not insist that the Bolsheviks did absolutely nothing for the poor; they did something for me. When the banks closed and the rich were paupered, some of the best-kept ladies in Europe were left in a pathetic, orphaned condition and were only too glad to accept the attentions of a scruffy young artist in the same income bracket as the church mice. I could invite the choicest cocotte to the Ritz Hotel and offer her a dish of sauerkraut.

As soon as Bela Kun came to power, he confiscated all the newsprint in the country and permitted only two papers: the *Red Flag* for the army, and the *Red Gazette* for civilians. Thus went my

Sensation with the crimson wind, and no one who was not a Hungarian in 1919 can possibly appreciate what a blow this suppression of the press meant to the intellectual life of our country. We were a nation of discord with myriads of little publications in which every shade of opinion could be aired. Such papers played nursemaid to satirists the way old-time vaudeville played nursemaid to many American comedians. And now we were bereft, with two rags only which anyone could read backwards and forwards with his eyes shut. We fell into idleness, sitting around in the journalists' club all day, venting our venom for nothing.

That the Soviets were willing to keep some of us alive, however, was demonstrated when they began to order propaganda posters and pamphlets praising the state. These were similar in spirit to American television advertising: they made smug claims, used gimmicky words, and took man for an imbecile. One poster by Marcel Vertès showed a Red soldier pointing at you with the question: "Are you with me or against me?" Marcel said, after it was all over: "I was against him." Tibor Polya, who had planted in me the seeds of insanity, illustrated a pamphlet promoting rural Communism. It was called: "Shall We Communize Sophie, the Farmer's Daughter?" This we did; we were young.

Foremost among the artists to declare the Hungarian Soviet as their personal property were the abstract painters. Unable to sell their pictures to the bourgeoisie, they had lived lives of slow starvation. Now their day of deliverance was at hand.

The same thing had happened in Russia. In 1925, when for the first time I saw Soviet paintings on display in Venice, they were all abstract: a red square within a white circle against a green background was entitled *Girl Milking Cow on a Collective Farm*. Then Stalin declared that art belonged to the people, and in 1937, in Paris, the Soviets exhibited giant post cards: *Lenin Talking to the Workers in the Putilov Factory*. Behind Lenin stood Stalin. At the New York World's Fair in 1939, another gargantuan post card represented *Stalin Talking to the Workers of the Putilov*

Factory. Behind Stalin stood Khrushchev. So far as I know, the only progress in art the Soviets have made since 1938 is that now Khrushchev is talking to the workers of the Putilov Factory, and who can say who, or what, stands behind him?

Another big change the Commune brought us journalists was that various Bolsheviks who had previously not been allowed to trespass in our journalists' club now began to hobnob with us, holding court and expounding the policies of the new regime. They liked to tell us "intellectual proletariat" about the wonderful life in store for us under the Soviet, when the state would take over the theater, motion pictures, and book publishing, and money would flow like mother's milk for murals, museums, plays, and so on. Artists and writers, they said, would be sorted into categories according to their talents, and the best of us would be on a par with the steelworkers—that is to say, in clover. A writer, Eugen Heltai, hazarded a question: "Tell me, Mr. Commissar, how can one emigrate from here?"

The commissar of motion-picture production, a Mr. Paulig, was a man we watched closely: when he showed up at the club with a murderous revolver in his holster, we knew that the Soviet was strong in the land; but when he came without the revolver, we knew that the government was shaky. Why a moving-picture producer should need a revolver at all is one thing we did not know.

Another visitor was a roly-poly, bullet-headed fellow, a deputy commissar by the name of Matyas Rosenberg. He wasn't worth sketching; I noticed him only because of his unusual face: he looked like a Kalmuck head cheese. Twenty-five years later, this face turned up in an American newspaper. "Look!" I exclaimed, "my old friend Matyi Rosenberg, the Kalmuck head cheese!" But now his name was Matthias Rakosi. He had fled the country in 1919, together with Bela Kun, and had gone to Russia, but he secretly returned to Hungary to organize Communist cells. On one occasion he was nabbed and jailed, but the Russians exchanged

him for some Hungarian flags captured by Cossacks in 1849 during
Kossuth's war of liberation. Whether the flags of freedom had
fallen in value or Rakosi's worth had gone up, I don't know; but
the Hungarians got the best of the deal. They got the flags, and
in 1945 they got Rakosi, too!

He was an ebullient, folksy speaker who knew exactly what
people wanted to hear, and how to say it. I noticed then his habit

of coining catchy phrases. Later, when he was Communist boss
in Hungary, his "salami tactics"—the act of patiently slicing down
one's opposition—became world famous. It is a loss to the
thesaurus of diplomatic lingo that he was eventually sliced down
by Nikita Khrushchev.

One day joyful news rang out in the journalists' club: in two
weeks the Hungarian Soviet government, as a special favor, would
invite the intellectual workers to dinner and meat would be
served. We counted the days. One more week to meat, five more
days to meat, three days to meat, tomorrow MEAT! By the middle of the afternoon, when I arrived, there was already a glad-
eyed line in front of the restaurant. At the doorstep stood a
bureaucrat, to whom we had to declare whether we wished to eat

roast chicken or turkey *chasseur*. Chicken-eaters got green tickets; turkey-eaters got red tickets. I took a red ticket, the turkey being a bigger bird and I being greedy. I ought to have known that a bona fide turkey, even in a dictatorship, positively begs to be roasted; and if it is *chasseur*, something is wrong with the turkey, or with the *chasseur*.

The *chasseur* turned out to be a thick sauce the color and smell of furniture polish, and its purpose was to cover up a stink that twisted my nose the moment the turkey made its debut in the restaurant. "I want roast chicken, roast chicken!" I shouted desperately to the waiter.

"Too late," said the waiter.

"Why too late?"

"Because you gave me your ticket. I gave it to the kitchen supervisor. He gave it to the chef. The chef gave me the turkey. I checked it out at the cash register, and there are just as many chicken tickets as chicken servings, and just as many turkey tickets as turkey servings, and you used up your turkey ticket, and I can't exchange it for a chicken ticket. It's gone." He took a side glance at my melancholy face and added with compassion: "Hja! That's Communism!"

Nothing less than that turkey *chasseur* could have made me give up my hopes of heaven under Bolshevism and conspire again to change my fate. I decided to go home to Györ. There my father, an *affreux bourgeois*, the director of an oil-and-soap factory, was engaged in a flourishing barter trade with the local peasants, successfully transmuting soap into chickens, geese, ducks, and even turkeys. I conceived a scheme to draw everybody in town, to hold an exhibition at which the pleased citizens would buy my drawings, and after that, with money in my pocket, to take further decisions about my future.

But when I arrived in Györ, I found it wasn't so easy, under Communism, to lay my head on my own pillow. My home was swarming with proletariat. A family of workers squatted in the front room, cooking goulash on an alcohol stove in the middle of my mother's best carpet. The bathroom was being used as a clubhouse by naked youngsters who, by special order of the local government, were taking daily baths in bourgeois homes; and they were having the time of their lives with the fixtures. My own room was occupied by a wine-swilling roadworker. All of this was by way of teaching us bourgeois a badly needed lesson on the brotherhood of man, and it took a special application, arguments, and a box of soap for the block commissar, before I could shove my brother out of my bed.

Here in the microcosm of my little town, where I knew intimately everyone concerned, I learned lessons about the species that makes revolutions, and I arrived at conclusions that have stood me in good stead in all the revolutionary years that followed.

In the beginning the Red revolution in Hungary was almost as gentlemanly as the Karolyi affair. According to Lincoln Steffens, Lenin had specifically instructed Bela Kun to avoid terror; but something must have gone wrong. For Hungarian terror troops, whose uniform was a scowl on the face, a leather jacket on the back, and a gun in hand, soon sprouted on the face of the land, and we called them the Lenin boys. They hated everybody, and especially a crowd. Once, in Budapest, the writer Iles Brody and I joined some onlookers around a barker who was selling toy dogs on the boulevard. The Lenin boys leapt to duty, and one stuck a gun in my belly and ordered me to move on. I'm still moving.

Toward the end, a housewives' counterrevolution broke out in Györ. The crowd, consisting of women and children, ransacked the home of a bigwig. They threw three hundred books and —how, I don't know—a piano through a window. They stole the piano piecemeal, but they didn't steal the books: they burned them. The Lenin boys were upon us in no time with guns at the ready. No one was killed in Györ, but in the neighboring towns of Papa and Csorna, where there was unrest also, some twenty-five persons were hanged on the trees of the public square. Among the spectators stood a man obviously of good class to whom the top

Lenin boy bellowed: "What's your name, what are you doing?"
The man said he was a lawyer.

"A lawyer! We don't need lawyers." And they hanged him with
the rest.

All in all, about four hundred persons were killed during the
Red Terror. I suppose it hardly seems worthy of the name; still,
we were terrified. In those days the Sunday driver had not yet come
on the scene, and we were not used to slaughter down the street,
or to the feeling that one might oneself be eliminated through the
awful whimsy of thugs.

By the time I finished drawing all the citizens of Györ, as well
as the entire Communist hierarchy, the local Soviet had fled. As
I prepared my exhibition, which was to be opened by the reinstated *Bürgermeister* and blessed by the bishop, who was now
firmly planted in his episcopal seat, I was warned that if I included the portraits of the late Soviet leaders, neither of these excellent events would take place. So I removed the drawings—
eighteen, I think—and placed them on top of a wardrobe, where
they gathered dust for years. My exhibition opened, the burghers
of Györ flocked in to admire their own portraits, and they told
me that I was a good lad and compared me favorably with the
local artist who carved the angels for the tombstones.

In 1935, on a visit home, I brought down the old drawings of the
Communist leaders and suggested to the town librarian that he
should buy them—after all, they were part of the history of
Györ. "A good idea," he said. "We'll put them in the Rogue's
Gallery." One drawing was missing—that of the president of the
local Soviet. "Never mind," I said. "I see him quite often in
Montparnasse. He is a journalist. I'll draw him there."

The librarian gave me 300 francs on the condition that I deliver
the missing drawing. I did.

One day the doorbell of my studio in Paris rang. Outside was a
messenger, who handed me a note from my model. He said he
couldn't pay his rent, he was locked out of his hotel room, his
typewriter was inside, and he couldn't make a living without it.

Would I, therefore, lend him 300 francs so he could retrieve his typewriter? That's the last I saw of this money. Thus did Hungarian Communism swallow up the little profit I made from it.

Now, I'm told, the present Communist regime has rescued these drawings from their ignominious fate and put them in a *place d'honneur* in the museum of Györ. How fine is the membrane between heroism and delinquency!

I remember the morning when my father, who had no use whatsoever for the Communists, awakened me with the words: "The bandits have run away." Little did he know that they would be replaced by new ones.

Operating under the shield of the Rumanian army, an improvised national army of Hungarians, with the traditional crane feather in their caps, was moving into the country under the command of Admiral Nicholas Horthy de Nagybanya; and Hungary opened to them like a princess in durance vile to her liberating knight. They came, all the best-decorated officers, Colonel Ostenburg, Colonel Pronay, Count Salm; and they went from village to village, where a list of names, drawn up by good Christians and containing the names of bad Christians, awaited them, and the bad Christians were hauled out of their homes and hanged on the acacia trees of the village square. At the head of each list would be the village Jew, ordinarily a man so humble as to be almost non-existent, who sold ribbons to the girls and wine to the boys, and he now paid with his life because Bela Kun was a worse Jew than he. Murder, rape, and castration were no longer atrocities: they had new names. They were "acts committed in national fervor," or "going too far." Men who were known to have committed as many as seventy or eighty murders went scot-free.

The strangest scourge that the Horthy Revolution brought upon us were those Rumanians. I've seen many an army, but this was the only one that wore lipstick, and whose officers had on corsets, rouge, powder, and smelled like a Bucharest bordello. I've wondered how this came about, and the best explanation I can offer is that Rumania was in ancient times a Roman colony, and, in the later empire, Roman generals picked up some dainty habits. The Emperor Vespasian told one of them who walked in a cloud of perfume: "I'd rather you smelled of garlic."

Our Rumanians smelled of garlic *and* perfume, and they packed up our factories and carried them home, lock, stock, and bulbs from the light sockets, and did not forget the spittoons. They achieved a sort of equity in looting: what the Germans had stolen from their country, they now stole back from ours.

The Red Terror burned into the White Terror, and at the root of both was the misery of four years of war, the humiliation of defeat, the economic and emotional insecurity of a country that had lost two thirds of its territory and had virtually collapsed. Like individuals, nations flee from an unbearable situation into *désarroi de l'esprit*, confusion of spirit. The White Terror took (according to Oskar Jaszi, of Oberlin College) four thousand lives. In 1919, Hungary of the sleepy pussycats became a Fascist land of concentration camps, terror troops, confiscated books, militarized children, rape, and summary execution—fit to be called by the *Neue Züricher Zeitung* "the first death spot in Europe's decomposing body." In later years Hungary's leaders proudly pointed out these pioneering merits to Hitler and Mussolini—as Count Ciano relates in his diary.

In the center of it all, riding a white horse, was Admiral Horthy. His personal poster showed two strong hands at the helm of a ship. Some Hungarians said: "I see the hands, but where is the brain?"

I met the regent at a reception in the twenties. He was a proud man, straight as a mast, with a commanding chest covered with ribbons, and bars, and a rich stamp collection. His nose resembled a lobster claw reaching out to pinch his jutting chin; and between lay a sunken mouth. Along with this formidable martiality he was blessed with a certain feminine grace, and he had made an early career as a courtier to H. M. Franz Josef I, ruler of the Hapsburg Empire, to whom he was aide-de-camp. He was a dyed-in-the-wool Austro-Hungarian. Malicious tongues said that once, at a hunting party, when told that a big bird he had shot was an eagle, he exclaimed: "An eagle! I thought eagles had two heads!"

Pompous in office, the regent at heart never lost the simple taste of the sailor for a girl in every port. When receiving girls at the Royal Palace, he posted medieval guardsmen in gorgeous uniforms and golden halberds in front of his office against a surprise visit

from Madame la Régente. Should the reader have any doubt that my informant was close to the admiral, I'll add the further details that his left arm bore a tattoo of a geisha girl holding a parasol.

This was the man who picked up the history of our country where my history books left off. His understanding of social problems reached no further than that rebels should be shot. Without a new idea in his head, he sought support for regaining Hungary's lost territories wherever it could be found, and he found it, inevitably, in Hitler's camp.

And that is his significance, I think: he proved that a Fascist regime, with all its organic sins, could be established, and accepted by well-meaning European statesmen; that it could even be forgiven in the person of such a *charmeur* as he was.

I suspect that just as there is an international of the prisoners of starvation, there is an international of the prisoners of elegance: hunting-horn tooters, pheasant shooters, horse-show watchers, wine-cellar owners. These people sense each other in a handshake, they understand and forgive one another.

Admiral Horthy is therefore remembered in most history books as a venerable, courtly head of state, a model of old-world dignity.

After World War II, when the regent was taken into custody by the Americans, the army found an officer who spoke Hungarian to be his guard. With characteristic realism, prisoner Horthy promptly offered the guard a high decoration.

"Sorry, Excellency," replied the boy, "I can't accept a decoration from you. But you've already done enough for me. You chased me out of Hungary because I was a Jew, and made it possible for me to become a lieutenant in the American army."

In the twenties the editors of the *Berliner Zeitung am Mittag* conducted a contest for the best headline. The winner was: ARCHDUKE FRANZ FERDINAND ALIVE—WORLD WAR FOR NOTHING.

I agree. World War I was for nothing. And what's worse, nobody wanted it. Not the Kaiser or the Tsar, not the British or the French. Not even Count Berchthold, foreign minister of the Hapsburg Empire, wanted a world war. But he did want a little police action against the saucy Serbs.

Count Karolyi says in his memoirs that Countess Berchthold told him that the night before the fateful ultimatum was delivered to the Serbs, "poor Leopold" hadn't slept a wink. He kept getting up and changing a word here, a word there, lest the Serbs should find it possible to accept it.

What a night's work that was! Once a count felt obliged to write a prize ultimatum. And today, half a century later, not one of us can rest easy in his bed.

Schellingstrasse, 41

Zero hour had arrived for me. I had to make a decision: whether to leave Hungary or stay. It was no longer true that *extra Hungariam non est vita*. Our three revolutions had set thousands of my countrymen fleeing like bugs from a bonfire.

For a Hungarian, to be a refugee is a way of life that began with Genghis Khan and continues to the present. There was a French emigration, a Russian, a Polish, and an Armenian one, but no other country has produced such a sustained wave of emigrés as Hungary, and I'm sure that a good statistician, provided he's Hungarian and knows how to juggle figures, could prove that there are more Hungarians living outside Hungary than in it. They turn up everywhere, from the swimming pools of Hollywood to the Pittsburgh coal mines. They shrink heads on Park Avenue, hunt them in Borneo. I dare say there are Hungarians among the emperor penguins of the South Pole.

Many have made their names sparkle, for instance Ferenc
Molnar, Arthur Koestler, Bela Bartok, Sir Alexander Korda. Vilma
Banky and Zsa Zsa Gabor delight the eye, Bela Lugosi and
Peter Lorre scare the daylights out of you. Some Hungarian Jews,
prevented by Horthy's laws from obtaining an education at home,
have invented magical drugs, or won the Nobel Prize, or built
atom bombs for foreigners in foreign lands.

And all of these Hungarians are united in a love of talk, a gift
of jibe, and a tremendous conceit in speaking a language nobody
else can understand. Now and then one of them writes a book
against the others. Legends arise: if you have a Hungarian friend
you don't need an enemy; if you go in a revolving door and a
Hungarian is behind you, he'll get out in front of you.

Many of my friends who left went to live in Vienna because
they suffered from the emigrants' delusion that they would soon
go home again: so why not camp on the doorstep? Others went to
Paris, and I wanted to do the same, but it was rather far for a
mamma's boy, and, besides, I felt diffident about living in a country
I was an ex-enemy of. I chose Munich, finally, for a special reason.
Our café in Györ had subscriptions to all the major German
humor magazines, and my father had taken a sub-subscription
from the busboy. After the intelligentsia of Györ had left their
thumbprints all over these magazines, they landed, in piles, in my
hands. They were my textbooks; and most of them were printed
in Munich. I decided to go to this cartoonists' Athens, enroll in an
art school, and amass a small fortune on the side by making drawings of dachshunds who had fallen into a pail of milk. I didn't
know that Munich already had a struggling artist: Adolf Hitler.

One knows cities by post cards. Paris is the Eiffel Tower, Venice
the Grand Canal, and so on. I knew Munich by its cartoon
types, and on my arrival I kept a sharp eye out, not for landmarks,
but for hippopotamus-sized, beer-guzzling, liver-dumpling-gob-
bling Bavarian burghers, unkempt artists in floppy caps, pipe-
smoking peasants from Tegernsee with leather shorts and a

chamois' beard on their hats. I found them. But I found, too, that
Munich was not all beer and *Leberknödl*. If anything, postwar
Munich was worse off than postwar Budapest. Ration stamps were
the rule, and the beer was only one per cent. There had been a
short-lived Communist *putsch* which had left traces of machine-
gun bullets on the façade of the Justizpalast. The political pend-
ulum, having swung too far to the left, had now swung over to the
right; and although I couldn't have grasped it then, quaint Mün-
chen of the fairy tales was now a kennel of barking Teuton nationalism, a hide-out of political murderers, the festering spot of hoarse
rabblerousers, a perfect setup for Adolf Hitler.

I couldn't help noticing his huge, blood-red posters calling the
Müncheners to a *Protestkundgebung* at the Circus Krone, or the
post cards in the store windows depicting Woodrow Wilson,
Clemenceau, and Poincaré as Jews, and Lloyd George as Semitic
as it is possible to make a Welshman look; nor could I overlook
the political police under the command of Dr. Wilhelm Frick,
later Hitler's minister of the interior, and boss of Heinrich
Himmler. Already a Nazi fellow traveler, he harassed foreigners,
especially Hungarians, whom he suspected automatically of being
Communists. In the early morning his cops would comb the
sauerkraut-scented pensions in search of stowaways who hid in
cold beds without proper papers. My papers were in order, thanks
to the protection of Marcel von Nemes, an art dealer—the one
who put El Greco on the market. But my new friend and colleague, André Dugo, had to change his abode every week in order
to elude these sniffling cops. One morning Dugo left his shoes
outside his door for a shine. A policeman noticed them. "Whose
shoes are these?" he asked. The landlady, a queen of landladies,
calmly replied: "They are mine."

"*Gut*," nodded the cop and went away. Only in Bavaria would
anyone believe that a woman would wear a man's shoes.

Thus politics then, like strontium 90 now, seeped through my
windows and settled in my bones; but I was unaware of this secret
contamination, even when I found myself right on the spot where
an immense chain reaction was about to start.

The trail that led me there began when an artist friend of mine named Boris burst into my lodgings one day with one of those ideas that make life worth living. He would publish an international magazine, all drawings, no text, and get it on the newsstands simultaneously in all the capitals of the world. The first issue, consisting entirely of drawings by Boris, would be devoted to love. The second issue, drawn entirely by me, would be devoted to children. The title of the magazine would be simply Y, emblazoned on the cover in howling pink.

In order to make the magazine easily identifiable with its editor, Boris had resolved henceforward to wear nothing but howling-pink neckties. He showed me some lengths of heavy silk he had brought from Paris and asked my assistance in having it made up, inexpensively, into ties. Within the hour, he had charmed my landlady, a dragon of a woman, into setting to work on the silk, transforming it into bow ties, long ties, and lavallières.

From this it can be seen that Boris possessed, in full measure, the Hungarian aptitude for adding two and two and making it sound like $E = mc^2$. Indeed, he sketched out the first issue, well larded with naked girls, and found a publisher for it, Buchgewerbehaus Mueller und Sohn, at Schellingstrasse, 41. In order to keep body and soul together while his fortune was in the making, he took a job as sports caricaturist for a magazine called *Fussball*, which had offices in the same building.

Boris's magazine never reached the stands. He was arrested by Dr. Frick's cops and escorted to the city limits. He went to Menton and there died of tuberculosis at the age of twenty-five.

Hastening toward his nearby goal, he shoved me a few steps toward my distant one. For before he left Munich, he bequeathed to me his job on *Fussball*.

And so I began to draw the square faces of Müncheners and others whose profession it is to chase one another up and down a soccer field. Every Sunday I attended the matches with my editor, Eugen Seybold, a man shaped like a snubbing post; and afterwards I helped him put the magazine to bed.

Our offices consisted of two rooms at Schellingstrasse, 41, just above the printing shop. The entire building was owned by the printers, Mueller und Sohn, and it was in three parts, separated by courtyards which were jammed with rolls of naked newsprint. Workers with black hands and blue smocks moved the rolls in and out; trucks rumbled back and forth, bringing new rolls and carrying away finished newspapers. The shop buzzed night and day, and

after dark the windows where the stereotypers worked flared with blinding blue lights.

The ruler of this inky kingdom was the *Sohn*, Adolf Mueller, a greasy potbellied burgher with a face of apoplectic mauve, who customarily shuffled around, huffing, puffing, in shirtsleeves, his unbuttoned vest held together with a golden watch chain. Summer and winter he sweated, and he always carried two handkerchiefs: one around his neck to catch the dribble, while with the other he blotted his forehead and nape. It was hard to talk to him because he was half deaf; hard to listen to him because he seemed not to know whether he spoke in a whisper or in a bellow.

Adi was a passionate hunter. Every Sunday he went out to his estate on the Tegernsee, and in the evening, about the time Herr

Seybold and I came back from the soccer matches, he would show up with the news that he hadn't got his rabbit. Herr Seybold comforted him: "Never mind, Herr Mueller, you gave them a good scare!"

What a queer old bird to go crashing into the world's stage machinery!

Adi Mueller printed papers of divers persuasions. He printed *Fussball*; and Cardinal Faulhaber's newsletter; and Boris's naughty magazine, *Y*; and he also printed the *Voelkischer Beobachter*.

And up and down the stairs, in and out the door, in the corridors and courts, and at the corner tavern—the Osteria Bavaria—I became familiar with faces which would one day inhabit the nightmares of the world. I couldn't know it then. I just watched them with the same innocent interest with which I study any face I see frequently. But like a ward politician, I never forget a face.

Often on weekend afternoons in the back courtyard, I'd loaf among the broken boxes and rusty machinery, watching groups of young workers doing military exercises, using sticks for guns. They included many of the workers at the print shop; but others came in trucks, and then the courtyard resounded with military barks. Adi Mueller showed no interest in these goings-on. He said to me: "I'm a businessman, I have to be on good terms with everybody. If the customer wants to do calisthenics in the back yard, he can do them."

But Ernst Roehm showed up sometimes, and when he did he would go around to the young men individually, shaking hands with them. He looked like a suburban pork butcher whose intimacy with pigs had ended in a resemblance; but he walked like a bear. He belonged to the broad-buttocked species of Germans and filled out his brown breeches well. With his cheek scarred by a shell wound, and no blink in his wild boar eyes, he looked, and was, a first-class roughneck, an unsavory combination of brute force and feminine suet.

Years later, in the New York Public Library, I happened to have in my hand the 1938 edition of *Who's Who in Germany*, and for curiosity's sake I looked up Adolf Mueller. After his name I read the words: "*Gründung der SA in den Geschäftsräumen der Druckerei*"—Founding of the SA in the premises of the printing shop.

Those whom I watched drilling there were the first storm troopers, boys to be honed to the ruthlessness of the hawk, the mercilessness of the beast of prey.

A face I saw often, and hauntingly, in the Schellingstrasse was that of Rudolf Hess. He had a striking likeness to my old friend, the Croat who used to stand at the window of the Klosterka complaining to his own reflection: *Nema chleba*—no bread. His downward-slanting bushy eyebrows and his anxious, blue, close-set eyes lent him the expression of a hunted beast. He tried desperately to hide his buck teeth by tightening his lips. In all the hundreds of photos I studied later, I found only one snapshot in which he smiled, revealing his teeth.

In this face, contrasts of weakness and strength were dramatic: the fragile centerpiece of the upper jaw was flanked by massive cheekbones and a baboon brow ridge, and was married to a sledgehammer lower jaw; all this bore witness to his violent, contradictory nature: timidity grafted to courage, sensitiveness to violence, and an abstract mind to muddle-headed mysticism.

Bushy eyebrows over close-set eyes can be indicative of a certain type of constitution, a trademark of the schizoid personality. As it happened to Nietzsche, and possibly to Stalin, so it happened to Hess when he made his famous solo flight to England: the sane schizoid had turned into an outright schizophrenic.

All this tragic waste of life I sensed in his face when I passed him at Adi Mueller's. He was a young man of my own age for whom I felt a certain sympathy—a shy, timid introvert among extroverts—and I never forgot him or ceased to feel for him right up to the day I saw him vulnerable, with shattered mind, in the dock at Nuremberg.

The day I saw Hitler's face in the Schellingstrasse is a day set apart from all other days.

I was in love as usual, with a *süsses deutsches Mädchen*, and all summer had been kissing her in the parks around the Pinakothek. But as the weather turned cooler I began to look for a warmer love nest. I remembered that Adi Mueller had given my friend Boris two rooms in our building in which to edit the magazine Y, and that when Boris had departed from Menton he had left the key with Herr Seybold. So I confided my *Liebeschmerz* to Seybold, and he gave me the key.

The following evening, arm in arm, hand in hand, my girl and I entered the corridors of Mueller und Sohn, and headed for the offices of Y. I opened the door and urged her tenderly into the room. Then we froze in our tracks. There was our nest demolished, the floor covered with debris, and a large hole torn out of the wall. Through the hole in the wall I saw the editorial staff of the *Voelkischer Beobachter*, until that moment hard at work. I stared at them; they stared back. One of those who stared was a man I had never seen before; he was none other than the man with the silly mustache.

I grabbed my Maedchen, and we hustled down the corridor to the offices of *Fussball*, where Herr Seybold was working at his desk. "Herr Seybold . . . a terrible thing. . . ."

"Oh yes," said Herr Seybold. "I've been trying to get you all day. The *Voelkischer Beobachter* has taken over the Y offices, and Herr Mueller has had workmen tearing the place to pieces."

"But I have a girl outside!"

"Take my room!" he said. And old Seybold, a good German if ever there was one, gathered together some manuscripts from his desk and silently stole away.

HITLER IN THE TWENTIES

Rapturously I hoisted my girl onto his desk and began to rain ardent kisses upon her pretty face. Suddenly she leaped off the desk with the howl of a wounded tigress. Between the masses of papers that lay scattered on Herr Seybold's desk, an army of thumbtacks stood in ambush.

So the day I first saw Hitler wound up with me picking thumbtacks out of my girl's bottom.

Now and then in Adi's printing shop I'd pick up the *Voelkischer Beobachter* hot off the press. It was an anti-Semitic sheet, badly written, good for a laugh; yet one day its headlines would blacken the heart, its very name become a tremor in the mind.

And how did this respectable, prosperous Münchener, Adolf

Mueller, become involved with Hitler's unsightly band, and why did he shuffle along with them through the years? He was a good-natured man who didn't snipe at Jews more than was proper for a member of the Catholic *Bayerische Volkspartei;* he couldn't even hit a rabbit when he tried.

After the first war, Hitler had been that most unemployed of creatures, an informer for the unemployed Reichswehr. His duty was to haunt the *Bierkellers* of Munich and report what those who were working were thinking. At the instance of Captain Roehm, he had joined a group of beer fanciers who called themselves the *Deutsche Arbeiter Partei.* There were six members in all. Hitler became number 7. Clearly, new blood was needed, so the seven set to work writing leaflets inviting the general public to their meetings. Hitler personally distributed these leaflets in the street. Nobody came.

The *Deutsche Arbeiter Partei* then decided to borrow some magic from Phineas T. Barnum and advertise. A cheap ad was placed in a dying paper called the *Münchener Beobachter,* which was printed by Adolf Mueller. The magic worked: one hundred and eleven people showed up. Hitler learned about the power of the press.

The bankrupt *Münchener Beobachter* happened to be for sale to anyone who would take over its debt to Herr Mueller. It was eventually bought by a wolf pack called the Thule Gesellschaft, to which Hitler's friends, Rudolf Hess and Alfred Rosenberg, belonged. They changed the paper's name to the *Münchener Beobachter und Sportblatt.* The main sports event covered was Jew-baiting. Its political tone was so obnoxious that the police clamped down and forbade its publication. In order to break the law without doing anything illegal, the owners changed the name to the *Voelkischer Beobachter* and continued to publish.

Eventually, Captain Roehm, with funds raised by his superior officer, General Ritter von Epp, muscled Hitler into the *Voelkischer Beobachter* as partner. Thus Hitler acquired a newspaper, and Adolf Mueller entered history: as a creditor.

The paper was published twice a week, Wednesday and Saturday, and the printing bill went unpaid twice a week. Adi Mueller was caught in Hitler's coils by virtue of the ancient axiom of commerce that a debtor holds his creditor's fate in his hands. Hitler threatened that if Adi didn't give him credit, Adi would never get his money back. He convinced Adi that he had big plans which would materialize shortly, and that he would end up chancellor of Germany. He even persuaded Adi to bring out the paper three times a week instead of twice, on the theory that he could get more advertising that way. Adi played ball for a while, then woke up shouting: "It isn't enough that you don't pay your bills twice a week? Now you want to owe me three times a week!" Hitler screamed at the top of his voice, but Adi kept his nerve, because he was hard of hearing. Right there in Schellingstrasse, 41, Hitler suffered his first cataclysmic defeat when the *Voelkischer Beobachter* resumed twice-weekly publication.

Sometimes the battle of the bills blasted away for hours in the office next door, with poor Adi rasping and blowing, and Hitler screaming. That dreadful sound would one day rend the air waves of the globe, but I heard it first through a wall. Afterwards, Adi would come into our office, sweating profusely, and tell Herr Seybold that he regretted the Hitler business like "a cat who had nine kittens."

He excused his leniency: "They haven't got money now, but Herr Hitler is a man with connections." Or: "I'm sick and tired of strikes, rising wages . . . you've got to admit, Herr Seybold, things can't go on like this."

As Adi ambled out, Herr Seybold jerked his thumb at Adi's back, saying to me: "*Ein Tepp!*"—an idiot!

There came the time when Hitler was jailed in Landsberg Prison, where he occupied himself with writing *Mein Kampf*. On the day he was released it was kind Adi Mueller who in person drove out to the fortress in his fine Daimler-Benz to pick him up, and subsequently he offered Hitler a home on his estate. And he, Adi, printed *Mein Kampf*—on credit!

In the mid-twenties I made a return trip to Munich and paid a visit to the Schellingstrasse, where I asked Adi about his investment in Herr Hitler. He showed me a copy of *Mein Kampf*, slamming it angrily on a table beside me. "The worst business I ever did," he said. "It's losing money every year."

Yet Herr Mueller hadn't missed many more rabbits before 1933 came around, and then the circulation of the Nazi Bible began to compete with that of God's. In 1936 a copy of that first edition sold at auction in New York for $250, while the police kept hostile demonstrators at a distance.

Today, if you wish merely to fondle one of Adi's copies, here is what you must do: Go to the main reference room on the third floor of the New York Public Library and fill out your request on a slip of paper. Take this down to the second floor, Room 210, and show it to the clerk. The clerk will ask you for identification, and if your papers do not appear to be those of a vandal, he will approve your request. You then return to the third floor, Room 303; you stop at a door that is locked and barred, and ring a bell. A clerk will put his head out, scrutinize you and your little piece of paper. Then he opens the door, you enter, you sit, he brings that book tenderly in his hands and watches you sharply while you leaf through it—that very book that Adi Mueller slapped upon the table, saying: "They're eating up my business."

All Adi's bills were paid in the end. Not only that, Goering gave *der Tepp* a fancy uniform and a shining title, naming him *Bayerischer Forst und Jägermeister*—Bavarian Forester and Hunting Master.

Adolf Mueller is an unsung hero of the Nazi revolution. No street was named after him, no statue placed in the park. His glory must shine only in the history book of a caricaturist. I can't help wondering what the world would be like today if he had been less kind and let Hitler continue to pass out leaflets in the street.

Across the road from Adolf Mueller's printing establishment, at Schellingstrasse, 50, lived a photographer named Heinrich Hoffmann. A little showcase attached to the outside wall displayed photos of newlyweds, interiors of houses, cats, and couples celebrating their silver wedding anniversaries. An inscription below the showcase read: "Studio in the Garden."

Hoffmann was my colleague on *Fussball*, where he worked as a press photographer. In 1920 this meant a status lower than a frog's behind. His assignment was to go to the soccer matches and snap the winning goal. He would stand just behind the net, stamping in the foggy cold, in a light overcoat, his trousers screwed into gray Alpine hose, waiting for the goal to happen.

And every Sunday evening when Seybold and I arrived at the office after the match, Herr Hoffmann would be waiting for us in the dark corridor in front of the closed door. "Now, Herr Hoffmann," Seybold would ask, "did you get the goals?"

"Yes, Herr Seybold," Hoffmann would answer with pride. "All three of them." Then there was the little ceremony of paying Herr Hoffmann for the goals, at five marks each.

This wretched man became Hitler's friend, made millions of dollars, and played a role in history that no photographer has played before or since. Because on that day in 1924, when Adi Mueller drove to the Landsberg Prison to get Hitler, he took good neighbor Hoffmann with him to photograph Hitler standing beside Adi's Daimler-Benz. Hitler, who had previously been camera-shy, gave Hoffmann the exclusive right to photograph him. I would never have dreamed there was so much money in that vulgar kisser.

Hoffmann was a hunchback without a hunch. With his long nose, gray, sapless skin parched against brittle bone, high shoulders, telescoped trunk, and rotund spider belly, he looked like a sickly troll escaped from the façade of a Gothic church. No joiner he, but a hungry, discontented misfit, one of the bruised. His was the vengeance of the dwarf. When you tell an *Untermensch* like him that he was born to look down on Slavs, Wops, Jews, you've got a good Nazi.

After World War II he was arrested by the American army and condemned to ten years in prison; he served five and a half years, including two years in solitary confinement. His huge fortune was confiscated.

These gloomy Nazi matters bothered my brains not at all. The beer was getting stronger in Munich, the sausage stamps had disappeared. In 1921 the carnival came back, in the Nockerberg the *Bockbierfest* was celebrated in the courtyard of the old brewery, and the smooth, brown nectar was served out of the tank that nursed it. They called the beer *Salvator*—Savior—and, indeed, one stein was enough to admit you to heaven. The brass band pumped old melodies, we yoohooed around the bandstand; and I didn't even notice that her right leg was shorter than her left. We waltzed and waltzed, and only in the morning light did I observe that she couldn't help moving *im drei viertel Takt*. Yes, Munich was her gay self again, enveloped in a vapor of beer, and it smelled to me like haystacks in which maidens roll.

I had been attending the art school of Hans Hofmann, who later became one of the leading exponents of expressionist art in the United States. His studio was immensely popular; it was crowded with aged spinsters and young Scandinavian girls. There we sat one day, amid the wonderful international perfume of art studios in which the scents of oil, turpentine, pipesmoke, and sweat mingled, waiting for a model to appear.

It happens occasionally in art schools that perverts pass themselves off as models. On this day a young man came palely loitering and presented himself as a model. He disappeared behind a screen and a few minutes later stepped up on the podium into the circle of old ladies, stripped naked, with a formidable erection. Screams, gasps, chairs banged, easels staggered! In the midst of the confusion a huge, gargantuan-bearded landscape painter from Bavaria heaved himself up and thundered at the young man:

"Gehst 'raus mit dein . . . dein Bohnenstangerl!"—Get out of here with your . . . your beanpole! And the young man, naked, with his clothes under his arm, ran for his life into the wintry streets.

Prowling through the art museum one day, I struck up an acquaintance with another Hungarian artist, André Dugo, who became my lifelong crony. Dugo had a summer-holiday acquaintance with Roda Roda, the most famous German humorist of the day—a warmhearted man with a warmhearted wife. Through their friendship, we two young men, far beyond our deserts, found ourselves having late suppers with some of the most celebrated men in Germany. There were the horsy Mann brothers, Thomas and Heinrich, both with close-set eyes, long upper lip, and small chin. Thomas chose to camouflage his long upper lip with a bristly mustache. Heinrich preferred to enhance his small chin with a goatee. Lion Feuchtwanger came: a little man with the smile of a rake, and unblinking, shining, raccoon eyes. For some reason I never fathomed, he would stare at me as if mesmerized.

And there was Kosor, the Serbian playwright who, whenever he bought a new pair of socks, cut off both toe and heel, saying: "That's where they wear out anyway."

Here a young fellow could gather pearls of wisdom as they fell from famous lips; for instance, Roda's "In Europe, the Orient begins where men no longer tuck their shirts inside their pants but leave them hanging out." At midnight, in company with other pickled philosophers, he would peel the sticky skins from the *Weisswurst* and throw them at the ceiling to see if they would stick.

Here in Roda's circle Germany's good wheat was growing. In Schellingstrasse, 41, the tares. I spent my time between the two, and never knew it.

My career on *Fussball* was progressing nicely. No important sports event took place without me, and I drew hundreds of soccer players. I recall especially a championship match between Fussball Club Nuremberg and Sport Verein Hamburg which had to be played three times because the teams collided with such Teutonic fury that more men were carried out than were left to finish the game. One of these murderous encounters took place in Cologne and, as was customary, the city gave a banquet the same evening in the town hall in honor of the visiting team. About half of the players were absent; they were in the hospital with broken legs and ribs. But the mayor of Cologne, Konrad Adenauer, did not fail us. He made a speech extolling the merits of sports in forming sound bodies, those vessels of sound minds.

Yes, it was the same choke-collared Adenauer, as skinny forty years ago as he is today, with a tiny head like a lemon on a flagpole. Now the lemon is shriveled, and with his slanting eyes and Mongoloid cheekbones, Adenauer could be the Grand Lama of Shangri-La.

I was a boy—father to the man—who followed his nose to food, and thus I became intimate with another species of Münchener, the members of the Baltic colony, less glamorous than Roda's friends, but equally hospitable and kind. They were *Auslands-Junker* really, refugees from the Bolsheviks. Their noses had that improbable upward twist I have discerned only in the faces of the denizens of the Baltic coast. They put jam instead of sugar in their tea, ate *pirogues*, baked cakes no German could concoct, and served them around samovars with a lavishness that could have come to Europe only with the hordes of the Great Khan.

While thinly veneered with Russian customs, they were French-rather than German-oriented, and talked light, bubbling nonsense, rare among the serious-minded Germans.

Yet these nice Balts played a black role in history and helped put an end to tea and cakes for years to come in Europe. They hated Russians because they were Junkers. They hated Communists because they had been landowners. They hated Jews because it is a Baltic custom to hate Jews. So these people, otherwise kind, became the bacillus-carriers of Nazism. They subscribed to the *Voelkischer Beobachter*, and also to the cheesepaper edited by the Catholic priest, Father Staempfli, who later did the final editing of *Mein Kampf*. For this service the Nazis were obliged to kill him; it isn't healthy to know that a dictator can't spell.

One Estonian family became my friends: she was stately, witty, and made excellent cakes; he was an engineer, meek, dyspeptic, a mumbler, and he answered to the name of Lutschy. In their house I met the artist who drew Woodrow Wilson and Lloyd

George as old rabbis; and Herr Alfred Rosenberg, chief philosopher of the Nazi party and later Hitler's mentor in foreign policy. He was a dreamy, fish-eyed pussycat with a long upper lip tightly buttoned over a tucked-in lower one, and a nose that ascended to heaven. Compared to the gorillas in the Schellingstrasse, Herr Rosenberg, I must admit, was Mr. Clean: dapper, urbane, polite; I am sure that Hitler in those seedy days must have been pleased to have such a well-groomed friend. Besides, Herr Rosenberg held an architect's diploma, while Hitler couldn't get near the school of architecture in Vienna.

Alfred Rosenberg had another attraction for Hitler: the Baltic complex of anti-Semitism, anti-Marxism, and anti-Moscowism. The pair of them developed what is called in psychiatry *folie à deux*, a happy common lunacy, and though Rosenberg was unan-

imously hated by other members of the Nazi party, he became
Hitler's most intimate political adviser.

These two men were guilty of emotional diplomacy, which is
just as dangerous as emotional arithmetic. They fooled themselves
about the determination of Britain, about the isolationism of the
United States. It was Rosenberg who planted in Hitler the idea of
the attack on the Soviet Union. As it turned out, they had mis-
calculated not only Russia's fighting spirit but the number of
Russian divisions available.

Herr Rosenberg was condemned and hanged in Nuremberg. It
couldn't have happened to a better-dressed man.

Around the corner from Lutschy's was the villa of their good
friend and frequent guest, a Harvard alumnus called Ernst Sedg-
wick Hanfstaengl, or Putzi. He was a big man with the hollow-
cheeked look of a hungry horse, and he was Munich's foremost art
publisher. I wooed him, naturally, but he wasn't interested in
Kelens. He preferred to collaborate with artists such as Raphael,
Rubens, and A. Hitler. Because he earned foreign currency, which
he kept abroad, he was able to feed the starving *Voelkischer
Beobachter* with good dollars, not inflated marks.

But it wasn't crude dollars that won him Hitler's heart: it was
Putzi's ability to play David to Hitler's Saul. For Putzi was a
pianist who could belt out Wagner with remarkable vehemence.
This talent had once got him ousted from the Harvard Club—the
piano couldn't take it any more. But Putzi's music acted like horse
balm on Hitler's kicking nerves.

I next met Putzi in Paris in 1928 when he came to the Louvre
and Luxembourg museums to select pictures for reproduction.
This was the first time after World War I that a German had received such permission from the French government. Putzi bore a
letter of recommendation to André Dugo from Lutschy's wife,
requesting his help in the long French conversations Putzi would
have with the directors of the museums. In addition he needed
copyists. Dugo and I dug them up for him. Millionaire Hanfs-

taengl began by offering these poor artists such miserly sums for their work that I stationed myself behind him and kept signaling: "Don't give in! He can pay!"

Putzi was a man of cascading mind, free-flowing, but it would hit hidden rocks and bumps which sent him glancing off in unexpected directions. As I was having coffee with him on the Montparnasse one day, I asked him about his old friend, Hitler, and he made a sweeping gesture with his arm: "*Aus!* I've had enough of him."

But when, in 1933, Hitler became chancellor, Putzi became a Nazi press officer and cascaded in splendor all over the Anglo-American press. His antics in the United States were such that Heywood Broun said: "It's good he came. Now we can see the truth of the Elizabethan saying: 'The devil is an ass.' "

As press officer he edited a very successful book of caricatures which Rudolf Hess had helped him to select and which had been approved by artist Hitler. It bore the title, *Hitler in World Caricature: Facts against Ink. Ink* in this case meant the drawings, or rather the distortions of devilish caricaturists. The *facts* were Putzi's comments. A publisher's foreword read: "In counterpoint against the symphony of the Fuehrer's success is the squeaky cat music of the world press."

I caterwauled over a full page. It showed a montage of headlines in all languages from the newspapers of Europe, condemning the Nazi murders. In front of them stood Hitler in triumphant salute. My caption was: "We've done it! We are more hateful now than in 1914!" Putzi's caption read: "*Le Rire* of Paris is trying to prove with this cartoon that there exists a United Front in the world against Hitler. *Fact*: Hitler's powerful efforts to establish order inside Germany led very early, in July 1933, to a United Front with England, Italy, and France for the safeguarding of European peace." (The Four Power Pact)

Well, well, Putzi, here I am, still falsifying world history!

The book closed with a photo of that ridiculous puss with its smudgy mustache, and the words: "Whatever they say about him, they are bound to envy us for him."

There came the inevitable time when Saul lifted his lance against David, and David fled. The mysterious circumstances surrounding this event reached me through the Baltic channel.

It came to Hitler's ears that, on occasion, Hanfstaengl men-

Deutschland über alles!
Hitler: Et maintenant nous voici aussi populaires qu'en 1914!
Nun sind wir glücklich wieder so beliebt wie 1914!

tioned his name to the press in an ironical tone of voice. Now there was something to scream about! Hitler called Putzi on the carpet and screamed. Putzi replied with dignity: "If you don't trust me, give me another assignment."

It was decided that Putzi should be sent to Spain. He took the Berlin–Madrid plane, together with a number of Nazi officers. Shortly after the plane left Tempelhof, Putzi heard a young lieutenant behind him saying in a loud whisper to his neighbor: "Don't forget! As soon as we reach Switzerland, *on the order of the Fuehrer*, we have to toss out this guy Hanfstaengl."

I don't know whether this was true, or just one of those hilarious German jokes. Anyway, Putzi got off at Leipzig, hired a taxi, and fled to Zurich. From Zurich he phoned Saul and reproached him. Saul sent his personal adjutant to try to coax Putzi home, but Putzi preferred to go to London.

Yes, but all his belongings were on the Berlin-Madrid plane, and there he was in a London fog without bedsocks. He wrote a letter to Lutschy's wife, asking her to go to his villa and pack some clothes for him. Mme Lutschy took a big basket and a maid and went to the Hanfstaengl villa, where they packed. As she left the building, she was arrested by two Gestapo men and taken to headquarters, where she was accused of conspiracy with the traitor, Hanfstaengl.

It was a horrid situation for kind Mme Lutschy. All she could do was produce Putzi's letter. The Gestapo colonel opened it and read it. Then his stern face softened. For the letter closed with these words: "In the bedroom closet, on the lower shelf, at the bottom, is a blanket. Don't forget to send it to me. This is the blanket with which the Fuehrer covered himself in the Landsberg prison. It is particularly dear to me."

What! Putzi a traitor? A man of such delicate sentiment? Never! Lutschy's wife was released.

Well, I don't know. There were no flies on Putzi. I never considered him to be an honest-to-goodness Nazi; he lacked the paranoid scowl with which I had become familiar in the Schellingstrasse.

I think he was just a sentimental musical clown who was inspired by German mysticism and a cash-and-carry fear of Communism, and whose cascading talents happened to bump him forth into the limelight.

Putzi Hanfstaengl was not the only German in Munich treading an invisible path to World War II. The town was full of those most bereaved of human souls, Reichswehr officers in mufti. For some mad reason these out-of-work officers had drifted into the film industry. A friend of mine, a guards officer of the Bavarian court, gave me a recommendation to Major Steinmetz, president of a motion-picture company, and he passed me on to a Captain Hoffmann, managing editor of a film magazine which needed a caricaturist. To my surprise, instead of asking whether I had ever been to art school, the captain wanted to know what I had done during the war. Upon learning that I had been a lieutenant in the Austro-Hungarian army, he made me an official caricaturist at once.

My first assignment was to draw Ernst Udet, a flying ace of World War I with sixty-two downed planes to his credit. Next to Baron Richthofen, he was the most renowned aviator in Germany, much better known than the Richthofen squadron's former commander, Hermann Goering.

Udet lived in a modest apartment and had no maid. He admitted me himself in a wine-colored robe, his naked legs sticking out from under. He was a stocky man with anxious blue wolf-eyes, and an easy but hard smile. There was a look about him of a small boy who loves a dare. Such was the man I saw, and drew, and when I had finished he said: "Now give me your pad, and I'll draw you."

I've had many models, some of them in high positions, who have felt compelled to get back at me by drawing my caricature; thus they reveal that they have a Udet syndrome: aggressive and mischievous people who love to shoot back.

Germany was forbidden, under the peace treaties, to have an air force, so Udet called himself a sports flyer, and as an aerial acrobat he put on shows in the capitals of Europe and made all sorts of spectacular flights: he flew over the Zugspitze, Mont Blanc, the Alps, Greenland; in 1931 he flew across Kenya, Uganda, Tanganyika, the Sudan, and Egypt. He always took with him a couple of cameramen. It seems incredible today, but in the twenties no one, so far as I know, saw the significance of these activities. Permission for his African excursion was kindly given by the director of the British Civil Aviation Service. Udet published an illustrated book entitled *Strange Bird Over Africa*, but it's safe to assume that his best prints went into the files of the Reichswehr.

In time, at Goering's persuasion, Udet joined Hitler's movement and became a commander in the SA air force, under Captain Roehm.

There comes a time in every revolution when wolf eats wolf. The time came for the Nazis in 1934 with the blood purge, when the fate of Danton, Robespierre, and Trotsky overtook Captain Roehm. He was arrested and jailed and given a revolver with which to shoot himself. But he refused to do that favor for Hitler. So two of his SA officers did it for him.

On the same night, Gauleiter Wagner, of Munich, gave a dinner party at the Ministry of the Interior, to which he invited ten SA commanders, among them Udet. The seating arrangement at the table was: a murderer, a victim, a murderer, a victim. They had a jolly time toasting one another's health until four o'clock in the morning when the telephone rang, announcing that Hitler had just landed at the Munich airfield. Wagner then gave a signal and each murderer killed his neighbor with revolver, cheese knife, beer stein, or whatever came to hand. Nine dead bodies were kicked under the table. But Udet's neighbor fumbled, and Udet, half out of his mind, managed to escape into the corridors of the ministry, where, as he was trying to find his way out, he ran into Hitler, who had just arrived from the airfield in his raincoat.

"Are you crazy?" he shouted to the Fuehrer. "What do you want from us?"

"Nothing will happen to you," Hitler told him, and Udet was saved. He joined the Air Ministry under Goering, and rose to the rank of air marshal of the Luftwaffe. When, in the fall of 1941, things began to go sour on the Russian front, Udet, rather than face another dinner party in Germany, killed himself.

Udet, I think, was another of those off-true-blue Nazis. He might have been happier as a lion tamer or going over Niagara Falls in a barrel. Not so General Franz Ritter von Epp, whom I also drew about this time. He was Roehm's commanding officer in the Reichswehr—the same man who raised 60,000 marks to buy the bankrupt *Voelkischer Beobachter* for Hitler.

The general stood proud as a horse at a wedding, and received me with a correct, thin-lipped smile which, however, went no deeper than his front teeth. As soon as he sat down to pose, there appeared on his face the scowl of a man-eating Nubian panther.

Mary Lincoln used to say of Abe, who ordinarily had a smiling face, that the moment he got before a camera his features would slip into a melancholy brooding expression—which, in fact, is the "Lincoln look" familiar to us. I have learned to watch keenly the differences between the social and the "posing" or photographic faces of my customers, for they reveal hidden aspects of the personality. Sometimes they express a concealed truth; sometimes they are but would-be faces. But always they tell tales.

General von Epp, the man who had exterminated the Hereros of German West Africa, chose to face the world as a savage Big Cat.

". . . My storm troops, as they were named from that day forth, attacked. Like wolves, in parties of eight or ten, they rushed again and again on the enemy. . . . After five minutes I could see hardly one who was not streaming with blood. I was beginning to know their qualities . . . one's heart almost rejoiced at such a revival of old war memories."

This paranoid orgasm is from *Mein Kampf*. Hitler is describing not the battle of the Bulge, but a brawl that took place in Munich while I was there, in the *Hofbrauhaussaal*, "filled with a howling mob above which numberless pint-pots flew like howitzer shells." It could not have happened without the benevolent wink of Dr. Frick's police.

In Munich, while I danced and drew, Hitler was plotting to exchange those pint-pots for bombs. I must say I failed to read world history on his face or even in the *Voelkischer Beobachter*. I didn't realize then that decent people could be made to swallow swill or to raise above themselves this mob of damaged, bruised pimps, homosexuals, drunks, drug addicts, brawlers, and convicted murderers.

In later years I looked well into Hitler's face; and in 1930, at the opening of the Reichstag, I saw his 107 booted deputies turn the German parliament into a barracks. I drew Goering, Goebbels, Frick, Gregor Strasser, Streicher, and the murderer Heines. My pencil knew their faces, traced their dysplasias, marked the paranoid scowl.

And it is still a mystery to me why sane businessmen, scholars, and statesmen failed to recognize them for what they were, why their lies were believed when the truth was blatant on their faces.

Did they suppose that a clean, scrubbed Hitler was a more honorable man than the beer-hall brawler or the man who butchered Roehm?

In a time of mass communication, beware the paranoid politician. The diagnosis is easy to make. He reveals himself when he talks violently and irrationally against someone or something. His eyes are dark with the baboon's frown. Between the smiles lurks the bitter snarl that bares his clenched eye teeth.

On the man himself is written the history he is making for us.

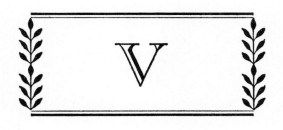

Peace Motions

AT THE Zurich-Munich International Bicycle Race, a Norwegian department-store owner in an astrakhan hat riffled through my sketchbook.

"Why don't you come to Norway?" he said. "We have plenty of sports champions there." He wasn't just exercising his voice. He had been his country's bicycle champion, and at home in Norway his small daughter, Sonja, was practicing to be Ice Queen of the world.

Mr. Henie's remark was a nudge in an obvious direction. The Reichsmark had collapsed. People were telling the puppy-on-the-carpet story in German. But for some time foreign newspapers had been picking up my drawings, so that I had little stockpiles of good cash in sports-minded countries such as Switzerland, Holland, and Norway. Like Putzi Hanfstaengl, I was an international financier who had foreign currency to play with.

So in 1922 I made for the Swiss border, and in Lindau-im-Bodensee, the last German town, spent my remaining marks on twelve hard-boiled eggs and a huge pole of salami, just to be on the safe side of starvation.

I went to Zurich, and there I was engaged by a sports weekly to travel from town to town, drawing soccer players of the Helvetic Confederation. From Zurich to Basel, from Basel to Bern we wandered, I and my salami; I had about three and a half inches left when we arrived at the Lausanne station, to find the platform jammed with journalists jostling, photographers lurching, gendarmes looming, and top-hatted Swiss dignitaries shuffling in their great shoes. Wherever I turned, I was brought up short by the invincible might of Boy Scouts spinning cordons with real ropes. So I stood with the crowd and stared, as everyone was staring, up-track, where the shimmering rails entwined like a sweep of seaweed. "What's going on?" I asked a bystander. And he told me.

The Near East Peace Conference was about to begin. The Simplon Express was due in from Paris bearing Lord Curzon and Poincaré. A *train de luxe* was on its way from Italy bringing the new Italian Prime Minister, Benito Mussolini. The three of them planned to meet in Lausanne for a little powwow before the opening of the conference the following day.

Now, I had three and a half years of world war in my bones, and three revolutions, pink, red, and white; I had just spent two years in the very snake pit of politics on the Schellingstrasse. Yet I had never read attentively the front page of a newspaper. I was as innocent of politics as the spring lamb you see on the meat packer's poster in the butcher shop. But here was a new thing. If I waited five minutes, I would find myself nose to nose with the portentous men of the time.

And so I waited with the crowd, craning my neck . . . and waited some more. But Mussolini's *train de luxe* did not arrive. He had changed his mind about meeting Curzon and Poincaré in Lausanne and had informed the British foreign minister and the French premier that if they wanted to powwow with him they had better continue to Territet, about thirty miles beyond. Poincaré was hopping mad at this piece of impudence from a wet-eared Italian prime minister, but Curzon, who loathed Poincaré, looked kindly on Mussolini's whim. So it happened that the Simplon Express moved heedlessly through the Lausanne station without stopping—past the Swiss dignitaries, the gendarmes, the press, the Boy Scouts, and me—and my only regret is that my salami was no longer with me.

Why did Mussolini play this childish prank? Well, it was glorious to crook a finger at the representatives of the two most powerful nations on earth and watch them come running; it was sweet to start getting even for the Treaty of Versailles, which had cheated Italy out of her rightful share of war loot. This "get even" spirit haunted Mussolini, I think, all the years of his life; it impelled him to attack Ethiopia, and took him out of the League of Nations, into the embrace of Hitler, and finally down history's drain. On the day he stopped his train at Territet, he had still another "get even" ploy, and that was against the Helvetic Confederation for certain events that had taken place in his youth, when he had lived in Lausanne in great misery. Starving, he had pounced on a lady in the park in order to snatch her watch. The lady screamed, the police came, Mussolini was arrested, and though he got off with a suspended sentence, he was expelled from Lausanne. This expulsion order was still in force.

Of course, now that he was returning as the prime minister of another nation and enjoyed diplomatic privileges, nobody would have brought the matter up. But Mussolini wanted that expulsion order rescinded.

Yes, but it was getting late, and Swiss bureaucrats, like bureaucrats everywhere, like to call it a day and go home and fall into their feather beds. It was quite a few hours before they could be routed out and made to change their minds in triplicate about Mussolini so that he could return without loss of face to Lausanne.

In the meantime I dumped my baggage in a hotel opposite the

railroad station and spent the rest of the evening cooling my heels with the world press in the lobby of the Hôtel Beau Rivage, where Mussolini was understood to have reservations; and here I noted for the first time that curious spectacle of wise men, some of them with white beards, waiting for hours on sore feet to ask questions of a jackass.

It was after midnight when he arrived, prancing into the lobby like his own equestrian statue. He stopped short when he saw our group, tossed his preposterous chin into the air, and without any plausible reason bugged his eyes like a lobster, so that the whites

shone around the iris and he seemed to be staring entranced at the Four Horsemen of the Apocalypse galloping in the distance. I didn't know whether to laugh or to call an ambulance. After a minute the eyes retreated, only to start the same amazing process all over again.

His complexion, which owing to certain strong modulations of the bone always photographed like patinaed bronze, in real life was a dirty yellow, like old, used tallow, and that jaw which would have served Samson to kill a thousand Philistines was shadowed by a creeping mold. His nose was a roughly finished job, his teeth healthy and yellowish, and when he laughed he clenched them tight as if he wanted to bite somebody.

And perhaps it took a caricaturist to observe his behavior when the arrival of the elevator brought the impromptu press conference to an end. He stepped into the elevator, turned his back upon us, and glanced at himself in the mirror. I, still absorbed in the bugging action of his eyes, caught the expression on his face. He glanced victoriously at his image. He bragged to his reflection: "You see! I did it!" There was even more in his look: "I did it," he told himself, "better than you could have done in my place!"

And as I stood there scribbling my impressions on my pad, Kismet made contact with me in the form of a plump Egyptian who breathed over my shoulder for a while and then offered me a fabulous sum of money for my drawing. As soon as I grasped the fact that I was living in a world where statesmen came higher than football players, I began to dote on them.

Politics, with me, was an acquired distaste.

That plump Egyptian, Azmi Bey, was the editor of a satirical Cairo magazine, *Al Kashkul*. He changed my life and set it in a groove from which I would see the end of his. Three decades later, while addressing the Security Council, as Nasser's chief delegate to the United Nations, he fell back in his chair, dead. I, directing the television cameras, recorded the event.

I saw Mussolini again after the formal opening of the conference, when he posed with Poincaré and Lord Curzon for one of those chummy photographs with which statesmen persuade peasants that God's in His heaven. With the eyes of the world on him, he had gotten himself up like an operetta diplomat: tight striped trousers, morning coat, winged collar, stiff cuffs, and that indispensable but inexcusable feature of Latin elegance, white spats. From his breast pocket peeked a white handkerchief, an object important to hygiene but better kept out of sight.

My eyes, however, were all for Poincaré, France's wartime president, father of the Entente Cordiale, and premier of the French Republic. He was a man who bestrode his times; for me he was the man who had engineered the downfall of my country.

He was an angry, yapping little schnauzer for whom the Versailles Treaty had not enough fangs in it. His profusion of gray hair had deserted the top of his head and camped entirely around the biting area; a light brown spot in the center marked the place where the onion soup made its entrance. He had deep, bone-sheltered eyes like cinders in a pit, and his forehead toppled over his brow as if placed by a drunken angel. He was pedantic in

grooming, as in everything else. Every gesture and word of his was clipped to the right size, and he had the defiant bearing of a provincial trial lawyer prosecuting someone for having swiped *Le Coq Gaulois*. The journalists called him old piss-vinegar, and he left an acid drop at every lamppost. Each look of his, each darting glance at Mussolini—and Lord Curzon, too—revealed that he took them both for lampposts.

It had become urgent for me to learn the reasons for this hulla-baloo in Lausanne, and I found my fountain of wisdom in the press bar of the Lausanne Palace Hotel. Opening from the lobby, it was decorated with all the flags of the world, and special prominence was shown to those of the whisky-drinking nations. The hotel's manager plenipotentiary, Colonel Steiner, a red-mustached musketeer in morning coat, had fortified it with everything a modern journalist might need: dice, cards, salted peanuts, a pretty barmaid behind the bottles, a piano for those who liked classical music, a slot machine for those who preferred modern.

After I had lost sufficient money on the slot machine, I found out that the Lausanne Conference had been called to revise the Treaty of Sèvres. This was one of the daughter treaties of the Treaty of Versailles, and after World War I it had given the Old Turks a dirty deal that the Young Turks felt they need no longer honor. They had already enforced their opinion by war. Now they wished to mop up the debris in a diplomatic manner.

There were all sorts of subsidiary problems which even today, almost half a century later, are as fresh as morning dew. First and foremost, of course, was British prestige in the Near East. Next, the prudent control of the Dardanelles, the sole outlet for the Soviet Union from its only warm-water port. And oil, which everybody wanted. And refugees, whom nobody wanted.

The battleground on which these issues were to be fought out was arranged as Clausewitz would have wanted it. Lausanne is built on the slope of a hill descending steeply toward Lake Geneva. At the top of the hill was the Lausanne Palace Hotel. On the shore of the lake was the Hôtel Beau Rivage. The French lived at the Lausanne Palace; the British at the Beau Rivage. The hotels were linked by public cable cars.

The Turks, at odds with the British, snuggled up to the French at the Lausanne Palace. The Italians, always jealous of the French, housed with the British at the Beau Rivage. The Americans, shy of entanglement, lived halfway between the two hotels, right where the ascending and descending cable cars met. The Russians lived the police knew where.

And all of us were cradled in a hollow of the Alps. Seen in a hundred views and moods from the glass-enclosed veranda of the press bar, the Alps would sometimes creep close and graze the nose, then fade to a breath in the blue distance. In late afternoon, soft smoky fog blanketed their feet, out of which jagged peaks rose like a menace; at twilight they burst into grenadine fire. On rainy days the whole picture was washed away by the sweeping mist.

I knew how war was made. Now from this eyrie I would see how peace was made.

Item. A secretary of the Turkish delegation, having come straight from the battlefield, leapt on a chambermaid and, meeting with resistance, bit off her ear.

Item. A British journalist found his Viennese fiancée in a love nest with an Italian ambassador and, seizing the nearest object to hand, which happened to be a bed lamp, broke the ambassador's head.

Item. Riza Nur, Turkish minister of finance, reached over the green baize conference table, grabbed the venerable white-bearded Greek statesman, Venizelos, by the neck and didn't let go until the beard turned blue.

Item. One of the members of the Turkish delegation eloped with the cash box, leaving the entire delegation penniless. This really isn't worth mentioning, because public money can always be replaced.

Item. A Russian émigré, Conradi, shot up the Soviet delegation at dinner.

Peace was wonderful!

One day the Chef de la Presse said to me: "Would you like to go to a reception tonight?"

Would I!

He handed me an invitation which began: *The Baron Pierre de Coubertin requests the honor.* . . .

Requests the honor! Me, a boy from Györ! I felt as if I had been awarded the *Légion d'honneur.*

I was in no doubt about what lay ahead of me. I had read the novels of Baroness Orczy, a compatriot of mine. A flunky would receive me at the door, knock on the parapet three times with a fancy mace, and in tones of ecclesiastical sonority pronounce my name. Proceeding into a crystal cathedral, I would shake hands with my host, breathe a reverent kiss upon my hostess' ring, and shimmer off into the throng of diademed dowagers, apostolic bishops, plenipotentiaries, attachés, ministers, generals, and consuls general, all richly bedecked with ribbons crosswise and crosses ribbonwise.

I took out my tail-coated evening suit. This costume had once belonged to my portly father, but our tailor in Györ had remodeled it to fit the skinny son. In order to look as much like the Prince of Wales as possible, I flattened it under my mattress and went to get a haircut. This was a considerable investment, but the occasion called for it. I could recoup by going without dinner and saving my appetite for the sumptuous buffet which even then was being prepared for me by world-famous chefs.

That evening, one step ahead of starvation, I arrived at a little hotel called Beau Séjour—or was it Beau Regard? One of those names that exist to be mixed up. I rang the bell at a door pointed out by the concierge. To my surprise it was opened not by a flunky but by a midget who pretended to be Baron de Coubertin, but I knew at once he was an impostor. The Chef de la Presse had briefed me that the Baron de Coubertin was none other than that famous sports lover who had revived the Olympic Games of classical Greece in twentieth-century Europe, an enterprise unthinkable for this shrimp who was looking at me out of velvety eyes like a little boy on Halloween who wears a false mustache and asks with his eyes because he doesn't know what to say.

I graciously entered, and he took my coat and led me into a salon furnished in an exquisite nineteenth-century *marché aux puces*, or flea market, style that only Swiss family pensions offer, at moderate prices, breakfast included. There were bowlegged chairs and lumpy sofas covered with surges and billows of dull red plush embroidered with golden acanthus leaves, and the windows were masked by rusty curtains festooned with bobtails as big as meatballs, their trails twisted up coquettishly, like Gibson girls. I was then placed in a red plush prison between two charming ladies whose combined ages were about a hundred and fifty. One of them had so much extra skin on her neck that she had tacked it up with a black velvet ribbon to which was pinned a golden locket containing, I'm sure, a hand-colored photo of her late husband and a lock of his hair.

By and by, two more guests arrived: the Marquis de Garroni, head of the Italian delegation (now that Mussolini had gone home), and one of his ambassadors. Lord Curzon had written to his wife that Garroni looked like a turtle but, as he sank deep onto a nest of broken springs, the breast of his evening shirt popped out of his vest, so he looked to me more like a destitute parrot on a rainy day.

A hotel chambermaid came around with cups of tea and wretched cookies at which I gazed with sore eyes: they would never replace the horse I was ready to eat.

And yet that evening proved to be one of those not to be missed, a climacteric to my youth. The doorbell rang again; the baron went to answer it and came back with a new guest. I turned to be introduced, and saw him—Nansen!—the hero of my schooldays, whose adventures on board his ship, the *Fram*, I'd devoured, and then devoured again.

Fridtjof Nansen was a great Norwegian who looked like a Great Dane. Pierre de Coubertin was a tiny Frenchman who looked like a Persian kitten. Photographed as they stood side by side on that red plush carpet, they would have made an attractive calendar illustration entitled *Friends*.

Nansen's face was arctic-colored: his cheeks frostbitten red, his eyes ice-blue and misty, his handlebar mustache snow white. He rose clear above the six-foot level, immense, muscular, broad-shouldered, and his great calves bulged visibly in tight trouser legs. He was the living illustration of a theory held by Professor Stockard of Cornell University that giant men and giant dogs have surplus skin, surplus bones, surplus boom, and surplus gloom. His face was hung with sorrow like a bull walrus on the muddy pavement of a zoo, dreaming of polar glitter.

I was to observe Nansen thoroughly for eight years. In that time I never caught him cracking a smile, this ponderous North-man, hard and lonely as Stonehenge, pugnacious, hard-hitting, straight-spitting. His diplomatic career came to an end when, as Norway's delegate to the First Assembly of the League of Nations, he was unable to control his use of undiplomatic language. But you cannot keep a doer from doing, and so he had picked up a burden that lay beside a rocky road: the refugees. He was their patron saint. He lent his massive strength, his massive prestige, to millions of Russians fleeing Bolshevism, Armenians and Greeks fleeing Turks, Hungarians fleeing Hungarians. They were Nansen's chicks, to whom the "Nansen passport" held out hope for a visa —to somewhere.

Why? Was it the stars, the arctic nights, "speaking peace as they do, those unchanging friends," that suggested to him a world's need, not of a bleeding heart, but of a stout one? To this day, you can get a Nansen medal for being kind to refugees.

I watched him holding the brittle teacup. My hero, who once, with tears streaming down his cheeks, had eaten his dogs, now munched cookies.

My stomach bayed with hollow rage. I got to my feet, bade the ladies good night, took my leave of the baron, shook Nansen's hand (and it felt like two hands), and fled from my first diplomatic reception giving forth a noise like thirty huskies in quest of a ham sandwich.

Poincaré and Mussolini had gone home directly after the open-ing speeches of the conference, leaving their ambassadors to cope with the rest. By far the most imposing figure left in Lausanne was British Foreign Minister Lord Curzon, Marquess of Kedleston. Everybody was acquainted with his resounding career as Viceroy of

India, his great diplomatic skill, and his positively psychic grasp of the "Oriental mind." A patrician, supercilious and remote, he was tagged in *Punch* with the lines:

> My name is George Nathaniel Curzon,
> I am a most superior person.

This reputation did not suffer from the statues that were erected to him in his lifetime, statues executed by court sculptors, who with their doglike mentalities presented him as an ermine-swathed hero, scanning the horizon for more yokels to conquer. Curzon approved of these alabaster penny post cards. It was his belief that members of the British ruling class, like himself, had been especially entrusted by the Almighty with the task of bringing light to lesser folk, particularly those of the Near and Far East. He dedicated one of his books: *To those who believe that the British Empire is, under Providence, the greatest instrument for good that the world has ever seen.*

What a happy marriage of idealism and imperialism!

All diplomats identify themselves with the country they represent, and it was quite natural for Lord Curzon to carry around with him the idea that the sun would never set on his baldish head. What he could not know—and none of us could know—was that he really stood in twilight, the last bastion at the *Exit* of an era; and that he was the first lordly lord to face a khaki-clad soldier who, with sword in hand, would cut to pieces a sacred treaty—one of those little chicks that were clustered around the Treaty of Versailles. When finally they had all gone to pot, World War II was at hand.

Looking with hindsight down the years, it seems to me that I can spy the very spot where Britain's glory began to seep away into the dark; and I was there. It was in the third-rate hotels and crumbly family pensions of Lausanne, where the scent of insecticide and dust blended so happily with that of *poulet rôti, pommes rissolées.* There a penny-pinching caricaturist found his natural home among others of wobbly social status: Shi'ite mullahs from

Persia, Sunnis from Iraq, Wahabis from the Hejaz, Zionists from Palestine, Kurds, Azerbaijanis, Macedonians, Gurkhas, Laks, and Lurs, who milled, swarmed, and plotted in an incessant rumbling, grumbling, undershudder to history. Each afternoon they would come to the surface and continue their sinister conspiracy to the tune of music at the *thé dansant* in the lobby of the Lausanne Palace Hotel. The British Empire stood solid only when a Parisian alley-ballerina, sparsely clad, appeared on the floor and performed calisthenics. Then all guttural plots ceased, and hundreds of Oriental eyes went pop.

Like a viceroy reviewing native troops, Lord Curzon progressed through the lobby, staring with glassy eyes past the ragtag and bobtail that cluttered the plush-carpeted floor. Yet, in three decades, how many of these scrubby characters were to become sparkling ambassadors, or prime ministers of independent countries, or delegates to the United Nations, holding appalling fate in the hollow of their hands!

But this was only 1922, and the foreign minister of Great Britain was the most illustrious man in Lausanne. He walked with an ebony cane, and when he sat down at the green baize-covered conference table, lackeys came forward to shove a green baize-covered footstool under his gout.

And I, noting this, thought that Lord Curzon's footstool seemed to be the little brother of the conference table.

My conscience as a chronicler compels me to tackle at this point the controversial matter of Lord Curzon's trousers. The affair of these pants, so interwoven with the last days of Empire, has already been described by Lord Zetland, friend and official biographer of Curzon, and by Harold Nicolson.

My story, however, is different from theirs. Sir Harold (as he is now entitled) was a member of Lord Curzon's staff and no doubt stood closer to his lordship's trousers than I did, so I beg future historians, digging for source material, to take his as the authorized version. My story is wholly biased and unauthorized, and I got it from a completely unreliable source: Lord Curzon's boozing valet.

Curzon arrived in Lausanne with a valet engaged just before his departure from London. His lordship soon found he had picked a lemon. This valet couldn't pack, he left his lordship's footstool behind, he was always drunk, was never there when wanted, and while his master was out he would sneak down from the second floor of the Hôtel Beau Rivage and dance in the lobby with the wives and daughters of ambassadors; or, preferably, he'd scoot over to the Casino de Montbenon, the rendezvous of Lausanne's adorable chambermaids, and not only dance but make dates.

One morning the telephone rang in Curzon's bedroom, and it happened that his lordship, personally, picked up the receiver.

"Hello, is that you?" asked a feminine voice.

"Who's speaking?" demanded Lord Curzon.

"Poopsie, don't you remember? We met yesterday at the Montbenon, and you said to call you. You even gave me your room number."

"This is Lord Curzon speaking," thundered Lord Curzon, and the caller hung up.

With split-second accuracy Curzon deduced that the call was for his valet. He issued a ukase whereby the valet was fired, effective at once.

That evening the marquess was to attend an official banquet. Lacking expert help, he dressed himself as best he could. He succeeded in welding winged collar to breastplate, then opened the wardrobe to get his trousers. They weren't there. Indeed, not only were the dress trousers missing, but all trousers, gray-striped, pin-striped, checked, worsted flannel, lounging, tweedy herringbone, all had vanished with his gentleman's gentleman.

A squadron of secretaries was dispatched to find the valet. I dare say the British Intelligence had to snap into action before the dragnet finally snagged the missing man in a sixth-rate hotel. He was commanded to hand over the pants. He refused.

Pacing up and down in heaven knows what costume, with Britain's prestige hanging on a button, Lord Curzon called into the chase that peerless diplomat, Sir William Tyrrell (later, as Lord Tyrrell, ambassador to Paris), a foreign-office nursling whose skill and tact could be depended upon to solve a situation fraught with danger. Tyrrell applied to his mission the full proceedings prescribed for peaceful settlement of a dispute: conciliation, arbitration, meditation. None of them worked.

"I'm keeping the trousers," said the valet, "until his lordship pays me what he owes me."

Tyrrell then menaced the man with the application of sanctions: "I warn you, there's a police force in Lausanne!"

"And I warn you, sir, there's a world press in Lausanne!"

This was a serious threat. Indeed, at that point in the talks his lordship's trousers would have come like manna from heaven to us bored journalists in the press bar. Sunk in thought, Tyrrell reported the deadlock to Lord Curzon. The marquess was outraged.

"I owe him nothing, and I'll pay him nothing!" he fumed. But Sir William told him that without payment the valet was determined to air the trousers in public, and Lord Curzon paid up. Sir William returned to the Beau Rivage with one more diplomatic victory to his credit and a pile of trousers over his arm.

Lord Zetland, in his biography, breathes but gently upon Lord Curzon's trousers. Sir Harold Nicolson states that the trousers were found the same day in the valet's room at the Beau Rivage, and is silent on the matter of the financial differences that separated the antagonists.

But I like my version because it shows British diplomacy at work. If there are questioners, I'll ask them a question: Who is more noted for telling the truth—caricaturists or diplomats?

Lord Curzon's opposite number at Lausanne was Ismet Pasha, a pint-sized general who later changed his name to Ismet Inonu after a village where he had won a battle. He was a follower of Kemal Pasha, who later embellished himself with the name Ataturk, Father of the Turks. Kemal had just thrown the Greeks out of that portion of Turkey allotted to them by the Treaty of Sèvres, in a blitz so swift that the Greek general who was to have been named commander-in-chief of the defense learned about his promotion in prison camp.

Ismet arrived in Lausanne with the mud of battle on his boots and on his head an army calpac made of sheepskin, which he wore throughout the conference, alternating it with his top hat.

The two men collided head on: Curzon, a marquess who looked like a marquess; Ismet, a general who looked like a toy soldier. Curzon had the poised arrogance of a British aristocrat; Ismet, the humility of an Oriental bourgeois. Curzon, an artist of improvisation, spoke chiseled, nuanced English and was a skillful diplomatic craftsman. Ismet shone in Turkish, if he shone at all, and as a soldier, he might be called the antithesis of a diplomat.

Curzon had come to Lausanne to see how much he could salvage of the Treaty of Sèvres; Ismet, how much he could destroy. At the beginning of the negotiation Ismet valiantly attempted a fighting speech, but his best efforts splintered against the architectural rhetoric of Lord Curzon. The rest of the conversation would take place in monologue, Curzon rising to the crest of eloquence and Ismet sinking deeper into silence while the crystalline words ricocheted against his head.

This would continue for hours. With clear, classic arguments, with fluted and convoluted phrases, Curzon built a Parthenon of words. But when at the end of his discourse he demanded of Ismet: "And what is your excellency's opinion?" Ismet woke up, shook himself, and answered: "No!"

Curzon thought, as anyone would: What a nincompoop! But Ismet, a military man, was aware that an army on the offensive uses up three times more energy than one on the defensive. He knew that eventually Lord Curzon, with his Greek pillars, would knock himself out cold.

Ismet's no was an effective forerunner of Russian *nyet* diplomacy, and I suppose both *no* and *nyet* are but diplomatic forms of Cambronne's *merde!* Never overlook the power of negative thinking in the shaping of world history.

I met Ismet Pasha on Christmas eve, 1922. The conference was in recess. Married delegates had gone home to spend the holidays with their families, and bachelors took to the mountains with skis. Only the Turks and I remained in Lausanne, the Turks being Moslems with no Christmas and I being an artist with no money.

That night there was no dancing at the Lausanne Palace, and the lights were dimmed. Only the multicolored bulbs of a gigantic Christmas tree loaded with tinsel, frosting, and sparkling trifles glimmered in the twilight of the lobby, which under normal conditions resembled the bazaar at Uskub. The jazz band, led by a Hungarian violinist, had been promoted to the status of a chamber-music orchestra and, with fiddles sordino, played *Silent Night*. Peace at last moved into the Peace Conference.

Under the Christmas tree sat two Unbelievers: Ismet Pasha and his aide-de-camp, crook-nosed Colonel Tewfik. Into the deserted lobby moved an errant *giaour*, myself, whereupon Ismet sent his aide to invite me to his table. The moment the orchestra leader saw me, a fellow Hungarian, sitting at the table of a mighty Pasha, he stepped out of *Silent Night* straight into the boots of the *Rakoczy March*.

Soon after, I don't know by what bug bitten but no doubt emboldened by my presence, the orchestra leader, fiddle under his arm and stick in hand after the tradition of the gypsy band leaders of Budapest, approached the table and, bowing to Ismet, asked him what his favorite song was.

The pasha, deaf as a cannon, turned to his aide-de-camp.

"What does he want?"

"What do you want?" snapped the colonel.

"I beg to ask His Excellency what song he would be most pleased to hear."

Colonel Tewfik leaned toward the pasha and bellowed a free translation: "He asks what he should play!"

The pasha opened his eyes wide, flung out his palms in amazement. "What should he play!" he exclaimed. "He should play what he wants!"

So died another Hungarian dream, noble in intention but ill conceived. Like a scalded cat, the ersatz gypsy slunk back to his podium and faded into the silent night. I, however, learned a lesson from the incident: that proper translations by competent dragomans are an absolute necessity in bringing about peace on earth and good will toward men.

My own conversations with Ismet that night were no more earthshaking than the orchestra leader's. The pasha was deaf, and I was deaf and dumb in French. But I wasn't blind in any language, and I took a good look at him.

Since childhood I had had a distorted view of Turkish pashas. Just as the heads of American youngsters are stuffed with cowboys and Indians, the heads of Hungarian children are full of Hungarians and dog-faced Turks, who in the fifteenth century fought heroic battles wherein the dog-faced Turks were always beaten. If, in spite of this, they held our beloved fatherland in bondage for a hundred and fifty years, it was undoubtedly due to the low cunning of bloodthirsty pashas like Ismet.

That those Turks were, by fifteenth-century standards, rather civilized and efficient administrators, and that all they wanted from Hungary were taxes and little boys for their armies (and, by the way, what does *your* civilized administration want from *you?*), was carefully concealed from us. Their ill repute was so solidly anchored in our minds that, five hundred years later, when a snail refused to come out of his shell we children would sing:

> *Snail, snail, put out your horn,*
> *Or else the Turk will come*
> *And break down your house.*

People have long memories; but children's memories are longer still.

And so I stared at Ismet Pasha, wide-eyed. A tiny man, he sat up at the table like a good little boy with bing cherry eyes and red cherry lips, his graceful hands fiddling with a golden watch chain.

He was a double-header; that is, his brain case had two distinct bumps like the back of a dromedary: a big bald one in front and a smaller one in the rear with a snow-white fringe around it. He had some difficulty carrying this improbable head on a rather frail neck, so his head floated from left to right, up and down, like a balloon on a windy day.

Because he was deaf, he could never be sure he had properly heard what was said to him, so he had developed an all-purpose smile, which he would turn on at any time, without apparent reason. He was too vain to wear a hearing aid in Lausanne, preferring to cup his ear elegantly with his hand. Later, as he grew older, he gave in and wore a microphone attached by a dangling wire to a hidden battery.

Ismet Inonu became, in the course of time, one of the Grand Turks of our age: prime minister under Ataturk and, after Ataturk's death, president of Turkey. Now in his late seventies, he is still a principal power in Turkish politics.

At the Montreux Conference in 1936, fourteen years after I had spent Christmas eve with the pasha in Lausanne, I was amused to note that on all sides young Turkish diplomats were cupping their ears, just as Ismet used to do. It seemed that the Turkish Foreign Office had developed a new species of deaf diplomat, just as you can develop new varieties of fruit fly. But what really flabbergasted me was that Numan Menemencioglu, head of the Foreign Office (and, later, foreign minister), admonished me when he sat for his portrait: "Don't forget my hearing aid."

I thought he was joking, so I left it out. We caricaturists, honor among thieves, don't poke fun at infirmities. But when Mr. Menemencioglu missed what amounted to his badge of office, he vigorously protested: "If you want your drawing to be popular in Ankara, you had better add the hearing aid." So I did.

Keeping a sharp eye out for diplomatic mimicry can help you make your way in a bewildering world. When Kaiser Franz Josef grew sideburns to balance his egg-shaped head, the entire Austrian general staff sprouted ridiculous tom-cat whiskers. You can identify leaders of the Second International such as Jaurès, Albert Thomas, de Brouckère, Stauning, and Kurt Eisner because they all sported Karl Marx's luscious beaver. Of the Third International, on the other hand, Trotsky, Chicherin, Dzerzhinsky, Lunacharsky, Maisky, Kamenev, Bulganin, and Kalinin, all favored Lenin's goatee. Joe Chamberlain's monocle dangling on a black shoelace (and that of his son, Austen) became a ruling-class symbol in England which was inherited like a title, and for a couple of generations we were treated to the intimidating spectacle of posh little English public-school boys with their shining morning faces denatured by a Cyclopean stare.

And let's not forget the Queen Alexandra limp, cultivated by English ladies with perfectly good ankles.

The law of monkey-see, monkey-do operates in diplomacy, bureaucracy, "society"—in fact in any pyramidal structure. As long as the hale imitate the physical infirmities of their leader, we can smile. But when the wise imitate a leader's mental infirmities, then we can begin to shiver and shake!

In Lausanne, Ismet used his deafness as a secret weapon against Lord Curzon. Even when he had heard perfectly well what Curzon told him, he would cup his ear, bend forward, and say: "I couldn't hear that. Would you repeat it, please?" Sometimes he'd make Curzon repeat the selfsame argument three times.

So one day Lord Curzon threw in the sponge and went home; and on home ground he suffered his *coup de grâce*, when the king passed him over for prime minister and called on an obscure M.P. named Stanley Baldwin instead. His career was shattered because he was personally shattered, and thus the last Englishman who really glittered faded into dusky history. When the conference reconvened in April 1923, his place was taken by redwood-faced, nerveless, bemonocled Sir Horace Rumbold, who for my money was the perfect exponent of the dictum: A British diplomat should always look more stupid than he really is—if possible. Sir Horace, a brilliant man, made the impossible possible.

I am not a votary of the great-man cult in politics, because when I scrutinize a great man closely enough to draw him it must be with pitiless objectivity, like a woman's. "What!" she says. "That little shrimp an ambassador!" Her first impression evaluates him purely for his biological import, relegating to second place his worldly status. Thus she leaps to an understanding which is not political science exactly, but is often very close to political reality.

My old on-the-spot drawings of Curzon reveal him to have been a far less formidable person than he looked. There is the proud pouter-pigeon chest, but it is shapeless, like that of a stuffed pouter pigeon, and his legs are spindly. I seemed to have the impression that his head was poorly sewn onto his body, and so I drew it, with a weak neck. The frontal bone is impressively molded, precipitating deeply between the saturnine eyebrows toward a beak-like nose; but the upper lip is skimpy, and there are sunken areas in the upper jaw that caused his smile to spread loosely and form-lessly from ear to ear. It is a bird face, but not that of an eagle; more of a young chicken hawk fallen out of its nest.

Curzon's face, in which so much strength was wedded to so much delicacy, suggested a man caught in a tug of war between incompatible traits of temperament. This would explain his tense-ness, touchiness, fussiness. Before coming to Lausanne, in Paris, Poincaré had given him the rough edge of his tongue; whereupon this Olympian had burst into tears and afterwards thrown a fit of sulks. On the Simplon Express that had carried them both to Lausanne—for which I had waited at the station—Curzon's *voiture salon* was in front of the train and Poincaré's in the rear. They had transacted the world's business—for instance, whether or not to meet Mussolini in Territet—by means of diplomatic couriers who staggered back and forth along the corridors.

What few of us suspected in Lausanne—I certainly did not know until many years later, when I read Lord Zetland's biography—was that his lordship's imperial posture, which earned him so many enemies among us members of the press, was in large measure due to an iron contraption he had been obliged to wear since his youth for curvature of the spine. In his correspondence with his wife, he referred to it as "my cage."

In all my drawings I had noticed the incongruity between the bombastic torso and the weak legs and neck; but I did not dream that so much seigneurial splendor was wrought of torturous bits of iron wire!

These events were followed from the press bar by as coruscating a company of journalists as I have ever seen gathered around one piano. In future years they were to become directors of great newspapers, write classics, found new religions, go to Hollywood, or get shot. French, Americans, British, Italians, Greeks: I was un-comfortable among them at first because most of them were enemy aliens to me, who had fought on the right side in the war. But I soon found that in the press bar the war was over and assaults were confined to bottles and barmaids, so I settled down in my home away from home to learn the art of waiting for news to break.

In those days great statesmen did not receive journalists in press conferences as they do today; they communicated by means of press officers. If a meeting lasted until dawn, journalists were obliged to wait until dawn for Ahrens of the Russian delegation or Sir William Tyrrell of trousers fame to come in and tell them everything it was good for them to know.

There was Lincoln Steffens, the great muckraker, who wore bangs to camouflage his oncoming baldness and dressed up as Whistler in flowing necktie and Van Dyke beard; "Jimmy" James, a little man with the stuffed breast of a bantam cock, thumbs in armpits, bowler tipped over his nose, and a big cigar screwed into his crooked mouth, who looked more like a successful bookmaker than the future managing editor of *The New York Times*; and Bill Forrest, one day to be managing editor of the New York *Herald Tribune*, with a mujik-face, pug-nosed and beaming.

Jo Davidson, a wild-eyed dumpling with an electric beard, gave daily demonstrations of American democracy, inviting his taxi drivers in for a drink. Jo made a very good thing of conferences, because statesmen seemed eager to sit for him. I expect they associate grandeur with sculpture rather than with painting, because busts can be easily set up in a square for pigeons to roost on.

There were the great political wizards of Europe, men such as Jules Sauerwein of *Le Matin* and Wickham Steed of the London *Times*, a cross between a southern colonel and Cardinal Richelieu. Such men never sat down at the common typewriters on the veranda but brought their own typists on expense accounts equal to those of great statesmen. Their conversation sparkled with the formula: ". . . as I told Curzon. . . ."

A frequent visitor was Lord Curzon's secretary, Harold Nicolson, who, though a diplomat, seemed to feel an irresistible attraction for the pagan atmosphere of the press bar. A brilliant essayist, he obligingly posed for his caricature and countersigned it with meager enthusiasm—for which I did not blame him. With round face, rosy cheeks, pink button nose, curly red hair, and white eyelashes over porcine eyes, he needed but an apple in his mouth.

I did not see a single press photographer brave enough to enter the press bar. Cameramen had no status then; they were outcasts, refugees from the county fair, who were not allowed to drag their foul boxes across sacred carpets.

As for me, I was an odd number: not a journalist, not a diplomat, and no expense account. Perhaps because of this I attracted around me people who were odd and oblique, such as the mysterious Italian, Conte Ponzone, an occasionally employed diplomat whose name, if mentioned in Italian society to this day, sets people bounding to touch a lamp to ward off the evil eye. Fernand de Brinon became my friend. Presuming, I imagine, that as a Hungarian I had a soft spot for the aristocracy, he whispered in my ear that his real name was Count de Brinon but that he didn't use the title in France because titles were not *bien vus* in the Third Republic. In afteryears, when he became Hitler's favorite journalist and later Vichy's ambassador to Berlin, he blossomed out as Count de Brinon—titles were well regarded in the Third Reich.

Arrested after World War II, de Brinon was shot, and died like a count after all, refusing the bandanna.

A young American holding a highball bumped into me. Spontaneous and confiding, a totally non-European lad, he said that he had just come back from Morocco, where he had dressed up as an Arab and crossed the battlefield of the Riff to interview the fierce rebel Abd-el-Krim in his own tents. But a single scoop did not admit such a baby-pink young man to the James–Forrest Big League, so Vincent Sheean for the time being was denied the company of Titans. He had two friends, myself and the piano; and, of the two, he treated me with more consideration.

When I first set foot in the press bar, Azmi Bey, with his Cairo magazine, was my only customer, and I wasn't happy at all to see formidable competition looming in the shape of another Hungarian caricaturist, Alois Derso. I had heard of Derso at home in Budapest; I had even brushed up against him during the Karolyi Revolution when we artists had gathered ourselves into a guild. But I had not dared to talk to him because he was gotten up like a *Graf-Baron* with a monocle and a loud checked overcoat down to his ankles.

But sartorial class differences don't count so much abroad, and we settled down together one evening in the bar to speak the Language. A veteran of the Genoa Conference, he told me how he had sat at a table scribbling caricatures while Geza Herczeg (formerly press chief of Count Karolyi, lately friend of Alexander King) had stood beside him, hawking them cheap to eager journalists, collecting the money on the spot, and putting it into a hat.

At dawn Derso said: "Well, I'm going home. Which way do you go?"

"Toward the railroad station."

"Good. We can go together."

We walked down the steep little rue de Petit-Chêne to the square in front of the station.

"I go left here," said Derso.

"So do I," I replied.

In front of the Hôtel Continental he stopped and offered me his hand.

"I'm home."

"So am I."

It turned out that we had both arrived in Lausanne at about the same time, had both gone to the nearest hotel, and that Derso had room 15 and I room 16. When we laid our heads to rest that night, we little dreamed that for thirty years we wouldn't get much farther away from each other than that.

Derso was a sensitively fashioned young man with small, collapsible hands and the sort of skinny legs that look wonderful when clothed in striped pants. Skeptical-eyed, slender-nosed, with a long upper lip and demonic smile, he gave the impression of a cardinal contemplating heresy. I noted that his working methods were eccentric. Nobody ever saw him with a sketch pad, and he never had a pencil in his pocket. He just prowled around the Lausanne Palace Hotel, head cocked, melancholy eyes riveted on his model. After a while, he'd get labor pains, borrow my pencil, scuttle to a quiet corner of the bar, and scribble profiles over every piece of paper within reach—wine lists, telegraph blanks, menus, his own passport—until he had created the absolute likeness of a man.

Once his caricature was born, he never forgot it. He walks about today with ten thousand portraits in his head, a morgue of caricatures.

Derso and I were sometimes favored in the press bar with the company of Ahrens, the wall-eyed, tumbleweed-haired press officer of the Russian delegation, and that of Dr. Christian Rakovsky, the Soviet ambassador to Paris and London and one of the founders of the Comintern. I expect they thought that as Hungarians we were bound to have nostalgic memories of Bela Kun's brief happy paradise.

Rakovsky dressed in traditional diplomatic uniform: striped pants and morning coat; but his cosmopolitanism showed up in his untraditional artist's mane, wing collar, and polka-dotted bow ties. Born in Bulgaria, he was a Rumanian citizen, had a French medical degree, spoke ten languages, and rattled incessantly in all of them.

One day he invited Derso and me to dinner with his delegation. When an ambassador invites a caricaturist to dinner, he is either an art lover or a publicity lover. The caricaturist accepts because he is a dinner lover. We found that the Russians were holed up in a hotel somewhat incongruously called Eden; on the way down I told Derso about the turkey *chasseur*, and how the Bolsheviks owed me a decent meal.

Derso and I sat on either side of Rakovsky. Ahrens was next to Derso, and next to him was Prince Mdivani, a relative of those two handsome lads, the Princes Mdivani who ennobled Barbara Hutton and Mae Murray. Georgians tell me that the title of prince indicated that in Georgia before the Revolution the man had owned two thousand sheep and a stone house. This one now owned mustachios like the horns of a black bull, a scimitar nose, furious eyes, and under the table a barrel belly, impatient for food. He stuck his napkin under his double chin and fought a battle of attrition with the *pommes dauphine.*

Opposite sat Vorovsky, an abstract-minded economist with a nonobjective beard, and he kept stretching his long neck like a short-sighted turtle. One can always recognize an economist by the precise way he eats *petits pois.* One can always recognize a press officer too, I reflected, watching Ahrens, by the hasty way he swallows his food without sufficient fletcherizing.

But of course my target for the evening was the middle-sized gentleman who sat directly opposite me, Foreign Commissar Georgy Vasilievich Chicherin, already a legendary figure among admirers of the Revolution, the man who had laid the foundation of Soviet diplomacy and who, not too long before, had torpedoed the Genoa Conference (the most important economic conference held since World War I) by signing a secret treaty at Rapallo with Germany's Rathenau.

Chicherin was the scion of an aristocratic family whose ancestors had held important posts under Catherine the Great. He had been a Tsarist diplomat, but in 1904 he had jumped the gun and joined the Socialist Party in Germany. He spent the war years writing pacifist articles in Britain, for which he was put in jail. But when Trotsky came to power, he pointed out to the British government that if it had the right to jail pacifist Russians in Britain, he would find it in his heart to jail British war enthusiasts in Russia. So Chicherin was released.

I saw him now, pudgy and stooped, looking at me with his almond-shaped eyes from the bottom up. With his sharp nose and saturnine eyebrows, he was the picture of a vodka-soaked bureaucrat in a Chekhov play. In Moscow he lived in a small room of the

Foreign Office with his cat; he never opened the windows, and he frustrated the charwoman's efforts to wash his tea glass and throw away precious old bits of lemon by hiding them in the drawer of his desk. He was lonely as a hermit, and it was a great day in the Foreign Commissariat when he invited a vet in to visit the cat.

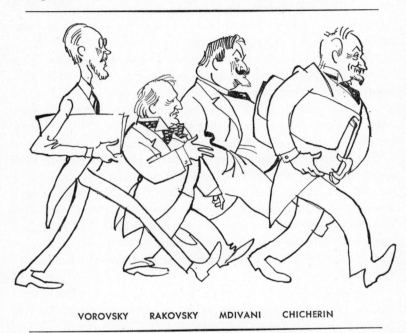

VOROVSKY   RAKOVSKY   MDIVANI   CHICHERIN

He was one of those *affreux* bureaucrats who never trusted secretaries to do a job he could do worse. He personally went to the railroad station to see that his couriers caught their trains. He worked at night and seldom slept by day. When exhausted, he played a little music on the piano; passers in the night would tell tales afterward about hearing the strains of Tchaikovsky seeping through his lone lighted window at the Foreign Ministry.

I suppose he had a touch of agoraphobia. I used to see him in the wide open places of the Lausanne Palace lobby, as lost as a blind beggar at a country fair, clinging helplessly to a column, then advancing in *valse hésitante*.

It was not unusual in those days to find an aristocrat among the Bolsheviks. There were many who objected to spending their lives as doormen to balalaika restaurants in Paris. In Chicherin's case, it is worth remembering that years before, in Paris, his father, who was counselor of the Paris Embassy, had been slapped in a night club; yet he had refused to fight a duel on religious grounds. I think it is fair to say that Chicherin became a revolutionist, not for power, or out of paranoia, certainly not for the sake of company. He is best placed in my revolutionary typology as a gentle man who thought the old ways weren't good enough for people, and had a vision of something better.

Sentiments of this sort were being rattled in our ears throughout the dinner by Rakovsky. He was selling us Chicherin. With his mouth full, he called the foreign commissar an idealist who had abandoned the forces of oppression to join with progressive forces for love of mankind, and the greatest Russian diplomat who ever lived. Throughout these hosannahs, Chicherin didn't say a word. His nose was buried in his plate. But when at the end of a long paragraph Rakovsky paused, Chicherin lifted his Oriental eyes and emitted his only significant utterance of the evening: *"Pas un mot est vrai!"*—Not a word is true.

Then he went back to his beef with *sauce bordelaise*, which by this time had soaked a slippery path down his auburn whiskers. A drop of sauce rolled to the end of a hair and hung there. He tried to catch it with a snap of his jaw.

How trivial is the mind of a caricaturist! Here I was, opposite this history-book figure; yet forty years after, when I remember him, I remember him snapping at the gravy like his own pussycat.

In those days of early Bolshevism, it was always possible to talk with a Russian, to exchange views, to doubt, to ask questions, to laugh together at a joke. But there is a world of difference between a capitalist-born Bolshevik and a Red-born Red. Today at the United Nations the Russians are silent, uncommunicative, and unresponsive. They walk around like men in fat iron masks. This is what Communist education has achieved in one generation: it has shut them up.

Of all the dinner guests that evening, only the caricaturists survived.

Chicherin was retired in 1939 and given a small apartment, where he lived with his cat and his piano. Presently his cat died, and so Chicherin died too. Nobody accompanied the hearse that carried his body to a distant cemetery: just a little music at the grave, short speeches by close collaborators.

The Georgian Prince Mdivani had a Georgian enemy, the son of a shoemaker, Stalin. Mdivani lived as long as Lenin lived; but when Lenin closed his slanted eyes, presto! Mdivani disappeared.

Our host, Rakovsky, got entangled in the Trotsky trial, and he vanished into thin air.

As for Vorovsky and Ahrens, during the second part of the Lausanne Conference, in April 1923, they were dining in that same room, at the same table, with a new member of the delegation, when a young Russian émigré named Conradi, whose family had been confectioners in Russia before the Revolution, shot them through an open French window.

Vorovsky fell dead, and the two others were badly wounded.

Max Beer of the official German Wolff Bureau got the scoop. He had been invited to dinner that night but had been delayed. He entered the dining room immediately after the shooting. The news reached me in the press bar, and I rushed to the Hotel Eden, where I found Vorovsky lying on the floor, under the table where we had dined together, his body covered by the tablecloth, on which there were damp stains of gravy. Vorovsky was long and the tablecloth short, and his feet were uncovered. Nothing is more macabre than a dead diplomat's feet.

The murder of Vorovsky had repercussions for a long time to come. Conradi was tried and acquitted. The outraged Russians broke off relations with Switzerland and, even after World War II, at the first meeting of the International Civil Aviation Organization, refused to sit at the same table with the Swiss. That the United Nations headquarters is in New York today, and not in

Geneva, is partly due to the events of that night, when Vorovsky's body lay on the floor, covered by the tablecloth upon which he had just dined.

My forebodings that Derso would have a number of good ideas before I did proved correct. He persuaded Colonel Steiner, manager of the Lausanne Palace Hotel, to commission him to do a dozen post cards caricaturing the principal delegates as seen in the lobby. Diplomats could then scrawl "I wish you were here" on the back of their own portraits and send them flying around the world. Seduced by these post cards, a rich Turkish bey ordered from Derso a souvenir album of original drawings.

One afternoon Derso's bey greeted me in the lobby.

"I've noticed that you are an artist, too. My brother-in-law wishes to order an album like the one Mr. Derso is doing for me." He then presented me to Prince Ali Hassan, a blue-eyed, petal-skinned Egyptian with a catfish mustache. We closed the deal at a princely price.

When both our albums were nearing completion, I was struck with an idea. I invited Derso for a little business conference.

"Look here, Derso," I said. "My prince and your bey are paying a fortune for these two albums, so there must be something in the idea. Let's put the albums together and publish a book that reasonable men can take home as a souvenir."

Derso tried to squirm out of this. He told me that he was planning to publish an album all by himself and was already in a very advanced stage of negotiation with a publisher.

"All right," said I. "Then I will publish an album all by myself."

This threat was pure hot air, as was his publisher.

Derso lived, and still lives, in quite a different style from that of other humans. He never retired before two in the morning, and for several hours thereafter read Nietzsche in bed. At dawn he turned out the light and spent another hour in the darkness yodeling "Cockadoodledoo!" out of sheer nerves. At last he would fall asleep and lie unconscious until four in the afternoon, when he would rise and shine and order breakfast from the tea menu in the press bar. Not until eleven at night was he in condition to draw caricatures.

I noticed this schedule and let Derso sleep. But shortly before he arose at teatime, I would enter his room, stand over his bed, wave my finger, and say to him in a hollow, ghostly voice: "Derso! Time is fleeting! The conference may end any minute. You are sleeping away the opportunity of your lifetime."

Derso would grunt, turn over, then go back to sleep.

This went on for two weeks. Conferences are as capricious as spinsters. One day it looks as if the world is saved, the next as if it is ripe for fire and brimstone. One afternoon I entered Derso's boudoir with the news that the Turkish delegation was packing and threatened to go home to Ankara.

"All right," he said. "Let's publish this album."

The next morning at eight I crept into his room: newspapers, clothes, and torn-up drawings littered the floor as if burglars had just departed. Derso was sleeping like a baby. I went to the sink, removed his toothbrush from the glass, filled the glass with cold water, and poured it over his head. Like a furious seal, Derso leapt from the depths, shot me a murderous look, then sat on the edge of the bed, gazing at his skinny feet. He then stood up and, having no idea what people do so early in the morning, sat at the table in his convict-striped pyjamas and began to scribble.

The first two weeks of our long collaboration, I dare say, consisted entirely of my pouring cold water on Derso. This was crude, but it served a double purpose: Derso was forced to get up, and since his bed was soaked, he was kept from falling back into it.

I began to draw furiously. I drew everybody, happy or miserable, I saw at the Lausanne Palace and the Beau Rivage. Occasionally I borrowed heads from Derso, and he from me. When on a single page he had lent me a Poincaré, a Curzon, a Mussolini, and an Ismet, I felt that he, too, should sign the drawing. So for the first time we used the double signature: Derso and Kelen.

Our album appeared with the title *Guignol à Lausanne* (Punch and Judy Show at Lausanne) and, in Arabic letters, *Caragheuze*.

The cover showed a British Punch and a Turkish Judy whacking each other with clubs. It was a success. Our laughter was airborne, and we had a whiff of how the Wright brothers must have felt.

Our paper airplane was something new in the world, a sign of the radically changing times that President Wilson had brought about for our benefit. Not only did the people have a right to know what their diplomats were talking about, but diplomats also had a right to know what they were doing. It was good to have a couple of caricaturists to tell them.

Still, laughing at Excellencies is bound to create a chill breeze somewhere. The superbly tailored, intelligent-eyed Sir William Tyrrell accosted me one day. He praised the album warmly and seemed especially enchanted by the splendid display allotted the Turkish delegation; and the portrait of Ismet—a perfect likeness! When he had me wagging my tail like a pup, he slid silkily to the point: Why had not the face of Sir Horace Rumbold, British High Commissioner in Constantinople, excited my artist's interest to the same degree as that of Ismet Pasha? My tailbone froze. I squeezed out the suggestion that if Sir Horace would honor me with a special sitting I would include his portrait in some supplementary pages that were in preparation.

I was honored in jig time in a salon of the Hôtel Beau Rivage. Sir Horace entered with Lady Rumbold and arranged himself upon a golden couch, his healthy, earthy face devoid of a smile, his thick lips drooping, a monocle soldered to his eye. I drew up a chair and began a left profile, on the side opposite the monocle. Lady Rumbold swished up and whispered in his ear. Sir Horace extracted the monocle and replaced it on my side.

Another time, I found next to me a fragile young man who moved slowly lest he should break: Mr. Naotake Sato, one of Japan's notable diplomats, who later became foreign minister and during World War II was ambassador to Moscow. I watched his fine hands and licorice eyes as he talked brilliantly in a subdued voice about Hiroshige and Hokusai, as if begging me to pronounce final judgment on these Japanese masters. One thing he did not mention was monkeys. And yet I knew he was thinking about monkeys. One of our compositions represented a fancy-dress ball in which His Excellency, Baron Gonsuke Hayashi, Japanese ambassador to the Court of St. James, was dressed as a monkey climbing up a tall Russian prince who was dressed as a telegraph pole.

Mr. Sato eventually wondered if a double-page drawing could be executed—of a size that might be inserted in every copy of the album—representing the entire Japanese delegation.

We drew the Japanese in evening dress, lounging elegantly in the Lausanne Palace lobby, watching younger colleagues dancing with lovely ladies. Not a monkey in sight.

Mme Bompard, the wife of the French ambassador, hailed us: "What sort of clodhoppers did you draw on my husband? Maurice! Show your feet to these gentlemen. Now! Aren't those the prettiest feet in the world? Why, they're like ladyfingers."

The ambassador looked at his feet and smiled diffidently at us. "My wife is right. They are like ladyfingers, but we are awfully sorry to bother you with them."

Eight months had flitted away—as far as I recall, a record for a conference. During that time the conference had broken up once and everybody had gone home. Lord Curzon broke up altogether and stayed home. The Turks were always packing to go home.

And was it a success? Of course. Any conference is a success which is followed by another conference instead of by a war.

The Turks came out of it with new boundaries that restored the original size of their country. An international commission, under a Turkish president, was appointed to control the straits. British prestige was in fine feather, although after everybody had gone home, a few trampled plumes were found under the tables by busboys cleaning up the Lausanne Palace *thé dansant*.

The question of Iraqi oil was left hanging, because oil questions can't be settled that quickly.

People are easier to dispose of. In the turmoil of war and the shuffling of boundaries, numerous Greeks were stranded in Turkey and numerous Turks were stranded in Greece. And neither nation wanted the Greeks or the Turks they got. So, in their eternal wisdom, the peacemakers agreed upon an exchange of populations. Greek and Turkish goatherds were to be transplanted to regions where only wine could be grown; and Greek and Turkish wine-growers were to be removed to regions fit only for goat raising. Everyone was to be compensated for the inconvenience.

Years later I asked a high official in the refugee market how such compensations worked out.

"More or less," he said.

"What do you mean, more or less?"

"Some people get more money than they are entitled to; some get less."

The Lausanne Treaty was the first postwar treaty that the victorious Allies negotiated, as distinct from imposed by consent. It was to be signed on July 24, 1923, a date which probably embitters the lives of Turkish schoolboys to this day. Derso and I prepared to celebrate it as best we could. We made a large lithograph: *The Apotheosis of Peace*. The scene was set in heaven, with Curzon beatified and the principal delegates as angels in lace nightgowns frolicking on pink clouds. Curzon had one arm around Poincaré, the other around Mussolini, who wore a black shirt and carried a club: this was a prophetic vision on the part of totally ignorant caricaturists.

In the center of the composition was a green baize table with the treaty spread out on it. We had the fancy idea of asking each participating power to sign our treaty in time to get it printed and on sale before the great day—that is, one week before the real treaty was to be signed. It was a most delicate diplomatic endeavor, requiring tact, prudence, and psychology.

I reviewed all possible candidates. I didn't dare approach Sir Horace Rumbold, because if he refused me, as well he might, the whole scheme would fall through. I thought I could get the French to sign, but even if they did, the British might still refuse, just to be haughty.

I concluded that the first to sign should be an American, a representative of a country old in democratic traditions and new to diplomatic snobbishness. So I presented the original drawing to Ambassador Joseph C. Grew. He didn't hesitate.

Thereafter I visited General Pellé, head of the delegation of France, a country where even a general is tolerant of humor. He signed.

Only then did I dare to approach Sir Horace Rumbold. Naturally, after two colleagues had affixed their distinguished signatures, he could not refuse.

Ismet signed with a chuckle. The rest just saw me coming and whipped out their pens.

And so our caricature of a treaty was signed one week before the real one. The original was bought by the Turks and reposes today in the archives of the Foreign Office in Ankara.

Yet, I don't look back on this incident as a major diplomatic victory. On July 24, sitting in my best clothes in University Hall watching the signatories step forward to take up, one by one, the golden goose-quill pen, I noted with humiliation that my decoy, Ambassador Joseph C. Grew, was not among them.

Not having been at war with Turkey, the United States had no reason to sign the Lausanne Treaty. The Americans were just having a little vacation in Lausanne while keeping an eye on Iraqi oil.

VI

The Courting Years

MAN is a chummy animal. From cave to conference some deep-sunk instinct urges him to unify: he forms families, clans, states, nations, and leagues. The Greeks had leagues, Napoleon dreamed of one, the British Commonwealth is one, the Iroquois Indians had a fine league of separate sovereign nations.

Man regards his historic leagues with pride, plagues his children with their names and dates, points with genuine regret to the ruins left after a league was shattered.

There is one league to which we do not point with pride. Its failure was too bitter, and the blame lies too close to home. Even the most thoughtful political wizards manage to avoid mentioning the unmentionable. It is as if fifteen years of history have been swept under the rug, so that all the grandeur has no power to sway us now and all the misery cannot serve to teach us. What a waste of years!

I shall have to break the embarrassed silence about the League of Nations, because my heart was bound to it almost from beginning to end. And wasn't it a great thing for a young man to be in love with, after all? Isn't it something to dance about that for the first time since man stopped scratching himself with his teeth, men tried to form a league that wasn't directed against any other group of men but was for every man?

As a schoolboy I always thought history lacked sex. Gibbon tried to correct this by writing a sexy *Fall of the Roman Empire*, but he put the juicy bits in Latin and the juiciest ones in Greek. That's no way to make history popular. In order to make my tale attractive to the very young and the very old, I'll liken the League of Nations to a jilted virgin. She was an odd, sad waif to begin with, born on the wrong side of the two-party blanket and abandoned by her Uncle Sam on the Quai Wilson. Lord Curzon—that famous humorist—thought she was the world's best joke. All she had to her name were a few Nobel Prize winners, some sugar daddies, two caricaturists, and a wisp of an olive branch.

First came the *Courting Years* from Versailles to Locarno in 1925; then the *Big Promise* from Locarno to the Japanese invasion of Manchuria in 1931; and then the *Rape* from 1931 to World War II, by which time the poor girl was anybody's trollop. It took twenty million deaths before the rapists could be brought to book and the maid's virginity repaired. No wonder it is not bon ton to mention her past, so instructive to virgins and rapists alike.

Derso and I, having come out of the Lausanne Peace Conference alive, surmised that Fate had placed in our hands the wand of a fine and ancient trade, that of court jesters; and that it behove us to follow not Majesties but Excellencies from conference to conference, to jibe, joke, jollify, and possibly make a living. We came to Geneva in the fall of 1923 to see whether we could enliven the Fourth General Assembly of the League of Nations.

We had not, however, come to reinforce Curzon's opinion that the League was the world's best joke, or Poincaré's quip that it was but a victors' club, or to add luster to President Harding's promise that he would not lead the United States into the club "by the side door, the back door, or the cellar door." With a world war still in our bones, all our good humor was drawn from Wilson's words that the League was "the world's first honest attempt to ensure permanent peace." We paid homage to this maxim, but in our own way, by jingling bells, turning somersaults, and occasionally administering bitter pills to delegates suffering from irregularities. We are by no means discontented with our descent from Scoggin. A jester sleeps with dogs, but in the great halls of kings he dines with priests, and that's as it should be, for what is a comedian but a moralist gone wrong?

In those courting years the League lived in hotels and kept her mountains of documents filed in empty bathtubs. The Assembly held its meetings in the Salle de la Réformation, an annex of the Hôtel Victoria which had to be entered through the lobby, where Philippe, the hotel porter, bowed to the arriving dignitaries. I recall him as a sort of Crô-Magnon ancestor of Comte Jehan de Noue, Chef de Protocole at the United Nations. Instead of the *Légion d'honneur*, he wore on his lapel the badge of a concierge, wrought of two crossed keys, and he borrowed additional dignity from a couple of potted palms. The quality of *chefs de protocole* has gone up, that of dignitaries has gone down. In those days most diplomats wore striped pants and a top hat and addressed one another with exquisite eighteenth-century courtesy. Today they wear evening beards in the morning, no hats, and for some of their diplomatic language their mouths should be washed out with soap.

This was the only lobby of any parliament in the world that had a piano with a lace doily on it and cute tables offering the prospectuses of shipping companies and Cook's tours. Ash trays were provided by a local department store, and the backs of wobbly plush armchairs were safeguarded from the hair-oil-using races of man by antimacassars. Here you could see, if you stayed long enough, a veritable Who's Who of the Roaring Twenties: the Aga Khan, majestic as a bullfrog; the flash-toothed Maharaja of Kapur-

thala; the wide-eyed Countess de Noailles; Baron Maurice de
Rothschild, looming and stooping like a brontosaur. Keeping an
eye on her husband's orphaned offspring was Mrs. Woodrow
Wilson, a stately woman with a baby face. As the years passed, she
lost her baby fat and hefty bones came to the surface; I can well
believe what some say, that during her husband's illness she became the first woman president of the United States.

Ignace Paderewski, the great pianist and former Polish prime
minister, was annually to be seen in that lobby; he never missed an
assembly so far as I recall. He stood proud, with a belly like a pregnant kangaroo, the kind that begins south of the belly button and
hangs like a bag, and he had everything a caricaturist demands of

a virtuoso: long hair, polka-dotted flowing tie, large-brimmed hat,
and gray morning coat. I watched him squinting nervously and
sketched that special blend of forms I was later to note frequently
in the faces of musicians: fragility in harmony with bullish masculinity. In Wagner, Liszt, Verdi, Gershwin, a weak upper jaw is
matched with a solid, impressive lantern jaw. In Paderewski's case
the chin was puny, but the forehead was ruggedly royal. Such men
feel deeply and have the strength to project what they feel; Paderewski was not only a great musician, he was also a fine orator.

He played piano and politics with unequal success. A close friend of Woodrow Wilson, it was he who inspired the thirteenth of the Fourteen Points, providing for an independent Poland with access to the sea. This became the "Polish Corridor" which separated East Prussia from Germany. Those nimble fingers improvised for us a polka that became a leitmotiv of German nationalistic agitation, and the Nazis' God-given excuse for tearing up the Treaty of Versailles.

It was Paderewski's greatest tune, but Hitler made us dance to it.

On the first floor of the Victoria, in a crowded hotel room, sat the highest body of the League, the Council. Never since my teens, when on a Saturday afternoon in Györ I bought for fifteen cents a "standing room only" ticket to see *The Merry Widow*, had I been so squeezed in a crowd. It had gathered to witness in living color a scene previously exhibited only in paintings in museums: diplomats deliberating on the affairs of the world.

On that first day in 1923 I drew sad-eyed, puffy Hjalmar Branting, a fine old walrus from Sweden and a renowned pacifist; and, peeking over his shoulders, Osten Unden, whose nose was a mere knob which kept his glasses from slipping. This chance drawing of Unden proved a good investment, because for his and my lifetime he has been Sweden's durable foreign minister. At that council table sat one of history's last truly resplendent handlebar mustaches, embellishing the person of Antonio Salandra. In 1915, when Italy declared war on the Austro-Hungarian Empire, thus plunging me into trouble on Monte San Gabriele, he was her prime minister. I took my humble revenge: I drew that great bucket head even greater than need be. Britain's Lord Cecil, a descendant of that Cecil who was chiefly responsible for the Elizabethan Age, was collapsed into himself like a wax candle on a hot mantelpiece; and over his shoulder appeared my toothy fellow veteran of Caporetto, Philip Noel-Baker. So well did we make peace at Geneva that he got a Nobel Prize for it.

Viscount Ishii of Japan, Quiñones de León of Spain, Rio Branco of Brazil—these names sound today like those of flying foxes of the Jurassic period; but in 1923 those foxes flew high. Their table was not horseshoe-shaped but oval. No microphones with a world-wide hookup interfered with their ear-to-ear whisperings. Simultaneous interpretation existed only as a bee in the bonnet of a Boston department-store owner named Mr. Filene. The interpreter, M. Parodi, sat at the council table, and whatever anyone said in English or French he translated, standing, into French or English.

Photographers were absolutely excluded. But on opening day a local photographer, M. Jullien, was admitted. He dragged after him a stepladder, which he used like an icebreaker to plow his way through the crowd. Then he set it up, climbed to the top, and, holding his magnesium powder high, commanded: *"Ne bougeons plus!"* Thunder and lightning broke loose, white clouds billowed to the ceiling, everyone began to cough, and those who regained their eyesight could buy the historic document for fifty centimes a copy.

If arrangements at the Hôtel Victoria were eccentric, those at the Hôtel National were well and truly pixilated. Here the Secretariat camped under the direction of Secretary General Sir Eric Drummond. It is believed he had been hand-picked for the job by Clemenceau. At the Paris Peace Conference the Tiger's attention had been caught by a young man behind Lord Balfour who was always giggling. "What's your name?" he had asked.

"Eric Drummond."

"Ah? Well, you're just the man to be secretary general of the League of Nations."

Sir Eric came to Geneva, bought the Hôtel National for five and a half million Swiss francs, and engaged the world's first international civil servants: M. Hottop, former director of the hotel, the concierge, several chambermaids, and a big, clumsy St. Bernard. The Germans, whose word for the League was **Völkerbund**, promptly labeled the dog the **Völkerhund**, and it spent its days bumbling sleepily in a neat garden where magnolia trees bloomed and a Negro lass, sparsely clad in a golden robe, held high a lamp, like Diogenes looking for an honest politician. There was also a sundial which told delegates—had they but looked—that it was later than they thought. The garden was separated from the lake drive by a palisade to which was attached a marble tablet inscribed: *To the Memory of Woodrow Wilson, President of the United States, Founder of the League of Nations.* Closer inspection revealed that the marble was really wood and that the engraving was only painted to look like engraving. In the fifteen years I spent in Geneva, Wilson never had a genuine marble tablet to his name.

The walls of the Hôtel National housed a Babel where delegates of fifty-odd nations who didn't know Peter from Pancho looked for their committee rooms like blind hens for grain. Once Maximos, the Greek foreign minister, got lost, and the committee over which he was supposed to preside waited vainly until eventually he was found presiding over a totally different committee. Another delegate discovered that for days he had been sitting in the wrong committee, making speeches on the wrong subject. Nobody had noticed. A young Hindu status-seeker bounded up to me in the crowd and pumped my arm out of joint, saying: "*Mon cher sénateur . . .*"

"You are mistaken," said I, "I am only a *dessinateur.*" And he melted away.

Sir Eric had recruited the secretarial staff largely from the members of the postwar planning commissions, in the belief that those who had worked so happily together in wartime could be salvaged for the benefit of peace. Among them was supposed to hatch the International Man. It seemed reasonable to hope that if they worked together toward a single goal, international solidarity would germinate, and that if they collided continually in the congested corridors, international conscience would spring to life.

Not since St. Paul baptized the uncircumcised and brought them home to eat *matzoth* on Passover had the brotherhood of man been under such stress. When it came to a showdown, it was found that cuckoo's eggs by the hundreds had been nurtured in the Secretariat: Englishmen who placed more faith in the stability of the British Empire than in a collective destiny; Frenchmen unable to disengage their hearts from *la belle France*; Hungarians with their "thousand-year-old Hungary." Even the nationals of tiny, helpless countries found more inspiration in, for example, "glorious Lithuania" than in Wilson's newfangled ideal.

So well anointed were they in nationalistic oil that, of those I drew in their modest cells in 1923, fifteen stepped straight into ambassadorial trousers, including the secretary general himself, who became Britain's ambassador to Fascist Italy.

And yet good eggs did hatch. I knew many, and I still know many at the United Nations, who found that a personal love of home sweet home did not necessarily conflict with a belief in man's interrelated destiny on his planet. For this curious viewpoint they have risked being deprived of their passports by their national governments.

The year Derso and I came to Geneva also saw the admission to the League of two new members: Ireland and Ethiopia.

The admission of the Irish Free State was supported by the British, who had done their best to prevent its existence. Ethiopia's entry was opposed by the British and sponsored by Mussolini, who, thirteen years later, did his best to put an end to its existence. No caricaturist can ever be as funny as statesmen.

My first pressing duty was to draw the members of these two delegations. It was my habit to arrange, through the press secretary, a visit to a delegation in its hotel. There I would transform one of the bedrooms into a torture chamber, moving furniture and lamps until I found the right position for a chair where, in strict diplomatic precedence, the members of the delegation would take their places: first the prime minister, then the foreign minister, and so on, down the line. I learned not to neglect the least cookie pusher, because it occasionally turns out that last year's cookie pusher is next year's immortal savior of mankind.

I set up such an interview with the delegation from Ireland, and drew the head of government, a famous Sinn Fein rebel, William Thomas Cosgrave, predecessor of de Valera. He was a man of girlish-pink complexion and blond hair so silky it could not be coaxed into a tidy garniture for the head, and he looked at me with

forget-me-not popeyes, through long white lashes. No Hollywood director would have cast him as a man to throw bricks, yet he had spent his life in and out of jail, and even as I drew him he was living dangerously. In fact, one president of the Executive Council had been bumped off.

The men of Erin came first to the League in an altogether un-neighborly spirit, bearing unreadable, unthinkable, druidic names. My sketchbook filled up with such anagrams as Marquis Mac-Suibhne Magh-Seanaghlas, and Adodh O. Cinnedigh. In later years, having proved to the whole world that the Irish can't spell, they dropped this habit so prejudicial to the brotherhood of man, and such names boiled down to Marquis MacSweeny of Mashono-glas, and plain Hugh Kennedy.

My next assault was upon the Ethiopians. Only once before had

I laid eyes on a black man and that was as a boy when a beer garden near my home engaged a troop of Negro singers and dancers to keep me awake at night with their strange howlings and stampings. By day, we urchins used to follow these black men through the streets of Györ, and so did droves of peasants with mouths agape. Once I saw a peasant woman staring at a bare black satin back. Unable to resist, she put out her forefinger and touched it. The man turned on her, snarling and flashing his brilliant teeth.

With such a memory in mind, I telephoned the headquarters of the Ethiopian delegation at the Hôtel de Russie. Somebody picked up the receiver, let me talk for a while, then said something in Amharic and hung up. I called again, and the same thing happened. After the third attempt I went to the hotel in person and asked the porter to announce me. He spoke a few words over the house phone and then directed me to the third floor. I knocked on the door of the delegation's suite. It opened slightly, and close to the top of the narrow slit the eye of a black-skinned giant appeared, peeping down on me. Then the door banged shut. I was about to retreat when a waiter arrived, wheeling two poached eggs on a little table. At his knock the door opened wide, the waiter rolled in, and so did I.

I found myself in a dark room with twin beds. On each bed, swathed in cheesecloth, lay a bushy-haired, electric-bearded Ethiopian in such a fashion that the heads were in the middle of the bed, while the black, bare legs hung airing over the bedstead. The moment they spotted me, both jumped up in alarm. Behind me, I could feel outrage emanating from the giant bodyguard, and I began to speak swiftly in French, English, German, struggling to explain myself, but they only shrugged. I resorted to sign language. I took out my drawing pad and made a lightning sketch of Lord Cecil. Then, jabbing my pencil toward one of the bushy gentlemen, I indicated that I wished to draw his portrait. He understood and nodded. He then squatted on the floor. I dared not attempt to seat him on a chair, so I squatted too. Above me towered the other delegate, and the giant bodyguard, who had lost his grasp of the situation and watched with grave anxiety what I was doing with my pencil.

Not until I had begun to draw did it strike me that I had no idea how Ethiopians might react to their own caricatures. I had seen some singular behavior in the last fifteen minutes, and in a sudden, searing glimpse into the future I saw myself flayed alive on the third floor of the Hôtel de Russie in honor of some antique prejudice. I thought fast: flattery, that was it! I ransacked my brain for the handsomest bearded man I could draw from memory and found him—Rabindranath Tagore. Onto the forehead and bush of the Ethiopian I tacked Tagore's face like a bearded Madonna, and handed it to my model. He was pleased. He smilingly caressed his wiry beard, which was snarled with feathers from the bed.

He passed the drawing to his colleague and the giant. They wagged their heads joyously. I got up from the floor, magnanimously presented to them my sketch of Tagore, and took to my heels through the door, which was now courteously held open for me by the bodyguard, and down the stairs straight to the nearest café, where I drew from memory the delegates from Ethiopia.

I saw them again the day they entered the assembly hall, when their country was ceremoniously received into the League. Each wore, in addition to his cheesecloth robe, an Italian Borsalino felt hat perched on top of his electric bush, a symbol that Western civilization was on the march in Ethiopia. When they passed the hat-check counter, feminine hands reached out to deprive them of these hats and they vibrated with alarm, their faces clearly registering: "No! Never!" A white man bobbed at their side; he was Comte Lagarde, Duc d'Entotto, Minister Plenipotentiary and High Counselor to the Ethiopian delegation, and he must have given them the high counsel to let go of their hats, for they did so. They didn't know what to do with the hat checks: the cheesecloth robes had no pockets.

When the president of the Fourth Assembly pronounced the historic words: "And now I invite the honorable delegates from

Ethiopia to occupy their seats in the Assembly of the League of Nations," the Ethiopians appeared at the doorway of the hall in their flowing white garments, clutching their hat checks, and glided toward the places reserved for them. Against the black mass of tail-coated diplomats, Ethiopia entered the League like a frightened ghost.

Throughout the years of the League, only two nations from black Africa were members: Ethiopia and Liberia. Just as Ethiopia was represented at meetings by a European, Comte Lagarde, Duc d'Entotto, the Liberians were headed by a Dutch banker, Baron Lehmann. Such titled white slaves were needed to guide the Africans through the quagmires of the white man's jungle.

Today at the United Nations the delegates' lounge looks like the *Bal Nègre*, full of jet gentlemen, some weighing a good part of a ton, others slender and graceful as jungle vines. They speak delicately accented English and French, wear Roman togas, and carry executive-type brief cases. Important of step, straight of eye, they have the air of men on their way to the future, and I ardently hope that when they get there they will find it is the place where they meant to go.

Whereas both new member nations were received into the League with amiable applause, our entry was vigorously contested by a lady delegate of some three hundred pounds, Mademoiselle Elena Vacarescu, of Rumania. In her leaner days she had been the mistress of King Ferdinand; she was the first, in fact, of the Vacarescu-Lambrino-Lupescu axis of Rumanian royal mistresses. English-born, Victorian-bred Queen Marie was no friend of royal romance, and she had caused Mlle Vacarescu to be exiled to Paris, where she found solace in writing poetry.

Still, there was no question that her services to the crown deserved recognition and reward; therefore, when the League was formed, Mlle Vacarescu was named a member of the Rumanian delegation, and she sat—of all places—on the Fifth Committee, wherein old maids of both sexes debated such questions as white slavery and obscene publications. It was the committee Polish dictator Pilsudski referred to when he said: "The League had better keep out of my affairs and stick to regulating the commerce in little girls."

Once Mlle Vacarescu halted suddenly in the middle of a speech and said, pointing to the Scottish interpreter, Captain Russell: "I want that man removed. Every time I mention white slavery an ironical smile appears on his face."

Mlle Vacarescu was a lady of expanded charms, and so was the female relative who served as her faithful chaperone in Geneva. The two ladies were wont to garnish their tonnage with heavy strings of Venetian beads and a bazaarful of trinkets, gaudy with moonstones and sunstones, onyx and sardonyx, and plain window glass. When they rolled, together, down the Quai Wilson, they looked like a couple of overflowing barrels of pirate treasure just fished out of the lake.

I drew Mlle Vacarescu as she was, in full fig and feather, with her arched black eyebrows grown together over her nose, her inquisitive squint, her lorgnette. This caricature burst into public sight in a colored lithograph depicting the council table of the League with the members and a few spectacular guests around it. Mademoiselle was outraged. She accused Derso and me of being agents of the Hungarian government sent to Geneva to ridicule the members of the Little Entente. The Rumanian delegation sent an official protest to the secretary general demanding that the lithograph be removed from the walls of the Secretariat and its sale prohibited in the hotels. The Secretariat complied.

The world press leapt like a stung lion: what was this muzzling of caricaturists? Why didn't we have the right to draw a fat delegate fat? Was the League a democratic institution or not? Mlle Vacarescu's poundage weighed heavily on the freedom of the press, and our lithograph sped around the world, bearing Mademoiselle upon it as on a magic carpet. Overnight we became known, and tasted some of the delights of fame when people who didn't know us bowed to us. Sir Eric bowed, too, to the might of the press, and our drawing was reinstated.

Mlle Vacarescu was not the only poetess in Geneva who

thirsted after our blood. One of the habitués of the League was
perky Comtesse Anne de Noailles, a lady with big cold eyes and
the sharp beak of a chicken hawk. She swooped upon Derso in the
lobby of a hotel, clutching a drawing. "So that's why you've been
following me around?" she screamed. "And I took you for an admirer. And see what you've done to me—the claws—the beak!
Look at me, you barbarian, I have the most beautiful eyes in the
world, and my hands—look at my hands—my lips . . ." With the
fury of a wounded chicken hawk she tore the drawing in two.

Quite a crowd had gathered, so the countess calmed herself
sufficiently to scribble a little poem for Derso on his drawing pad.
In it she informed him that when she was dead her ghost would
be gayer than he and her cinders fierier than his life.

Emily Hahn makes the point somewhere that people who don't
want to be written about should not invite writers to tea. I'll add
that those who can't stand to be caricatured should eschew public
life.

The most important aspect of a human being is the truth about
him, and this is exactly what so many people can't endure. The
caricaturist, by his very nature, can't suppress the revelation of
truth. Even if he is well disposed, his hand betrays him. The result
is a bitter pill for the ladies, I know, because they are surrounded
by *couturiers, corsetiers, coiffeurs,* masseurs, husbands, and lovers
who conspire with the womanly vanity of each to build in her
mind an altogether false image of what she looks like. I am not
a *coiffeur.* Besides, for me the unpawed, unprinked woman gives
forth the real magic, whether she likes it or not.

Mr. Khrushchev has warned us about the hazards of the cult of
personality; yet I dare say it is here to stay as long as she elephants
follow bulls. I myself am in the service of that cult, and the more
spectacular, or absurd, or terrifying a personality is, the more I dote
on it.

You might say it is a good thing in an international organization
that a brainy delegate from a small country is enabled to play a

mighty role on the world stage. The drawback is that an outstanding man might lend his country's affairs a prestige and weight they don't deserve. In the early twenties you could easily have gained the impression from the antics of Messrs. Beneš and Titulescu that the two most important nations on earth were Czechoslovakia and Rumania.

Sometimes I reflect: what was Eduard Beneš really? Was he a great statesman or a petty intriguer? A dreamer or a realist? Or just a shrewd bird with a longer beak than he could see the end of? Such questions were unposable in his day, and perhaps, to many, unthinkable now, for Beneš is remembered as a "personality," a patriot, and a champion of the League.

He was a bowlegged schoolteacher, a dachshund always in a hurry, and a fidgety model for me because no sooner had I got him seated than he tried to jump up and run away. When he smiled, such a network of crow's-feet appeared that it was hard to know which wrinkle was the eye. It took some time for one to capture that foxy smirk, which had nothing cheerful about it; it was tight-lipped, demi-sec, with a bitter bouquet. As I drew, Mme Beneš stood guard behind me, flashing messages in Czech code to her husband. From the reaction of a wife to her husband's caricature I often gain insight into their relationship. Once an ambassador's wife, looking at my drawing, remarked: "I always said he looked like a camel." Shortly afterward, she eloped with the third attaché.

Judging by the cold potato-salad cheer with which Mme Beneš viewed my efforts, she lived with her husband in cloudless bliss.

Beneš stood out from the common crush of diplomats by dint of a cream-colored flat-top beany cocked high on his brain case and a ready-made raglan coat; he looked like a shoemaker decked out in his Sunday best. He was unsnobbish and easily accessible; communicative, yet he never opened up completely. Deep in his system he nursed a gripe and a fright, both clearly expressed in his mechanical, lemonish smile. Some frightened people turn to alcohol or drugs; Beneš was a work addict. He labored eighteen hours a day and was to be seen in the evenings coming out of a meeting with stacks of homework under his arm. The next morning he would return with the most thoroughgoing *rapport* on any subject what-soever, from the reform of the calendar to the protection of nursing sperm whales. It could not have happened to him, as it once happened to Sir Austen Chamberlain, that he carelessly read the *rapport* of his neighbor, Senator Dandurand of Canada, who in turn picked up Sir Austen's *rapport* and read it.

Gripe and fright are not the best advisers for statesmen. Beneš's bogy was the fear of a Hapsburg restoration. This prevented him from bringing Czechoslovakia together with other peoples of the former Austro-Hungarian Empire into a strong Danubian confederation. It wasn't his fault alone; yet it was faulty of him to imagine that security could rest on a country composed of Sudeten Germans who did not wish to be Czechs, Hungarians who did not wish to be Slovaks, and Slovaks who did not wish to be Czecho-slovaks.

He was a creation and a creature of the Treaty of Versailles, and when in Munich France broke with the policy laid down in this treaty and assiduously pursued in Geneva for eighteen years, that was the end of "Little Beneš" and of Czechoslovakia. The pieces were snapped up by Hitler and, after Hitler, by Stalin.

Beneš was not the only victim of that time-honored misconception that places reliance on armaments and counterarmaments, alliances and counteralliances woven around jerry-built nations. It caused his downfall; and it caused the downfall of practically everybody in this book.

Whereas Beneš, with his upturned nose, looked unmistakably Czech, Titulescu of Rumania looked like no member of the human race described in any anthropological What's What. He had a small head like a greengage, mongoloid cheekbones, a low forehead, parchment complexion, big baby eyes, and no trace of beard or mustache, but a rich, feminine growth of hair. His fingers were unusually long and doughy, and he gangled in every limb, walking with long, elastic steps, his arms flailing like windmills. He had the shrill voice of a witch.

Such a strange caricature of a statesman was he that people quite often asked me, a caricaturist, for my expert opinion. The answer lies in textbooks of medical psychology. In such a book, under the heading "elongated eunuchoids" (*eunuchoider Hochwuchs*), I found described the same short neck, short trunk, narrow shoulders, broad soft hips, and exceedingly long legs and arms.

Eunuchs, in fact, make splendid diplomats. Their sharpened intelligence, feminine intuition, flexibility, and above all the skepticism natural to men living on the margins of social acceptance and biological conformity, all combine to equip them for slippery and subtle jobs. The Arabs have long known this: in the heyday of the Moslem civilization, they used to turn out eunuchs, both black and white, on the disassembly line, and trained them to become competent administrators, Viziers, Sofas, Divans. Some of them even usurped the thrones of kings.

American history is enlivened by a prize eunuchoid: John Randolph of Roanoke, Jefferson's leader in the House of Representatives. Like many eunuchoids, he sought to compensate for his infirmities by a wicked use of words. He was a master of the insult beautiful. When a political antagonist dared to bring up his lack of virility, he replied superbly: "You pride yourself upon an animal faculty in respect to which the jackass is infinitely your superior." Of another opponent he said: "He shines and stinks like rotten mackerel by moonlight."

Titu, as we called him, commanded the same snap wit and graceless language. But being a Rumanian instead of an early Virginian, every time he insulted a colleague he sent him a gold watch the following day. Once Pierre Laval remarked: "He owes me a gold grandfather's clock."

Eunuchoids tend to simulate masculinity. One symptom that strikes my eye is the typical dashing gait, with the foot never coming down quite firmly enough, so that they walk like swashbuckling jellyfish. Randolph fought duels, he appeared in Congress booted and spurred, carrying a riding whip and followed by his favorite hound. Titu spread money around himself like incense, gave opulent parties, and treated his herds of admirers with grand-seigneurial generosity and contempt. He was loud, presumptuous, and domineering. When Mussolini attacked Ethiopia, Titu swung into the lobby of the Hôtel des Bergues at cocktail time and across

the crowd of distinguished diplomats and their ladies shrilled out: "Mussolini has got us up to our necks in *merde,* and now he wants us to eat it." (When the incident was reported to Mussolini, he said: "Exactly.")

Brilliant, superficial, crooked, rootless, this one-man spectacle, surrounded by journalists, attracted far more attention to his business in Geneva than it deserved. For fifteen years all Europe followed the debates between this noseless, beardless man-woman and Cyrano-nozzled, hairy he-man Count Albert Apponyi. Titu fought tooth and claw, lying at a tangent like a hysterical woman; Apponyi lied back with the dignity of a Jesuit-educated old piece of pemmican. And the subject of these arguments? Well, they concerned certain disgruntled Hungarians, the so-called "optants," who owned property in Transylvania but didn't wish to stay there and call themselves Rumanians; the Rumanian government objected to compensating them for their confiscated properties.

During the debates, Titu sat at the council table in a fur coat and plaid scarf, though the room was well heated. He repeatedly pulled a golden snuffbox out of his pocket, dipped in his doughy fingers, and pinched snuff. I am doomed to remember the unmemorable. Once the tobacco juice like a curious little mouse peeked out of his nostril and in the passion of argument he let it run.

Randolph of Roanoke died insane. Titu died a drug addict. I am told that toward the end of his life he underwent hormone treatment and a miracle took place: he grew a beard, divorced his wife, and in the south of France developed a way with ladies that made up for much lost glory.

I have noticed many eunuchoids among diplomats, politicians, statesmen, and even in the army, where I'm sure they shine at tactics as did their eminent predecessor, Narses of Byzantium. I cannot name them, of course. You can call a "great man" an ape if you choose, but not a eunuch. That hurts.

Their degree of eunuchoidism is not always the same. Some of them are married and have children. But wherever I see long legs, loose-swinging arms, a short trunk, feminine hips, a scant beard, luxuriant silky hair, and that characteristic dashing-dainty step, and hear the high-pitched voice, I look next for the strain of feminine intelligence, frivolity, cynicism, eel-like flexibility, and capriciousness even in grave matters. I look also for fundamental negativism like that of Randolph, who remains a smaller man in his nation's memory than he was in life; and that of Titu, who strained brilliantly at gnats and left nothing behind him but a tale for a caricaturist's history book.

People generally do not recognize such symptoms in their leaders. But they suffer the consequences.

If God in his wrath should decide to destroy the British ruling class as once he destroyed Sodom and Gomorrah, unless ten righteous men could be found among them, Robert, Viscount Cecil of Chelwood, would be one of those righteous men. He was the British member of Wilson's three musketeers who had fought so valiantly for the League at the Paris Peace Conference. The French musketeer, old Senator Léon Bourgeois, had to be pushed to meetings in Geneva in a wheelchair; the other, General Jan Christiaan Smuts, did not come to Geneva at all. This left Lord Cecil, the League's elder uncle and parfit gentil knight.

In Hungarian we occasionally use the expression, "elegant as an English lord." Cecil was an undoubted lord, his name was sprinkled with history as with a golden powder; his Elizabethan forebears had helped mold England at a time when many a lord's ancestor had poached for his dinner. But was he elegant?

He could have been a giant if he had tried, but he walked stooped and sloppy as an old mackintosh dangling from a coat hanger. He lived in a state of declared war with a soft black felt hat. He clasped it under his arm, stuffed it in his coat pocket, squashed it in the middle, dropped it, sat on it, swatted flies with it, used it as a fan. Only rarely did he put it on his head.

He wore a collar of terrifying altitude. His coat was shorter in the back than in the front. His arms were so long they might have been a spare pair of Titulescu's; his coat sleeves began to give up the ghost at the elbows. What had been subtracted from the sleeves his honest tailor had tacked onto the trousers, which bagged at the knees and fell in concertina folds around the ankles. They were very old pants. Only at the seat did they shine like new.

And yet Lord Cecil was the most elegant man in Geneva; because elegance is not a matter of pants, it is a matter of head. He had the domed bald pate of a Dürer prophet, garnished with a curly fluff at the fringes. Deep-set in oblique shadows beneath the vaulted brow, a pair of burning eyes stood vigil. His nose was bold as a falcon's beak, and his long upper lip protruded like a monkey's. His face was not at rest for a moment. He could laugh like a child, and he was forever sucking on that long upper lip or thrusting it out suddenly.

Modest, friendly, direct, Lord Cecil nevertheless lived in a world within, remote from the world without. During the long sessions at the council table he would slide farther and farther down in his chair until all that was visible of him was the top of the apostolic bald head and his bony fingers, crossed as in prayer, and he stared at the ceiling as if he saw a vision there. Collapsed in an armchair in the crowded lobby of the Hôtel Victoria, he stretched his long legs out as far as they would go, never noticing that passers-by had to jump over them.

When, by and by, the League passed out of the hands of apostles and into the hands of foreign ministers, Cecil was pushed aside by men like Sir Austen Chamberlain, Sir John Simon, and Anthony Eden, and never again did he slide under the council table. Yet he did not forsake his duty to the Maid. He came to Geneva as the representative of the powerful British League of Nations Association, through which he had organized in England a solid mass support for the League.

We drew him as Savonarola; we drew him as a bald eagle atop lofty heights; we drew him as Moses bringing down the tablets of the law from Mount Salève. In 1934 a frail little lady visited our exhibition in London and expressed a desire to buy this Moses drawing. She handed me her card: it was Lady Cecil. I'm scared of my models' wives; they seem to know what their husbands look like better than I do. Lady Cecil sensed the apologies welling up in me and said: "Oh, he's just like that, Mr. Kelen—always playing about with the tablets of the law."

There is a widespread delusion that a man chooses his profession; the truth is that his profession chooses him. That is why men of similar careers, whether executives or executioners, will, when carefully observed, fall fairly neatly into commonly repeated types, as if Nature, in creating them, had dipped her hand into the same barrels and bottles.

In a large profession such as politics, you can isolate dozens of such "types." These four men whom I drew in 1923, so prominent in the courting years of the League, were to be reincarnated for me again and again. Beneš, as I see him, was a busy beaver, a patient builder of dams. Such a man hews down mighty oaks with his little nibbling teeth, but his foresight cannot encompass the splash of that oak when it comes tumbling down.

Titulescu was a brilliant prestidigitator who could saw a pair of striped pants in two before your eyes, stuff them into a top hat, and pull out a dove of peace. The dove was dead, but you could take it home with you.

Apponyi was a legal eagle with eyes fixed on a book and feet planted on treaties. A legal eagle builds his nest on inaccessible heights and lays hard-boiled eggs in it.

Lord Cecil was a prophet, a man of too much character and crystalline morality. He glowed with cold passion for lofty ideals. Such men inevitably knock themselves out of the perfidious game of *Realpolitik*, but continue to flicker like will-o'-the-wisps over the bad conscience of their times.

Now and again I find a man with kindness and humor in his eye, strength in brow and jaw, taking shape under my pencil. In politics he adds up to the *enlightened doer*, and he's rare enough, but I drew such a man in 1923: Albert Thomas, the founding father and first director of the International Labor Organization. In my innocence I might have overlooked him had he not worn a fine auburn beard and walked around town alongside another auburn beard, this second one decorating his Chef de Cabinet, M. Viple.

With this M. Viple as matchmaker, I made an appointment to draw Thomas at his home—to my dismay, at 8 o'clock in the morning. Even at that hour Thomas was bouncy, talkative, ebullient, and sunny. Like so many labor leaders, he was shaped like a meatball, with a round belly in which I think he kept a gyroscope that enabled him to stay afloat in the most furious crosscurrents of political intrigue.

He was a French Social Democrat, and that auburn bush proclaimed that he had sprung fully armed from the beard of Karl Marx, a member of the Second International, separated by a few thousand hairs from goateed Lenin and Trotsky. You might think it easy to draw a man who is all beard: just draw a mattress and you can't miss. Not so; a beard is a hairy problem, subtly shaped and shaded in conformance with the face beneath, bristling, wisping, rippling, flowing, curling, whorling in a manner as intensely personal as a fingerprint, and tamed, like any other pet, to its owner's habits.

There is a legend of old Vienna (the home town of psychology) that by a beard you can tell whether a man pays his bills or not. The man with the straight-flowing beard caresses it smoothly downward, saying to himself: "I shall pay." The man whose beard ends in two separate points first caresses the right tress, asking himself: "Shall I pay?" He then caresses the left tress, saying: "Or shall I not pay?" The man who lets his beard grow but shaves his mustache says: "I will pay half." And the man with the Van Dyke goatee grabs his beard with one downward yank and snaps: "I won't pay!" This last they call the *zahl nix* beard, and how truly so is proved by Lenin, who never paid a penny of Tsarist Russia's war debts.

Albert Thomas had the cleft beard of the man who ponders both sides of a question, and I noticed how he played with it, right, then left, curling the ends upward. While I sketched, his nine-year-old daughter entered the room, carrying a neatly wrapped ham sandwich, and when the drawing was finished, Thomas sandwiched this sandwich between a heap of documents and stuffed the lot into a brief case. Then he showed me proudly around the ILO building; for though the League lived *en passage* in hotels, the daughter organization was well set up in a building which from the outside looked like a convent and on the inside like a hospital. Each glass window, each piece of furniture, Thomas told me, was the gift of a different government. This was news to me, but I have since learned that international organizations (including the United Nations) are furnished like the homes of penniless newlyweds, each chair from another relative.

I came to know this warmhearted, brilliant man well over the

years, drew him dozens of times as he ate, worked, and joked; and I caught the perpetual point of interrogation in his blue eyes: "What can I do for you?"

When after an opulent dinner in a Paris restaurant a fatal heart attack felled him, the men and women of the ILO wept bitterly. I was not to see such an outburst of emotion again for many years, not until the news of the death of Dag Hammarskjold reached the UN. International civil servants tend by occupation to be skeptics. But I've got to admit they know when to cry.

The ILO represents one of the remarkable new concepts that took shape around the League, drew strength from her, and remained strong after the League died. The United States did not join the League but did join the ILO; Japan, on the other hand, left the League but did not leave the ILO. The organization continued throughout the war, bloomed bigger and better after

San Francisco, and stands today, with the Soviet Union as a member, for principles unimaginable to our grandfathers: that a man has a right to work in healthful conditions for decent pay and a right to time for rest. Ever since the angel with flaming sword drove us forth to scrabble for our living, the ILO has been the first helping hand we've had; it proves, too, that when man makes a League, he doesn't make it in vain.

Posterity decided to erect a statue to Albert Thomas, and France's *sculpteur d'Etat*, Paul Landowsky, *Grand Prix de Rome*, was commissioned to execute it. Landowsky had not met Thomas, and he straightaway came up against that beard. M. Viple asked me to provide sketches of Thomas's beard which would help Landowsky, and I gladly did so. The monument now stands in front of the ILO building in Geneva, and I have often made a pilgrimage to the statue of my immortal friend and looked up at him, thinking: "*Mon cher directeur*, how you have changed!"

What a sensation it was for us in Geneva when a genuine Indian chief came to town! A whiff of Peter Pan was just what I needed for our album, and so I stalked him through the corridors of the Hôtel National. I was desolate to find him wearing a neat brown business suit and at his side no moccasined brave but a common- or garden-variety, vulturous paleface lawyer. I sketched the chief, who favored my drawing with a benevolent smile. The lawyer, however, snatched it out of the chief's hand, tore it to pieces, and threw it on the floor. Then he grinned at me with his false teeth to show me there were no hard feelings.

The chief took this situation in hand by presenting me with his card, upon which was engraved: *Deskaheh, Chief of the Cayuga Nation, Ontario, Canada*. The lawyer informed me that the chief had weighty complaints against the Canadian government and had come to Geneva to lay them before those charged with the welfare of racial minorities.

North Americans are accustomed to Indian troubles. They are aware, from earliest childhood, that everything that has happened to the Indians since the landing of the Pilgrim Fathers has been bad for the Indians and that there is absolutely nothing they can do about it, least of all go back where they came from. But for us in Geneva, forever embroiled with peevish Lithuanian Germans, Czechoslovak Poles, and Transylvanian Hungarians, it was refreshing to greet this malcontent from across the sea.

It was true that a certain section of the Secretariat heard the complaints of racial minorities, but mainly those created by the peace treaties, which had seen to it that in some countries the majority of people were minorities. The nations concerned had signed obligations granting their minorities the privilege of appealing to the League when they felt they were being stepped on. Canada, however, had accepted no such obligation, and the Secretariat therefore had no notion what to do with the chief, who further complicated matters by trying to register with the League several strips of wampum representing treaties his ancestors had concluded with the paleface; these documents he carried in a buffalo-skin pouch. For several days they let him cool his heels in the corridor; then they advised him to present his complaint in writing.

Well, the chief had not come this far to write letters that he could have written from home. What's more, a day would come when he would have to render to the Cayuga Nation an account of his accomplishments before the League. Bogged down as he was in bureaucratic mud, the offer of a theatrical agent came in handy. It was proposed that the chief should appear on a local stage and there present the grievances of the Cayuga Nation to the people of Geneva. The lawyer was in favor of this solution.

The following day huge posters were pasted all over the city, announcing that Deskaheh, the Great Chief, descended from Eagle Eye and Game Killer, would be on exhibition on the premises of the Salle Centrale at 8:30 that evening, admission 1 fr., children half price.

The Salle Centrale was filled to capacity with old ladies from the pensions and Genevese mammas with their children simmering with excitement at the prospect of seeing a live Indian. Hiding in the rear were a few curious members of the Secretariat. Above the stage was flung a wide pennant which cried out: JUSTICE FOR THE CAYUGA NATION!

The curtain went up; Deskaheh appeared dressed in the regalia of a Cayuga chief, feathers and all, and, with the air of a magician, placed his buffalo pouch upon a little table. In an undertaker's hollow voice he unfolded the trials of his people. He told how the paleface real-estate agents had swindled them out of their land and how the government had withdrawn their ancient hunting and fishing privileges one by one. He pulled a wooden pipe out of the pouch and held it high. "Here is the pipe of peace which my ancestors smoked with the Canadians. And here are the agreements. . . . The black beads represent my ancestors, the white beads stand for the paleface. With your own eyes you can see that at the end hangs a black and white fringe. This means that the agreement was concluded in accordance with the law."

He then handed the wampum down from the stage to the mothers seated in the first row, who admired the needlework and forbade their children to touch it. "And all these agreements the Canadian government has broken!" perorated Deskaheh. A murmur of indignation arose at the Canadian government's contempt for such beautiful handiwork.

The following day Deskaheh was on his way back to Ontario. I went to the railroad station, shook his hand, and sent my warmest sympathies to the Cayuga Nation. Deep down, I felt the impact of his tragedy. Only gradually was life and observation to unfold to me its desperate symbolism: that a League formed of nations whose sovereignty is totally intact must leave hundreds, thousands, millions of people at the mercy of their governments, whether mildly selfish or utterly insane. Deskaheh foreshadowed the unfortunate Jews of Europe; he foreshadowed apartheid; the "freedom fighters" of Hungary; he foreshadowed another chief, not a Hawk, but a Lion of Judah, who, once he had been gobbled up by a jackal, could find no help in the League, or anywhere else.

Once a woman went to her pastor to request a funeral oration for her defunct husband. "I have various prices," said the pastor. "I have a speech for $2 that makes the women and children cry; another for $3 that makes the men cry too. And for $5, I can make my voice tremble."

All the speeches I heard in 1923 were $5 speeches. It was typical of the early Assemblies that not one prime minister or foreign minister of a great power appeared in our album, but we drew five winners of the Nobel Prize for Peace: Lord Cecil, Léon Bourgeois, Nansen, Branting, and Lange of Norway. Under their guidance a Treaty of Mutual Assistance was drafted, tightening loopholes in the League Covenant, and requesting member nations to make definite engagements for the maintenance of peace.

The governments did what you and I do when we get a disagreeable letter: they didn't answer.

And at about the time these Nobel Prize winners were pronouncing their speeches with trembling voices, three Italian officers of the Albanian-Greek boundary mission were slain on the Greek side of the border. Mussolini's eyes bulged. He thrust out his gorilla jaw and sent a blistering ultimatum to the Greek government, which contritely bowed to all his demands, except a few that were judged incompatible with national honor.

Mussolini then ordered his navy to bomb Corfu and occupy it.

The League was stunned. Here was a flagrant breach of the Covenant wherein member nations were pledged never to make war on a fellow member until all possibilities of peaceful settlement had been exhausted. The Council convened. Excitement ran high, and I was elated to think that I would see high diplomacy in action. Because I had gone freely to Council meetings while the League considered the sorry case of a Macedonian boy beaten by his Greek schoolmaster for speaking Serbian with a Bulgarian accent, I actually believed that secret diplomacy was a thing of the past. I was dumfounded when the usher pointed to the sign on the door: PRIVATE MEETING.

All I could do was what the other journalists were doing: I waited in front of the closed doors and, whenever they opened, tried to read on the face of a hurrying secretary what was going on inside. I waited until the end of the meeting on the chance of catching an unguarded word of the departing members from which historical deductions could be made.

Since then, I have waited in front of royal palaces, in the Gobelin-decorated halls of the Quai d'Orsay, in the austere corridors of the British Foreign Office. I have waited on hot days before the Locarno Palace Hotel and on cold nights in the courtyard of the Haag Binnenhof. I have waited in St. James's Palace before the golden door of Queen Anne's room while inside Ribbentrop defended the occupation of the Rhineland. In September 1923, outside the closed doors of the League of Nations Council, I was initiated into that most familiar antic of the diplomatic press: waiting.

We know now what went on behind those doors, how the disciples of Wilson—Belgian Foreign Minister Paul Hymans, Sweden's Branting, and Lord Cecil—fought like lions for the Covenant, and how the little Greek lawyer, Politis, and the huge-headed Italian, Salandra, almost came to blows. But Mussolini refused to admit that the Council was competent to judge him. He insisted that the case be placed before the Conference of Ambassadors, which was a transmogrified form of the Supreme Council of Allied Powers. In the end, the League accepted this humiliation.

I was far from appreciating the implications of the affair at the time, but I well remember the efforts of a French politician to explain it to me. "The interests of peace," he said, "must come before the prestige of the League."

Now I'm old, and I know that world organizations and young virgins live on their prestige.

Locarno Idyll

A LITTLE Italian village festooned with flowers and flags, a polished lake sliding to meet the sky, candles of black cypress standing vigil over red roofs, a summer dying a balmy death: this was the setting in which the Big Promise was made to the olive-crowned maid.

I had seen Italian villages before, but only on battlefields, where chimneys stood without houses and the charred fingers of bare walls stretched toward heaven to beg mercy. Here the chimneys had houses, and at night the harmonica's sentimental sound seeped through open windows. Strings of rainbow-colored electric lights garlanded the quays, and girls twittered in the grenadine twilight. There are pageants that displace more air, but the threepenny idyll in a village on Lago Maggiore wafted a gentle breath over Europe, the breath of hope.

In the rustic Town Hall were gathered eight delegates from seven nations: France, Germany, Britain, Italy, Belgium, Poland,

and Czechoslovakia. It was the first time since the end of World War I that former enemies had faced each other to talk of peace.

What was the main obstacle to peace in Europe? The peace treaties, naturally. The Locarno Conference was to revise them and to replace them with a new pact that Germany could sign, not under duress, but freely by agreement, preparatory to her honorable admission to the League of Nations. It was precisely here, at the threshold of the League, that a dead dog lay. The League's Covenant was part of the Treaty of Versailles, which spelled out Germany's war guilt; signing the Covenant would have been tantamount to an admission of that guilt to which all the humiliations, occupations, reparations, and separations were pegged. You might just as well have asked George III to sign the Declaration of Independence.

As we all know, a treaty is sacred; you can't just tear it up, especially when it took more than a year to concoct. But a treaty can be buried alive under new treaties, and that is exactly what the Locarno Conference set out to do. For fifteen days the gentlemen in the Town Hall busied themselves like gophers under a heap of dry beanstalks made of "treaties of mutual guarantee," "arbitration conventions between first parties and respective second parties," "boundaries individually and collectively guaranteed," all to be paraphrased, signed, sealed, filed, and possibly not forgotten.

History's memory is capricious. It makes much of such instant statesmen as Ribbentrop and Ciano, keeps alive the names of little crooks such as Goebbels and grand butchers such as Hitler and Mussolini, and Stalin, whose cold hand is still at our necks. It broods on the umbrella of Neville Chamberlain, but does not recall the monocle of his half brother, Austen; and Briand and Stresemann are hardly visible in the sandhills of encyclopedias.

Blessed are the peacemakers, but their names are soon forgotten.

"What a beautiful man!" exclaimed a German lady-journalist peeking over my shoulder. My drawing, however, showed a fragile Frenchman on wobbly legs, stooped under the weight of a shaggy head, looking like a poet who has just received twelve rejection slips on an empty stomach. His transparent paper nose, eyes cold as blue-point oysters, mustache drooping over a crooked mouth that opened right oblique—all these I had been drawing piece-meal, but together they made up more than their sum: they made up Briand, and Briand the Gestalt was a beautiful man.

Stresemann was a cartoon German, both opulent and stiff, pug-nosed, porcine-eyed, full-lipped, and his bald head had rusty shadows around the edges. He carried his embonpoint with the self-assurance of a Prussian police inspector on his day off; his trousers were too wide for his legs; he smoked cigars in paper holders; and, just to make doubly sure, he wore two dueling scars on his left cheek. In the Sudan such scars indicate membership in one's tribe; in Germany they signify a college education.

Tweedy Austen Chamberlain had a monocle dangling on a black shoelace, and his mouth curled down in a permanent grimace, precisely like a stage Englishman in the act of adjusting his monocle. His other eye was glassy too, and it popped with the anguish of a mother hen who, having hatched a brood of duck-lings, sees them troop into the water. Slim and trim, he stood and walked square-shouldered, as if he had swallowed a coat hanger.

Briand, Stresemann, and Austen Chamberlain: each man was prototypical of his nation, as if the Archangel in charge of International Affairs had especially picked him out of the gilded moth-ball atmosphere of each separate Chancellery and then set all three down together in the autumn of their lives in an autumn landscape, saying: "There! You have soon to make peace with your Creator: make it first with your fellow men."

And they tried. There were knots in the skein of negotiations, but in the bucolic air of Locarno they loosened and retied them-selves into bows. Briand invited his colleagues for a little sail on the lake aboard a white boat, *Fleur d'oranger*, Orangeblossom. Lady Chamberlain was invited too, because many years before, on their honeymoon, the Chamberlains had sailed on that very boat, which now with the smooth grace of a swan glided past the Isola

Bella, the Isola dei Pescatori, silver-coasted islands spangled with bright villas among the palms. Champagne was served, the company chatted, and by the time the maraschino sun plunged behind the blue Alps and the *Orangeblossom* came home to rest, an agreement had been reached on Germany's admission to the League.

Stresemann could not speak French, nor Briand German. Reichschancellor Hans Luther, however, spoke perfect French, so Briand again arranged a little picnic, inviting him to spend the afternoon at Ascona, a village not far away, on the lake shore. There, beneath the vine-covered arbor of the Albergo Elvezia, Briand communicated for the first time to a German his dream of European reconciliation. As the chancellor listened, he held on his lap the Elvezia's purring pussycat; the cat must have been a spy, because Briand's words became known: "We were separated by the war," he said, "you a German, I a Frenchman. Perhaps at this point we have differences. But I can be a good Frenchman and a good European, and two good Europeans ought to understand each other."

The following day I took a young lady in a motorboat to Ascona to have tea under that arbor. The vine leaves blushed in the autumn sun, a caressing breeze came from the lake, bored chickens scratched the dust for lost grains, and now the cat sat purring on the young lady's lap—it was a professional pussycat who purred for everybody. I drew this cat, eyewitness to history, and sold the drawing widely.

This was the pastoral atmosphere from which the Spirit of Locarno first drew breath. It was interrupted by the martial advent of Mussolini. He traveled in a style conforming to his own dictum: live dangerously. He took a special train from Rome to Milan; from Milan he personally drove a racing car to Stresa; and at Stresa he changed to a speedboat in which he roared across the lake to Locarno. He brought with him a shipload of gorillas in black shirts. Now the nights were loud with shrieks of *Eia! Eia! Alalá!*, the trampling of boots, and the singing of the *Giovinezza*.

Mussolini announced that he would receive the press in the Locarno Palace Hotel. Most journalists boycotted the interview as a protest against his muzzling of the Italian press, but I went to see him because, as a caricaturist, it was unfriendlier for me to go. He hadn't changed since our first meeting in Lausanne; he still looked hungry and pale, for he suffered from a stomach ulcer to which—as he said—his opposition attached rosy hopes. His eyes still popped. By this time I knew these popeyes by their expensive name, *basedevoid*, and I had observed two varieties. One kind pops, but it is partly hooded by heavy lids like a heifer's eye, and it is a mark of a depressed and melancholy disposition; but the other kind, which shows the white all around the iris, like the eyes of Hitler, Salvador Dali, Jerry Colonna, and Mussolini, signifies high tension. This was also evident in Mussolini's stuck-up posture, strutting gait, and the popcorn delivery of his speech. His rough skin, coarse hair, gorilla jaw, and the straight line of the back of his head and neck were all part and parcel of the stocky type of muscleman, courageous, persevering, aggressive, in love with risk and women. Above all, such a man believes he is always right. It was no chance slogan, but symptomatic, anchored in the foundation of his temperament, that Mussolini painted on every street corner in Italy: *Il Duce ha sempre raggione*—Il Duce is always right!

He wore a morning coat, striped trousers, and white spats, still masquerading as a show-window statesman, but I noticed that he bit off every word as he spoke it, and I drew the bitter grimace at the corner of his mouth. He awaited each question with an "I scorn the imputation" look on his face. Before answering, he stiffened, drew himself tall, then retracted his mouth, baring the great grinders, half closed his eye, turned pale, and with a canine snarl flung back an answer. Afterwards, he stood immobile, looking down his nose, bulging his eyes, pouting his lower lip, as if savoring complete victory.

These expressions of emotion that flare and die on the face of a statesman are a peephole to the inner man, more informative than all his biographers and political urinalists. Why is it that from the first day Mussolini and Hitler appeared on the world stage, my colleagues the caricaturists, Low in England. Sennep in France, Rollin Kirby and Fitzpatrick in the United States, recognized them for what they were, whereas responsible statesmen who dealt with them fell into their trap? I suppose we are just innocents, like the child in the story who, while all the citizens admired the king's new clothes, pointed and piped: "The king is naked!"

Mussolini dismissed us and, flanked by a dozen black-shirted stalwarts, left the room. I sped after him for a closer look, and I noticed that, after all, he had changed—and for the better! In Lausanne I had glimpsed briefly, squatting dead center on the crown of his head, a wart about the size of a Scotch barleycorn. Now in Locarno I saw that the years had brought increase and it had grown into an early June pea. Ten years later, at Stresa, there was the wart again, the twin brother of a juniper berry.

I am a wart buff; I weigh and count them in preparation for my epic, *Warts Shaping Our Future*. Growing on coarse skin, they advertise a predominant muscular streak in a man's make-up and are a sign of pugnacity even when they appear on such a man as Abe Lincoln, who had one on his right cheek. Cromwell had plenty of warts, and I have counted eight so far on Khrushchev and three on Mme Khrushchev; Mao Tse-tung has a beauty on the left side of his chin.

For a while I asked myself why such a vain man as Mussolini did not have the wart removed. A plausible answer reposes in the Vatican Museum (I think): a bust of Julius Caesar, full of warts.

In pursuit of Mussolini's wart, I arrived with him outside the conference room, and there an incident occurred which has been reported variously by several historians. Since I heard every word, I'll set it down as it really happened. Our little platoon bumped into a group of journalists who had boycotted the press conference; these included George Slocombe of the Socialist *Daily Herald*; Nypels from Holland; and Henri Barde from France. The Duce,

visibly annoyed at having been snubbed by his former colleagues,
stopped before red-bearded, violet-eyed Slocombe and, with the
arrogance of a grouse in the mating season, fired the question:
"*Comment va le Communisme?*"—How is Communism doing?

"I don't know, *Monsieur le Président*," replied Slocombe. "I am
not a Communist."

"But you were at the Zimmerwald Conference!"[1]

"No, sir, I was not."

"Then I'm mistaken," said Mussolini, and here George Nypels
cut in with: "*Ça vous arrive souvent!*"—That happens to you
often.

Mussolini was too taken aback to reply. His Fascist bird dogs
twitched with rage. For a moment it looked like a brawl, then
Mussolini, his eyes bulging in a truly frightening way, bit out:
"*Peut-être*"—Maybe—and stalked away.

However, *Il Duce ha sempre raggione.* Later in the day, a
detachment of blackshirts walked up to bemonocled Henri Barde
and slapped his face so hard that his monocle flew out of his eye.

There had been no need for Mussolini to come to Locarno, but
he was like a dog who loves action for action's sake and runs after
a wheel, barking, just because it is turning. He did not participate
in the deliberations at the Town Hall; Italy was represented by his
old and wise legal adviser, Vittorio Scialoja, from whom Mussolini
took more knuckle-rapping than from anyone else. When this job
was offered to the taciturn sage, he had said: "I'll take it under
one condition: that I don't have to work the Fascist way."

"What do you mean, the Fascist way?"

"Quick and bad."

President Eisenhower pronounced a truism of the ages when he
said Khrushchev wants peace, but on his terms.

So does everybody else. Before a compromise can be worked out,

---

[1] In 1915, Europe's Socialist leaders met at Zimmerwald, Switzerland, to
co-ordinate their efforts against World War I. At this meeting Lenin submitted a motion that laid the foundation for the Third International. The
minutes were drawn up by Trotsky.

even a honeymoon like the Locarno Conference passes through phases akin to a gypsy horsetrade. Rumors leak out, delegations pretend to pack to go home, false accusations and false denials fly wildly, flocks of *canards*—ducks—symbols, in French, of false news, darken the horizons, and nobody knows where they came from or where they will go home to roost. Statesmen, even the soberest, rely on such juvenile trickery in part because they are playing to a juvenile audience. First, they have an opposition at home for whom they must put on a show of valiant battle; then, they have public opinion at home and abroad to which they must cater for applause; what's more, they are really trying to get peace on their own terms. The diplomatic press becomes an instrument to be manipulated, the *canards* are let loose, and it is the journalists' job to shoot down the right bird.

In such a flap I bumped into George Stewart, press officer of the British delegation. "Come with me to the hotel," he said. "In four days Sir Austen is having his sixty-second birthday. We are giving him a dinner party, and we want you to draw a menu."

"But, George," I said, wide-eyed, "the conference is dead, the Germans are going home, they've already ordered their sleeping cars."

"Never mind all that," he said. "Just come with me." I followed him to the delegation headquarters and there learned that the conference was far from dead, that peace was in the bag, and that on October 16, 1925, as a birthday present for Chamberlain, the Locarno Treaty was to be initialed. "Keep it under your hat," admonished George Stewart. "Just draw a menu." He gave me a jocular order of dishes.

Caviar garanti
Consommé juridique
Truite formule du bateau
Canard hebdomadaire
Sauce pacifique
Surprise d'Ascona
Fruit de pacte

With this happy secret under my belt, I drew merry pictures of British delegates offering orangeblossom bouquets to Sir Austen and Lady Chamberlain, while my journalist colleagues sent off dark dispatches about the failure of the conference. Sure enough, as the birthday neared, the air began to shimmer again with success. Two journalists pounced on me in the local pastry shop that served as our press club and told me that the representatives of the world press had decided to give a luncheon in honor of the delegates, and that they too wanted a humorous menu card by Derso and Kelen within two hours. I rushed home. It was only three o'clock in the afternoon, so I was sure of finding Derso in bed. We had no trouble coming up with a subject; it was plucked right out of the air; *canards*, false news. But now I knew where these irritating birds came from: they came from the delegations themselves. So we drew the ministers as angels of peace, serving *canards* to the press.

The luncheon took place at the Palace Hotel on October 15, 1925, and with some excitement, for it was the first time that the former belligerents had sat down publicly to break bread with the press.

It was also the first time that highly placed luncheon guests had had their legs pulled publicly by caricaturists, and we were by no means certain how they would take it. The menu card was large, 11 by 15 inches, and there was one at every place. The guests began to enter, and the first to notice the menu was Briand. I watched him anxiously as he examined it with care. Then, beneath his shaggy mustache, a smile was born.

After lunch Briand spoke, holding our drawing in his hand; he talked about *canards*, and statesmanship and the press, and the new dream that had just begun in Locarno. He was such a frail man, but his voice was like a booming church organ and it could make the marrow tremble in your bones. Chamberlain spoke next, and his voice sounded as if it were spoken into an empty salad bowl. Stresemann took note of our *canards* in his husky, mutating, goiter baritone. He spoke in German, and who do you suppose translated? Pasty-faced Paul Schmidt, Hitler's future interpreter, and he may have been good enough for the Fuehrer, but not for me. Hanging on his words, I didn't think he did full justice to the gratifying sermon Herr Stresemann was delivering on the subject of Derso and Kelen's menu card; but perhaps my head was turned, for my ducks were flying high that day and all the beatings I had taken from schoolmasters for drawing their caricatures on the blackboard had come to glory. And as for Derso, he was right in having chosen the artist's life in seedy hotels instead of inheriting his parents' grand hotel with gypsy band.

This luncheon in Locarno established a tradition for us. Each year thereafter, as long as the League existed, whenever the world press received statesmen, we provided menu cards elaborately portraying the political situation at hand and putting large numbers of statesmen in their proper roles. When speech time came, our drawings sometimes suggested important statements that made the headlines of the day. In any case, they offered gaiety to ease tension, and contributed in their way, I think, to the remarkable optimism of those years.

The next day, as predicted by George Stewart, the Locarno Treaty was initialed as a birthday present for Austen Chamberlain, the Spirit of Locarno rose over Europe, and at 7 o'clock the people of the countryside crowded in front of the Town Hall to see the treaty held up in the window. The sound of bells from the little church of the Madonna del Sasso rang out across the lake, and it was down in the dust with the women, the old mothers crossing themselves, and up with the children in their fathers' arms; and as the last banners of light were flung out against the fading sky, thousands of Japanese lanterns took the place of the sun, and later, fireworks burst next to the stars, candles burned in every window, and for young men, who would never have to go to war, it was dancing in the village square with their sweethearts.

The Locarno Treaty was signed in London in December of the

same year. I went there, not because I had business, but as one goes to the wedding of a childhood love. It was my first visit to London and about the only thing I could say in English was *ros-bif*.

The ceremony took place in a small salon of the Foreign Office, where, even with the room still empty, we of the press were vacuum-packed like skinless, boneless sardines. In the corner a high platform had been constructed where movie- and still-cameramen roosted, bumping their heads on the ceiling. In the center of the room was a large table covered with dark blue baize, and on it reposed a black coffin containing all the *paperasse* referring to the Locarno negotiations.

At a signal the klieg lights began to zish, inundating the salon with a violet glow, and opposite us a double-winged door opened with *éclat*. The eight men of Locarno entered, and after them, in a majestically moving wave, the entire British political rabbinate in morning coats and their grandfathers' high-winged collars; at the crest of the wave was Stanley Baldwin with a head like a chopping block, and Neville Chamberlain with his microcephalic bird face. The lords of England trooped in, splendidly clad in names like the cast in a Shakespearean play: fatherly Lord Balfour, portly Lord Hailsham, and Lord Runciman, who would one day make mincemeat of Czechoslovakia.

The speeches were brief. Austen Chamberlain read the king's greetings, and then Briand spoke in his compelling way: "Among the letters I have received there's one alone that makes me think this act to be the most important of my political career. In a few simple lines an unknown woman of the crowd writes, 'May a mother congratulate you. . . . Now I will be able to look at my children and love them without fear.' "

They signed the treaty, and the cameramen and kings departed. Through it all I had noticed a young man with a face put together like early rose potatoes, laughing, joking, whispering right and left, seeming to mock the solemnity. It was Winston Churchill, the man of destiny, but an odd potato when peace was in the air.

I woke the next day to that phenomenon everybody knows about and Charles II tried to do something about: a genuine London pea-soup fog. It isn't a fog really, because the densest fog has a cottony shimmer; and it isn't midnight at noon, because the darkest midnight has a bluish glimmer. It is midnight in the anus of an inkfish in mourning. Street lights seem to be veiled in black organdy and give no light, towers of orange fire burn on the street corners, their summits sucked into vaults of darkness. In my hotel room I had an eerie feeling that something was watching me—and it was. Fog had seeped through cracks in the walls and now crouched in the corner of the room like a hobgoblin—or perhaps it was the Spirit of Locarno.

In the fall of 1926, after some bickering, Germany entered the League with Mrs. Wilson in the gallery and, near her, Mrs. Stresemann. The Assembly was chock full, and it was Briand's day. He pronounced the greatest speech of my life. Like rumblings from the profundity of a holy cave came his warm, vibrating voice: "Ended is the long war between us, ended the long veils of mourning for sufferings that time cannot heal . . . away with the rifles, machine guns, and cannons! Make way for . . . peace!"

A caricaturist is not supposed to let oratory get into his system, but this speech raised lumps in my larynx, and I paid homage as best I could, passionately jotting down his dramatic gestures; and when later, with his cheeks, like mine, rosy with emotion, he wandered half dazed into the lobby of the Hôtel Victoria, I approached him in the shadow of the paper palms, showed him my drawing, and asked for an inscription.

"What are you going to do with it?" he inquired.

"I shall publish it in a German magazine."

Briand fell silent. He pondered, studying the drawing. Then he walked slowly over to the doily-covered piano and, leaning on it, he wrote on the drawing a sentence from his speech—however, with a slight modification: *"Il faut que désormais la guerre soit*

finie entre nous"—From now on the war *must end* between us.
Was it prudence, or had his passion cooled? I don't know.

Briand's voice and his magnetic spirit lifted tides of men toward peace as later Churchill's carried us through years of war. He
never spoke from notes. He used to say: "A speech is not a literary
work, it is an act. It is not to be read, it is meant to be heard. Its
form is secondary, its effect is what counts." When a journalist
asked for the text of a forthcoming speech, he said: "If I gave you
the text today, I'd say something else tomorrow."

Our menu card that year reflected the warmth and conviviality
he brought to the high affairs of state. The new horseshoe-shaped
council table was bedecked not with documents and bottles of
ink but with flowers, lobsters, filets mignons, and bottles, and at
the head of it Briand and Stresemann touched glasses over Austen
Chamberlain's head. At the luncheon, Stresemann said: ". . . and
now I'll realize your drawing." He stood up, along with Briand,
their glasses full, and clink! a cartoon scene came to life. This was
on September 10, 1926, the twelfth anniversary of the battle of
the Marne, when French soldiers had gone from Paris in red taxi-
cabs to fight the most crucial engagement of World War I.

It was clear weather in Geneva, but some clouds floated on the
horizon: there was the cumulus cloud of reparations, and the
evacuation of the Rhine with thunderheads. Briand now set about
dispersing these in the manner of a civilized Frenchman. One
might call it bistro diplomacy.

Statesmen and journalists are like man and woman, united in
wanting the very opposite: the statesman tries to keep his secret,
the journalist tries to find it out. Briand used to invent little games
of hide and seek in order to elude journalists. He brought a touch
of Hitchcock to the Thoiry affair.

On September 17, 1926, Briand invited Stresemann to meet
him for luncheon in the village of Thoiry in the French Jura. It
was meant to be as secret as a meeting between illicit lovers.
Stresemann drove in his car to a point on the lake shore outside

DÉJEUNER
de
L'ASSOCIATION
des
JOURNALISTES
accrédités auprés
de la
S . D . N .
en l'honneur
des MEMBRES DU CONSEIL
et du PRÉSIDENT de la
VII -ième ASSEMBLÉE
MENU
HORS D'OEUVRES
Truits du Lac
Caneton chez soi
SALADES   FROMAGES
Tartes   aux pruneaux

Derso et Kelen

Copyright
by DERSO et KELEN

GENÈVE LE 10 SEPTEMBRE 1926

Geneva, boarded a motorboat, and meandered aimlessly for a while. Reporters watching him might have supposed he was just getting some fresh air. But then, in a convenient cove on the opposite shore of the lake, he stole off the boat and into a car, in which he drove over the French border to Thoiry. There, at Mère Léger's hotel, Briand awaited him after having made a similar hare-and-hounds journey from a different direction.

To make absolutely certain that their destination should not be detected by newspapermen who might be tailing them, the French border police had been instructed to hold up all cars containing journalists and shuffle their papers around for at least twenty minutes. Thus, the newsmen would be sure to lose track of the ministerial vehicles.

And yet, when, after their luncheon, Briand and Stresemann emerged from Mère Léger's hotel, they were greeted by a pack of reporters. How had the journalists run the ministers to earth?

Well, one of the journalists had a motorcycle. The border police had dutifully held up all *cars* containing journalists, but the man on the motorcycle had been allowed to pass into France without delay. He dogged the ministers to Thoiry, then obligingly returned to guide his colleagues to the vital spot.

There was in Geneva a certain D. Fitzgerald, foreign minister of the Irish Free State in Cosgrave's cabinet, who differed from all other foreign ministers in that he didn't possess a hat. Like Jack Kennedy, he had one of those great Irish death-to-hats growths of hair. He was a friend of mine. As a Hungarian, I had a certain appeal for the Irish revolutionists, because they were all much attached to my great countryman, Kossuth, and the mantle of his glory fell on me. Fitzgerald's life was further complicated by a wife who was such a staunch supporter of de Valera that she told him: "I'll not buy you an egg with the rotten money you bring home serving the traitor Cosgrave." They starved happily together in blissful disharmony until the next election brought de Valera to power. Thereafter, Fitzgerald was able to have eggs for breakfast.

This ex-jailbird and foreign minister had his delegation's car at his command. The day after Thoiry, he proposed that we should go and inspect the suddenly renowned establishment of Mère Léger. It was only twenty minutes' drive to Thoiry, a tiny village with one street, one church, one hotel, and opposite the hotel a dunghill with a pitchfork in it. Mère Léger, a short peasant woman, came out of her kitchen, wiped her hands on her apron, and shook hands with us.

She showed us the room where the historic luncheon had taken place. Like the scene of a murder, it hadn't been touched. "We are waiting for the photographers," she said.

In the center of the room were a round table and a few chairs with seats of woven straw. The wallpaper was a festival of flowers; flies played tag around a naked electric bulb that hung from a low ceiling; the only wall decoration was a dusty poster for Apéritif Diablerets; and there was an artificial palm set in artificial moss. A pleasant stable smell blew in through the open window, for the benefit of nature lovers.

On the table among the swooning napkins and dying chrysanthemums I noted a saucer filled with the butts of cheap caporals; no doubt this had been Briand's place. Opposite, on an ash tray, were two paper holders with cigar butts in them; here had sat Stresemann. One cigar, hardly touched, lay in the ash tray.

Four empty wine bottles, one champagne bottle, one bottle of Evian mineral water were casualties upon the table. Nice work for two statesmen and two interpreters! I picked up the champagne cork and put it in my pocket as a souvenir.

Here, after all the years of postwar wrangling, the questions of reparations and the evacuation of the Rhineland were threshed out and agreed upon in principle by the two ministers. Peace is not fussy about décor. It can be born in a hotel room like this, as well as in a stable.

After the lunch a slight scuffle had developed over the bill. "No," said Briand to Stresemann. "I'll pay for the lunch. You take care of the reparations!"

I asked Mère Léger to prepare for us exactly the same dishes she had served to the foreign ministers, and she brought in *saucisson chaud, truite meunière, civet de lièvre, poule au pot, pigeon, compote* and cheese. There was some difference of opinion about dessert, which Fitzgerald solved after the fashion of foreign ministers, by tossing a coin.

He won; they always do.

The next important consequence of this outbreak of peace was that Uncle Sam glanced across the Atlantic and saw the maid he had abandoned, now radiant, courted, vitamin-rich. The people of the United States observed that Europeans were perfectly capable of behaving like good Americans if only they put their minds to it.

Briand started it all in a New Year's message to the American people in which he voiced one of his eccentric notions that nations ought to renounce war as an instrument of national policy. No one was more surprised than he when this idea was taken seriously in Washington. But Washington in those days, with Calvin Coolidge in the White House, looked with favor on any idea that was against sin, so long as it entailed no other obligation.

Before long, Secretary of State Frank B. Kellogg came to Paris with a bouquet of white lilies in one hand and in the other a pen to sign a pact. He was a little old man who looked like a little old woman who resembles a little old man: a round face with close-set vigilant eyes, no neck, but lots of snow-white hair worked painstakingly into garlands like icing on a wedding cake.

Stresemann came too; this was the first time a German foreign minister had visited Paris since the Franco-Prussian War of 1871. But he was gravely ill, and when he went to pay his respects to Prime Minister Poincaré, a doctor waited in the anteroom. After an hour the doctor sent a written message to Poincaré beseeching him to order Stresemann home to bed.

The Kellogg-Briand Pact was signed on August 27, 1928, at the Quai d'Orsay in the Salle de l'Horloge, amid an orgy of marbles, velvets, silks, all exquisitely blended, spiced with silver and gold, and stewed in tomato sauce. From the ceiling hung gigantic chandeliers, weighing at least a ton each and sparkling with prisms and imitation candles, the crystals streaming down, the candles streaking up, all icy splendor and filigreed flame. The *pièce de résistance* was the alabaster fireplace that held *l'horloge*, the clock from which it took its name. *L'horloge* was cajoled out of rich metals into an embroilment of acanthus leaves, flowers, and gilded warts, and it sat like a queen enthroned, clad in dizzy magnificence, staring down upon the horseshoe table set for the signing of the treaty.

The scenery must have been pleasing to Richelieu's ghost; but this was an American affair, and the secretary of state was not going to sign a pact behind a bush. Now for the first time I saw Hollywood intrude into the plush-carpeted sanctum of a Foreign Office. Eight heavy-duty klieg lights showed their uncouth faces; miles of black cables snaked like pythons over the red carpet; platoons of sweating technicans in shirtsleeves installed 35-millimeter film howitzers that spied down upon the horseshoe table where "those guys" (as I learned engineers refer to ministers) would perform. As the statesmen entered the room (Poincaré stumbling over the cables), the klieg lights exploded in a pink glow, and all the eighteenth-century Venetian luster of crystal and candles was snuffed out by the crude and sober floodlight of twentieth-century technology.

The pact was signed by fifteen nations, with a heavy gold fountain pen especially manufactured for the occasion. It bore the inscription: "If you want peace, prepare for peace." Kellogg took up the pen with trembling hand, but it was too heavy for the old man, and a French secretary had to help him affix his name.

The Kellogg-Briand Pact has been ineffective in practice every time it has been invoked. The last notable occasion was at the Nuremberg trials.

It was not a pact, after all, so much as a declaration against sin. Yes, but so were the Ten Commandments, which were held up to the multitude and the next instant smashed. A correct thought is formulated in the minds of men, and out of the mist a track emerges toward the unimaginable goal. No matter whether the Kellogg-Briand Pact satisfies the legal eagles; it makes a big difference, when you are a warmaker in the dock, with a dozen gallows hidden in the closet, whether the judge is against sin or not.

The bells of Locarno, Mère Léger's rabbit stew, Mr. Kellogg's gold pen—that was the closest we came to peace between the world wars. Briand and Stresemann tried to establish a strong European policy over the heads of the national jingoists. Austen Chamberlain acted in the role of an honest matchmaker who, seeing two parties in love, stakes his career and throws all his influence into furthering the match.

The villagers of Locarno had knelt and crossed themselves when they saw the treaty in the window of their Town Hall; but when Stresemann returned to Berlin, special security measures had to be taken, not to keep the jubilant crowds away, but to prevent them from shooting him as they had shot Erzberger and Rathenau, two who had tried to make peace before him. After Thoiry, Briand was received at the Gare de Lyon with catcalls, and M. Seydoux, a high official, said: "Herr Stresemann thinks that Franco-German problems can be contained in a liqueur glass." The editor of the *Deutsche Tageszeitung* offered me quite a lot of marks for my champagne cork, with the obvious intention of using it as an exhibit against Stresemann; but I kept it in my pocket.

Briand, when he was a young lawyer at Saint-Nazaire, had been caught with a young lady in a forest by a game warden in a situation the French call, with remarkable elegance, *attentat à la pudeur*—that is, he was performing in broad daylight what respectable people reserve for the cinema. He was disbarred, then reinstated, the president of the bar observing that he had been young once himself. But at the most exalted point in his career, when he stood as a symbol of Europe's noblest strivings, royalists

like Léon Daudet never referred to him in print except as
maquereau, pimp. Even a drawing of ours was turned against him.
We had drawn Briand, spatula in hand, with a pail of cement,
laying the cornerstone of the Palais des Nations. Ludendorff
figured out, in his glorious and fat head, that we had "unmasked
Briand for what he really is: a Freemason."

The kernel of this nuttiness was the Treaty of Versailles, which
the French regarded as Holy Writ, and the Germans as obscene
literature.

Peace? Of course everybody wanted peace. But they followed
the age-old dictum: "If you want peace, prepare for war." And
the pen that signed the Kellogg-Briand Pact was not only too
heavy for old Kellogg; it was too heavy for Europe.

The French wanted peace, but they wanted reparations too,
for they were being hard pressed by the United States for
repayment of war debts, and they saw in the occupation of the
Rhineland a guarantee that Germany would pay. The Germans
wanted peace, but they also wanted the evacuation of the Rhineland, and what other weapon was left to a beaten, disarmed,
poverty-stricken Germany than not to pay her debts? That much
anybody can understand about world politics.

When Briand and Stresemann, in Thoiry, had agreed in principle on the questions of reparations and evacuation, the hurrah
patriots at home snorted and spat in disgust. Berlin termed
Stresemann a traitor who ought to be jailed; Paris called Briand
an incorrigible optimist bleating about peace, and they accused
him of trying to sell France's friends, Poland and Czechoslovakia,
down the river.

Well, at any rate he would have spared them the trouble of
doing it later, at Munich.

A stalemate developed, one of those familiar the-chicken-or-the-
egg stalemates: the French wanted reparations first; the Germans,
evacuation first. The tussle lasted several years, and then, on
October 3, 1929, Stresemann died.

From that time on, we went downhill with the irresistible speed of a bicycle without brakes. The Spirit of Locarno turned poltergeist. The reasons are many, and I'll leave it to historians to fathom their interplay. As a caricaturist, I look at men, and here I see three men formulating a policy together. None of them represents himself; behind each is a complex structure built out of all the conflicting forces of his nation. When one man dies, his structure begins to wobble and heave, seeking a new balance, and it disturbs the balance of the two others. It is just about impossible to re-establish the political and spiritual equilibrium. The same thing happened when, after agreeing upon a policy with Churchill and Stalin, Roosevelt died.

Politics cannot rest on a frail scaffolding of mortal men; it must rest on eternal, inviolable principles. Nations must find a way to impose on themselves at least as much discipline as exists in a nursery school: "Don't hit, don't grab, share toys, and the next one to scream is a monkey's uncle."

I could not have imagined three more disparate men than Chamberlain, Stresemann, and Briand. Chamberlain was a British Tory, stiff, cold, pedantic, pompous, and protocolaire. Stresemann, portly and irritable, was an efficient German businessman who had written his doctor's thesis on the utilization of empty beer bottles, and exhibited all outward signs of having contributed heavily toward emptying same. Briand was a small-town lawyer in need of a haircut, with a built-in allergy toward documents and protocol.

Friendship and marriage are held together as much by differences as by similarities. No doubt Briand admired in his friends the qualities he didn't possess: Chamberlain's tidiness, Stresemann's practicality; and both of them sensed in him the unkempt genius. What they had in common was good will, an unselfish desire to serve, and personal integrity—a rare combination in one politician, let alone in three foreign ministers of major powers meeting at the same instant in time.

Of the statesmen I drew in my young years, Aristide Briand

LA DANSE DE LA FINANCE...

...AUTOUR DU VEAU D'OR

provided for me a standard for all the rest. At the time of Locarno there were not too many years between me and the boy who wanted to climb on a barrel and shout *Pax!* to the enemy, and it is natural that I should have hero-worshipped the man who dared to do just that. But now I am in the same decade of life as he was then, and I still cherish him.

He was frail, wobbly, with exceedingly delicate hands and feet; just a touch of roundness hid under his vest, and a double chin filled his winged collar. His strength was all in that marvelous head, the Zeus brow and Saturn eyebrows; and there were visions in the cold eyes that seemed always to be gazing from a mountain top.

He was simple, sentimental, ironical, ponderous, and lazy. Once he rebuked a Latin American diplomat who brought him a heap of documents to study. "You don't suppose I've lost my incapacity for work, do you?"

As a politician he was a freelance, not fitting into any party; in fact he had been kicked out of one. He meandered among his well-groomed colleagues in Geneva like a stray *Monparno*, his hand in his coat pocket, a cheap cigarette glued to the corner of his mouth: a philosopher among politicians, a poet among diplomats; also, a wit among caricaturists. In 1927, when disarmament was the rage in Geneva, our menu card represented Mars, a stupendous God of War, being dismantled by delegates with such instruments as forks, corkscrews, nail clippers. In an after-lunch speech, Briand picked up the drawing and poked fun at himself: "I see a stooped little man standing on the shoulders of a formidable God of War, trying to convince him. . . ." He continued for a while in his velvety way, the very model of an easy-witted Frenchman. Then his tone changed and he dropped the picture on the table. "They say," he thundered, "that all I do here is bleat about peace." His eyes took on the steel blue of Breton waters, his cheeks flushed, his voice dropped. Almost in a whisper he said: "Yes, with my last breath I will bleat about peace," and

LES LÉVITES

sat down. There was a stunned silence, and not friend or foe present but felt the impact of his sincerity.

He combined terrestrial shrewdness with celestial zeal, like one of those traveling padres who whammed out the Gospel to the loudmouthed, horse-thieving, pistol-toting badmen of the wild and woolly West.

A truly great statesman, I think, is more than a super-bureaucrat, a parliamentary wizard, a wire-puller, a know-better, an outguesser, a favorite uncle, or even a man with a good-looking wife. He inhabits regions removed from the tribal idolatry of political parties and above the heads of the straggly line of customs officials who guard the nation's borders. There is something in him of the religious leader: his values arise from deep sources, his actions seek a strait gate along a narrow path, he serves mankind and trades in imperishable wares that political fashions and slogans can't make obsolete. He often fails in a confused world. But his failures are a better guide for us than other people's successes.

Briand said: "It is not enough to act, one must dream a little."

In 1930, just before his death, perhaps sensing the wind of the grave, he came forth with the idea of European union: too late for him, too early for Europe. This notion, so simple and realistic, was just as unacceptable in old, overdeveloped Europe as it is impossible today in new, underdeveloped Africa. Continents made up of small nation-states have this in common: everybody wants to be prime minister, nobody wants to be dogcatcher.

Briand's idea of a United States of Europe was submitted to his fellow delegates at a luncheon in Geneva. The League set up a study commission—that's a sort of mausoleum for ideas. Derso and I drew him as Moses, pointing with his cigarette toward the Promised Land he was never to be permitted to enter. The last speech he made in Geneva concerned this drawing. When he returned to Paris, he sent a messenger to me requesting five copies, and shortly afterwards the man who said: "As long as I am here, there will be no war," died.

He hadn't been a churchgoer, he was an agnostic, and in France he had framed the law separating church and state. But when the remains of his frail body lay in state on a catafalque in the lobby of the Quai d'Orsay, the Cardinal Archbishop of Paris sensed the breath of God in him and came to bless the apostate.

I visited his tiny apartment—two or three rooms—on the avenue Kléber. His valet, Emil, showed me his possessions, which were almost as modest as a saint's: a few paintings on the wall, presents from artist friends; a couple of cheap ash trays. And I saw lying there the copies of our drawing showing him as Moses.

"Imagine," sighed the police inspector who had been his bodyguard, "a man who disposed of the government's secret funds for so many years, dying poor!"

Some time afterwards, in a newsreel theater, his tombstone was shown, and on it a gimmick-happy producer had superimposed Briand's face. He gazed at me through the vibrating haze with his cold eyes . . . I felt a shiver through my spine as old words of his flashed to my mind: "Politics would be an idyll if one were chastised only for the evil one has done."

I'm not the only one he can move across the years. Recently I talked to Vernon Bartlett, a British M.P. and veteran of the League. He told me he had visited Geneva and lunched in the Brasserie Bavaria, whose walls are decorated with some hundred and fifty of our caricatures. Directly above his head was a drawing of Briand.

Some young American tourists were there, a boy and a girl of that generation for which we can afford every gift except the gift of tranquillity Briand wished them to have. The boy came to study the drawing.

"Bryand," he called to his companion. "Bryand? Who is Bryand?"

And Bartlett said: "I could have cried."

VIII

The League
Around the League

Hungarians have a maxim: It is better to live in the smallest room of a big hotel than in the biggest room of a small hotel. When Derso and I first established ourselves in Geneva, we naturally went to the Hôtel Richemond and engaged a garret so small that when one man came in, two had to get out. There was hardly room for a bed and the weekly bill.

A member of the League Secretariat, Signor Ganzoni, rebuked us: "*Mais, chers enfants,* artists don't live in luxury hotels!" He advised us to find rooms in one of the family pensions that abound in Geneva. In a humbled mood we took lodgings at the Pension Primrose, a tall building in danger of immediate collapse.

A particular hazard was a red carpet that crawled shakily up the staircase, with holes and snags to ensnare the feet, and loose brass bars to snap at them. There was also a nightmarish elevator, a matchbox that could be set in motion by means of two frayed cables which ran through holes in the floor and ceiling. If you pulled one cable, it took you up; if you pulled the other, it took you to the cellar. But which cable to pull? Both looked alike. It was like Russian roulette.

The Pension Primrose was run by an exceedingly pretty widow with two children. The boy had reached the age of flirting with chambermaids. The girl was in her late teens, a distraction to young waiters. Their mother was careful to employ only gargoyles of medieval repulsiveness.

The pension was the haunt of retired cheese merchants and widows of Indian Army officers whose pittances sustained life only in the Pension Primrose. There were also a number of spinsters who looked like a flock of elderly pelicans. Eleven months of the year they pickled in the pension, but in September, when Assembly time came around, new life bubbled as the camp-followers of the League of Nations checked in: destitute journalists, disgruntled colonials, self-appointed prophets, appointed spies, prime ministers of non-existent governments in exile, dotty old club ladies, caricaturists, and English girls as freckled as turkeys' eggs who had taken temporary clerical jobs at the League.

All of us had two things in common: we carried a great harvest of mimeographed papers, and we had no money.

Apartheid was observed between the two sets of guests. Respectable *pensionnaires* generally appeared first in the dining room, whose scarlet velvet drapes had been drained of all brilliance by sun and dust. We kibitzers of high diplomacy drifted in late, to sit at our assigned tables next to our napkin rings and to eat old crow inadequately disguised with a brown sauce as chicken.

Collapsed over his soup was an anteater-faced Polish priest whose name was a bottleneck of consonants. He represented a Catholic publication and he brought home with him every piece of paper the League published, which he read while he ate, using his thin nose as a pointer.

An American spinster who followed the League's debates on behalf of a woman's pacifist association in Minnesota sat stiffly upright, wearing a pince-nez on a silver chain and a hat adorned with a stuffed woodpecker. A soulful-eyed Viennese lady sat hatless next to her husband, a retired English Army captain. Kind and modest, they made it their business to care for destitute children in the mountains of Illyria, and they came to Geneva yearly to find new inspiration and new funds.

Like any seedy pension in Europe, we had our Russian émigrés: Miliukov, the Menshevik leader, and Nemanov, a revolutionary Socialist who never allowed the name of Maxim Litvinov to cross his lips. He referred to him only by his family name of Wallach.

These men had known Lenin, Trotsky, Zinoviev—had fought them. They had lost the Revolution, but gained wisdom, and they lived out their years as elder pension-statesmen. Such mellowed old Russians left over from the turbulent times are today a dying species, like whooping cranes. But in those days they were plentiful, and to talk to them was like watching the world go around.

We had in our midst a stumpy-legged Bulgar by the name of Todoroff. I had drawn him at the Lausanne Conference when he was his country's finance minister; but in that capacity he had lacked the foresight to steal enough money to stay on his feet when his prime minister, Stambulisky, was assassinated. He now made his living as, of all things, a caricaturist. We'd talk shop together. "How's business, *Monsieur le Ministre?*" I'd say, and he'd show me his sketches. From the look of them I guessed he must have a sideline. One day he told me that he had just paid a visit to Belgrade. "The Macedonian Black Hand Society sent two men to kill me. Ah, but Todoroff is smart," he said, pointing to his temple. "I taught them how to swim in the Danube— underwater."

The rascal just couldn't leave the old game of diplomacy alone!

Our most highly placed *convive* was His Excellency, M. Kara-baghian, prime minister of the government-in-exile of the Republic of Azerbaidzhan. He was always alone, and I had a suspicion that he was the sole member of his cabinet. But he carried in his pocket a round rubber stamp, and after dinner he spent hours writing long reports, which he then stamped with great vehemence.

Once, in that sullen after-dinner hour when guests in a family pension begin to ferment, he came over to my table and asked permission to sit down. For the next five minutes he laid bare to me the turpitude of the behavior of the Russian Communist government toward Azerbaidzhan. Then he said: "Mr. Kelen, I have a highly confidential matter to discuss with you. I have decided, on behalf of my government, to declare war on Russia. But I don't quite know how to proceed. Could you advise me?"

"Your Excellency," said I—for I always addressed him by his proper title—"this is a drastic step you are contemplating. I think you are making a grave mistake."

"Do you really think so?" He sat back with a question mark on his face. "Perhaps I should sleep on it," he said.

The following day, after dinner, he came again to my table and, seizing my hand in both of his, he said in earnest tones: "Mr. Kelen, you have done a great service to my country and to the people of Azerbaidzhan. To express our gratitude, my government has decided to name a river after you." And right there among the breadcrumbs he wrote out a document, in his own hand, announcing that the name of the Kura River was changed then and there to the Kelen River; and he banged this document with a rubber stamp. Thus I did my bit for peace, and to those whom it may concern I say that, come the counterrevolution, I am going to Azerbaidzhan to collect my river.

We had a tableful of Portuguese journalists from poverty-stricken newspapers; yet they represented elegant living in our pension. I have a notion that old-world courtliness, born in the eighteenth century and carried on through nineteenth-century-operetta chivalry, is kept alive today like an eternal flame mostly among Poles, Portuguese, and Hungarians, who habitually kiss ladies' hands, turn corners with a pretty pirouette, and stand with their heads bent slightly forward and to the side in an attitude of deference. I don't know how Poles and Portuguese come by these manners, but we Hungarians learn them as little boys at dancing school.

In that old furniture depot which was the dining room of the Pension Primrose, our Portuguese colony sat with an air of ascetic majesty, like mocha noblemen painted by El Greco at the funeral of the Count de Orgaz. Their star performer was one Vasco da Costa, a journalist from Lisbon with a frayed waistcoat that did not match his trousers, a monocle that fitted his face, and white spats that went with everything. He suffered from an affliction known as priapism—consult your doctor for further details of this enviable disease. Certainly, Portugal is an unfortunate place to have it in because there even the prostitutes walk with chaperones. Vasco arrived in Geneva in a hungry condition, and nightly, like a black panther, he slunk out of the pension to hang about the bushes in the park, waiting for a woman, any woman, to come along. On rainy nights he would have to stay home and raid his own chicken coop—our clutch of monstrous chambermaids, of which there was not a fryer in the lot.

But once a year, when the Portuguese delegation gave a sumptuous reception at the Hôtel des Bergues, Vasco would invite one of these unsightly maids to accompany him. He would dance attendance on her as if she were a *grande dame*, and present her to his minister with a flourish.

A middle-aged spinster from Bayswater who lived in the room next to Vasco complained. She said that the nocturnal traffic was so heavy that she couldn't sleep a wink, and she asked our landlady for another room. "I don't know what to do with you," said our pretty landlady to Vasco. "I certainly am not going to give you the room next to mine!"

One night the spinster was seen peeking through Vasco's keyhole. I do not know what she saw, but presently she joined a missionary society and went to Africa to convert savages.

Once I too got a chance to be chivalrous to one of our chambermaids. She asked me to put in a good word for her at the League of Nations committee in charge of hiring cleaning women. I did, and she got the job. One day I met her pursuing her duties in a corridor, and she poured out to me her complaints about the world organization. "We have a supervisor," she wailed, "who doesn't know the first thing about mopping a floor. She used to be a cigarette girl in a night club. But what can I do?" She turned a look of scorn on me. "She got *her* job through a member of the League Council."

I declared myself beaten.

When I discover a cheap pension, I spread the good news among the poor. The time came when Derso and I wanted rooms and found the place full of eggs I'd laid myself.

Among the last guests I introduced were a Hungarian spy and a bogus journalist.

Our spy, Almassy, was from Transylvania, a tall, swarthy, squiggle-eyed individual who carried a big cigar between yellow teeth. He did not tell me for whom he spied, but this became evident from his conversation.

In 1919, when Transylvania—which had formerly been part of Hungary—was handed by the Allies to Rumania, his job was to create confusion for the new Rumanian administration. He told me with pride about his first successful mission: he had blown up a viaduct at the very moment a troop train carrying 250 Rumanian soldiers was passing over it. His next assignment, together with a Hungarian team mate, was to burn down the port of Constanza.

"We settled in Constanza," he said, "and opened an exterminator's business, which we operated for a year. Then by bribery we got the job of exterminating the cockroaches in the granaries along the harbor. Once inside, we detached the electric wires and swathed them in cotton. Then we short-circuited them. The entire harbor burned down."

The saboteurs were caught. There being no death penalty in Rumania, Almassy was sentenced to twenty years in a chain gang. He asked me: "Do you know how to take off your trousers with chains on your legs?" I did not, so he explained.

"First you push down your pants as far as the chain. Then you push the right leg of your pants through the ring around your right ankle, just enough to get your right foot out of them. Then you pull the right leg of your trousers back through the same ring, and afterwards pull the whole thing through the iron ring around your left ankle. After that, you free your left foot. Do you know how to put *on* your trousers with chains on your legs?"

He then explained the reverse of the exercise. I'm glad I know these things.

Almassy was released from jail after the Hungarian Secret Police held up the Budapest–Bucharest train and in the suitcases of two distinguished Rumanian businessmen found stolen documents—which the police had just planted there. The innocent businessmen were arrested, condemned to death as spies, and then exchanged for Almassy and his team mate.

"How does the Rumanian delegation in Geneva feel about you?" I asked.

"They feel fine," he answered. "Titulescu would never think of passing me without asking after my health—in Rumanian."

Almassy eventually left the Pension Primrose to move in with a blond widow. One of his colleagues, a Hungarian spy who, in order to make ends meet, worked also for the Rumanian government, noted that every night one of the League of Nations guards would empty the secretary general's wastebasket and carry its contents to Almassy's apartment. Since he had a covetous eye on that wastebasket, he notified the police. The guard was dismissed, but not a thing could be done about Almassy: there's no law against collecting trash. But in 1934, when King Alexander I of Yugoslavia and French Foreign Minister Barthou were assassinated in Marseilles by a member of a Croat terrorist organization, the Ustachis, the murderer stopped in Annemasse, on the

Swiss-French border, and Almassy had a rendezvous with him. He was then expelled from Switzerland.

My bogus journalist friend was also a Hungarian, named Peterfy, and he has a special place in my memory because he demolished my belief in recorded history once and for all. He was really a law student at the University of Geneva; but when the Assembly convened, a Budapest paper, in order to save the expense of maintaining a special correspondent, hired him to write up the Geneva news.

When Count Apponyi died in Geneva, Peterfy felt it fitting that the great Hungarian debater should have pronounced some immortal last words. So he invented a few.

The following day, *Az Est*, the most important evening paper in Hungary, printed in immense headlines the last words of Count Apponyi: "HUNGARIANS! HOLD THE LINE! VICTORY IS IN SIGHT!"

Today that copy of *Az Est* is kept in the national library, where, centuries hence, a historian who on a grant from the Academy will write his definitive book on *The Life and Times of Albert Apponyi* will find it. The very fact that he will find it will make it true. I wonder how many such "well researched" facts have wiggled their way into history books?

What cannot be found in the national library is that Peterfy was fired for the hoax and died in an insane asylum. Before his internment he had time to propose a business scheme on a fifty-fifty financial basis: the founding of a False News Agency to be called FNA. He explained to me that there is always some news in the air which editors expect to happen. For instance, he said, when the Pope is gravely ill, what newspaper would resist buying a dispatch: "THE POPE IS DEAD"? When Amundsen is lost in the Arctic, how could we fail to sell an article called "AMUNDSEN FOUND!"? No editor would dare risk refusing such scoops.

He admitted an administrative difficulty: collection of fees would have to be quick.

It would be selfish to claim that all the lunatics in Geneva were poor and lived at the Pension Primrose. As we climbed higher up the scale of lodgings, we found them everywhere, and there was a generous sprinkling of them in the luxury hotels and establishments of importance. I have the tenderest feelings for lunatics; in fact, I suspect that in every new idea there is a grain of lunacy—and in every lunacy, the grain of a new idea.

Dr. Eugen Bleuler reports, in his *Textbook of Psychiatry*, that one of his schizophrenic patients invented a cleaning fluid while he was in the asylum and made a fortune.

I had a friend, Dmitri, a Russian refugee who had operated a chain of pawnshops in Macao. Having made enough money for his needs, he had come to Geneva to do something for mankind.

"How do people make war?" he asked me. "By floating war bonds! Why not peace bonds? If people invested money in peace at four and a half per cent interest, we'd have no wars. Right?"

Right.

Forty years later, in a lunatic world, when governments refused to foot the bills for the United Nations' peace effort in the Congo and on the Gaza strip, the UN floated peace bonds.

Horacio Díaz de Oliviera, a Brazilian who had made money in the building industry, shared his sumptuous office, which overlooked snowcapped Mont Blanc, with an Amazon parrot. Whenever I visited there, it sneaked out from behind the sofa and pinched my ankle with its sharp beak.

"The trouble with the world today," said Horacio, "is that the walls of houses are too thin. In the days when we built houses with walls that were six feet thick, there was no economic crisis."

He published pamphlets, gave lavish parties, buttonholed ambassadors in order to sell the world on six-foot-thick walls. Some said he was a bore, others that he was mad. I say he was a man of foresight who advocated sane economy through crazy spending, the very axis on which the world turns today.

Each year Count Coudenhove-Kalergi came to Geneva, peddling his dream for a Pan-Europa, a United States of Europe. Being a count, he was of course invited everywhere, regardless of his twilight condition. Yet to this very day, with the European Common Market a reality, some old Geneva hands recall him laughingly as a Utopian.

But it is for those humble crackpots of the pensions, those friends, that I keep a soft spot in my heart. My English captain and his wife were modest as a pair of mustard seeds; but whatever moved them to care for Illyrian war orphans now moves UNICEF. Our lady pacifist from Minnesota wore a funny hat, but women's pacifism is not funny. And all those eccentric old ladies of every nation who, with their eternal nagging, ear-chewing, button-twisting, and petition-pushing, disturbed the delegates in their earnest endeavors to pave the way for World War II had at heart the welfare of countless millions of people too "normal" to do anything but mind their own business.

A story went around during the Disarmament Conference about one of these dotty old ladies. In the early hours of dawn she telephoned Arthur Henderson, the president of the conference, and the sleepy voice of a secretary answered the phone.

"I must speak to the president," said the old lady. "I just had a dream about how to bring about general disarmament. I want to tell it to Mr. Henderson right away."

"But the president is in bed. Won't you tell me your dream, and I will tell it to the president?"

After some argument, the old lady told her dream to the secretary, who then said: "Now I'll tell it to the president." He covered the mouthpiece with the palm of his hand for a while, then spoke again: "The president thanks you very kindly, and he asks me to tell you that last night he had exactly the same dream."

Politicians believe that what they are doing is *Realpolitik*. But sometimes I wonder if the dreams of the dear old ladies who in their years have seen small worlds immolated, lives emptied, hopes buried in foreign fields, are not our *Realpolitik*: if only somebody would *listen* to them!

The first year of our stay in Geneva, we discovered a *brasserie* called the Bavaria, in a narrow passage between the rue du Rhône and the Grand Quai. It was at that time a dimly lit dumping grounds for local beer fanciers. Internationalism had infiltrated only as far as a single table under the presidency of owlish M. Pierre Comert, chief of the Information Section, who over the beer and pretzels served information to journalists. As the League grew, more shady-looking foreigners moved in, and gradually the local burghers eased themselves out.

One afternoon I looked up from my *choucroute garnie* to find M. Neiger, the owner, standing over me. He said that he might be in the market for a few Derso and Kelen caricatures to put on his walls. We sold him some, and then some more. In time, our caricatures covered the walls, and whenever M. Neiger bought a drawing, he would send his devoted waitress, Berthe, to the proper delegation to get it autographed. It became the fashion for prime ministers to add their jokes to ours. Aristide Briand wrote under his portrait: "A certified copy of the original." Litvinov, finding himself scrutinized suspiciously through Austen Chamberlain's monocle, wrote one of those fine old Slavic prophecies: "He will look at me differently in the future."

The Brasserie Bavaria became one of the most celebrated *potinières* between the two world wars. Perhaps it was favored more by the beer-drinking, sauerkraut-eating nations than by the tea-drinking, pudding-eating ones; but, generally speaking, no statesmen or journalist, certainly no tourist who passed Geneva would have failed to eat a frankfurter there. Here you might have found yourself sitting at the next table to Briand, Stresemann, Austen Chamberlain, Ramsay MacDonald, Beneš, Litvinov. Failing that, there was the gallery of portraits signed with the names that signed treaties. Ministers of small countries, before being hanged through their own efforts, were eager to hang in the Bavaria, through ours. They would send us special envoys, who knew how to express themselves in a discreet and slippery manner, to suggest who our next model ought to be.

Derso called the Bavaria our Beerhall of Fame.

Above all, the Bavaria was a conclave of journalists. The policy of open diplomacy had by no means solved the newspaperman's problems. Diplomacy is like a wedding: the public ceremony is more spectacular, but the secret part is better worth watching. In order to guess what is going on at midnight in a dark bedroom, the journalists need a place, open late, where they can meet, consult, sift gossip, thresh out the latest diplomatic whodunit, and find answers to important questions, such as what do you know, what do you think, and what will you have? Many a stein of light and dark passed into history before people anywhere read the latest news from Geneva in the morning papers. Conflicts between a journalist and the management were dealt with by M. Neiger in a diplomatic manner: he removed the journalist's portrait from the wall and condemned it to solitary confinement in a drawer until penance was done.

Each Assembly saw the visit of H. V. Kaltenborn, who inevitably published our annual press-luncheon menu cards in the *Brooklyn Daily Eagle*. Here we sat with the cowboy humorist, Will Rogers; and little, narrow-faced Bill Hard, who made the first transatlantic broadcast from Geneva to the United States; and Liddell Hart, the Englishman who carried great tomes of military knowledge in his small head. Here, pale, transparent Mme Geneviève Tabouis, wonderchild of the French press, walked in on toothpick legs.

I recall William Shirer, always conscientious and composed as a bank teller. I suppose he was already stacking, in neat piles, the events that would one day add up to *The Rise and Fall of the Third Reich*. John Gunther came from Vienna, a humble general practitioner in those days, not yet a famous internist of politics. Bill Hillman, Truman's future biographer, barrel-chested as the sheriff of Tombstone, pronounced direct criticisms of the League out of the side of his mouth. And there was the correspondent of a French newspaper who went to Belgrade to cover the funeral of King Alexander I. He got drunk on the local *slivovitz* and telephoned his paper the most hilarious report of a royal funeral ever written.

Miss Sylvia Pankhurst, Georg Bernhardt of the *Vossische Zeitung*, Pertinax, all these great ones of journalism are but memories today. But a figure from the past I still encounter at the United Nations is Max Beer, the brilliant and witty correspondent of the *Neue Züricher Zeitung*, who smoked an eternal cigar. Once I was drawing him with this cigar in his mouth when he suddenly put it out and lighted a cigarette. "Well, Herr Doktor, do you smoke cigars or cigarettes?" I asked.

"I smoke cigarettes," he said. "I eat cigars."

In 1928 Bernard Shaw visited us in golf trousers, tall, steep, and stiff-necked. The right side of his face was narrower than the left, and he wore his left eyebrow higher than the right. From under these eyebrows he squinted with pale blue eyes. His red beard was already undergoing a conversion to off-white, and from under his whiskers peeped a pair of vampire's incisors: he looked like the devil's Santa Claus. He said of the Naval Disarmament Conference: "This is more an economic than a disarmament conference. What they want to know is whether it is more economical to fire an 18-inch gun, or two 9-inch guns."

The Bavaria was one of those key spots where, if you stayed long enough, you would sooner or later see every important person in Europe; and you would hear every good story about them. The journalist Edmund Demaître told me how as a very young man he had interviewed a very old man, Clemenceau.

"I have jotted down a few questions, *Monsieur le Président*," said Demaître. "If you would be so kind as to answer them?"

"Certainly."

"In your opinion, should the French Army have occupied Berlin in 1918?"

"*Je m'en fous!*" replied Clemenceau, which, roughly translated, means: "I don't give a fig."

"Do you think, *Monsieur le Président*, that the reparations payments were too high for Germany to pay?"

"Je m'en fous!"

"Is it your opinion, sir, that the Allies should have arrested the Kaiser?"

"Je m'en fous!"

Ten questions were asked by Demaître, and ten times the answer was the same. But after the tenth question Clemenceau the Tiger —whose actions at Versailles had laid the foundation for World War II—said: "Young man, when you are my age and a young journalist comes to you and asks you the same questions, you'll give the same answer."

Demaître once wrote to ask for an interview with Bernard Shaw. Shaw replied: "You want to talk to me and sell what I have to say to you. When I can sell what you have to say to me, I shall give you an interview."

What Shaw did not know was that, underneath his French name, Edmund Demaître was a Hungarian. He sold Shaw's letter to the *Daily Telegraph* for ten pounds.

One of the culture heroes of French storytellers in those days was Tristan Bernard, the playwright. He was known to be strongly allergic to female writers. Once a lady journalist was seated next to him at a press luncheon, and she said: "*Cher maître*, forget that I am a woman. Treat me as you would a male colleague."

Throughout the luncheon, Tristan spoke not one word to her. But after luncheon he tapped her on the shoulder and said: "*Allons pisser.*"

From Egon Erwin Kisch, a shaggy Communist reporter, I heard the following story. In 1918, when the revolution broke out in Vienna, he had been working for the influential *Neue Freie Presse*. His brother, a well-groomed bourgeois, worked for the same paper. On one of those turbulent days, the brother arrived at the press building and anxiously asked the porter: "Is the managing editor in?"

"There's no more managing editor. Your brother has fired him and grabbed his office."

The bourgeois Kisch rushed up the staircase and saw his brother

Erwin standing on the managing editor's sacred desk, haranguing the editorial staff. For a while Kisch stood at the door, listening to his brother communizing the newspaper. Then he lifted a warning finger and said: "Erwin! I'll tell Mamma!"

As the years fled and I grew old on Mme Neiger's frankfurters, I found myself sitting at a table in the Bavaria with the four architects who had designed the grand new palace which was now being built for our Geneva maid. Three hundred and seventy-seven plans from all over the world had been submitted in open competition, but no one plan was judged satisfactory. In the end, the committee had chosen parts of five separate plans and commanded the architects to work out a compromise in the best diplomatic tradition. The present Palais des Nations in Geneva is the result.

One of the architects was Joseph Vago, a hawk-nosed Hungarian with a goatee dyed black and eyes as crazed as Macbeth's. He had tussled with the law in Horthy's Hungary, where all architects, in order to carry on their profession, were required to give an account of their behavior during the 1919 Bela Kun Bolshevik regime. Vago refused to do so. Now he was able to place his name in the Budapest telephone directory: Joseph Vago, no profession, builder of the Palais des Nations.

We were brothers under the skin. What is an architect but an artist who scrubs his neck? Broggi had the brotherly idea that the League should buy the originals of the menu cards we drew for press luncheons, annually ticking off the years of open diplomacy. He had them framed in silver and he hung them on his marble walls in the Palais des Nations; and there they hang to this day, a procession both melancholy and merry of old promises kept and broken, old hopes and jokes and meals gone by.

Throughout these many years, a running argument developed between Mme Neiger and me: had our drawings made the Bavaria famous, or had the Bavaria made us famous? She subscribed unreservedly to Oscar Wilde's opinion that a caricature is a tribute mediocrity pays to greatness; the greatness she had in mind was, of course, her incomparable frankfurters and beer.

So far as I'm concerned the question was never settled, but I'll
say this much: when M. Neiger died, we had to borrow twenty
francs to send our old friend a wreath.

Mme Neiger also has the endorsement of Ambassador Ernest
Gross of the United States, whom I remember as a pinkish youngster studying political science under the wing of Sir Alfred Zimmern. Quite recently, he told me that he had dined at the Bavaria
and that many of our old drawings were still hanging there. I informed him that the best collection of our Geneva drawings is
now displayed at the Rockefeller Library, and I urged him to go
and see them the next time he was in Geneva.

"Well—er—" he hedged, "but they don't serve beer there."

What is a caricature which, when served with sauerkraut, can be
one man's fortune and another man's unpaid bill?

The art of caricature is not simply a matter of drawing a big
nose bigger and a floppy ear floppier. It involves an evaluation of
the inner man through his outward features. A good caricature
is the result of long and careful observation of the model.

The message any form of art conveys is the truth, be it beauty,
ugliness, spirituality, sensuality, or any other thought or emotion.
The specific message of a caricature should be the model's personality. It is the artist's opinion. It must be told simply, and to make
it unmistakable, it has to be emphasized. The more it is emphasized, the more humorous, or ultimately the more grotesque, it
becomes. Between the sublime and the grotesque there are endless
gradations, and the borderline where the grotesque—or the caricature—begins is in the mind of the individual artist, or of his view-
ers.

Many sublime artists—for instance, Leonardo da Vinci—have
played at caricature. In my opinion, the personality in all of Goya's
portraits is so strongly underlined that they brush the caricature.

I never met Max Beerbohm, an eminent caricaturist, but I am
told by those who knew him that he was a kindly man who did
not enjoy hurting other people's feelings. But he was a man of

opinions, and when he was face to face with blank paper these opinions came forth with elementary frankness. His portraits of famous contemporaries are not distortions or clever calligraphy. They are graphic satire at its best, which at times can confer grandeur upon the mediocre.

In the United States, managing editors have a persistent bad habit: they give some hungry artist a photograph and command him to torture it into a caricature. I wish I could persuade some of these camera-happy gentlemen to go to the library and look at the various caricatures Beerbohm made of Oscar Wilde from life. They will be studied as long as anyone studies Wilde, because in them you can see, unmistakably, all of his grandeur and decadence, all of his wit and his folly.

I used to admire greatly the caricatures of my countryman, Henry Major; and those of Sem, the chronicler of the *haut monde* in Paris. I think my colleague, Derso, who does not carry a sketch-book but prowls after his model, staring until he sees his astral body, is one of the best caricaturists of our times. I dare say he would argue the point. The only comparison I have ever heard him make of himself with da Vinci is that while Leonardo was left-handed, Derso is ambidextrous. Not only can he draw with both hands, he can write two letters at the same time; but the gift is wasted, because he never writes letters.

One of my cronies at the Brasserie Bavaria was a young Swiss doctor named Ernst Friedheim, who in the early twenties was occupied with dissecting corpses at the Hôpital Cantonal. I held forth to him one evening on my conviction, which had been growing ever since my Klosterka days, that you can judge the personality of people by the bones of their face and the way they are fitted together. He remarked: "I'd feel happier about your idea if you'd send the heads of your ambassadors down to the morgue so that I could boil them down and measure the bones of their facial skeletons."

An enticing scheme, but hard to manage.

In spite of his skepticism, Friedheim lent me a book, *Körperbau und Charakter* (Physique and Character) by Dr. Ernst Kretschmer, professor of psychiatry at the University of Tuebingen. To this day, he has not got it back. This book changed my outlook on my fellow men and ultimately on political and social affairs; and it greatly affected my work as a caricaturist. It gave backbone to my observations, put them in order, and anchored them within the body of growing knowledge called "constitutional psychology."

Since the subject keeps popping up in this volume, I will tell you briefly what constitutional psychology has to tell me; as well as where I depart from it.

Dr. Kretschmer looked around his insane asylum and noted that among the patients suffering from manic-depressive insanity (whose moods swing between the poles of manic agitation and deep depression), round-headed, stocky, compact fellows were in the majority. Among those who suffered from epilepsy or catatonic schizophrenia (the latter are the "living statues" I saw in the Klosterka), the muscular physique predominated. Finally, among the patients suffering from schizophrenia (or split personality), skinny fellows were noticeably numerous.

Dr. Kretschmer then looked beyond the walls of the insane asylum and studied the close relatives of his patients. He discovered that those of his patients' kinsmen who physically resembled them showed peculiarities of personality reminiscent of their hospitalized relatives—though they remained well within the bounds of the normal. That is, among the kinsfolk of his manic depressives, he found those plump people who habitually teeter between jolliness and sadness. Among the huskier relatives of epileptics or catatonics, he found explosive brawlers and stiff-necks. Among the skinny relatives of his schizophrenics, he found those abstract-minded, eccentric people who live with their heads in the clouds.

Kretschmer postulated what, in fact, I had sensed in a primitive way in the Klosterka: that no hard and fast line separates the sane from the insane and that a particular type of mind, sane or insane, prefers to live in a particular type of body.

Kretschmer described in great detail (and with an artistic pen) the three main body types and their corresponding temperaments —by which is meant the simplest personality traits.

Kretschmer was not the first to recognize basic human types. They have been observed since the days of Hippocrates, and down the centuries to the present day every observer has attached to them names that sound like teeth rattling in a cold shower. I am accustomed to naming them, in basic English, Round Man, Muscleman, and Thin Man. In fiction and legend, Mr. Pickwick, Sancho Panza, and Falstaff are Round Men. Tarzan, Paul Bunyan, and Hercules are Musclemen. Ichabod Crane, Don Quixote, and Caspar Milquetoast are Thin Men. You know how these men look and how they behave.

The difficulty is that no human being is a "pure type." Nature has shaken every man into a rather complicated cocktail.

This part of the problem has been attacked by an American, W. H. Sheldon of Harvard University. He said, in effect: "The trouble is that Kretschmer based his observations on mixed types. We must think of the three types in theoretically pure form, and see what happens to mind and body when they get crossed as they do in you and me."

Sheldon called his types endomorph, mesomorph, and ectomorph, and to determine the proportion of each in any given individual, he would measure the body carefully with calipers and tapes. He devised a system of expressing his mixtures simply with numerals.

When he came to study the temperaments of his subjects, he found that in the crossing of types the temperamental traits follow along, if not exactly in step, close at the heels of the physical crossing.

I am an artist and I own neither calipers nor measuring tape. I rely on my eyes. Here is where I part company with the gentlemen on the academic bench. They are bound to gross body measurements which can be expressed numerically. While by no means overlooking the body, I contend that the careful eye can discern, in the anatomy and morphology of the face, the proportion of the three types in any individual.

This is not in contradiction to the scientists. Kretschmer observed: "The face is the visiting card of the constitution."

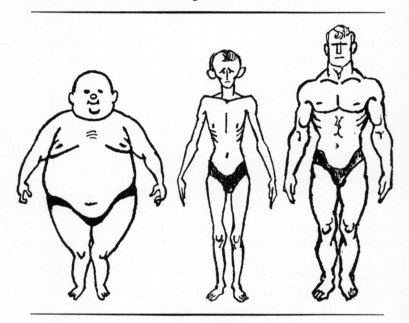

But the face is unmeasurable by any scientific means we have so far found. The judgment of the eye, however, instantaneously grasps the "character" of a face and, with some training, clearly perceives the scaffolding behind it, and thus the participation of the three main types in its make-up. In addition to the statics of the face, the eye also grasps its mimetics, which reveal the dynamic aspect of the personality.

It is my belief that such popularly known faces as hatchet face, or baby face, or faces with such common features as a lantern jaw, buck teeth, angular profile, are produced by specific crossings of the three main types, and therefore are correlated with definite patterns of temperament.

In this book I talk about pig face, owl face, horse face, monkey face, and so forth. I do it because I know the reader will understand at once what sort of face I mean. Men and beasts have the same bones in the face. A likeness to an ape or to a fox indicates a similarity in the arrangement and proportion of the facial skeleton.

Should we assume that there is a resemblance on the temperamental level between men and beasts who look alike?

If we do, we're in interesting company. Four thousand years ago, the Code of Hammurabi advised judges to evaluate the men who appeared before them by their likeness to animals. Aristotle wrote a treatise on this subject in which there are some very astute observations. Leonardo da Vinci left many drawings which indicate that he had devoted thought to it. In the sixteenth century the Italian physician, Giambattista della Porta, described the resemblances between men and birds. Darwin demonstrated the analogy in the expression of emotions in men and animals. In 1930, Professor Charles R. Stockard of Cornell University, in his book, *The Physical Basis of Personality*, pointed out that similar glandular anomalies in men and dogs produce similarities in physique and temperament. For instance, glandular insufficiencies produce, in both men and dogs, midgets with yapping voices and perky locomotion—as, for example, the Pekinese. Glandular oversecretion results in giants with surplus skin, booming voice, and sluggish locomotion—as in the St. Bernard.

I think that the resemblance between men and animals is well worth thinking about, and not only on the part of caricaturists. Besides, I have a philosophical opinion: I believe in—because I see it—the existence of a universal pool of form and function, out of which men, beasts, plants, and objects in endless variations draw a share. These forms and their functions are inseparably interrelated.

From this vantage point, I can suppose that resemblances between men and animals may have more significance than meets the eye.

A controversy rages among psychologists: what is more important in the shaping of human personality—heredity or environment?

In our time the environmentalists have won hands down. Partly this is because of the overwhelming impact the views of Sigmund Freud have had upon our way of life.

In the United States practically everyone feels equipped to psychoanalyze himself, his neighbor, and his wife and kids. But constitutional psychology—which deals with the hereditary side of the personality and which has been advanced so far by an American, Sheldon—is almost unknown even to highly educated people. To an American there is something downright undemocratic in judging people by the way they look. Thus, he ignores the existence of hereditary factors. He half-judges himself and others and is in turn half-judged and half-understood, particularly in those all-important report cards, diplomas, questionnaires and all the rest of the tyrannical paper work which governs his business life.

What is more important in ordering a suit—the material or the tailor? Obviously both are important.

In order to evaluate properly the powerful effect of environment, we must know, first, what it affects. We must learn to judge the material life works with, the innate aptitudes of a person, his temperament, which is part and parcel of his constitution and thus can be recognized in his face and body.

Once the broad area in which the temperament moves has been defined, the field can be narrowed by observing posture, locomotion, quality of voice, delivery of speech, haberdashery, grooming, taste in women, dogs, sports, cars, and everything else wherein the total personality—including the brand marks of environment—might find expression.

Teachers, parents, judges, social workers, truant officers, foremen, family counselors—all who have serious responsibilities toward their fellow men—should know a great deal more than they do about the findings of Kretschmer and Sheldon.

I urge all diplomats to study the works of these men, second only to those of Niccolò Machiavelli. And surely Darwin's wonderful and neglected book, *The Expression of Emotions in Men and Animals,* should have something to say to them.

But most particularly I recommend constitutional psychology to everyone who, like me, loves to lie on a crowded beach and gape at the infinite variety of the human race which God, in a happy mood, created.

I talked shop once with my colleague, the Swedish caricaturist, Stefan Strobl. He told me that at one time he had worked at the Stockholm prison hospital in order to study the faces of criminals. One day, the prison psychologist brought in a new prisoner and said to Strobl: "Well, what do you think of this one?"

Strobl looked at the man and answered: "He is a thief and a pathological liar."

"We shall see," said the psychologist. He then submitted the prisoner to the laboratory third degree, the Szondy test, the Rorschach test, and so forth. In three weeks, the psychologist came back to Strobl and said: "You were right. The man is a thief and a pathological liar. How did you know?"

Said Strobl: "I saw it."

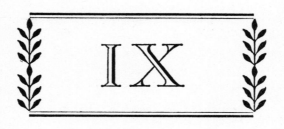

Prelude
to Pearl Harbor

BRIAND presented his plan for European Union in September 1930. The same month the German elections gave Hitler a hundred and seven deputies in the Reichstag instead of the previous twelve. I decided that as soon as the Assembly was over I would go to Germany and take a longer look at these Nazis.

First I made my usual pilgrimage to the Schellingstrasse in Munich, the cradle of Hitler's career and mine. I found Herr Seybold scratching his head. "Funny things are happening in this country," he told me. Adolf Mueller, on the other hand, was shining like a man who learns that perfect faith bringeth heart's desire: his money back.

I bumped into a fellow countryman of mine, Stefan Lorant,

editor of the *Münchner Illustrierte,* and one of those Hungarians
who wander the world, laying golden eggs-of-Columbus: he does
things some likelier person ought to have thought of first. In England, a land full of mackintosh pockets, he brought out the first
pocket magazine, *Lilliput.* In the United States he composed the
first picture biography of Abraham Lincoln.

It was the time of the *Oktoberfest,* and together with Lorant
and Karl Arnold, boozy cartoonist of *Simplicissimus,* I took a tram
to the fairgrounds, where Munich's famed breweries had set up
their colossal tents and filled them with barrels of beer, enough to
soak two thousand Bavarians in one wave; and they fed them with
hunks of oxen barbecued in majestic entirety on the premises. To
keep the juices of hops and barley flowing steadily, ceremonial
carriages loaded with barrels went back and forth, pulled by six
Mecklenburg horses gorgeously caparisoned in feathers, ribbons,
and jangling brass chains. The coachmen were dressed as Bavarian
mountaineers and, bellowing like Abominable Snowmen, drove
giddily through the dense crowds, operating on the popular belief
that a horse will never tread on a drunken man.

All this I remembered from years before and it is still my tenderest memory of Germany.

But in 1930 something new had been added: in the brewery
tents there was an occupation army of thousands of brown-shirted
storm troopers, steins in hand, arms around the frilly shoulders of
süsse deutsche Mädchen, yodeling and singing to the brassy winds
of shirtsleeved peasant bands in mossy hats and milkweed plumes.
Golden blond and handsome, nevertheless they seemed savage in
their mindless strength, and if God had not created them savage
they were made to look so by *kepis* strapped to their jaws like steel
helmets with the rims far down over their eyes.

My colleague, Karl Arnold, was a social reformer; scratch a social
reformer, find a brawler. Two steins of dark beer did the scratching,
and Arnold, red and loudmouthed, began to hurl insults in the
direction of the golden boys: he called out *Nazi Schweine! Scheiss-
kerle! Rindviecher! Dummoxe!* and other selected pearls from the

rich Bavarian treasury of insults. I said my last prayer, but nothing happened, the boys took it in good part. Evidently even a Nazi storm trooper, when his arm is around a maiden, goes deaf, like a grouse in the mating season.

Before leaving Munich I saw Lorant again, and he invited me to tea with his friend, Count Arco, the assassin of Kurt Eisner, who in 1919, as the Social Democratic prime minister of the newly established Bavarian Republic, had admitted Germany's war guilt.

"Tell Kelen about it," Lorant said to him. And the short, bucket-headed count with untamed hair told me his wild and wasteful tale.

He had been a young career officer in the Bavarian army, and a monarchist. On that February morning he had awakened, bathed, breakfasted, and bundled himself in an extra set of warm clothes, to the surprise of his chambermaid; but he had told her: "It's cold in jail." Then he waited on the street for Kurt Eisner, who eventually appeared walking with two men. Arco slipped behind them, unlocking the safety catch of the revolver in his pocket. Stepping forward swiftly, he shot Eisner in the back twice, from close range. Eisner fell dead, and Arco fell, too, with four bullets in him. From the ground, he saw the man who had shot him, smoking revolver in hand. He realized there were still two bullets in that revolver, and he pretended to be dead.

He was taken to a hospital, where a howling mob soon gathered, wanting to lynch him. Eisner had been a much-loved man. Even before his blood had dried on the street, the people had brought flowers to put over it and set up a sign reading: "Proletarians! Take off your hats to Kurt Eisner's blood." That night the mob stole Arco from the hospital. They took him to a school, where a kangaroo court was organized, and Arco was tried by hysterical women and teen-age boys and sentenced to death. Two Red guards were delegated to take him to the Luitpold Gymnasium and shoot him; but one of the guards had been in Arco's regiment in the army, and he remembered him kindly. He persuaded his comrade to sneak him back into the hospital.

After Eisner's death, the Communists took over, and when the regime fell and von Epp's soldiers executed the Red guards, Arco managed to save the lives of these two men.

"Tell Kelen," prompted Lorant, "how you regret killing Eisner."

"I regret it," said Count Arco. "I didn't understand the situation. He was a good man. And I didn't know that, the day before, he had resigned as prime minister. I carry this murder on my heart like a cross, and I can't forgive myself."

When the Nazis came to power, Arco was arrested as a rabid monarchist. He was in a concentration camp for a time, and then he died, a man who had lived with an albatross around his neck.

After Munich I went to Frankfurt, because Adolf Hitler was there. Thousands of brownshirts engulfed the streets, sweeping down roadways and sidewalks like a muddy tidal wave, howling, roaring, red in the face, deliriously breaking windows and plundering Jewish stores. With Wolf von Dewall, political editor of the *Frankfurter Zeitung*, I went to the meeting where Hitler was expected to speak; without von Dewall's ash-blond head beside me, I shouldn't have had the courage to press through the hard-muscled mass. Hitler entered, with his barely remembered, commonplace face, and it seemed to me a mad world in which the sight of this face awakened hysterical adulation in the crowd. Wailing and shrieking broke out, and for minutes on end the hoarse sound of *Sieg Heil!* tore at the joints of the walls.

What struck me first as I looked at Hitler were those beautiful shining white teeth that my friend, Ward Price, had described with heartfelt admiration in the *Daily Mail*. What struck me second was that they obviously belonged to his dentist: the looseness of his mouth as he spoke revealed some irreplaceable emptiness. His eyes were buttermilk-cold, and they did not bulge like Mussolini's but popped and stared like those of a patient who has followed overlong the watch a psychologist dangles before his nose. One of the unsightly features of his face was the tremendous brow ridge, a swollen bumper like that of a boxer who has been battered. A massive brow ridge is impressive if it is in harmonious balance with the rest of the face, but Hitler's was strikingly out of proportion to the sunken upper jaw which the little mustache was inadequate to coax out, and to the receding and unimpressive chin. These blatant dysplasias and the staring eyes were outward signs of the tension that triggered Hitler to sudden explosions such as I used to hear through the walls of Schellingstrasse, 41, and which later made him bang the floor with his fists and (according to some) chew the rug.

I am a nose-watcher. I think that noses are welded and molded of a number of constitutional components; they are a sort of test-tube culture of the constitution, a generalized formula of a man. Hitler's nose was crudely hacked out, unfinished, a vulgar proboscis, coarse and inconsistent. At the root it was mildly depressed and narrow, then it jumped brutally to a broad bump, only to slope thinly down and end in a hard, plebeian tip which was pointed and yet square like a die, showing hideously the two-part cartilage that formed it. The flares of the nostrils were fleshy but hard as unripe plums and thrust forward, cutting into the tip. Anthropoid apes have no nose tips, only nose wings, and my feeling is that when the human nose wing blatantly dominates and cuts into the tip, some primitive and brutal forces can be looked for in the personality.

Incongruities ran up and down the man. The occiput was too small to balance that bulging brow ridge, and the narrow shoulders ill matched his wide hips. After he became Reichschancellor, an expensive tailor corrected the feminine softness of Hitler's body, but in Frankfurt it was evident, and I noted too a curious attitude of his: as he spoke, gesturing, he kept bringing his hands down over the lower abdomen as if protecting his amorous armature. There is a school of thought, kinesics, which holds that habitual postures and gestures reveal some aspects of the personality. For example, a girl who habitually sits with knees pressed tightly together may be afraid of advances; but one who sits with knees habitually apart invites them.

I've studied scores of Hitler's photos, and many have caught him in this kewpie posture I noted first in Frankfurt. I mentioned this to a psychologist friend, who said: "Ah, yes, that's where he was vulnerable."

From Frankfurt I went to Berlin for the opening of the Reichstag. I had done the same the previous year, 1929. At that time the Nazis had twelve deputies, among them Goebbels, Goering, and the political cop of my Munich days, Dr. Wilhelm Frick. I had ignored them totally. I drew instead, fast asleep in an armchair, Herr von Kahr, a bearded Bavarian Neptune who in 1923 had suppressed Hitler's *putsch*. In 1934 he was sleeping just as peacefully in his bed when the Nazis dragged him from it, killed him, and threw his body in the lake.

I also drew a pumpkin-faced Socialist deputy named Ebert, a young man with a budding belly which would one day achieve the barrel-shaped proportions of that of his father, the first president of the Weimar Republic. Today young Ebert is the mayor of East Berlin.

I stood in the foyer as they arrived in batches, Goebbels running up the steps as he always did lest you notice that he had a club foot. A priest named Munchmeier, who had jumped the pulpit to become a Nazi, saw me drawing and offered himself as my guide,

pointing out the plums, patiently spelling out names. It was forbidden in Social Democratic Prussia to wear uniforms, and so all
of these Nazis had come bundled in overcoats and raincoats, but
once inside the Reichstag they took them off and stood revealed in
boots and brown shirts, swastikas on their arms. Still, they were
far from the elegant Nazis we knew later: Count Reventlow wore
his tuxedo pants tucked into his boots; my guide, Munchmeier,

wore a polka-dot tie with his brown shirt. The brown shirts were
not all precisely brown; they ranged in color from khaki yellow to
khaki green, whatever material of a muddy color could be scraped
together.

But their manners were uniform: overbearing and loud. They
were an island of badmen, and in the corridors and restaurants they
kept themselves isolated from the rest of the deputies. The Reichstag I'd known the year before, a dignified, civilian parliament that
smelled of floor polish, had become a uniformed barracks with a
whiff of garlic and old shoes.

Goering was present, not the beef steer he later became, but an
angry bull calf holding his head ready to butt. Since the Nazis were
the second largest party, he automatically became vice president of
the Reichstag, which three years later he burned to the ground.

Frick, always with papers under his arm, was the image of the order-loving German bureaucrat, gazing sternly from under his caterpillar eyebrows; Gregor Strasser, whom four years later Hitler slew, was a mountainous wrestler with convex lips like a parrot's,

and his shaved bullet head looked bruised and irregular, as if it had been pulled out from under an oxcart.

There was one among the hundred and seven who struck both my eye and my mind, so that he became my nightmare-by-day— and still is—a shape symbolic of these ill-constructed half-men who dismembered a good world. I had heard of him before: Edmund Heines, an officer of the Black Reichswehr, an illegal army of about twenty thousand men which operated clandestinely in 1920–23 on the Polish border, terrorizing Poles and Germans alike. Germans who reported their activities to the Allied Control Commission were dragged at night from their beds, tried by kangaroo court, and brutally put to death. These were the notorious "Feme murders," and Heines had to face trial for them, but when the judge serves the state and not justice, justice comes second.

Heines became the leader of the storm troopers in Munich. He was a friend of Roehm and a fellow homosexual, and so, for a while, the brave blond lads under his command had the job of scouting the town for suitable lovers for their commanders. Now he was a deputy of the Reichstag, and I was drawing him—his broad shoulders, bull neck, and sledgehammer jaw. I was horrified by the shape of the ill-fitting upper head, the brain case squeezed as if between two boards, narrowing toward the top and ending in a point like a sugarloaf with the summit decorated by a patch of naturally curly parsley, which was blond, to show the difference between an Aryan and an ape.

This is called a "tower skull." According to Kretschmer, it often turns up among schizophrenics. According to me, it is a disaster among leaders of men.

I couldn't have missed Heines that day, for he made a distinguished contribution to the debates. He didn't speak, but he never sat down either; he just stood next to his bench in the aisle, and while others who were not Nazis spoke, he pulled out a whistle and whistled. He demonstrated clearly and by design what the Nazis thought of parliaments. When, in 1960, Nikita Khrushchev took off his shoes at the United Nations and banged the desk with them, I wondered what he thinks, really, about the Parliament of Man.

Not all the murderers in Germany were deputies in the Reichstag; some were in jail, and on an assignment from the Ullstein press I visited the Alexanderplatz, the police headquarters, to draw some twenty police inspectors. My guide was Ullstein's well-known police reporter, nicknamed "Corpse" Gutmann because he was roused to such a pitch of cheerfulness whenever a dead body was pulled out of the river Spree.

The chief of the political police was a Jew, Bernhard Weiss. "I'll show you something that ought to interest a caricaturist," he said, and he opened a side door into a room empty except for a mountain of cartoon books entitled *Das Buch Isidor*. The target of the humor was Herr Weiss himself. "A chap called Joseph Goebbels wrote it," he told me. "He's a very clever man. But of course I had to confiscate it."

The next time I heard of Herr Weiss, he was a refugee in Denmark.

Gutmann greeted the inspector of the homicide squad as if he were his twin brother. I asked the inspector to ignore me while I drew him as he proceeded with the interrogation of a murderer; and I drew the murderer too, for he fascinated me, especially his eyes. He was unable to keep them on one object, but twitched them about in anguish and aggression. What's more, I recognized those eyes: I had just drawn them in the Reichstag, the unresting eyes of Heines, whose every movement was jerky and abrupt like the murderer's. One poor wretch was in jail; the other was a deputy of his country, and the power of life and death would be delegated to him by Hitler. Among the Nazis I drew there were too many like him: Roehm, Bormann, Greiser, Sepp Dietrich were all birds of a feather.

In 1934, in the Blood Purge, Heines was found in bed with a young boy, and he was murdered. Was Hitler aware of his disturbing character, and that of Roehm and the others? Of course he knew, just as those who adopted Hitler as their strong bulwark against Bolshevism knew that Roehm and Heines were his friends.

I watched the Nazis sowing dragon's teeth in the fall of 1930. A year later the Japanese invaded Manchuria.

The Japanese had a simple explanation for their action: Chinese bandits had blown up the track of the South Manchurian Railway near Mukden, and they had been obliged to intervene. It wasn't an original excuse, but it contained practical wisdom useful to remember for those who observe dealings among nations: "He who wishes to drown his dog accuses it first of madness."

A winter's day in 1932 found the Japanese outside Shanghai. Before attacking, they had cooked up an ultimatum for China. I'll never forget the time, in Geneva, it was to expire: 19 hours, 30 minutes.

In deadly silence we listened to the deliberations of the council. The clock on the wall ticked to the fatal hour. I watched Japanese delegate Yoshizawa sitting at the council table, poker-faced as a dried prune, in his mouth a cigar as long-barreled as a navy gun. Dr. Yen, the Chinese delegate, stooped over the table, sunk in

thought. The interpreters droned on. Everyone sat stolid as bowling pins. Time ran out.

Cables began to arrive, secretaries entered in a rush to place them before the Chinese delegate. They told of panic, of refugees, of hospitals bombed, of women and children slain in the streets. In an hour there was a pile of papers in front of Dr. Yen.

I was a casualty of a sort that day. An incident of my childhood came to my mind: a large mill had caught fire in my home town; the flour had exploded, and people had jumped to their deaths out of flaming windows. For some time afterwards we kept hearing about one or another person we knew who had died or been injured there. For the first time since I came to the League I felt the full impact of what Briand had taught us all along—that at the other end of diplomatic proceedings, of tedious speeches, of consecutive translations, and of dusty communiqués, there are people in anguish.

Sam Dashill, of the United Press, couldn't take this lying down, so he took it standing up with a glass in his hand at the bar of Chez Maxim. There, on the dance floor, he noticed a Japanese with thirty-six teeth, all grinning with a pearly gleam.

"Dirty rat!" shouted Sam. "Yellow-bellied scum! Nippon gibbon!" The Asian just grinned in his direction, and that was more than a full boozed American could take Chez Maxim. He stalked onto the dance floor determined to knock out at least fifty per cent of those teeth, but he was waylaid by the manager and a Swiss bouncer. Those mountaineers are good at this sort of thing, and the party, Sam, Japanese, and all interested bystanders, soon found themselves under the plane trees of the square.

"Put 'em up!" shouted Sam.

"You are mistaken, sir," countered the Mongoloid, his teeth turned on to their highest power, "I am not Japanese. I am Chinese."

"Chinese! Why the hell didn't you say so?"

"Why should I? I would have interrupted your insulting the Japanese in public."

The spirit of Chez Maxim did not reach as far as the council table. To Japan's weak explanations, M. Paul-Boncour of France and Sir John Simon of Britain gave weak replies. These gentlemen, politicians who had replaced prophets in the service of the maid, served with their lips, but not with their hearts. In their hearts, indeed, they understood Japan's position: here was an overpopulated country whose people, a bit yellower, perhaps, than respectable Empire-builders ought to be, but vigorous, efficient, "modernized," had nowhere to expand. So why should they not expand to China, where four hundred million peasants no doubt had plenty of room.

"After all," said Sir John Simon to the journalists, "what is China? A geographic expression."[1]

A stalemate ensued. Slippery statements and arguments folded back on themselves and doubled over again like apple strudel.

[1] George Slocombe: *Mirror to Geneva* (New York: Henry Holt & Company; 1938), p. 279.

Never once was mention made of "war." The Japanese talked only of "unfortunate disturbed conditions in East Asia." Once, when by an appalling slip of the tongue, Japanese delegate Mr. Sato pronounced the word *war* the interpreter obligingly translated it as "incident."

So the Japanese occupied Shanghai, and men, women, and children were slaughtered every day; and there was no one in Geneva with the courage to stand up and say: "Japan has invaded the territory of a sovereign state; she has violated the Briand-Kellogg Pact and the Covenant of the League of Nations, and she is therefore an *aggressor*."

However, a yip was heard from the kennels where the court jesters sleep. Derso and I prepared a cartoon in which Mr. Naotake Sato was the central figure. He was a sliver of a man, polished and polite, the same who in Lausanne had ordered from us a lithograph representing the Japanese delegation, a rather poor image of an aggressor facing a Council-ful of eleven Western giants. But we depicted him in a belligerent posture, standing before the horseshoe table, pointing his finger at President Paul-Boncour. That hand of Sato's was the focus of the drawing: was it just the pointing hand of argument, or was it a gun? Anyway, all the members of the Council were standing, their hands up in surrender.

This cartoon doesn't pack the punch of many a daily cartoon in a daily paper; but in the careful realm of diplomacy and double-talk it was like the danger flag that shows you where the ice is thin on a smooth pond. William Martin had to have courage to publish it on the front page of his *Journal de Genève*, which in those days was almost a semi-official publication of the League of Nations.

The following afternoon, when the meeting opened, most members of the Council had the drawing in hand; they pushed it under one another's noses as if it were a contraband copy of *Ulysses*. We felt rather guilty about our victim, Mr. Sato. We liked him personally, and thought that Fate had dealt him a sorry role, as it had to us, his critics. Diplomats, like caricaturists, obey higher orders. To our astonishment, no sooner had the meeting ended than Mr. Sato

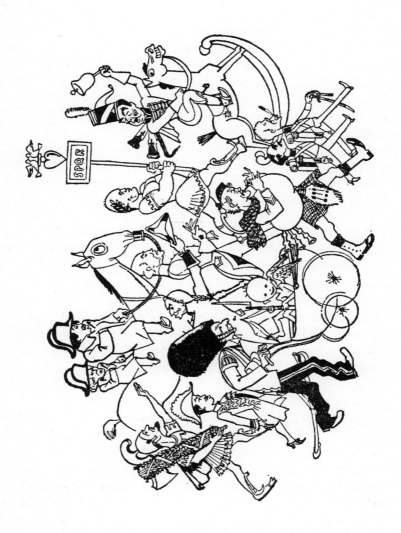

approached us in the corridors with open arms; he wanted to buy the original. For him it seemed a triumph that he had held a gun to the world's best hope for peace.

Did the drawing make any difference really? One can't know, of course. It released for the moment some pent-up anger, brought into the open an image of the Council that hadn't been admitted before. The effect an experience has on anyone is hard to fathom, especially on politicians, but even such a small experience as the sight of a caricature leaves tiny fingerprints upon the mind. In the end, the Council brought themselves to send out a commission under Lord Lytton to investigate "the unfortunate disturbed conditions in East Asia."

One of the good things about living long is that one sometimes sees the third-act curtain of certain episodes. Mr. Sato became foreign minister of Japan, then ambassador to Moscow; and after Pearl Harbor he was in charge of the affairs of stranded American diplomats in Japan—Ambassador Joseph C. Grew was not happy with his help. When, after the war, Japan joined the United Nations, Mr. Sato was a member of the delegation, and we met in New York as survivors of a vanished world. I asked him if he still had our drawing, and he replied in a melancholy mood: "During the war, American bombers hit my house, it burned, everything I owned perished, including your drawing."

At the turn of 1932, with a respectable war going on in China, the first World Disarmament Conference was called in Geneva. Derso and I planned an elaborate album to celebrate such a well-timed event, and all around us the other camp followers of international diplomacy, the restaurant owners, the pension mothers, the hotel busboys, the horse-and-buggy coachmen, prepared feverishly to catch the shower of gold which they judged would rain on them for at least ten years. This proved to be a conservative estimate, because if you count the five years of war—which is only a quick, efficient way for nations to disarm each other—the Disarmament Conference hasn't really ended to this day.

Foremost among us rejoicers were the madams and brothel-masters far and wide who mobilized and threw up a veritable Maginot line of *maisons closes* around Geneva. These establishments were not permitted in the City of Calvin proper. When I first arrived, in 1923, Geneva had been in the midst of one of her historic guilt spasms, and all the bordellos that had sprung up within the city walls were to be abolished. The Swiss settle such matters in a democratic way, by plebiscite, and the street corners were loud with posters demonstrating that public opinion was split straight down the fairway: women were abolitionists, men weren't. One poster read: Do you want our wives and daughters to be raped in public parks? Then vote for the abolition of the *maisons publiques*. It was signed, The Father of a Family.

The ladies won, of course, and so, at the time of the Disarmament Conference, the houses formed a *ceinture de chasteté* around the city on the French side of the border.

A distinguished visitor dressed in black and white like Salvador Dali, who might have been the envoy of a Caribbean republic, or perhaps the director of a funeral parlor, knocked on the door of M. Carlos García-Palacios, an eminent member of the League of Nations Secretariat. "I understand that you are attached to the Fifth Committee?" he said, shedding his black gloves.

"Yes, sir. What can I do for you?"

"Your committee is concerned with—ah—certain social problems? I, sir, am the owner of a *maison close* at Annecy, and I follow its work with the keenest interest. I wish to inquire about a resolution you are preparing regarding the abolition of white slavery. My lease expires next month. In view of the forthcoming Disarmament Conference, I am inclined to sign a new five-year lease. But considering the effective work of your committee, I do not know whether this would be advisable. Tell me, Monsieur, what should a prudent businessman do in my position? What would you do?"

García-Palacios did what any prudent international civil servant would do: he handed the prudent businessman a great pile of *procès-verbaux*, minutes, press releases, summaries, memoranda—

twenty-five pounds of mimeographed verbosity from the Fifth Committee—with such an air that the gentleman from Annecy felt he was receiving secret documents of state. He was much obliged. He told Palacios: "If ever you should find yourself in Annecy, don't fail to drop in at Aux Belles Poules. You shall be received as if it were home."

Among the more distinguished houses was one called La Maison Blanche, the White House, no doubt because of the important business conducted there. Exercising the utmost precautions to protect the anonymity of its guests, La Maison employed a special superintendent who was in charge of slipping capotes, little sacks, over the diplomatic license plates of cars stationed in front of the house. Inevitably, the day came when the superintendent forgot to remove one of these sacks, and presently a limousine with its license plate in modest purdah entered the city and parked before the Hôtel Métropole, proclaiming to all the world and its brother that Monsieur l'Ambassadeur had just presented his credentials at the White House.

A journalist friend of mine once met an ambassador leaving La Maison with his overcoat over his arm. "Ambassador!" cried the journalist. "What are you doing here!"

"You won't believe me," replied His Excellency, "but I was having my overcoat pressed."

A still more exciting feature of the Disarmament Conference was that the Americans were going to be in it. President Harding had promised not to lead the United States into the League via the front door, the back door, or the cellar door; but now someone had discovered a little side door where you parked your guns. The titular head of the delegation was Secretary Stimson, but he came as an observer, really; the working man was Hugh Gibson, with the splendid head of a Hollywood Indian, and one of the most elegant men in Geneva. At his side was Senator Claude A. Swanson, whose mustache needed a good clipping, but his frown did not, as it was already clipped to his face by a pince-nez lest it slide off his beaky nose; and old Geneva hand Norman H. Davis, a quiet silver fox whose lips looked eternally chapped by the Geneva *bise*.

I went with Derso to the Hôtel de Russie for an appointment we had set up through Major James B. Ord with the delegates of the United States. We found them sitting in a semicircle of basket chairs in the middle of the lobby. We approached; Major Ord came forward to meet us; and, as he did so, the entire formidable force of generals and admirals jumped to their feet as one man and stood at attention like so many ninepins.

The sight of American brass, all atwinkle with stars, standing at attention for two caricaturists, was one of the most exhilarating of my life, and for two pins I'd have turned around and walked back in for an encore.

We signaled "at ease," sat down on straight chairs, and began to draw. We drew Brigadier General George S. Simonds, Rear Admiral Arthur J. Hepburn, Lieutenant Colonel George V. Strong—known in World War II as Godalmighty Strong—and so on, down the line to the last major. After that first dazzling display of military etiquette, I noted that the Americans had easy manners, with nothing of the snap, crackle, and pop stiffness of German generals, nor even the more urbane martiality of the French species. They were like any bunch of civilians drilled to sit straighter than absolutely necessary; and that, of course, is where Tojo and I went wrong.

I sketched the profile of a man sitting in one of the basket chairs, with alert, yet timid black-currant eyes, insignificant nose and chin, smooth round forehead, and a little puff of air in his jowls: a small boy with bubblegum, thinking of some mischief he was too well behaved to carry out. It was Thomas C. Kinkaid, who under Mac-Arthur was to become Commander of the Seventh Fleet; but on his own merits he was a hero of the Pacific, in the thick of it from the first day at Midway, Guadalcanal, the Solomon Islands, and the Aleutians. At first his armada consisted of Pearl Harbor leftovers, but Kinkaid, with leftovers, was able to serve up a full-course war.

Yet I saw and drew in his face far less aggressiveness than I have seen in the faces of many an American businessman; and in the course of my life I was to observe that a great many military leaders today are not as ferocious-looking as the men they lead and, as a group, not as formidable of countenance as the great-boned generals of my youth. Asthenic components seem to be seeping into the constitution of the high brass as expressed in the birdlike faces of Generals de Gaulle, Montgomery, Mark Clark; in Hyman Rickover's hard-boiled-egg head; in the vigilant simian looks of General Marshall; in Lauris Norstad's elongated face, which looks as if El Greco had designed it; and most of these men have strikingly alert eyes and delicate chins.

All this suggests to me that the more the military shifts toward science and technology, the more it chooses for its own men of thought rather than men of physical force; dog-faced soldiers such as Lord Kitchener and Earl Haig are on their way out. It is true, of course, that some "military geniuses" showed a certain degree of delicacy of feature—Lord Nelson and Napoleon are good examples. The point is that bookish looks are trickling down over the summits of command and if the trend continues there'll be nothing left of what we once considered the model of a modern major general.

Derso and I, when collecting the hundreds of portraits necessary for an elaborate album, divide our head-hunting labors according to the types each of us can draw more easily. Derso is a master of the fine-drawn line proper to decadent and precious faces. I am more at home with rugged, bony faces that give me something to chew on. Asians fall automatically into my jurisdiction. I therefore made an appointment to visit the Hôtel Métropole, abode of the Japanese delegation, alone.

Once a committee of experts under the presidency of Owen D. Young was holding meetings in Paris in great secrecy behind closed doors. Nevertheless, a Japanese newspaper published, word for word, conversations held in the committee. It turned out that the correspondent of the newspaper had simply walked into the committee room and sat down behind the Japanese delegation. Mr.

Young scolded the secretary, who said in despair: "How could I know? All Japanese look alike!"

They don't, of course. Not even sheep look alike, and the shepherd can tell them apart by their faces. The character of a face, in sheep and men, depends largely on how the different bones of the facial skeleton are fitted together. The various races have certain common rules of facial composition, but once you have looked at enough of them, they sort themselves out in miraculous variety.

I am fond of Japanese faces; I enjoy their well-defined hairlines, their linear eyes, the craggy facial skeletons. I therefore went eagerly to the Métropole, especially as I knew that, with a fine war in progress in China, the Japanese had felt it prudent to mobilize for the Disarmament Conference their first line of diplomatic defense.

I was treated to coffee and one of those pleasant Japanese discussions about Hiroshige and Hokusai. Afterwards, two chairs were placed in the center of the room, and the procession began, according to protocol, with Viscount Matsudaira, chief of the delegation and father-in-law of the Emperor's brother, Prince Chichibu. Next, His Excellency Nagaoka, ambassador to Paris, an old acquaintance, for I had already drawn him ten years before, in Lausanne. Cute and round as a kitten, he gave me a shrewd squint and took his place. At once his neck wilted, his eyes slumbered, his head slowly sank toward his necktie. He caught it halfway, shot me an apologetic and fading smile, then like a bird at evening tucked his face into his collar and fell asleep. What has the book of diplomatic etiquette to say under "Ambassador, sleeping, awakening of, by caricaturist"? A glass of cold water would have done the job, or a buzz fly—no such luck. I started a great rustle of papers, cleared my throat repeatedly; I shuffled, coughed, creaked my chair, and grunted, but to no avail, until, like all other international conflicts, this one was resolved by time. His Excellency suddenly emitted a roar of a snore, woke himself up, and stared at me dumfounded, forgetting to close his mouth. "Thank you, Ambassador," I shouted. "Hold that pose."

Next, Hiroshi M. Saito, ambassador to Washington, whose face

I always observed with curiosity, for he was one of those ageless Asians who between twenty and eighty look the same. He died in the United States, and the American government, as a special courtesy, sent his remains to Japan on a battleship to be buried with Shinto ceremony. This calls for favorite foods to be buried with the departed, and after his years of service abroad, a bottle of Old Parr whiskey stood on the altar to warm him on his shadowy journey, and three of his favorite brands of cigarettes were burned in the incense.

And so my pencil skipped through the ambassadorial physiognomies, and at last I was ready to attack the militia: first, General Iwane Matsui, Supreme Military Adviser to the delegation, a waddling, wispy skeleton topped by a shrunken head, a shining light of the Asiatic League, which wanted to chase non-Orientals out of Far Eastern affairs.

My next customer approached the model's chair carrying his tremendous brawn on short bowlegs, walking with a wide, waddling Mongoloid gait. I could see, under his civilian clothes, his musculature bulging like knackwurst, and though he walked slowly, his muscular tension led him to perform a stiff, unexpected little dance as he came toward me.

You've heard of bullet heads; well, once bullets were made of rough-hewn rocks and shot from wooden guns, and that's the kind of bullet head Admiral Osami Nagano had. It was rugged, craggy, dangerous, and primitive: a rocky brow ridge, high granite cheekbones, a very small nose with hard, open nostrils, a long, convex mustache area, a Crô-Magnon jaw. He watched me with black eyes, close set, fearful, and vigilant.

I had not heard of the admiral before, and I can't tell fortunes, but sometimes fortune peeps through a drawing. He had the face of the history he made. Nine years later, as chief of the naval general staff, he gave the order for the attack on Pearl Harbor. It was an infamous drawing I made of him, because I know a gorilla when I see one, whether he is riding in a limousine or on a bicycle. I like Japanese writing, and after I had finished, I asked him to sign his name on the drawing. I remember wondering whether he actually had written his name or something disobliging about my mother.

Still, Nagano was a samurai. When he was arrested by the United States forces, he accepted full personal responsibility for the attack on Pearl Harbor and the fifty-five counts of war crimes for which he was indicted, including murder at Hong Kong, Shanghai, and in the Philippines. Like his fellow commanders among the Japanese, he cut a better figure than the German rabble, who, like slum gangsters, pointed their fingers at one another to save their hides. Nagano escaped hanging by dying of a heart attack complicated by pneumonia.

The faces I drew at the Hôtel Métropole that afternoon are in themselves ideographs of their country's twixt-war history. Most of these men were "moderates," particularly Matsudaira and Saito. At home the military occasionally butchered such moderates; but in Geneva they lived for the time being in the same hotels, posed for their caricatures, and worked crossword puzzles, as did other civilized statesmen. In later years the military murdered some of my favorite models: Baron Hayashi, whom in Lausanne I had drawn as a monkey climbing a Russian Prince; Takahashi, whose murderer entered his home and, having shot him and then whacked him to pieces with his sword, according to Ambassador Grew, apologized to the household for the inconvenience;[2] and nice old pudgy Admiral Saito, whom I drew in Geneva, was riddled with thirty-six bullets. Though an admiral, it was he who said: "Those whose careers depend on war always want war."

It is a melancholy feeling for a caricaturist, leafing through his piles of drawings from years gone by, to look at faces he has drawn in a blithe mood and reflect how many have come to a hideous end. A caricaturist's sketchbook is an odd place to find evidence of the savagery of our times; but you do find it there.

[2] Joseph C. Grew: *Ten Years in Japan* (New York: Simon and Schuster; 1944).

If the Disarmament Conference was not to be delivered entirely into the hands of the court jesters, something had to be done to find out who had unfortunately disturbed conditions in East Asia. The League of Nations therefore sent out a commission consisting of a stocky German doctor, an outdated French general, a skinny American general, and an Italian count with a monocle. They were under the presidency of Lord Lytton, an Englishman

who resembled a nannygoat. They traveled by horseback, by rickshaw, by auto, by cart; they talked to soldiers, bureaucrats, farmers in the rice fields; and they came back to Geneva convinced that those Chinese bandits were Japanese.

The publication of the Lytton Report on October 1, 1932, was awaited in Geneva and throughout the world with great expectations. The correspondent of a large American news agency, an acquaintance of mine, offered a printer's helper two thousand francs for each page he sneaked out before publication. The printer reported this mischief to the League of Nations; a League official confided it to me; but not a word was said to the newspaperman, who possibly still doesn't know that his skulduggery was discovered.

Twenty-four hours before the report was made public, Lord Lytton was to speak to the world from the League's newly

erected radio studio. I asked Arthur Sweetser, an American
member of the League Information Section, to take me with him
to the studio, where I might ask Lord Lytton to pose for me.
"On one condition," he said, "that you hold him long enough
so that I can have a chat with him."

Actually, I can draw a nannygoat in no time flat, but I
pretended to be bogged down in Lord Lytton's lineaments. For
twenty minutes I listened to the conversation, and I spent most
of it kicking myself for being too much of a rabbit to run out
and sell the information to my acquaintance for all those francs.
Lord Lytton delivered himself of his personal and private opinions regarding the East Asiatic affair. It was his view that nobody
would ever be able to clean the Japanese out of China, but that
China was so massive that in the course of time the war would
bleed Japan white.

A similar opinion came to me about this time from another
observer of world affairs: I was traveling between Paris and
Geneva and had fallen in with an American writer, Frank
Simonds. We were sitting in his compartment, chatting, when an
unkempt country bumpkin appeared at the door. "Will!" shouted
Simonds. "Come in!" He turned to me: "You must meet this man
—he is the foremost humorist of America." That's how I met
Will Rogers.

Humorists are not necessarily funny-looking. David Low has
a tearful expression; Ferenc Molnar never let out a hearty laugh
in his life; Bernard Shaw preferred to look diabolic; and my
colleague Derso looks like a pensive chamois. But Will Rogers
was funny and he looked funny. His mischievous mind, tuned
to jokes, had arranged the wrinkles on his face so that they
reflected jocularity like the funny mirrors in a fun house, and,
talking to him, one's own paralyzed smile muscles leapt for joy.
He had a peanut face: the upper and lower parts of his head
were broad, but there was a squeezed section in between, so that
the eyes were very close-set, even inward-slanting as if pinched for
room; and they were blue as the Oklahoma sky. There was

strength in Will, but it was well balanced by sensitivity, idealism, and humanism, which twinkled in those eyes. You'll see the same contradiction in his humor, which rode bareback and roughshod but was shot through with penetrating wisdom. One saying of his in those days stays in my mind: "Small nations haven't got the right to be small." It was true then, but how much truer today, in an age Will Rogers couldn't have foreseen.

On the train from Paris to Geneva, with the battle of Manchuria raging, he told us the following joke: "The first day of the battle the Japanese killed 30 Chinese, and the Chinese killed 3 Japanese. On the second day the Japanese killed 300 Chinese and the Chinese killed 30 Japanese. On the third day the Japanese killed 3,000 Chinese, and the Chinese killed 300 Japanese.

"If things continue at this rate," concluded Will triumphantly, "there'll be no Japanese left!"

It was a good joke, but that terror of numbers exists today and it isn't only Japan that isn't laughing at it.

Deeming the presence of eight front-line (but moderate) diplomats insufficient to deal with the Lytton Report, the Japanese now dispatched to Geneva a very large potato in the person of Yosuke Matsuoka, president of the South Manchurian Railway and, later, foreign minister. He was a little peppercorn of a man— tiny, but strong—and more than any other single person, so far as we can know, he set his country on the road to Hiroshima. He brought Tokyo into the Rome-Berlin Axis. He swallowed Hitler's nonsense that the Japanese were a sort of Mongoloid Aryan. He

joined Hitler and Mussolini in the perfidious nonaggression pact with Russia.

He was, from the artist's viewpoint, "dysplastic," with his small head and long neck sloping to narrow shoulders, in misalliance with the short and heavy chassis. The selfsame dysplasia could have been admired on the body of Heinrich Himmler; and, long before either of them were heard of, Thomas Theodore Heine, the founder of *Simplicissimus*, used to draw the devil with this body build, sensing, as any artist must, Sheldon's constitutional outlook on delinquency: a striking contrast of contradictory personality traits expressing itself strikingly in an ill-balanced physique. He was a sort of un-Japanese Japanese, a Christian, and a law graduate of the University of Oregon. His cheekbones were not very salient, the nose was small and pointed, his protruding upper lips sported a Hitler mustache. At night he would descend in a brown kimono and sandals into the lobby of the Hôtel Métropole carrying a bottle of cognac in his hand. As the level of the cognac sank in the bottle, Matsuoka's effusions rose; around three in the morning you wouldn't have dreamed there was such a thing as an inscrutable Oriental.

It was February 24, 1933. In Geneva, in the General Assembly of the League of Nations, forty-two nations adopted the Lytton Report, which condemned Japan as an aggressor. There was one resounding "No!" It came from Yosuke Matsuoka. He walked to the rostrum and made a short speech declaring that the vote made Japan's membership in the League impossible. At his words, in different corners of the chamber small figures stood up and walked through the haze of cigarette smoke toward a door, like children toddling to school through the fog. The plunging of little hoofs ceased; there was a gloomy silence broken by a blow of the gavel. Belgian Foreign Minister Paul Hymans then adjourned the meeting.

Four days later, Hitler, who had been Reichschancellor for just a month, suspended all constitutional rights in Germany.

Through these ominous events the Disarmament Conference plodded ahead to infinity, and it seemed to hold for me the promise of a lifetime job, for, as governments rose and fell, they provided a limitless immigration of new faces for my sketchbook. Secretary Stimson faded from the scene, but the newly inaugurated president of the United States, Franklin D. Roosevelt, sent us Cordell Hull. Briand was gone; in his place came Tardieu, like a tiger shark with a bitter grin. For the Germans it was a quick-change act throughout the year. They had started out with Heinrich Brüning of the Catholic Center Party; by summer they switched to the "Government of the Barons," with Franz von Papen as chancellor; now the new year of 1933 brought us the Nazis.

As a first measure, in order not to breathe the same air

Stresemann had breathed, the German delegation moved from the Hôtel Métropole to the Hôtel Carlton.

The Nazis sent to Geneva a young "expert," a former naval officer, and now an SS Gruppenfuehrer: Reinhard Heydrich. He was there to explain to the Disarmament Committee the *raison d'être* of those fierce young men in uniform, the SA troops I had seen yodeling at the *Oktoberfest*. They numbered in the millions now, and while Captain Roehm was alive they menaced the very existence of Hitler. Ah, said Heydrich, they were only gymnasts, aiming at Strength through Joy. He explained they were engaged in what Dr. Paul Schmidt, the interpreter (who was a bit of a linguistic gymnast), translated into English as "defense sport."

"Defense sport!" exclaimed British General Temperley. "What sort of nonsense is that?" The SA was officially labeled part of the armed forces of Germany.

But Heydrich took the opportunity to show the world the stuff Nazis are made of. He began by berating his delegation for having permitted some of his remarks before the committee to be translated by a Jewish translator, Hans Jacob. Then, without consulting them, he had the black, red, and gold flag of the Weimar Republic hauled down from the front of the Hôtel Carlton and replaced by the Nazi swastika. Ambassador Nadolny (who wasn't at all sold on Heydrich) snapped: "A German delegation abroad is like a ship at sea, and I'm the commander." Off went Hitler's flag.

I needn't recall to anyone who lived through the years that followed the name of "Hangman Heydrich," deputy chief of the Gestapo under Himmler, chief of the Secret Service, architect of death camps and genius of the final solution. He met his own final solution at Lidice when his car was blown up by British saboteurs in Czechoslovakia, and the burden of guilt was placed by the government upon the nearby village of Lidice, which was razed, annihilated, and its male population exterminated; so that strange word, Lidice, remains in our many languages as a symbol of the gruesome wrath of absolute powers.

Looking back, I try to assess whether I guessed the bestial brutality of Hangman Heydrich. I never would have drawn him, a minor German among many, but for the fact that when I was sitting in the Brasserie Bavaria one day he took a table near me, and I watched him. He was a blond "Aryan," taller than Hitler or Himmler, but not a giant; perhaps six foot two. His shoulders were

squeezed; his neck was too long, and his head was birdlike and delicate for such a big body. This was a long-drawn narrow face with a massive beaky nose and voluptuous fleshy lips, eyes very close together, slitted and freezing blue, an arctic fox's eyes, but with a piggy watchfulness in them.

Photos of Heydrich show him smart as paint, but I remember some sloppiness in his posture as I watched him walking through the restaurant. Altogether, I think that, like his subordinate Eichmann, Heydrich was a weak man. There must have been something in the life history of men like these that embittered them and developed in them the paranoid streak which in Hitler's world was rewarded with a title and a uniform.

From Geneva he went home to tell Hitler all about Jewish

interpreters and ambassadors allergic to the Nazi flag. So Hitler, that same fall, sent Joseph Goebbels to investigate whether it was worthwhile staying on at the Hôtel Carlton at all.

In 1933, just as there were two Japans, there were also two Germanys: that of the barons and that of the brawlers. The barons, accustomed to thinking of themselves as the end-product of German civilization, did not imagine that the brawlers were equal inheritors of the Teutonic tradition. For them, the awful corporal was a willing tool to be led by the mustache, used to shake off creeping socialism, and then dropped. "As long as I'm alive," said Hindenburg, "the Austrian corporal will not be Reichschancellor."

Little did the barons suppose that Hitler was using them to give a splash of style and honor to his purpose. Herr Propaganda-minister Goebbels came to Geneva escorted by a bevy of exquisitely tailored noblemen, Barons von Neurath, von Weizsäcker, von Rheinbaben, and they surrounded him and showed him off to crowds as if he were a macaque with the gift of performing miracles. He received the press at the Hôtel Carlton, and I was there early to get a front seat. I had already drawn Goebbels in Berlin, but now I wanted a look at his tonsils. He entered, as always, at a run, because if he hadn't he would have limped, and behind him ran Nazi secret-service men, and I could see by the shape of their coat pockets that their hands were on the trigger.

What a queer little cabinet minister he was! Someone had given him a mock scientific name: *nachgedunkelter Schrumpfgermane*—shrunken, browned Teuton. The rostrum came up to his neck, and only his egghead was visible. The big brown eyes were feverish and underscored with green shadows, the cheeks hollow, the chin a tiny triangle like a kitten's, the nose just a short little bulb, upturned so that the upper lip looked even longer than it was; and over this hastily nipped-out facial skeleton presided a domed forehead rising to a huge, overcapacious brain case. All this was supported by a long, stringy neck in which the Adam's apple jumped up and down like a monkey behind bars.

He looked like a sickly child. As a child he must have looked like a sickly tarsier. One shudders to think how much pity must have been visited upon a child like this.

He spoke in German. What he said was Nazi buncombe, but how he said it was revealing. Two features fascinated me: his mouth, and his hands in action.

Confucius observed: Nothing is clearer than what is hidden, nothing is more manifest than what is minute. When I listen to a man or a woman, I watch what emotion shades the corners of his mouth. Some people have the pinch of a smile even when they are expressing condolence; others show contempt even when they tell you that tomorrow is Wednesday.

As Goebbels spoke, I watched the loathing contempt, the sneering hate that twisted his lips. Furrows cut into his face, descending from the cheekbones down, framing his chin, and they provided a cruel setting for the rancorous mouth. This was the deep Goebbels, a split-second revelation of the driving emotional dynamo of the man. Mussolini, a more flamboyant figure altogether, actually gnashed his fangs. The little doctor never frowned, and his feverish eyes looked indifferent, but his lips were bitter with bile, and he seconded every word he uttered with cramped fingers like branches of a barren tree.

When the conference ended and Goebbels stepped down from the rostrum, most journalists simply walked out, but a certain motley crowd converged on him like minnows on the bait and began to harass him with loaded questions about concentration camps, anti-Semitism, and Aryans. They were the reporters of little Jewish publications in Czechoslovakia, Hungary, Poland, and they had not many more holidays to spend at their childhood homes. I don't know if Goebbels believed they were the correspondents of *The New York Times,* or the *Manchester Guardian,* but he debated with them for an hour, while the barons, sleek and contented, smiled indulgently at the gesticulating assembly. Then they led their pet back into his cage.

Twelve years later, in a Berlin bunker, Goebbels saw the denouement of this discussion. He had wiped out millions of families; now with his own hand he destroyed his own seed: six children, then his wife, and finally himself. I saw his body in a newsreel, lying on its back looking at the sky, his fingers cramped as in life. Goebbels was one of the greatest scoundrels in history and he deserved death a thousand times, and yet I must confess that when I saw his charred, cramped hands and that charred profile so familiar to me, I pitied him.

Through all the ins and outs of German government, one figure stood firm in Geneva like the proverbial reed which flourishes while great oaks fall. He came with Brüning, and he survived the barons and remained under Hitler, whose field marshal he became, then minister of war and commander in chief of the armed forces: General Werner von Blomberg.

The tall, lanky Blomberg glinted grayly at me out of eyes sharp and perplexed, as his aide-de-camp, Major Tschunke, introduced me. I rather thought I was facing a bewildered female gibbon in a cage, and I couldn't get rid of this quite incongruous impression as I followed his stylish progression down the staircase of the Hôtel Métropole.

We found chairs and I drew him; and as I did so, it dawned on me that he was a sort of Prussian Titulescu in a general's uniform. My drawing showed, though in lesser degree, every item in the package known as *eunuchoider Hochwuchs:* overlong extremities, short trunk, loose hips, narrow shoulders, small head, scant growth of beard in sharp contrast to feminine growth of hair. His cheeks were rosy as a milkmaid's, and his voice was pinched.

This amount of femininity in a mighty general accounts for his rubbery backbone and also for his durability. A compliant servant of Hitler, he delivered the Reichswehr to him and stood by, shivering in his boots, while the Fuehrer marched into the Rhineland. To be sure, he helped liquidate Roehm; but then he had the backing of Hindenburg and the barons.

Blomberg had five children. Eunuchoids are not eunuchs; but they are discombobulated, and I was not astonished some years later to learn that poor Blomberg was a sex casualty. He fell in love with a certain Fräulein Gruhn and wished to marry her. For a high-ranking army officer to propose to marry a commoner, even in a Third Reich composed largely of characters out of the bottom drawer, should have called for some Dutch-uncle advice from drug-addict Goering and paperhanger Hitler. But they raised no objections. Hitler even consented to be a witness at the wedding, which took place in January 1938. No sooner had the happy couple departed on their honeymoon than wild rumors spread abroad, anonymous telephone calls were received, and by and by a snoopy police inspector produced the dossier of one Erna Gruhn, who had a police record as a prostitute and had been convicted of having posed for salacious pictures. To Goering, who aspired to Blomberg's job, this dossier came as manna from heaven, and he quickly showed it to Hitler. The Fuehrer, a man of huge public morality, blew up. Sixty-year-old Blomberg was sacked, and he returned to Erna in Capri. A naval officer paid him a visit and thrust the well-known revolver into his hand. The prospect of an honorable, Hitler-face-saving end did not tempt him. He continued to enjoy the good life with Erna.

My guess is that the aging marshal, probably unaware of the nature of his complex sex life, had belatedly found the perfect woman for him, and he was content to have done with rank, title, command, place in history, honorable suicides, and all the rest of the awful claptrap of a militaristic state.

I am sorry to say he did not live happily ever after. He died in his pyjamas in the Nuremberg jail.

In the office of Fritz Schnabel, chief of the printing section at the League of Nations, hung a Daumier lithograph from the war of 1871 which represented a German and a French soldier standing in front of a door marked DISARMAMENT. They were in Alphonse-Gaston attitudes, each inviting the other: "After you."

The situation was the same in 1932. It is exactly the same today, except that now the soldiers are dressed up in Russian and American uniforms. In 1932 we called the deadlock "security first, disarmament after"; today we call it "inspection first, disarmament after"; but it comes to the same thing.

Day after day, Commander Kinkaid sat in the same committee with his future enemy, Admiral Nagano; General Blomberg sat across from Red Army General Simon Ventzoff; French General Marie-Gustave Gamelin sat side by side with Ugo Cavallero, Mussolini's chief of staff.

The phraseology was the same as it is today: disarmament or doom, the folly of an armaments race, man's yearning for peace. Everybody had a plan. It is dispiriting to recall Japanese delegate Matsudaira, nine years before Pearl Harbor, calling for a reduction in aircraft carriers, or Italian Foreign Minister Dino Grandi presenting his Seven Point Plan for beating machine guns into ploughshares—four years before Mussolini turned Ethiopia into a garden of fire.

Russia presented a plan for General and Total Disarmament, the very plan that Mr. Khrushchev submitted to the United Nations in 1959; and she was just as safe in submitting it in 1932 as she was in 1959. Even then the Russians were becoming crafty at catching the sly bird by the beak and stealing the eggs from the propaganda nest.

These days the disarmament delegates return each year to the United Nations sessions in Geneva, like swallows to Capistrano. It was observed that while the French, Spanish, English, and Russian interpreters rattled away, the Chinese was silent. Once in a while he barked into his microphone: "*Chü nien de lao diao diao.*" When someone congratulated him upon the remarkable conciseness of the Chinese language, he replied: "Nothing to it. I just say: 'Same speech, last year.' "

In 1932, Spanish delegate and historian Salvador de Madariaga pronounced the speech which is the précis of all disarmament speeches, and it has been widely borrowed by cartoonists and humorists to the present day. I don't remember his exact words, so I'll repeat it the way I borrow it.

"Once upon a time the animals held a Disarmament Conference.

" 'We'll abolish all beaks and antlers,' said the Lion, 'but I need my fangs for self-defense.'

" 'Fangs and antlers must go,' said the Eagle, 'but what's so bad about an innocent beak?'

" 'Beaks and fangs have to be abolished,' said the Stag, 'but my antlers represent a long and glorious tradition.'

" 'Comrades,' interrupted the Russian Bear. 'Let's be friends, abolish everything, and give one another a nice big hug!' "

CIAMAC. Do you remember what these enigmatic letters stand for? They are the initials of the French for International Confederation of the Association of War Veterans and Amputees.

In 1932, this limbless, eyeless, scar-faced organization of Germans, French, British, Italians, Hungarians, Poles, Czechs, and all the rest had the notion of holding a conference of its own, and it would be held in the very chamber where the general committee of the Disarmament Conference held its meetings.

It was a Sunday morning in the month of May, the magnolias in the garden of the Hôtel National balanced their pink chalices, and little girls in white held on to their mothers' hands on the Quai Wilson. Automobile horns tooted on the lake drive as they always did, and in the cool committee room Arthur Henderson, president of the Disarmament Conference, banged his gavel as he always did; and the interpreter, George Mathieu, settled himself and patted his papers as he always did. But at the table, and in the delegates' seats, the faces were different. Men sat there who had no faces at all; they had been erased by bombs, and some had had their sight snuffed out, and there were those whose crutches stood guard beside their seats. Old honest Henderson spoke to them, but what could he say? He knew the truth; and so he lied to them like the doctor who lies to the incurable patient, and his voice of false hope was translated by Mathieu from English into French, standing at the same place where only the day before he had translated other perfidious utterances. He wound up with President Henderson's promise—and this was sincere, at least, for he was a man close to the grave—that he would do everything in his power to lead the Disarmament Conference to a successful conclusion. The blind men clapped their hands, and those who had no hands hit the desk, or just shouted: "Hear, hear!"

It was a sad conference. When it adjourned and the delegates left, the halt led the blind, and those with hands pushed wheelchairs. They were French, German, British, Italian, Hungarian, Czech, and all the rest; but somehow they had learned to help one another.

They had one more moment before leaving the building.

The day the Disarmament Conference opened, mothers, grandmothers, and children had brought petitions and laid them at the foot of the rostrum. There were fifty-four million of them. They came from all over the world. Mary A. Dingman of the United States alone brought eight million petitions. The line of women was so long that while the head of the procession deposited the first package at the rostrum, the end of it wound around the corner of the street. Afterwards, the League of Nations sanitation department came to gather them up and take them away in trucks, but 8,003,674 of these petitions were deposited in a glass coffin and placed at the end of a corridor in the Disarmament Building. After a while, the delegates got used to this glass coffin and they ceased to look at it, just as I stop looking at the pile of bills and threatening letters on the top of my TV set.

But the delegates of CIAMAC paused to look at the coffin. Slowly their wheelchairs rolled by, and they stared at the dusty bundles, all done up in ribbons of different national colors. They paused and stared.

Some letters from children were exhibited there. A little girl from Greece wrote: "I learned in school that the lives of animals and plants are sacred, and yet war destroys everything. This is unjust."

Thomas King, 11, United States, wrote: "I understand the Disarmament Conference is bogged down. I have a proposition. Take away the guns of those who want to fight at any price, let them fight with rotten eggs, tomatoes, maybe grapefruit, or popguns."

Thomas King, American, should be forty-four years old. Did he survive World War II, I wonder? And will his son, if he has one, be shot at with popguns if we fail him—as up to now we always have?

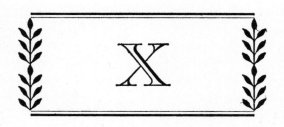

I Must Reduce
Myself to Zero

WHEN I was a boy in Hungary I learned that India was a country full of elephants, maharajas, and British. I learned that the elephants were poor and the maharajas rich, but that the British had their portraits on the postage stamps.

The first time I met a maharaja was in Geneva in 1923. Our album about the Fourth Assembly had just seen the light of day when, in the lobby of the Hôtel Victoria, behind the potted palms, where diplomats and caricaturists alike might steal the hotel stationery, a stringy Englishman tapped my shoulder and conveyed to me a message that His Highness Jam Saheb, of Navanagar, desired to make my acquaintance. The desire was mutual, for this maharaja, under the nickname of "Ranji," was the former cricket champion of the world. He had even played in the United States, where cricket is less popular than appendicitis. What's more, the stringy Englishman was none other than C. B. Fry, also a renowned world champion, who upon retiring from the sport entered into Ranji's service. I therefore accompanied Mr.

Fry at once to the Hôtel de la Paix, a sizable hunk of which the maharaja had rented.

His Highness looked at me with one eye, which was all he had, and expressed the wish that I draw his official and unofficial family. A man of dignified belly, he sat in an easy chair which served him well as a throne. Behind it were stationed two oak-sized Bengal Lancers in mufti with bristling, mission-accomplished mustaches. A lower-echelon secretary placed a chair for me at the maharaja's left, and another empty one for my models; and he called in the first victim. She entered, a doe-eyed girl in a pink sari who came forward with hands clasped in prayer, bowing humbly at each step. She stood before the master of her fate and waited, bewildered, for a life or death sentence. He commanded

her to sit on the chair in front of me, for what reason the poor
girl couldn't imagine, and she sat trembling under my scrutiny.
Two older women came next, and some men, all with praying
hands and bated breath, looking mystified at the empty chair
and at the stranger with a pencil and a face like Ran the Kite; and
the small children of India, dressed in tinseled garments, eyes huge,
shining black, and soft, like cherries in cherries jubilee, shadowed
by lashes thick as the petals of black asters.

Then an old patriarch entered, clad in a black robe with a
silvery beard streaming down the front of it. A white turban
framed his old, bone-colored face on which age had incised the
marks of wisdom and humility, and his eyes were melancholy and
sublimely kind. He was introduced to me as Sir Prabhashankar
Pattani, His Highness's prime minister. The sage stood with praying hands, bent knees, head bowed sideways before his prince, who
was half his years, and I was struck with compassion at the timeless
injustice of age humble before youth wielding power.

When I had drawn some twenty-five portraits, the maharaja
said to me: "Now you may draw me," and he took the chair, with
his good eye toward me, adding: "Don't be cruel! You know my
people in India look on me as a god." God asking mercy!

When we came to discuss my fees, he said: "Don't confuse
me with rich maharajas like Kashmir and Patiala. I'm only a poor
maharaja." When a poor maharaja and a rich caricaturist do
business, an adequate settlement can always be reached.

The Indian Round Table Conference was called in London, in
November 1930, to draw up a new constitution for India. In order
that this might be accomplished with as little nuisance as possible,
the participating delegation was heavily laced with persons who
actually enjoyed watching white men carry burdens: tame
knighted Indians; rajas, maharajas, and maharajirajas with names
like diamond-studded tapeworms; shahs, nawabs, khans, and their
retinues; knights and barons from all British political parties, and
their ghost writers. There was also a sprinkling of Indian Indians

such as Dr. Ambedkar, the Untouchable leader, and, on the whole, there was someone there to represent, however arguably, most of the myriad races and religions of India: Hindus, Muslims, Parsis, Sikhs, Afghans, Gurkhas, people of all castes and colors. Only one body of men was not represented: the Congress

RAMSAY MACDONALD

Party. Only one man was absent from this super-spectacular: its star, Gandhi.

Gandhi was not invited because Gandhi had been bad. The previous April he had taken a little walk of a few hundred miles to the sea, and Indians from village, field, and town had dropped whatever they were doing and followed him by the thousands. When he reached the sea, he sat down on the beach and began to boil salt water until he obtained a residue of evil-smelling salt, and all those myriads of Indians did precisely the same. It was a foolish and provocative demonstration. For a few annas he could have bought all the salt he needed at the market. There was one thing wrong with the salt he could have bought, the same thing that was wrong with Boston tea: it was taxed.

"Pack your toothbrushes, boys," Mrs. Naidu had advised her companions in crime. "We're on our way to jail!" About one hundred thousand of them were arrested, including Gandhi.

Imagine the House of Lords gone mad. I sat in the balcony listening to King George V opening the Round Table Conference, and spread below me were great banks of turbans, fluorescent in the Gothic dusk, sulphur yellow, hellish red, poison green, and shocking pink, and when the king had done they came to life and popped about like fireflies. Some were piled up in domes of pearl and gold like the Taj Mahal, others floated like the crests of whooping cranes or were tightly fitted like gauze around a broken head. In shape, color, and fit, these turbans reflected the many races and religious sects of India, and it occurred to me that the British had been able to rule India for centuries because of their ability to tell turbans apart and play them against one another.

By this time the turbans and I had reached the cloakroom and I was treated to the spectacle of packs of princes and hordes of lords lined up like ordinary concert-goers to get their overcoats. The Aga Khan was swaddled in pure gold, the Maharaja of Alvar had come as a rainbow wearing a red silk tiara, the Gaekwar of Baroda wore a crimson beany, Patiala had diamonds the size of mockingbird's eggs dangling from his ears; and almost everyone was roped up with beads and bracelets knobbed and gouted with colored fire. That day in the cloakroom of the House of Lords, staggered by beards, headgear galore, and faces of every architecture and complexion, I determined to draw them all and paint them in living color.

I might not have realized this ambition so easily, but walking on the Strand one day, I was hailed by an Indian diplomat named

Jarmani Dass. He was the same man who years before in Geneva had pumped my arm when he thought I was a *sénateur* instead of a *dessinateur*. I had tabbed him as a place-seeker then, but now he was fatly placed as minister-in-waiting to His Highness the Maharaja of Kapurthala, and he was eager to pass his joy in life on

MAHARAJAH OF BIKANER

to others. He greeted my idea of an India album with enthusiasm and generously offered to hand me around from prince to prince. Before long I found myself having coffee with half of royal India at the Mayfair Hotel as guest of the Maharaja of Dholpur, a wispy, virginal sort of man with a black, incredibly pointed mustache and great, shy, tender, velvet eyes.

My pen is too meek to describe, my arithmetic too weak to tot up the riches I encountered that afternoon; but my memory is fresh enough to remember the gossip. There was that masterpiece of a maharaja, a Mogul emperor straight out of a miniature: the ruler of Patiala, tall and barrel-chested, whose overweight was but an attribute of royal dignity. He was a Sikh, not permitted to cut his beard, but to prevent it from dipping in his soup he wore it rolled into great black sausages, which aptly framed his magnifi-

MAHARAJAH OF PATIALA

cent jowls. He had more debts than any other ruling prince, and several hundred wives.

And there was the Maharajiraja of Darbhanga, a landowner of Bihar, a fat boy in a huge fluffy striped turban. He was reputed to be the moneylender among princes. It is hard to believe that maharajas have budget troubles like you and me, but they do, and the maharajiraja stood ready to assist his brothers with loans at a moderate interest rate.

I drew the portrait of the Nawab of Bhopal, a Muslim prince, the best polo player in India. He was short and stocky and dragged his feet. Jarmani Dass, who followed me about whispering exotic gossip in my ear, said the Nawab had fallen from a horse so often that every bone in his body had been broken twice. He had no son, his heir was a daughter, but he had raised her like a boy, and she was there, a swashbuckling sight in white breeches, boots, and a riding whip in hand.

Moving intermittently through the lobby of the Hotel Mayfair was His Highness the Aga Khan, opulent, knock-kneed, his eyes filling the entire orbital area. He was friendly in a patronizing way, and like so many people accustomed to standing in reception lines, his handshake was a blessing as well as a dismissal. His third begum, Jeanne-Andrée Carron, whom the French called La Belle Chocolatière because he had fallen in love with her when she was serving in a bonbon shop, complained that she wanted to wear white to her wedding but the Aga had compelled her to dress in green and brown, the colors of his racing stable.

Not long after Dholpur's party, I made the acquaintance of a young woman who looked like a Malayan princess and walked like a Persian gazelle; and she had an eternal cigarette dangling from her lips. She was Menaka, the dancer who had been touring Europe with a Hindu ballet company presenting religious dances. In private life her name was Leila Sokhey, and she was the wife of the director of the Haffkine Institute of Bombay, an important research center for tropical diseases.

Through Menaka I met her friend the Maharani of Baroda, and I know that many readers will greet this princess like an old acquaintance, for some part of her is said to have gone into the fashioning of Louis Bromfield's splendiferous maharani in *The Rains Came*; and there is a goodly splash of her husband, the Gaekwar of Baroda, in Bromfield's fictitious maharaja. The scene of the novel resembles their state of Baroda; and that mad literary palace exists in real life, the opium dream of a pastry cook, made of *spumoni*, *tortoni*, and *petits fours* twisted into towers and topped with cat's-eye marbles. In the fantastic labyrinth of coves, alcoves, dimples, and dents, thousands of sacred monkeys roost. My sister Margit was a guest for some time in that palace, and one day, while she sat soaking in her solid-onyx bathtub, one of the sacred monkeys came in through the window and began to eat the soap.

The maharani was a delightful person with the dolorous face of a Hindu madonna; she was wise and kind, her common sense not at all spoiled by princely quarantine. She enjoyed collecting about her people of a literary, artistic, and political turn of mind, and they enjoyed being collected by her because she was such a good listener. The Barodas had a palace in Paris, and I became a frequent visitor and was caught up for a while in the pleasures both simple and sumptuous of maharajas abroad. I'd take the ladies through the byways of Paris to the artists' cafés and studios, the carnivals and curio shops. Sometimes we parked the princely Rolls-Royce, which bore the insignia of the house of Baroda, on the rue Lafayette, around the corner from the little streets where one obscure jeweler's shop nestled next to another. I was assured that great discoveries could be made here and bought cheap, and Menaka and the maharani plunged into this jungle, like huntsmen, with many a view halloo. This Indian queen of course could have bought the whole street and wrapped it in cloth of gold and sent it home to Baroda, airmail. But it was sport she was after; the joy of bargaining, the hard-won haggle, this was the breath of life to her. She would circle like a tigress around a bauble, wheeling about, pretending to walk away, floating back on reluctant feet, opposed at every step by a flint-eyed Franco-Polish-Levantine-Jew.

The Baroda ménage drifted back and forth between Paris and London, where the gaekwar was participating in the Round Table Conference. In London the maharani organized a charity ball for the benefit of the Charing Cross Hospital. Sandwiched between the *trillalla* of opera singers and Mrs. Sarojini Naidu reciting poetry, I drew caricatures of the notables present. With half the ready cash in the British Empire flying around that ballroom, I had the pious agony of seeing my drawings bring benefits to the sick which they never vouchsafed a healthy artist.

There was a banquet connected with this ball, in the crystal dining room of the Dorchester Hotel, at which I was the only European present. The lone waiter delegated to my service brought me a procession of British culinary efforts. Everyone else feasted on Indian food prepared by the large kitchen retinue without which the Gaekwar of Baroda never traveled. I was miffed by this discrimination, and seeing the company munching some half-crown-sized biscuits, I expressed to the maharani my desire to taste one. She said I wouldn't like it; it was too hot. I reminded her that I hailed from Hungary, where babies are fed paprika, so she gave me a biscuit. One crumb of it felt as if a thousand needle-pricks had attacked my mouth. Yet the Indians were chewing whole needles with pleasure, perspiring profusely at the bridge of the nose, and occasionally gasping for air.

Opposite me sat Mrs. Sarojini Naidu, the poetess, wit, feminist, and staunch disciple of Gandhi. I am sorry to say that this lady joined the ranks of poetesses such as Vacarescu and de Noailles who eat Hungarian caricaturists for breakfast. Her generous mouth followed a broad upward curve and ended in a malicious curl underscored by the shadow of a mustache. She had planted a patch of white camellias in her luxuriant black hair, which flowed to her nape in heavy waves, and she walked about like a pouter pigeon. In drawing her, I couldn't disregard her ample graces or the fact that she shared Vacarescu's conviction that a bazaarful of trinkets can disguise a barrelful of charms. Could she have expected me not to make something of the heavy ornament, rather like a golden cowbell, which she wore around her short neck? I am not an evilly disposed man. I admired Mrs. Naidu greatly. I enjoyed her wit and came to appreciate the courageous way she contributed to her country's social turmoil. But face to face with my white paper, I become an ugly truth-teller. From the day I drew Mrs. Naidu's portrait for the benefit the Charing Cross Hospital, and half of Who's Who roared, I lost a valued friend, and ever afterwards she looked through me as if I were some sort of gas, lighter than air.

Fat poetesses! I am one with Luther at the Diet of Worms: "Here I stand, I cannot do otherwise. God help me! Amen."

The Baroda princesses were famous for their beauty. One of them, the Maharani of Cooch Behar, was a widow and the only ruling princess in India at that time, and she had a daughter of twelve, already glamorous, with a mellow complexion like pale peanut butter in the sunset. Now she is the politicking Maharani of Jaipur, Nehru's prettiest foe.

The Gaekwar of Baroda, like most short-legged bulldog-faced men, was both generous and selfish. Fate decreed that he should fall in love with a Hungarian girl, and one I'd known for years, since the time she had lifted her leg lackadaisically in the third row of the ballet of an operatic theater in Budapest. She became one of those demi-Pompadours which along with salami and paprika are among our country's most popular exports to the West.

In my capacity of caricaturist-in-waiting to maharajas, I met many princely mistresses. They were not queenly ladies, but rather the sort of unexceptional girls I used to wait for in my youth at the back doors of shops and modest night clubs. Just as at one time *nouveaux riches* Americans used to come to Europe and shop for paintings, and snapped up absolutely anything with a French name on it, so these maharajas gobbled up absolutely anything dyed blonde. It was the lack of a standard, I suppose, by which to judge European looks; it is remarkable, though, that while these princes were born with jeweler's lenses for eyes, and while, when it came to fabrics, furs, cars, yachts, palaces, they insisted upon the most fabulous and unique, they chose mistresses from the dime-a-dozen counter.

I found the gaekwar's *inamorata* brassy and tough. However, she possessed the particular quality of Hungarian demimondaines in that she had about her an air halfway between the harem and home-sweet-home. She was domesticated and companionable, a lover who could cook: pretty, but not so pretty as to keep her man on pins and needles of jealousy; bright, but not so educated as to put him in the shade. The gaekwar, advanced in age but young in heart, was ensnared.

This did not upset the maharani one wit. As Gandhi said, the Indian woman is the Incarnation of Tolerance.

THE GAEKWAR OF BARODA

But the gaekwar committed an error: he invited my compatriot to visit him in Baroda. This was more than the Incarnation could tolerate. The literary maharani of Mr. Bromfield's book, cut off from British help, with common sense and ancestral majesty guided her state safely through flood, plague, fire. But this real-life maharani, faced with the natural calamity of a husband half out of his mind, made no bones about calling in the India Office, those guardians of the chaste family life of princes. Two handsome Englishmen set sail with the lady. They were really operatives of the British Intelligence on one of their delicate assignments. The journey was long, the nights romantic. The gaekwar's girl friend was seduced twice this side of the Red Sea. At Aden she was taken off the ship and a detailed report of both affairs sent to the India Office, with carbon copies to the maharani, which she handed to her princely husband with the words: "Read this, you old fool!"

I had the great good fortune to find for myself one of those typical London hotels where the proprietor is Italian, the maître d'hôtel Swiss, and the pastry cook Alsatian. It was close by the St. James and Green Park, and I spent my days drifting between there and the meetings of the Round Table Conference, which were held in St. James's Palace so that any delegate who felt so inclined could employ toilet paper bearing the inscription: "His Majesty's Government."

For me these faces from the Indian subcontinent were curious because I found among them all types familiar to me in Europe— from the high-cheeked, slant-eyed Slavic to the horse-faced Nordic or the long-nosed Armenoid. Some of them had the map of Ireland all over them, but the map had browned in the sun. The color range was great, from jet black to ivory white; but Indian palefaces often bear huge, romantic-looking shadows under the eyes, as some Greeks and Arabs do.

Some of these delegates showed up later at the United Nations. I recall particularly Sir Ramaswami Mudaliar from Madras, first president of the Economic and Social Council; Zafrulla Khan, fat in London, lean in Lake Success, where as foreign minister of Pakistan he established a record for long-distance oratory with a seven-hour speech. This record was broken only by Krishna Menon, who made a speech of seven and three quarters hours.

I chose the thirty-six leading men of the conference and published a portfolio containing thirty-six loose, hand-colored, full-length portraits. It had two editions. One was for rajas and maharajas, bound in genuine imitation snakeskin for forty dollars a copy. The other was clothbound, for Englishmen and Untouchables, and cost only twenty-five dollars a copy.

For a while these portfolios were passed around London like chapatties before the Great Mutiny. Then trouble broke out. Every album I've ever published with Derso or without him has stirred up a tempest, but never such a one as these Indian drawings. Indians are witty people with a wicked sense of humor. Each of my models laughed thirty-five times at my album, but the thirty-sixth time he did not laugh. A long procession of secretaries began to show up at the Hotel Stafford to invite me to grow hair, clip beards, and perform plastic surgery on double chins.

Rao Bahadur Sir Annepu Parasuramadas Patro Garu was willing to buy an album if I would alter his legs to make them as long as his name. Sir Pheroze Sethna, B.A., Kt., O.B.E., J.A., would buy one on condition that I make his nose shorter. He came to my hotel in person to suggest that I give him a discount of 33⅓ per cent—which I should anyway have to donate to the bookseller around the corner. I told him I would cut off his nose, but not the bookseller's.

Will Rogers asked me in Geneva: "Do you really *see* these birds the way you draw them?" I replied that I draw what I see, feel, and think. A caricature is not supposed to be a photograph, it is an opinion. I told Will about the diplomatic incident with Count Bernstorff, the Kaiser's last ambassador to Washington.

Bernstorff was a familiar figure in Geneva; he looked like a comic *papa* in a Viennese operetta at the turn of the century. His hair was fluffed up on the sides, he wore winged collars and polka-dot bow ties, a monocle dangled down his chest, and he chewed bonbons. When I drew him, I naturally drew him in checked pants.

One day the count accosted me in the corridor of the League of Nations building. "Why do you always draw me in checked trousers? I have never worn checked trousers in my life."

"No matter what trousers you have on, your Excellency," I said, "I see them checked."

One of my models in London was Nawab Sir Muhammed Akbar Hydari, the prime minister of Hyderabad. He was a little old man with a beak nose to which a white goatee paid an occasional visit. I drew him all in black, his top hat falling over his ears, a morning coat bunched high on his shoulders, a yellow brief case in one hand. I showed him carrying an umbrella with his free hand. I don't know why, except that whenever I saw the nawab his whole being seemed to me to cry out for a red umbrella, so I made him a present of one.

It was one of the most successful drawings in the album, except to the nawab. He had a private talk with me. He wanted me to redraw the page, making the red umbrella invisible, and have it reprinted—he would pay all the expenses. The new page could then be substituted in all albums. I said I was sorry, this would be impossible. He then ordered several copies of the album, but stipulated that I operate on every one of them and remove the umbrella. I did so.

But to prove I am not blind and that other people see as I do, I presently received a letter from India, from the secretary of His Highness the Nizam of Hyderabad, ordering five albums; but it was sternly specified that in these copies the Nawab Sir Muhammed *should have the red umbrella in his hand.*

This nizam is the one they used to call the richest man in the world; it was said he had pearls piled up to the ceiling in his palace. He was also a man who hit a gold piece twice against his teeth before he spent it. I regret to say, therefore, that the state of Hyderabad owns five copies of my album but only in the Untouchable Edition.

The Round Table Conference progressed into the winter of 1930–31. Meanwhile, back on the ranch, Lord Irwin, Viceroy of India, released Gandhi from prison. They met in Delhi, and after some bickering back and forth about whether Gandhi's Civil Disobedience Movement should be suspended, or discontinued, or neither, on March 5, 1931, they signed the Delhi Pact, which provided, among other things, for the Congress Party to be represented at the Round Table Conference. The following fall,

Gandhi came to London to attend the second part of the conference.

Gandhi arrived in London accompanied by a goat and dressed like anyone in Far Rockaway who after a swim in the ocean bundles up in a bathtowel and walks back to his hotel. There were some who were outraged that he had come in such non-Savile Row attire to negotiate with the leaders of Empire. The caricaturists were satisfied: my only complaint was that he never took his goat for a walk in St. James's Palace.

Gandhi refused to live with other delegates to the conference in the posh hotels where the tab was picked up by the British government. He established himself in the East End among the poor, and this district became a favorite haunt of mine for its own sake. Not far away, in Petticoat Lane, was a market where you could buy anything you can't buy at Macy's, from secondhand cribs and bibs to stolen coffin nails.

Gandhi also took a town house at 88 Knightsbridge, where he conducted daily business, and this is where I first saw him. In the murky London autumn I passed through a clammy iron gate to a desolate front yard and entered the building. At the foot of a narrow staircase I was greeted by two friendly detectives from Scotland Yard. It is easy to spot a Scotland Yard detective; they all look like Edgar Wallace, well fed and rosy, with a perpetual cold-cut smile. They go about their business with aboriginal cunning, lulling you with fables, and asking sudden questions out of context.

One of these detectives told me that he had a daughter, aged three, who was good at art. If only he knew an artist to whom she could show her drawings! Could she show me the drawings? Well, might he ask for my address? He noted it down in a notebook, and of course the infant genius never showed up, but my address did, I suppose, in the files of Scotland Yard. I've learned to look out for secret-service men and their anxiety neurosis, and to save time I spill the beans on the spot. I told these gentlemen I had come to assassinate Gandhi with caricatures. They looked pleased at that.

In the meantime, coming down the staircase was Mira Ben. Her name had been Madeleine Slade, and she was the daughter of a British admiral. She had cut her life in two, had betrayed (as they said in those days) "her race and class," to become a disciple of Gandhi. She was dressed from head to foot in an eggshell-colored homespun robe, and from the hood of it a great scimitar nose thrust out like Savonarola's. Miss Slade was a man-woman in need of a shave. Her job in the Gandhi ménage was the preparation of the Mahatma's food, no great culinary achievement since he lived on mush and pap. Scotland Yard handed me over to this lady, who escorted me up the staircase into the inner sanctum.

I was more than eager to see in skin and bone this man whose toothless grin, banana nose, and coconut head were already part of my daily fare. All over London you'd see street urchins making an arrangement of cut-out paper and matchsticks which they stuck between the knuckles of a clenched fist; then they put a grubby handkerchief around this creation and held it in front of your nose: it was Gandhi to the life, goggling and putting out his tongue at you.

Was he a crank or a fake fakir? Or a man something like Christ?—even in England there were many who thought so. On the other hand, the newspaper articles that hailed his coming quoted liberally from his autobiography in which he described himself as a black sinner, a former liar, a thief who stole money from the servants to buy cigarettes, a coward who dared not leave the house in the dark for fear of ghosts, an insatiable lover who tormented his wife with senseless jealousy, and made her clean his law clerk's chamber pot, and beat her when she did not do it cheerfully.

The inner sanctum where Gandhi spent his days in London was about fifteen by twenty feet. There was a fireplace, a ratty sofa, and two windows. The moment I entered I felt I had come home. This was no holy shrine of a saint, but an unholy art studio smelling of linseed oil, turpentine, and body odor. Along the wall sat old ladies behind easels who held their brushes at arm's length and squinted with one eye at Gandhi's head; and hairy sculptors behind tripods, punching mud. In a corner of the room, seated on a brown skin of God knows what, sat the Mahatma, looking for all the world like a professional model masquerading as Gandhi at seventy-five cents an hour. He was utterly remote and detached from the surrounding Greenwich Village goings-on. He was operating a spinning wheel—not the big colonial-type wheel such as appears sometimes in his photos, but a portable wheel which lay flat on the floor. Gandhi worked it by turning a horizontal disc with his right hand while with the left he milked the yarn.

My first impression was of a pyramid of homespun cloth topped with a dried prune. The prune seemed minuscule compared to the mountain of coarse fabric. His cranium was covered with scrappy gray fuzz, but from his crown five or six hairs had been allowed to grow and they hung like a fuzzy flag down his back. It is my business to notice such oddities and conduct a thorough investigation. I did my research among the chorus of old ladies with paintbrushes, and they told me that by this tuft, when Gandhi died, the angels would whisk him off to heaven. I later found that it answered to the name of *sikha* and was an external symbol of Hinduism. As a young law student in London he had cut off this *sikha* lest he look ridiculous, but it was quite evident in 1931 that he no longer cared how ridiculous he looked.

I took out my sketchbook and joined my colleagues in squinting at Gandhi. As soon as I began to draw, I was struck by the childlike proportions of his head: a balloon-shaped brain case floating over a relatively delicate facial skeleton. The frontal bone was ridgeless, polished, and mild, like that of an adolescent. When he laughed, as he very often did at something his secretary read to him, his laughter was toothless and innocent as that of a babe. In my opinion this infantile look of Gandhi's was his secret weapon; it attracted the maternal affection of women and disarmed men. The British arrested Gandhi seventeen times and put him in jail; but they did it with the loving care with which one puts a child in a corner, not so much to punish him as to keep him out of mischief. "My best deals were made behind bars," he used to say.

But these pronounced childlike elements in Gandhi's physique are signals to my mind of his more private gift of childhood: the ability to be one with the universe, on equal footing with birds, bees, flowers, stars, and animals both real and stuffed. We call it the world of make-believe; but is it perhaps the all-embracing divine reality in which children are at home, and also saints?

Gandhi gazed at me from beady, elephant eyes embedded in a dark nest of benevolent wrinkles, inquisitive, mischievous, and above all humorous. These lively shiny blackberries advertised the presence of a wheel inside him that never stopped spinning. Here was Gandhi the Whip, the "beloved slave driver," who energized everyone around him.

These two prime elements of childishness and dynamism were immediately apparent, graphically illustrated in him. They denoted both Gandhi the dreamer and Gandhi the pusher; Gandhi the cross between a prophet and a ward politician.

Gandhi the prophet was shy, sensitive, introspective, abstract-minded, idealistic; Gandhi the ward politician was tenacious, assertive, uncompromising, extrovert in the sense of being impelled to action.

I returned time and again to 88 Knightsbridge to see him; he had for me an endless fascination. They said he was a man of "spiritual strength." The very phrase is an opposition of terms: the spirit with its delicacy, strength with its hard stubbornness. So, in the body of a man of "spiritual strength" you have to find opposites. Delicacy showed up on Gandhi in such features as his small chin, narrow chest, thin, fine skin; strength was in his big hands and feet, knobby knuckles, stringy musculature, broad knees and elbows.

Such contrasting tendencies do not live in peace, and when they are as evenly balanced as in Gandhi they may result in sudden outbursts of energy, and then deadlock. Both of these caused him woe. Here's the young man who was cruel to his wife, and suffered for it. Here's why he visited brothels in his youth, and why he sat tongue-tied on a girl's bed until she threw him out with insults. Here is the ravenous eater, whose inhibitions prevented him from asking for a second slice of bread in his London boardinghouse.

Saints are terrible people, really. I'm sure Mrs. Gandhi would bear me out. They are not half as tame as you and I, who forgive ourselves our load of faults, trusting to luck they won't be noticed.

But a saint, a Gandhi, is so self-analytical that he appears in his own eyes an insufferable monster; he is so easily bruised that the whole world's bruises become his. Having an extra dose of coldness in his nature, he might reject people and withdraw to the top of a pillar like Simeon Stylites. Having an extra dose of warmth, he may lend himself with love to his fellow man. This was Gandhi.

He was by no means a religious Hindu; in fact he had been expelled from his own caste, the Vaisya, the third highest of the Hindu castes. But in his childish simplicity he had grasped the key principle of all religions: unqualified love. And of all things, he applied this principle to politics.

Gandhi celebrated his sixty-second birthday on October 2, 1931, and through the good offices of my friend, Tibor Weber, who had become involved with the Gandhi group as a writer, I received an invitation to his birthday party, which was held in the Student Movement House. Gandhi sat among us at a flower-decked table with a pile of presents from the Indian students in front of him, not sumptuous gifts, just bananas, oranges, and some mangoes.

Mrs. Naidu was the principal speaker. "Look at him," she said. "How shall I describe him? He looks to me like the Mickey Mouse of history!"

Gandhi burst into laughter so loud that his few remaining teeth almost fell out of his head.

People were always thinking up names for Gandhi. Lady Astor called him the "wild man of God." Churchill called him the "naked fakir." To his disciple, Umar Sobani, he was "beloved slave driver." He didn't care what anyone called him as long as they didn't call him a saint. "They say I am a saint trying to be a politician," he said. "But I am only a politician trying to be a saint." Don't you wish every politician would?

I like the Mickey Mouse appellation best, not just because Gandhi had big ears and no chin, but because both were so improbably successful. Do you remember how that mouse swept the world off its feet, leaped across oceans, invaded five continents, and everywhere you looked you saw Mickey in pins, pens, watches, ornaments, and you could buy them in celluloid and plaster, and in diamonds and gold? Mickey won the love of young and old, rich and poor, all over the world, for one reason: because he was GOOD.

Mickey was born good, but it took Gandhi thirty-seven years to become good by prayer and self-discipline. Because he was an architect of systems, he kept loading himself all along the way with fancy fads and kinky cranks to which he stuck with mulish resolution. As a fairly prosperous lawyer in South Africa, he had washed his own laundry, starched his own collars, clipped his own hair. "In front it was all right," he wrote, "but in the back it was a mess." Of course he imposed his dietetic hocus-pocus upon his family and everyone about him with the severity of a top sergeant.

At the time I met Gandhi he was already an accomplished saint who had graduated from purgatory. He had tamed the brute in him and harnessed its energies to the service of the spirit. The same selfish energy that had caused him so much spiritual pain became now his spiritual strength, the steel girder of his character, and the wire mesh of his perseverance. The former coward now taught the ultimate degree of fearlessness to millions of people; the tongue-tied lawyer was a toothless but irresistible orator.

I can affirm, though, that the Gandhi who sat before me was

no embodiment of Hindu quietism, no yogi-type saint. He was a tense, fidgety man. As he dictated letters to a secretary, he would make sudden sweeping gestures with his dry hands as if chasing away a fly, and at the same time jerk his head in the opposite direction in a gesture of no; this, I learned later, is the Hindu way of nodding yes. He wasn't still for a moment and I believe that his spinning wheel, which is now the motif of the flag of India, was not only an object of social significance; it also gave the Mahatma something to do with his hands.

When I finished his portrait one day, I showed it to him and handed him my pencil, requesting his autograph. He studied the caricature, his head open in toothless laughter, and slowly he wrote out his signature on my pad. Then he asked me: "Did you learn to draw before you knew how to write?"

"Yes," I said, "I have been drawing since I was three."

"You see," he said, pointing to his autograph, "I have terrible handwriting because I never learned how to draw. I believe children should be taught to draw first, and then to write."

"But my handwriting looks like the footprints of a drunken cockroach who has fallen into the ink and is looking for a place to sleep. How do you explain that, Mr. Gandhi?"

I showed him some samples of my handwriting, and he agreed that it was awful. He seemed not at all put out by the collapse of one of his beautifully thought-out theories.

Gandhi's handwriting was delicate and continuous, wrought of spiderweb threads without pressure on the pencil, and his autograph as a whole had a wispy, ascending tendency like the frizzle by which the angels would lift him to heaven. Many years later, penniless in New York, I sold my autographed caricature of Gandhi for $25 to Dr. Ernst Friedheim, the Swiss doctor who had introduced me to my other hero, Kretschmer. By this time he had become a distinguished biologist and owned a roomful of white mice. It was a wrench for me to turn the drawing over to this mouse-nabob, but it was Christmas 1939, and the hotel where I had been staying had locked me out of my room and would not permit me to get my toothbrush; and for $25 I would have sold autographed caricatures of the Three Magi.

Every Monday Gandhi held a silent day for the peace of his soul when he would say not one word to anybody. This was a most unwelcome intrusion into the Round Table Conference, which was already dedicated to two silent days: the English weekend. Only four working days a week were left. But Gandhi was intransigent. I went to observe him on a silent day at 88 Knightsbridge, and I caught Gandhi the saint compromising with Gandhi the politician. He said not a word, indeed, but he listened to every word his secretary was reading to him, and then he wrote answers on a pad that lay at his side.

He winked an eye now and then at his vow of poverty. He lived like the poorest, always traveled third class, ate mostly fruit. But he raised no outcry when a costly ventilation system was installed in his third-class compartment, or when his followers presented him with rare, expensive fruits. "People have no idea," remarked Mrs. Naidu, "how much it costs to keep the Mahatma poor."

One afternoon I was sitting with Gandhi on his dilapidated sofa, finishing some sketches, when he was visited by Miss Masaryk, daughter of Tomáš Masaryk, president of the Czechoslovak Republic. She sat down at our side, and I overheard their conversation.

"How much money does your father make a year?" asked Gandhi.

"About a million Czechoslovak kronen," was the reply—about $30,000 a year.

Then Gandhi explained to Miss Masaryk why he had asked such an indiscreet question. He was trying to figure out, he said —if the annual income of the viceroy of India was $125,000 a year, and the average income of an Indian was $26 a year—what the proportion was between the income of the Czech president and that of a Czech citizen.

Many evenings I'd stay for the evening prayer. All the lights were turned out and through a side door men and women came on tiptoe to gather around Gandhi: Devadas, his stumpy son; Miss Madeleine Slade with her *khadi*, the homespun robe, thrown over her head like a monk's cowl; Mrs. Naidu all in jewels, Pandit Malavya all in white, Hitler's friend Chandra Bose all in black, and whoever else happened to be about the house. They stood in the twilight and chanted.

We listened awestruck, the painters and the sculptors, the Scotland Yard detectives, the circumcised and the uncircumcised. Through the walls we heard the rumblings of the city of London, the yapping of taxis, the growling of buses, the shrieking of brakes. Little did I realize Gandhi's grandeur at the time. But one evening, when the fog outside was pink, and inside the strange prayer wailed and moaned, and the orange light of the fireplace flung shadows against the wall, I noticed among the shadows that of Gandhi apart from all the rest, and huge. I'll never forget that giant pyramidal shadow with the head of a child.

In London society Gandhi was all the rage. He visited Oxford and Cambridge, was the guest of the Bishop of Chichester and of the Red Dean of Canterbury. Lord Lothian introduced him to Lady Astor, a misalliance, you would have thought. Lady Astor began by lecturing Gandhi, calling him a humbug; the Indians had never had it so good, she said. When Gandhi finally got a word in edgewise and explained his case, these two odd-balls became excellent friends, and Nancy's "wild man of God" became a favored visitor at her house. Once she said at a public meeting that she had observed that Gandhi had considerable difficulty holding on to his clothes. "I believe that is one of the problems of the East," she added. "What should we do if we had to hold on to our clothes all the time? No wonder they don't get anywhere!"[1]

[1] Maurice Collis: *Nancy Astor* (New York: E. P. Dutton & Co.; 1960), p. 154.

It was learned that Gandhi did not like to be called "Mahatma," great soul. "The woes of Mahatmas are known to Mahatmas alone," he said. He preferred the common Indian address of friendly respect: Gandhiji, which means "dear little Gandhi," and it sounded charming or ridiculous, according to your politics.

Next door to England lives another ancient race of malcontents, the Welsh, and they too have the habit of tacking absurd syllables like *fach*, dear, or *bach*, little, to one another's names whenever they please. Gandhi was invited to visit the greatest of these Welshmen, Lloyd George, at his country house at Churt.

There they sat, Lloyd George *bach*, and Gandhiji; Lloyd George with naughty eyes, Gandhi with innocent ones. It was a perfectly symmetrical interview at which a caricaturist ought to have been present. For years Lloyd George had been playing hob with English affairs at home, as Gandhi was now doing in the Empire. Both men were radical reformers, helmsmen of their countries in rocky waters; both had made themselves the voice of voiceless multitudes. Each was in his opposite way a nature boy, and both were pains-in-the-neck to their families.

The day was wintry and Gandhi traveled scantily dressed. The conversation revolved around the subject of clothing: is it a protection against sickness, or not? The two statesmen reached full agreement that Polynesians were healthier before they were introduced to pants. While this was being threshed out, a strange black cat never before seen at Churt walked up to Gandhi, who was sitting cross-legged on Lloyd George's sofa, and established itself on his lap.

When Gandhi departed, the cat departed and was not seen again—until Miss Madeleine Slade, Gandhi's English disciple, visited Churt and sat on the same sofa. Then this bizarre cat returned to sit on Miss Slade's lap, but with her departure it disappeared forever.

This story was told by Lloyd George to Louis Fischer, who checked it with Gandhi.

No doubt we are dealing here with a case of transmigration of souls, and I am still wondering whose soul was housed in that cat. Was it Disraeli, wanting to be stroked for having provided Gandhi with an Indian problem? Some sympathetic Welshman such as Owen Glendower, who had had his troubles with Anglo-Saxons? Or Lord Curzon, homesick?

It might have been a caricaturist, but I don't know what caricaturist would have had the courage to sit on the lap of Miss Madeleine Slade.

Gandhi's most spectacular appearance was at a party at Buckingham Palace. Among the lords and princes of Empire, splendid in their Sunday best, he stood in his swaddling clothes, with naked toes sticking out of sandals made of the skin of a goat that had died a natural death. King George V, *en grande tenue* of an Admiral of the Fleet richly bedizened in the ornaments royal persons so generously bestow upon themselves, drew him aside and said to him, in substance: "Mr. Gandhi, I remember twenty years ago when I traveled in South Africa you greeted me with a magnificent speech. What made you change your mind? You know the British are generous, but we can also be stern if need be."

Gandhi replied to the king in his now famous "midnight speech," delivered at the closing of the Round Table Conference. He announced that the Civil Disobedience Movement would be resumed, and, against it, he said, ". . . your airplanes and cannons will be like toys!"

Gandhi's disciples at 88 Knightsbridge hadn't liked his hobnobbing with the lights of London society. The consensus was that the Mahatma had fallen into bad company and that the sooner he returned to the simple life under the sacred-monkey-laden trees of India, the better it would be. I was at the Knightsbridge house that foggy December day when Gandhi packed his toothbrush. I followed him down the staircase out to the wet pavement, where he gave his trailing train a swish with a Mae West gesture, and on skinny legs, with long steps like a wading bird, disappeared into a taxicab. On his way home, in Italy, he asked for an audience with the Pope, but it was not granted. I imagine every church has enough problems with its own prophets.

He left London on December 1, 1931. On January 4, 1932, at 3 a.m. he arrived in Poona—at the jail.

I became a Gandhi-addict not for any holy reason but simply because the Mahatma gently tickled my funnybone. I'd been alerted to his sense of self-mockery by the Mickey Mouse incident, and his autobiography is full of such evidence. Because of his devotion to self-medication he pronounced himself a quack. Once when he was very ill and a stranger suggested packing his entire body in ice, he wrote: "As soon as he entered the room, I knew he was a crank like me."

A man with a sense of self-mockery can look at himself objectively. Self-mockery is the recognition of one's own fallibility, and thus the beginning of humility. I am wary of statesmen without self-mockery, because they feel infallible, and infallible statesmen are dangerous. Dictators by nature have no sense of self-mockery. Among the great men I've drawn, it is people such as Gandhi, Briand, Einstein, and Lord Cecil who gave me a feeling of safe anchorage. They are fully aware of their own strength, and yet the real key to their natures is Gandhi's *I must reduce myself to zero*.

When Gandhi was shot, potentates who would not dream of following his example said he was "the greatest man of our time." Jan Christiaan Smuts, who had clapped him in jail in South Africa, said he was a "prince among men." Bernard Shaw said: "It shows how dangerous it is to be too good."[2]

I say this of Gandhi: politically, his greatest significance lies in that he had the comical idea of applying goodness to politics, and he was successful. You may reply he was lucky that he had to face the British, not Hitler, Tojo, or Stalin; and that two world wars came along and helped him to his end. This is true, but he may

[2] *The New York Times*, January 31, 1948.

be imitated not because he was good, but because he was successful. Today the Negroes of the southern United States are imitating him.

When I look along the palisade of centuries, I seem to discern
that at every age man has been given some problem to solve—and
solve it, moreover, on the side of the angels. Often some great
man of the moment is there to point out the problem. I believe
that Gandhi was one of these men, incomparably taller than any
other figure in this book, who has pointed out to us our next
problem: we must learn how to settle disagreements non-violently.

He was a messenger of creeping morality which in so many dis-
guises and tortuous ways has been pushing us along from the
beginning of time.

In 1931 there were already intimations of immortality about
Gandhi; but it was only in the line of business that I drew Ali
Jinnah, the founder of Pakistan.

Gandhi was near-naked but vital. Ali Jinnah was stiff, cold, dry-
eyed, and he dressed in a tight morning coat, striped pants, and a
six-inch white collar. Jinnah's hair posed for me the old problem:
is a zebra a black horse with white stripes or a white horse with
black stripes? It had black and white stripes, two inches wide; and
I do not know which were dyed, but they might well have been
calculated to match his striped pants and neckties.

Gandhi pulled in his neck like a shivering marabou. Jinnah
stretched his, like a hawk spotting a sparrow. Gandhi cackled and
mocked himself. Jinnah never laughed and he took himself dead
seriously. Psychologists have a word for the starchy, rigid type of
man who stands and moves like a ramrod that has swallowed a
poker: tetanoid. Such people have lockjaw of the mind. Tetanoid
politicians frequently make tetanoid political troubles.

When Gandhi was a young law student in Bayswater, a suburb
of London, he founded a vegetarian club of which he was secretary. Many decades later, the man who mobilized and organized
hundreds of millions of people and brought them to independence,

in describing this vegetarian club, made one of his endearing statements: "This brief and modest experience gave me some little training in organization and conducting institutions."[3]

I'm sure it did. And perhaps it gave him a hint of graver things to come. For there was factionalism in Gandhi's little group of

ALI JINNAH

cranks. Some of them ate no meat but did eat fish; others abstained from meat and fish but ate eggs; Gandhi abstained from meat, fish, and eggs, and reduced his friends to squirming embarrassment when he made stern inquiries in a restaurant whether or not his pudding contained an egg.

If factionalism weighed heavily upon vegetarians in Bayswater, how could it be absent from the Congress Party?

[3] *Gandhi's Autobiography* (Washington, D.C.: Public Affairs Press; 1948), pp. 79–80.

The Moslem League was formed, and when Jinnah became its rigid, arid, irrevocable leader, he was the wrong Indian for Gandhi to plead with: "You can cut me in two, but don't cut India in two."

Jinnah did both.

My acquaintance with the princes of India did not give me a greater regard for crowned heads than I had the day I talked back to Charles IV, wartime king of Hungary. It would be unjust to throw them all into the same golden basket. The Gaekwar of Baroda, for instance, was a good ruler of his state and an exceptional man.

Most of them were educated by the keddah system: this is a method, invented by elephant hunters, of pegging down a wild elephant between tame ones and keeping him there until he stops threshing about. The government surrounded small princes with English tutors and aides-de-camp, then sent them to Eton, Harrow, Oxford, Cambridge, until their political selves became docile, tamed to the notion of the British Raj.

But those who remember Charles Laughton's portrayal of Henry VIII will have in mind a good caricature of most of these princes: sheltered from reality, pampered by adulation, their wishes promptly gratified, they became grown-up spoiled children, vain, capricious, sometimes cruel. Innocent of a sense of reality, they surrounded themselves with flatterers and thieves who battened on them.

When such men were set to fashioning a new constitution for India in the face of the unrest which was stirring the country, that enterprise was doomed. Perhaps among those who stood in their jewels in St. James's Palace watching a comic little man walk in with careful, naked steps, there were some who guessed that Gandhi, and nobody but Gandhi, was shaping the future India.

No new constitution came out of the conference. The princes

went home to enjoy yet another sixteen years of royal privilege.
Then Nehru dismissed them.

Nehru dismissed them generously, giving them plenty of
pocket money, and for useful princes he found useful jobs. Perhaps the most desperate among them is Patiala's heir, who found
himself responsible for his father's innumerable wives and a multitude of half sisters and half brothers. He married off as many
mothers as he could and gave the rest money with which to live
modestly. But these ladies and their royal children had not been
trained to live modestly. They organized a sit-down strike in the
courtyard of the palace.

There's a young man with troubles!

I was introduced to His Highness the Maharaja of Jammu and
Kashmir by Jarmani Dass at the first Indian party I attended,
whose host was Dholpur.

Not long afterwards I received a letter from Major Kushru
Jung, aide-de-camp to His Highness, asking me if I would
undertake to draw all eighty-six delegates to the Round Table
Conference in single, full-length portraits, and also do a large
composition with all eighty-six around the round table in the
exact seating arrangement. There were to be two sets of original
drawings, and what were my conditions?

When a maharaja wants to commission a caricaturist, the caricaturist faces two problems: not to ask too much, and not to ask
too little. If he asks too much, he might drive his gilded customer
away; if he asks too little, he'd have to shoot himself.

I ruminated all day and hit on the nice round sum of £2,000—
that was about ten thousand dollars in those days; then I tossed
on a sleepless bed. Around dawn I sat up, called myself a blood-
sucker, and on the maharaja's behalf rejected this preposterously
high demand. I was in such a sweat that I didn't answer the maharaja's letter for three months. By that time the end of the
first phase of the conference was approaching, so I pulled myself
together and argued with impregnable logic: I did not have the

right to reject my offer. So I replied, quoting my sum, and it was accepted at once. Obviously I had asked too little.

I didn't realize then the maharaja's astronomical income, nor had I grasped the Lola Montez psychology of princes: "What Lola wants, Lola gets."

Once the matter was settled, the maharaja threw himself into these caricatures as if they were the new constitution of India. Lorenzo the Magnificent could not have been more attentive. The first thing was the paper. I told him truthfully that good paper was important for good drawing, and he assisted me in selecting the absolute best: it was like a thick holy wafer. Paints like crushed jewels, brushes of precious fur, all these were sent to my hotel, and as my sketches progressed, the maharaja took a personal interest in each one. Where I was kind, he called me remiss; and where I was unkind, he pointed out how I could do better. He was particularly helpful when it came to making Englishmen look silly. It was evident that the ruler of Kashmir was a born caricaturist who was just using me to do the rough work, that of drawing.

In almost every romance I've read about India since Kipling, there has been mention of that mysterious phenomenon, the Oriental grapevine, which spreads news with the speed of sound from Calcutta to Calicut. I wish to inform the British Intelligence that I have unraveled the mystery: Indians gossip, Englishmen don't. Englishmen hem and haw so much about subjects it is not correct to mention in public, or even think about in public, that they have become a race of inscrutable Occidentals. Indians are garrulous, they say whatever comes into their minds, and if nothing comes, they do what Hungarians do: they make something up.

No sooner was I observed next to the Maharaja of Kashmir than there were dozens of lips to tell me the exciting story of his life and hands to illustrate it with motions. When he was still Sir Hari Singh, heir-presumptive to the throne, he had a British military aide. This man naturally wished to make his fortune out of the East, as Robert Clive, Heathcliff, and other Englishmen had done. He arranged that Sir Hari should be surprised in a Paris hotel room with a Mrs. Maudie Robinson by a man claiming to be Mrs. Robinson's husband. Nothing, but nothing, could assuage this man's bleeding heart except money. Eager to avoid a scandal which might have compromised his chances of succession, Sir Hari was milked of $750,000.

Lord Darling, the British judge, managed to keep the prince's name out of the court proceedings. He was referred to only as Mr. A. Still, truth must out, especially when you are but a twig on an Oriental grapevine. Mr. A's right name might just as well have been bellowed through a megaphone.

Sir Hari's British aide went to jail, Sir Hari shaved his mustache and underwent purification ceremonies before withdrawing into the jungle for a period of exile. After six months his uncle died, and Sir Hari emerged as maharaja of one of the greatest and richest princely states. He was crowned to the tune of a million dollars, including food for the poor.

At the time I met him this scandal was a mere buzzing in the ear. He was a stout gentleman with an oversized peanut-shaped head and green marble eyes in a sooty setting. In his case, I do not think the keddah system had been too successful. He did not confide subversive views to me, but I had the impression that he was a secret admirer of Gandhi. Also, he had silver and gold mines in Kashmir which he refrained from exploiting in order not to pay taxes to the Crown.

At the close of the conference, not wishing to abandon his work on my caricatures, the maharaja asked me to join him for a holiday in Cannes. He set out for Cannes with one wife; countless ladies-in-waiting dressed in Persian splendor; a full team of young polo players, every one of whom was a captain in the Kashmir army; secretaries; cooks; servants; and twenty-two Hungarians. One Hungarian was a caricaturist, and the rest were horses. I discovered on this occasion that in addition to the best salami, paprika, and cocottes, the best polo ponies come from Hungary.

We put up at the Hôtel Martinez, where the maharaja and his suite occupied the fourth floor, with the servants sleeping on either

side of the doors. I slept on the second floor. The polo ponies got
separate quarters near their place of business, the polo field.

The members of the household were in a state of electrification
because the maharani was about to have a baby; and this event
was sensational because for the last three hundred years no maha-

MAHARAJAH OF KASHMIR

raja in Kashmir had begotten a male heir. Life in the hotel revolved around the lady, a frail little person, pale as the snow on
the peaks of Karakorum, and pink of cheek as a rose in the valley
of the Indus. Each morning at eleven she descended into the
lobby bearing the luminous and beatific mien of all expectant
mothers; and flanked by ladies and an equine English doctor, she
went for the ritual walk of pregnant women. In every eye there
lurked the question: will it be a boy or a girl? As the fateful day
approached, some curious characters appeared at the hotel, all

wanting to sell something to the maharaja: a Bavarian veterinarian
with two hazel-colored dachshund puppies in tow; a man from
Toulouse who had invented a cradle that played sweet melodies
when rocked; two chicken-boned Italian engineers dressed as diplomats, from the Isotta-Fraschini motor company; a Hungarian
horse-dealer with diamond rings on his fingers, which were juicy
as frankfurters; and, finally, a six-foot male lady dressed as an
Egyptian queen, covered with oversized silver coins and smoking
a black cigar. This was Cynthia, the most venerable astrologer in
Paris.

Every day, when I got tired of drawing, I would repair to the
lobby, where this company sat waiting for the arrival of the prince.
In the evening the maharaja would occasionally ask me to accompany him to the casino, where no sooner had he entered the
Salle des Jeux than a trail of cocottes formed after him like a
school of dolphin; each hoped to sit near him and as *mascotte*
collect something when he won. But the maharaja was a fisherman and a polo player, not a gambler. He'd sit down at a twenty-
franc table, play a round or two of chemin-de-fer, then give the
signal which was a command: "Let's go home to bed."

In fact, the gambling at the casino was a pale thing compared
to the excitement at the Hôtel Martinez, where the bookies offered
two to one on a girl. My horse-dealing compatriot inveigled me
into a flutter. I bet him the price of a ticket to Budapest that the
baby would be a boy. He wanted it this way. He said he was a
man who from birth had always lost his bets. In this case, if he
lost, the price of the polo ponies he would unload on the maharaja would make it a pleasure for him to buy me a ticket to Budapest. If he won, the money I'd pay him would help defray his
overhead.

One morning a seaplane landed on the shore beside the Hôtel
Martinez. One of London's most distinguished obstetricians ran
bareheaded through the lobby. Simultaneously we learned that
a Paris jeweler of great fame had registered at the hotel. D-day
had come.

We delegated M. Behar, the Turkish manager of the hotel, to throw an Oriental grapevine around the fourth floor. Bettors were pacing up and down the lobby like fathers in a family comedy. O cruel incertitude! What disenchantment when M. Behar came down the stairs shrugging his shoulders, pouting his lower lip, and showing his palms in a way that meant, in any language, no news.

No Hungarian horse-dealer, Parisian jeweler, British obstetrician, or cigar-smoking astrologer can predict the exact time of the arrival of a baby. Only the baby knows. The loneliest man in the world during those hours of anguish was the maharaja, who closeted himself in his apartment. Imagine the thoughts of a man who any moment might become the first maharaja of Kashmir in three centuries to produce an heir to his throne; or else just another flub. His polo players were out of sight, but the Bavarian veterinary crossed the lobby regularly with his dachshund puppies. Not even a royal birth could stay them from their appointed rounds.

It was late in the day when the otherwise unperturbable Turk, M. Behar, thumped down the staircase, waving his arms and shouting for joy: "It's a boy! It's a boy!"

The maharaja beamed; the Parisian jeweler sold him, with no effort, $300,000 worth of earrings, bracelets, necklaces, which the happy father showered upon his little wife; the Hungarian horse-dealer sold him a dozen polo ponies on the hoof; the Isotta-Fraschini people unloaded half a dozen motorboats with which to make a hell of Shalimar; the servants and the hotel staff shone with well-oiled looks. I am sorry to say, however, that the inventor of the musical cradle went home to Toulouse miserable. The maharaja did not want a musical cradle.

I drew a special greeting card showing all the princes of the Round Table Conference offering flowers to the babe. Miss Cynthia made up an exquisite horoscope, and I asked her what it predicted, but professional ethics sealed her lips.

Was she able to put down in black and white, I wonder, that

this little boy would never ascend his princely throne? That no sooner would he arrive home in Kashmir than Muslim tribesmen would swoop down and be fought back with British help? That in 1947, when India gained her independence, his father would secede to India, and turn to Nehru for help, and that his beautiful land whose very name makes the heart melt would become the battleground of a shooting war with Pakistan? That all these matters would press heavily upon the Security Council of the United Nations, as they still do?

Did she foresee that this prince would have a serious automobile accident and be pieced together anew in New York City, at the Hospital for Special Surgery, hard by the United Nations? Or that the selfsame caricaturist who had greeted his arrival in Cannes with a card would then, as TV director, be in charge of the telecasts of the Kashmir debates, and send them flashing around the world?

If you live long enough, the stories that have intruded into your life come to some astounding conclusions.

Karan Singh recovered, and he is now a trim young man in his thirties. He is head of the state of Kashmir.

You will have noted that just as I had a Maecenas, like Virgil, so did I have a Virgil, like Dante, to guide me through the divine comedy in London. Mr. Jarmani Dass was my Virgil who tirelessly introduced me to people, simply to be amiable. I now wanted to reward him with the only gift a caricaturist may offer: immortality. I had been commanded to execute eighty-six drawings of eighty-six people on holy paper, twice. The maharaja had not told me for whom he intended the twin copies. Perhaps it was some library or government building in India, which might last forever in that durable country. So I took an eighty-seventh piece of holy paper for each album, and on it I drew and colored the image of Mr. Jarmani Dass, so that for thousands of years his name would live among princes.

I delivered my artwork to the maharaja. He carefully examined every single drawing in each portfolio, comparing each portrait with its twin, one in his right hand, the other in his left. Then he came to the portraits of Jarmani Dass and stared at them for a moment with a puzzled frown.

"That one," he said, "I don't want!" And he laid both portraits aside.

There came a day in Marseilles when I bade the maharaja of Jammu and Kashmir goodbye. He set sail with two albums of caricatures, thirty-three polo ponies, two dachshunds, six motorboats, ladies unnumbered, and a newborn prince.

As for me, I had more money than I ever had in my life. For some time I had been eager to give myself free rein on the tables of the Cannes casino. Every single evening I entered the casino and did not leave it till broad daylight. It took me six weeks of hard labor to lose the money the maharaja had given me, but in the end, like Gandhi, I reduced myself to zero.

I have never gambled again, except in a telephone booth, where the apparatus sometimes gives you your dime back and sometimes does not.

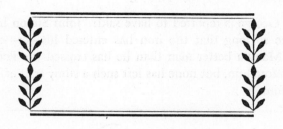

Intermezzo

In 1934 Derso and I survived the greatest days of our professional lives. Since these have so little relation to recorded history, I'll squeeze them between chapters in a fashion favored by Bernard Shaw for dealing with irrelevancies.

In those days we held an exhibition in London which was opened by British Foreign Minister Sir John Simon in the presence of ambassadors accredited to the Court of St. James.

Sir John Simon, from 1931 to 1935, was one of the most unpopular foreign ministers ever to go abroad and give England a bad name. His chief crimes were supporting Japan in the Manchurian crisis, weakening the League of Nations, and wrecking the Disarmament Conference. As chairman of the Simon Commission in India, he came up with a report hundreds of pages long in which he accorded hardly a paragraph to Imperial Enemy Number One, Mahatma Gandhi.

Lloyd George is reported to have said: "John Simon has sat on the fence so long that the iron has entered his—er—soul." He wrote: "Many a better man than he has crossed the floor of this House before him, but none has left such a slimy trail of hypocrisy behind him."[1]

SIR JOHN SIMON

Possibly the worst thing ever said of him was: "He understands things only through his mind."

Sir John, as I saw him, was a lean, craggy man with a bald, pointed head much too small for his body. His perpetual smirk bore no humor; rather, it was the outward expression of inner awkwardness. Added to sleepy, ice-cold eyes, a broken nose, stiff neck, and stooped but rigid posture, it completed the picture of

[1] John Gunther: *Inside Europe* (New York: Harper & Brothers; 1936), pp. 252–3.

an unworldly, clammy lawyer who, if he wanted to be chummy, put his arms around your shoulders and called you by the wrong first name.

When the cataclysmic news broke that he had opened the exhibition of two Hungarian caricaturists in London, one newspaper wrote that he had done it "to show that he was human." As one of the beneficiaries, I am obliged to point out that for once Sir John had hit upon a very human thing to do.

I have forgotten how it all started, but the original plan was for Sir John and our British colleague, David Low, to open the exhibition together. A snag arose when Low absolutely refused to be in the same room with Sir John. Derso attempted arbitration. He told Low that Sir John ran around with Low cartoons—which always represented him as a pinhead—in his pocket, and drew them out at appropriate occasions and told everybody in Geneva what a great artist Low was. But Low was adamant. In the end it was decided that our exhibition should have a two-pronged opening, one by Low for the press, and another the next day, by Sir John, for diplomats.

The day Low opened our exhibition, the managing editor of the *News Chronicle*, a paper that belonged to the "Cocoa Press" owned by the chocolate manufacturer, Cadbury, gave a dinner for us in the Savoy Hotel to which all British caricaturists were invited.

When you give a bone to a dog, it growls. Diplomats, and even caricaturists, who should know better, make after-dinner speeches. Derso refused to growl, and it was left to me to make a speech in bad English for which I have never forgiven the Cadbury Chocolate Company.

It was, of course, splendid for Derso and me—as it must be for anyone who has had the luck to achieve some celebrity in this world which is so big and has so little room at the top—to hear the compliments of our English colleagues; but these are memorable only to us. After dinner, some of us moved to the Café Royal, because artists, after a posh party, like to move back to

Bohemian quarters to wash the cleanness off. Next to me was Will Dyson, caricaturist for the *Daily Herald*. The talk was of cabbages and kings and probably the weather; I've forgotten just what. But at one point Will Dyson said something to me which I remembered ever after: "Don't you think that anything the mind of man can conceive is somehow in the realm of the possible?"

I am still pondering that provocative sentence I heard the night our cup ran over.

The following day the exhibition was reopened by Sir John Simon. Protocol demanded that when the foreign minister officiated at such a function, the entire army of ambassadors accredited to the Court of St. James had to turn out too, whether they were art lovers or not. Since ambassadors to Britain are usually chosen from among the most distinguished men in their countries, it followed that this opening would be a scene of concentrated splendor, starring Derso and Kelen.

We got there early, and so did the mayor of Westminster, who looked like a sommelier with a silver chain around his neck. He was so jumpy while awaiting the arrival of the foreign minister that I attempted to put him at his ease with a little conversation, but he seemed not to appreciate my kindly effort. When Sir John arrived, the mayor got rid of me in an imperial manner by shoving me out of the way.

Sir John was ceremonially received by the mayor. He then made a speech in which he told the distinguished audience that he found everyone's caricature immediately recognizable, except his own. He said that that very morning he had received a visit at the Foreign Office from Italian Ambassador Count Dino Grandi and that they had discussed the origin of the word *caricature*. They had agreed that it derived from the Italian *caricare*, to charge, in the sense of "overload." Indeed, a French expression for caricature is *portrait chargé*. What happy days those were, when the British foreign minister and the Italian ambassador had nothing else to thresh out but etymological problems!

Sir John then declared the exhibition officially open, and I stepped forward to be crowned with laurels.

Have you ever thrown a piece of bread into a goldfish pond and watched a myriad of shining fish dart forward to snap at it? In this crowd of vastly powerful people, I was thrust aside, literally discarded, as the ambassadors swarmed toward Sir John and the lionesses of Mayfair swooped upon the ambassadors.

The main trouble with the greatest day in our lives was that Derso and I were the only unimportant people present.

Yet, there was one guest who stood by—the Hungarian minister to the Court of St. James, Count Laszlo Szechenyi. His luminous name in the history of Hungary was matched by his interesting looks. Long before Madison Avenue discovered the sinister distinction a black eye-patch confers, the count wore one. He had lost the eye in an automobile accident.

The Szechenyis live in our national memory as a brainy order of aristocrats. One of them, Count Laszlo's ancestor, Count Istvan, had founded the Hungarian Academy of Sciences on the proceeds of his income, which he had given up for the purpose for one year. When asked how he would live during that year, he replied: "My friends will support me." His action earned him the cognomen, "The Greatest Hungarian," and his words offered a way of life to thousands of his countrymen scattered like sands across the earth.

Count Istvan traveled extensively in Western Europe. When he returned home, he commanded large audiences of peasants from his estates to gather so that they might profit from his experiences. He told them: "Englishmen honor work. And they love to work!"

"Poor Englishmen," sighed a voice from the back.

He had a more favorable response when he introduced another English custom to Hungary—horse racing—and he is remembered with special tenderness by horse breeders and bookmakers.

It was a special pleasure for Derso and me when a man wearing a name we had learned in school invited us to luncheon at the embassy. We ate chicken paprika served by footmen dressed in black-braided dark-blue Hussar uniforms, like footmen in a novel by Baroness Orczy. The countess spoke excellent Hungarian, to our surprise, for she had been born Gladys Vanderbilt. She was a slight, but hard-knit woman, serene and pale, with black eyebrows and dark eyes that were slits framed by naturally rich eyelashes. Two little countesses, who resembled their red-cheeked father, joined us. Hungary was never a colonial power, but here, apparently, was a Vanderbilt totally colonized.

Meanwhile, back at the gallery, famous and infamous people came to buy drawings of each other. Count Laszlo bought several, but he insisted that one of them be twin self-portraits of Derso and Kelen dressed as deep-sea divers exploring the murky waters of politics. This was an awe-inspiring demonstration of *noblesse oblige* which went far to heal the bruises we had received from the elbows of Mayfair.

After opening day, Derso and I regained possession of our exhibition, and we spent much of our time at the gallery. One day a middle-aged, corpulent lady entered holding a lorgnette at the ready; she wandered from room to room, carefully examining the drawings. Suddenly she broke into a hysterical scream: "That's what they've done to our peace! That's what they've done to our peace!"

We helped her to a chair, brought her a glass of water, and called an attendant; but all the time she sat there gasping, she moaned: "That's what they've done to our peace!"

Our diplomatic caricatures were meant to entertain statesmen as well as to "charge" them. But our opinions were there, and so were dire prophecies with all too short a range for those who examined them carefully through a lorgnette.

The year was 1934.

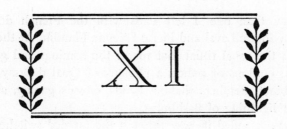

XI

Summer in Venice

In my time, I have met two political geniuses, Gandhi and Hitler: Gandhi because he played politics with absolute honesty, Hitler because he played politics with absolute dishonesty. Each appealed to opposite facets of human nature, and each moved people beyond belief.

In Europe, Hitler committed his people to violence. Now more and more the faces that filled my sketchbook were those of men who looked violent and who talked in violent language. They faced frightened men who tried to deal with them by cunning or by compromise.

The prophets retired into the wilderness. Earnest men of good will wandered aimlessly on the edges of crowds.

On April 16, 1935, I attended a conference held at Stresa, on the Italian side of Lake Maggiore, opposite Locarno—opposite in more ways than one. I left Paris with the French delegation headed by Pierre Laval and Pierre Étienne Flandin. At the station there was the usual ritual that marks the comings and goings of ministers: cordons of police, a phalanx of Quai d'Orsay bureaucrats, cabinet members shaking hands, crowds gaping, all under the sheet lightning of flashbulbs.

The train wended its way through the tangled switches of the

Gare de Lyon, Laval donned his *béret basque* and grinned like a charcoal peddler brushing his teeth in front of a mirror. At Dijon the people of France gathered to shout and clap their confidence in him. Could they not have looked twice at his double-dealing face and guessed that in ten years they would have to shoot him?

We crossed the Italian border at Domodossola, and thick-haired, ruddy young men wearing Fascist insignia on their lapels invaded our train. They were Mussolini's bowwows and they patrolled the corridors, spying with dour eyebrows into our compartments.

Then a regrettable incident occurred. In the dining car I had ordered a bottle of Lachryma Christi, which was cooling its heels in a silver ice bucket at the corner of the table when a waiter inadvertently knocked it off. Bucket and bottle fell to the floor with a clang and a crash. At that same instant, from either end of the diner six husky detectives stormed in, converged upon the scene of the crime, and searched thoroughly under my table for dead bodies. When they found only a broken bottle and scattered ice, they retired from the scene, but not before giving me an ugly look.

I had pushed my chair back, and threw an apologetic glance at the ministerial table next to mine. I saw Messieurs Laval and Flandin, pale of face and looking anxious. Now here was a fine thing—French statesmen trembling because some Lachryma Christi had spilled on the floor.

The Stresa Conference was an attempt by England and France to detach Mussolini from Hitler; had they succeeded, it would have made war improbable in Europe.

At that time, Mussolini was already amassing Fascist troops along the Red Sea, for what reason one could only guess. But it was rumored that Laval had privately promised Mussolini a free hand in Ethiopia if only he would remain loyal to his wartime allies. It was said that the director of the Foreign Office had remonstrated with him: "But *Monsieur le Président,* what have you done? Ethiopia is a member of the League of Nations!" Laval answered, in mock surprise: "Ah?"

The conference at Stresa was meant to be a reassurance of peace. Stresa itself was an armed camp. On the street corners,

M. FLANDIN

sentinels in steel helmets stood guard with fixed bayonets. *Arditi,* Fascist storm troopers, patrolled the square. Seaplanes circled over the lake and at night huge searchlights probed the skies for aggressors. The Hotel des Borromées, headquarters of the conference, was surrounded by armed men. The Spirit of Locarno, born ten years earlier on the other side of the lake, did not attend the conference.

Mussolini had learned his lesson. Not once did he receive the press. He barricaded himself on one of the well-guarded off-shore islands of the Borromées and came to Stresa only three times.

One day, around noon, I saw a group of people entering the

Hotel des Borromées. I followed them the way a woman follows a crowd to the bargain basement, and thus passed freely through a wall of secret agents. I found myself in a little salon among distinguished guests sipping cocktails, face to face with Mussolini. Our eyes met and he glared. I felt a shooting stab of fear. The last time I had seen him in Locarno, I had been standing close to Nypels, the Dutch journalist, when he had told Il Duce that he was often wrong; and later the Fascist plug-uglies had sent Henry Barde's monocle flying through the air. I swiftly lost myself among the people and observed him from behind a glass of champagne.

He had put on weight. His eyes no longer bulged, because they were firmly embedded in fat. He had shed his coy disguise of diplomat, wore the field gray of a victorious general, and beneath the belt his belly bobbed when he laughed. But his grin was not a sign of gaiety, it was more of a paralytic contortion, and his gaze diverged alarmingly, a sign to me that he was suffering the endemic affliction of statesmen: he badly needed sleep.

When I'd taken this in, I slipped among the guests and left the place as freely as I had entered. The adventure convinced me that in Italy anyone whose business it is to take the lives of dictators can do so easily, if only he is tired of his own.

When Mussolini came to Stresa again to attend a meeting of the conference, I was waiting for him outside the hotel, and I saw a spectacle that first took away, then gave me back my faith in the Italian people. It was dinnertime and April weather: over the lake shadowy clouds rolled against a sulphur sky. A squadron of steel-helmeted *arditi* stood dead at attention as Mussolini's limousine slid past the black and gold lacquered fence of the Hotel des Borromées and stopped at the entrance. No sooner had Il Duce's stocky silhouette been swallowed into the glowing doors than the tidy rank and file of the honor guard exploded. The *arditi* shouldered their arms, rushed to the gates, seized the bars overhead, pressing their steel-helmeted faces between them, and howled: "Du-u-u-uce! A noi! Du-u-u-uce! A noi!" It was not a sound of ordinary human voices, but what one might expect to hear from lovesick cavemen. I have never seen such a spontaneous outburst of animal devotion for one man. For ten minutes it continued: Duce! Duce! Duce!

Then the skies opened and a sudden April shower drenched the streets. With no hesitation at all the honor guard forgot all about Mussolini, they dropped off the fence, pulled their cloaks around them and ran for their lives. Later, as in the still of night I hurried home, a couple of them scared the daylights out of me with the glitter of their bayonets in the shadow of a doorway of a ladies' drapers, where they had taken shelter from the rain.

It was Mussolini's chronic heartache that he couldn't transform the easy-tempered, fun-loving Italians into glorious brutes like the Germans. He confided to Ciano: "The Italian race is a race of sheep. Eighteen years is not enough to change them. We must keep them disciplined and in uniform from morning until night, beat them and beat them and beat them . . . send them into battle even if you have to kick them in the pants. This is what I am going to do."[1]

Repeated advice from Hitler, Goebbels, and Company had led him to a pseudo-anthropological turn of mind. "The war will make of the Neopolitans," he said, "a Nordic race!"[2]

Mussolini attributed the peaceful disposition of his people to the mild climate of Italy. During one of the rare snowfalls in Rome he looked through the window: "This snow and cold are very good. In this way our good-for-nothing Italians, this mediocre race, will be improved. One of the main reasons I have desired the reforestation of the Apennines has been to make Italy colder and snowier."[3]

Try as he would, he couldn't convert his Fascisti into Nazis. Some of the young Italian ambassadors such as Dino Alfieri or

---

[1] *Ciano's Diary*, 1939-1943 (London: William Heinemann Ltd.; 1947, 1950), Foreword, p. x.
[2] Ibid., p. 369.
[3] Ibid., p. 321.

Baron Indelli were more like birds of paradise than ruthless hawks.
Ciano himself could have been a coveted gigolo in any Paris café.
The Nazis conspired in beer halls, the Fascists in cocktail lounges.
The brownshirts were made of cotton and wool; the blackshirts of
silk and satin.

The Nazis were rapists, the Fascists were *séducteurs*. There was
only one rapist among them and that was the boss, Mussolini. But
he gave his young Valentinos what they most wanted, fringed
fancy hats, uniforms emblazoned with fasces and eagles, stamp
collections all over their chests, everything an Italian could possibly need to parade on the Corso before the eyes of the girls.
For himself, he devised a strange headgear, incomparable in the
history of world conquerors: it was a steel helmet, but to it was
attached a tall plume of a snowy aigrette which stuck three feet
into the air.

It was unkind of Mussolini to force the goosestep on his Italians, who since the time of the Doges have practiced a swish-and-
sway style of elegance in motion. But Ciano's diary tells us Il
Duce introduced a stimulating accompaniment to the goosestep:
". . . drums and trumpets to be played at the same time. . . . It
was he who chose the bandleader's baton . . . changed the proportion and design of the batons."[4]

Now here was a statesman!

Though he secreted himself in the Borromées, Mussolini did
not fail to arrange a little entertainment for his guests at Stresa.
You will recall that my wartime adventures landed me atop Monte
San Gabriele watching the Austro-Hungarian army and the Germans force the Italian army into the famous retreat from Caporetto described in *A Farewell to Arms*. The Generalissimo who
lost this battle was Luigi Cadorna, Chief of the General Staff, and
he was fired, *prestissimo*.

Because nationalism must always turn defeat into victory and
raise generals on horseback, even generals *manqués*, Mussolini

---

[4] Ibid., p. 18.

resolved to unveil a statue to Cadorna at his birthplace, the town of Pallanza, near Stresa. Ever since Il Duce had come to power, he had been growling about Italy's having been cheated of her legitimate share of the victor's spoils at the peace conferences. Here was a splendid opportunity to rub the noses of British Prime Minister Ramsay MacDonald and French Prime Minister Pierre Étienne Flandin in Italy's war sacrifices. He therefore insisted that these ministers honor the ceremony with their presence.

Special permits were issued to the press, but of course when I went to pick up mine the man in charge was out to lunch. By this time I had become such a warm admirer of Italian officialdom that I did not wish to puzzle anyone by proffering a bona fide permit, so I just hopped in a taxi and went to Pallanza.

The fifteen-mile road was under heavy military occupation. At every bridge, crossroad, and viaduct were stationed squadrons of stern soldiers who brought my taxi to a full stop while officers swished forward to demand my permit. I handed over my half-price ticket for the Swiss Railways which had my photo on it and also the rubber stamp of the Swiss Federal Railway System. The officers examined it carefully, looked at me and at the photo, then handed the document back with a snappy salute. In this way I passed unmolested through dozens of controls, paying homage all the way to the Italian way of life, because I find humanly conducted disorder infinitely preferable to inhuman discipline.

I arrived at the monument before which the twenty-five best-decorated veterans of World War I stood at attention under the eye of Signor F. Suvich, undersecretary of state, waiting for the ministers to arrive. It was a cold and windy day, and Mussolini, true to his belief that people ought to live dangerously, had had Ramsay MacDonald, Pierre Laval, and President Flandin, in their top hats and morning coats, transported to Pallanza by open motorboat. He had the common sense not to come himself, though he had promised to be present. In his stead he sent Achille Starace, secretary of the Fascist Party, an ominous buffoon with rooster feathers in his large-brimmed *Bersaglieri* hat, who swayed

at the hips and pursed his lips preciously while fluttering his eyebrows. He looked like an old-time burlesque comic mimicking a
prostitute. He was to tell the Duce: "The Italian women are
happy about the war because they will receive six *lire* a day and
will not have the encumbrance of their husbands."[5]

In the presence of Cadorna's statue and Italy's twenty-five best-
decorated heroes and the country folk who had gathered there,

these men, both sinister and weak, made speeches about war and
peace. There was one there who thought about his comrades dead
at Caporetto, and the Italian boy on the mountainside; but he
was only a caricaturist.

You might call the Stresa Conference a turning point in history,
but there's no such thing. History turns twenty-four hours a day.
Yet there are banana peels where history slips, and Stresa was such
a banana peel.

The final communiqué from Stresa was innocent: it piously up-
held the Locarno Treaty, and the independence of Austria, and
other doomed notions. But I am not a student of communiqués.
The men who concoct them are my business. Everything I saw in

[5] Ibid., p. 137.

Stresa leads me to believe that at that time Mussolini had already made up his mind to conquer Ethiopia, and that the real question settled in Stresa was whether he would do it with the blessing of the French and the English, or with that of Hitler.

I have told of the three times in my life I scrutinized Mussolini closely, at Lausanne, Locarno, and Stresa. Each time I noted disturbing features in his face and demeanor. Yet the people who negotiated with him, who saw him daily and intimately, our leaders who appeased him and granted him a hunting license in Africa with people as his game, apparently could not see that he was but a half-man dressed up in the uniform of power.

It was an inner-circle secret during Mussolini's lifetime that as a young man he had been an out-patient, treated for syphilis, in a Swiss hospital. I have it from a doctor friend in Geneva that when he came to power, the documents pertaining to his case were stolen. The fact must have been known to his entourage, because Air Marshal Balbo repeatedly referred to Mussolini as a "product of syphilis." Ciano in his diary notes: "I used to object to these words, but I wonder now if this judgment of Mussolini is not correct. . . . The Duce has decayed intellectually and physically."[6]

Syphilis leads to a condition known as paresis. Dr. Eugen Bleuler, in his textbook of psychiatry, describes the symptoms: grandiose ideas, sudden outbursts of anger, judgment impaired by desires demanding immediate fulfillment. He describes a paretic who jumped from a high window to get a cigar butt.

I do not think Mussolini wanted to bring about a world war. But his "I dare you" posture, his "who but me?" gait, his eccentric helmet with the aigrette plume, the incongruous staging of the Stresa Peace Conference, all this suggests to me that he wanted above all to be regarded as a conquering hero. When he saw Ethiopia on the map, he thought it was a cigar butt, and utterly ignoring the consequences, he jumped after it.

The emotional makeup of a statesman is not his private affair;

[6] Ibid., p. 387.

we should all be aware of it. I feel grieved when I see that among the military, legal, economic, and monetary experts who are so influential in public affairs, the psychologist is absent.

In Stresa, Derso and I met a distinguished Italian gentleman with black eyes and a white Van Dyke beard by the name of Cavaliere Campione. He was the director of CIGA, the concern that owned the luxury hotels of Italy. He invited both of us to spend the summer at the Hotel Excelsior on the Lido, in Venice.

THE MAHARAJAH OF KAPURTHALA

The Excelsior was a rich man's sanctuary impenetrable for photographers and autograph hunters; but if one night it had burned down you could have seen most of Elsa Maxwell's best friends fleeing in their nightshirts. It was the time of the 1935 Venice Film Festival, and as it turned out, it was also the eve of the Ethiopian campaign. With the society cheetahs mingled screen stars, film magnates, international munitions peddlers, secret agents, generals, and the entire Fascist hierarchy, all of them in swimsuits. I suppose Signor Campione felt that in such a crowd two Hungarian caricaturists were all that was missing. He no doubt hoped too that our pencils would be busy drawing notables, and that these drawings would speed to the capitals of Europe bearing the legend: "As seen on the terrace of the Hotel Excelsior, the Lido."

The first man I ran into when I walked onto the terrace was the playwright Ferenc Molnar.

This most celebrated of Hungarians held a special mystique for provincial boys of my generation. First of all, he was our childhood idol, and we had wept in our pillows at the tragedy of Nemecsek in *The Paul Street Boys*. Then, as we grew older, our eyes turned naturally toward our capital of Budapest, the way Moslems turn to Mecca. There was but one city for us, and Molnar was its prophet. Each of his characters was hand-picked from the byways of our city, and whoever read Molnar or saw his plays could gaze into the sentimental, sophisticated, frivolous, and skeptical heart of the Budapest of the Hapsburgs, just as anyone reading Mark Twain may sense the heart of America.

When I was sixteen I was taken to Budapest, and Molnar was pointed out to me sitting in a straw hat at a sidewalk café. Then I was shown the marble-topped table where, they told me, he had written *Liliom*, and I sat down at it and swelled in pride.

He was not just a famous man, a name for a gossip column; we owned him, we had inherited him, he was our totem ancestor. We who aspired to fame knew that if we ever amounted to anything, there'd be the breath of Molnar in it. We thought more of ourselves because we were dining in the same restaurant as Molnar. As we made our way in the world, we won the right to sit at tables on the fringe of his group, silent when he spoke, so that we could say afterwards: "Molnar told me. . . ." And when Molnar said something in Budapest, there were Hungarians in Paris and Berlin who the next day said: "Molnar told me. . . ."

The first time Molnar called me by name and invited me to sit at his table, he might just as well have drawn a sword and knighted me. An earldom was mine the day someone said: "Molnar told me . . ." and related a joke I'd told Molnar!

But in 1935 my totem ancestor had not spoken a word to me for five years. It was on account of a caricature, of course. Well, he had been getting plump, and the day we met him on the terrace of the Hotel Excelsior, he was quite stout. He greeted Derso cordially, then turned to me.

"Kelen," he said. "It's like this between you and me: Once a farmer and his hired man and his pipe were traveling home from market along a country road in a cart. It was night and pitch dark. 'Wait,' said the farmer. 'I have to stop here a bit.'

" 'Better go into the bushes,' said the hired man."

I listened to this saga, anticipating the unsavory turn it was taking. In another minute I'd be slain by a gag which would travel on the goulash circuit from Venice to Valparaiso.

"Eventually the farmer reappeared," continued Molnar, "mounted the cart, and they continued on their journey. 'Wait!' cried the farmer, 'I've left my pipe behind.'

"They went back. The farmer went into the bushes—it was

pitch dark—and began to grope around on the ground. After a while his companion became impatient: 'Have you found your pipe?'

" 'No!' shouted the farmer. 'But I've found the mess three times!'

"That's how it is with you and me, Kelen," concluded Molnar. "When I travel abroad I run across all sorts of Hungarians, but I never find you. How are you?"

I was the pipe! I could have shouted with relief. I was so shaken that I gave Molnar the greeting I usually reserved for my mother: "I kiss your hand!"

Naturally, he did not forgive me outright, nor ignore my offense. But among the flowers, beside the blue Adriatic, he officially enumerated all my crimes and expounded to me his kindly philosophy: "A belly is merely a matter of lung. Some people can hold it in, some people can't." Then he offered me his solemn and magnanimous absolution.

In that crowd of millionaires and empty-headed dignitaries and their ambitious mistresses, Derso and I found the hearth of home in Molnar, in his humanity, simplicity, and naturalness. Like Hungarians everywhere, we found a nest for ourselves away from the pomp of the Excelsior: a little restaurant on the shore, called La Vida, where in a dusty garden by the light of a glass-covered candle on a red-checked tablecloth we ate our dinner. La Signora who served us *manicotti* was perhaps not so punctilious as the Rudolph Valentinos in tuxedos who served the *scampi* at the Excelsior; but our mosquitoes were twice as big.

One night I came late to La Vida. Molnar had already dined and sat with Derso at a bare table among empty liqueur glasses. He gave me a scolding glance, justly: it was not right to have an appointment with Molnar and keep him waiting. But all Hungarians recognize a *force majeure*, women, and so I laid my tale before him. She was from Philadelphia and it had been love at first sight at the Excelsior *thé dansant*. She had come to see me that afternoon, thrown her strong, supple arms around my neck, and time had stood still.

But that wasn't why I was late. The young lady had left in good time, but afterwards I'd felt a strange pull between my shoulder blades, a spot hard to reach. Straining back, I touched something coarse like the crust of a wound. She had probably used her nails on me, and in my amorous rapture I hadn't even felt it. But when with some effort I succeeded in displacing the "scab," I found she had parked her chewing gum on the hairs in the valley of my back. It took me an hour and considerable pain to get it off.

Molnar understood, and forgave me.

Hungarians are like termites: where there's one, there are more. My colleague Derso being a dead loss for luncheon, I dug up another compatriot, Bela Daranyi, a young man, but no small potato: his uncle Ignacz had been an illustrious minister of commerce under the dual monarchy, and another kinsman of his, Kalman, was prime minister in 1936 and as such announced to the world that Hungary was committed to Hitler, by making a speech in my home town, proclaiming the first anti-Jewish legislation. Beluska was the director of Futura, the Hungarian government's wheat purchasing and exporting agency. You could see he was a good patriot because he wore a paprika-colored shirt.

Beluska hadn't come to Venice solely to eat *prosciutto con melone* with me. War was in the making, and he was busily selling Hungarian wheat to the Italians. He stood at the bar at two o'clock in the morning concluding million-dollar trans-actions in barley and wheat. In the dining room, a tidy little family camped next to our table: a pretty wife, a three-year-old child, a uniformed nurse, and a husband who looked very much like a caricature of a capitalist in *Izvestia* on May Day. He was Fritz Mandl, the Austrian munitions pasha. His presence was no less innocent in regard to the oncoming African campaign than was Beluska's.

Mrs. Mandl was the very antithesis of her husband. She was transparent as a lily, sensitive as an Arabian gazelle, with a face aristocratically molded except for the upturned nose of a gamine; she had a cluster of black eyelashes around forget-me-not eyes, and jet-black hair against a complexion of skim milk. Destiny had in store for her a career in Hollywood as Hedy Lamarr; and in the dining room of the Excelsior it was evident that Frau Mandl of Vienna had the arcane, romantic gift of beauty.

Frau Mandl had already had a brush with the motion-picture industry. A few years before, she had played the title role in a film called *Ecstasy*. Today we'd think it not much more naughty than *September Morn*, but then it was the only film yet made in which the star had appeared in the nude. She had been eighteen and plump as a squab. I had the tenderest recollection of her bare back as she ran into the bushes. Now, as Frau Mandl, her silhouette was queenly, and as she walked out of the dining room our eyes went with her. "That can't be the one," grumbled Beluska. "It's too small. I'll bet my head that posterior was played by a double!"

Around noon this family was to be seen on the porch of their bathing cabin, Hedy in a generous bathing suit, the white-veiled nurse with a watchful eye on the little girl, who was busy building fortresses of sand. In the shadow of the cabin, the munitions magnate sat in swimming trunks talking the Lord knows what sinister shop with his friend, Ernst Rüdiger, Prince von Starhemberg, Commander of the Heimwehr, the Austrian Fascist militia, and soon to be vice chancellor under Schuschnigg. But what he really was was Mussolini's *Gauleiter* in Austria.

The prince was in his mid-thirties, about my age, a great handsome hunk of a man with a slightly balding head, a ruffian with a streak of noble Austrian irresponsibility in him. Like me he was a graduate of the battle of Caporetto, but things must have been different on the Piave where he fought, because he had not been cured of bellicosity for life. He had soon gone to Munich to battle in the Oberland Organization under von Epp and Roehm and had taken part in Heines's terrorist campaign with the Black Reichswehr on the Polish border. He met Hitler in Munich and participated in the Beer Hall *Putsch* of 1923. After this escapade, his mother, Fanny, whose hollow cheeks and sickle nose I had once drawn in Geneva, brought him home and fashioned out of the vulgar Nazi a fancy Fascist, whose Heimwehr troops took part in a *"putsch"* that bombarded some modern worker's dwellings the Social Democrats had built. They killed a thousand men, women, and children.

This prince's ancestors had been rulers before the Hapsburgs. From the age of three he must have been told the story of how his forefather, Rüdiger, had saved Vienna from the infidel Turks in 1683. He needed no prestige. What he needed was money, and it came to him from Italy, from Herr Mandl and others like him. That is why Prince von Starhemberg sat in his swimming trunks and made deals with infidels.

The former Princess Mdivani was summering on the Lido, but now she was only Countess Haugwitz-Reventlow, and later she was to demote herself to plain Mrs. Cary Grant. In my eyes, Barbara Hutton's reputation as a glamour queen sat falsely on her. Black eyebrows on a white skin, black eyelashes against slate-blue eyes, baby-faced and pretty as a milkweed, she was the picture, it seemed to me, of the "girl next door," who ought to have had more children than husbands instead of the other way around. The count was dry and stiff like salted codfish, which needs to soak for three days before you can make a *bacalao* out of it. He wore shorts, Babs wore pants and a Chinese blouse with dragons feeding on giant flowers that lent warmth to her pallor. Their sumptuous yacht was anchored in the hotel's private cove, hard to relate to that string of humble "five-and-tens."

In a crowd like this, where is the oddball in whom a caricaturist can find a friend? Only in royalty, earning its living. I formed a nightly bar-fly fellowship with a tall, lonely, sad-eyed auto-salesman, Prince René de Bourbon Parme, brother-in-law of Emperor Charles, on whose account I was almost beheaded in

Chapter I. By day he drifted about trying to talk somebody into buying a Cadillac.

And that's how it was in Venice in the summer of 1935. By day there was Josephine Baker in very tight pants, and Serge Lifar of the Paris Opera ballet doing naked pirouettes on the

hot sand. By night, under the marquee of an evening sky sprinkled with the golden dust of far-off suns, the band played an imported tango, and well-placed reflectors made a heaven's gate of the hotel front. On the glass dance floor, lighted from below with amethyst and ruby lamps, black shoes and golden shoes whirled in a spinning kaleidoscope, and in and out of the sharp shadows and lights of the terrace, men in black and white and women inadequately covered by lamé and ermine swarmed and wooed.

And through it all, generals, admirals, wheat merchants, financiers, and politicians sat in their swimming trunks and prepared for a war which would change the shape of the world. Perhaps they imagined they were only changing the shape of Ethiopia. As it happened, Ethiopia is one of the few spots on the globe that emerged from that war unchanged, ruled by the same Negus, living almost the same life it has lived since Biblical times.

But the rest of us in Europe and Asia, and in the United States, we have changed.

One day Signor Campione alerted me that the Hotel Excelsior was about to be invaded by high Fascisti.

At about ten o'clock in the morning a white seaplane settled upon the blue waves in front of the hotel, and a speedboat brought to shore four men: Dino Alfieri, a splendid fellow with the profile of a movie idol and flashing black eyes, who later became Mussolini's ambassador to Berlin; Luigi Freddi, giant boss of the film industry; Bonomi, a dyspeptic, wilted thistle who was minister of tourism; and finally the *pièce de résistance*, Mussolini's son-in-law and future foreign minister, Count Galeazzo Ciano.

Within the hour Ciano descended the steps of the hotel in bathing trunks, flanked by six secret service men. He threw himself into the cool waters, but not before the detectives had swum far out to the right and left, forming an arc of wide privacy for Ciano. No one was permitted to come within splashing distance of Mussolini's son-in-law except the official photographer, who followed him about on a hydro-bicycle, faithfully snapping each stroke of his crawl. We mainland rats watched this unbelievable spectacle from the shore and realized that when Mussolini talked about *mare nostrum* that is exactly what he meant.

There was to be a special preview of the films Italy would present at the Venice film festival for the Fascist high priesthood: Ciano's father Costanzo, president of the Chamber of Deputies and minister of communications, who in these capacities had managed to acquire a gigantic belly and a still greater fortune; Ciano's wife, Edda Mussolini; Count Volpi, minister of

finance, with the kind of white-pointed *zahl nix* beard that all
finance ministers ought to wear; General Teruzzi, with his
divided shall-I-pay-or-not-pay beard; and Roberto Farinacci, the
man with the broken nose who was called the Italian Streicher,
and whose brutality was too much even for Mussolini.

Only a selected few were admitted to the showing of the
film. Derso and I were invited by Signor Campione. We sat in
the dark. A newsreel was to precede the feature film. The
screen lighted and flickered; we saw Italian soldiers embarking
Italian mules upon an Italian ship at the port of Naples. They
were on their way to Africa.

All at once, in the front seats, pandemonium broke loose:
shouts in the dark, gesticulating silhouettes. For a moment it
seemed that some pacifist had infiltrated our ranks and was
demonstrating against the mules, but then I recognized in the
flashing light Ciano, Alfieri, Freddi, and all the others shouting
hysterically: "A *noi!* A *noi! Viva Il Duce! Evviva l'Italia!*" and
then they began to sing the *Giovinezza* wildly in chorus.

At that time the invasion of Ethiopia had not yet begun, and of
course it was not officially recognized that any such invasion
was intended. But these high Fascists knew why those soldiers
were embarking for Africa. And now we knew, too. In those
yells we could hear the authentic voice of nationalism about to
cover itself with glory.

After some time, the outburst calmed down and the feature
film began.

Its title was immense upon the screen: *QUO VADIS?*

It is certainly an advantage for a caricaturist to see his model
nude. Usually this entails insuperable difficulties. In the case of
Count Ciano, I could see that he was a fat boy with surplus lard
on his belly, chest, and haunches. Like almost anybody with a
great deal of subcutaneous blubber—sea elephants, for example
—he loved to flop about in the water.

He was knock-kneed and walked sway-buttocked like a woman.

He had some difficulty in imitating the martial gait his father-
in-law believed proper to Fascisti. The best he could do was walk
like a rather daring gigolo. His face was soft in outline, his eyes
large and velvety, his mouth shaped in infantile defiance, and
he carried his chin high. It was written all over him: a weak
child in need of a father, with a large streak of feminine vanity;
a soft object, indeed, to fall into the hands of Mussolini.

What Ciano lacked in masculinity, his wife, Edda, had in a
large dose. She was Mussolini's undoubted daughter, with great
cheekbones, broad jaw, and short neck. Her longish nose was
bent at the tip as if to peek into her large mouth. She was a
stubborn, domineering, self-righteous, iron-panted woman who
feuded incessantly with her husband. She wanted to go to war on
the side of Hitler and told her father so. Ciano did not want
to go to war on the side of Hitler and told his father-in-law so.

Yet eight years later, after Mussolini had ordered Ciano shot,
Edda did a surprising thing. She got hold of Ciano's diaries
written in prison, smuggled them out of Italy, and arranged for
their publication.

Today the published diary can be bought cut-rate on the
remainder counters. In fact, it ought to be read widely. Because
of the vain, mad, ambitious nincompoops who people this book,
decent folk surrendered their common sense, morality, children,
and their lives. And they will do it again and again until they
learn to look at a king and see when he is naked.

The summer bent toward its end. For some time Beluska
had attracted my attention, first on account of his paprika-
colored shirt, next because he seemed to be wearing dark glasses
when he looked at Frau Mandl. Now he advised me that on
September 1 the annual Congress of Pansies would open in
Venice. This came as a complete surprise to me. I had observed,
of course, that an international freemasonry of homosexuals
cuts across national, racial, and class boundaries; but I didn't
know that they met each year like Rotarians. Beluska assured

me, however, that in September, when the regular tourists go home, homosexuals take charge in Venice, and he knew the names of the committee members who were already on hand preparing all sorts of good times which it would be a pity for me to miss. But I had decided that I had just time to jump home and see my family in Budapest before the regular Assembly of the League of Nations opened in Geneva.

It would have been good to wind up my summer in Venice watching pansies feeding pigeons; but I was moving toward a different ending. On the train to Trieste I studied the map of northern Italy, picking out familiar place-names around Monte San Gabriele. I made a fantastic discovery: one could approach Gorizia from the Italian side, too. Somehow it had never occurred to me that in order to get to this place one needn't start out from Vienna, travel via Klagenfurt and Laibach to Heidenschaft, there take a narrow gauge train, change to mule-back, and so to San Gabriele, where one would sneak up on Gorizia and capture it. There is a theory of learning that holds that once a stimulus has paved its way to the brain it will take that route again before changing to another. Now, looking at the map, I realized that the next station was Monfalcone, which had been the end of our front line on the Adriatic, and on the night of October 20, 1917, I'd seen the fighting there from the top of San Gabriele. It would be quite simple to get out at Monfalcone and take the train to Gorizia.

There was no time to lose: the train stopped for a minute at Monfalcone and started again while I was making up my mind. I threw my bag out the window and hurtled off the moving train.

The depot was bedecked with flags, a *Bersaglieri* brass band had broken up and was loitering on the platform with trumpets at ease. Along the road peasants were approaching in their Sunday best, black suits, white shirts, and no necktie. As I had two hours to wait for my train to Gorizia, I walked in the direction the peasants were coming from and ended up in a cemetery, a pleasant, neat, country cemetery with many flowers, bounded in a square by a low stone wall. What better reading matter for a Sunday afternoon between trains than the inscriptions on the tombstones of a village cemetery? But I soon found that these tombstones in Monfalcone were not easy reading. There were many large white statues of kneeling angels praying for village souls, and the names on these were clear enough. But I saw many modest gray stones, hardly bigger than the milestones on a road- side, with inscriptions that were fragmentary and recondite like the names of centurions dead ages ago. B LA N GY; FE NC K ACS; I studied them: there was something about them—and suddenly I read them clear! They were the familiar names of Hungary, names like Bela Nagy, Ferenc Kovacs, but so badly mauled that only another Hungarian could guess what they meant. Some of the little stones said simply *Austriaco Ignoto*— Unknown Austrian. These were the graves of my comrades of the battle of Tolmein. The good people of Monfalcone had gathered their bodies from the hills, from the trenches and from among the rocks, rescued them from the indecency of shell holes, and laid them to rest in their own cemetery.

In World War I, we Austrians didn't have the metal dogtags G.I.'s have today. Our identification consisted of a metal folder with a paper inside on which the name was scribbled in ink, and if a soldier's body had lain in the rain a couple of weeks, the ink ran and the name became illegible. Yet someone in Mon- falcone had looked carefully at these names, treasured the clear letters, and placed them with their owners, on the little stones.

One stone bore the inscription: An Herrn . . . Krauss. Obviously this poor fellow had no identification, but rather than call him *Austriaco Ignoto* they had fished out of his pocket a letter addressed to him and copied the first line of it; it was a most moving epitaph.

I found out too what the flags, the flowers, the peasants in their best and the brass band were all about. In this cemetery of Monfalcone had been buried a man by the name of Enrico Toti. He was a war hero who had lost a leg in battle, and yet he had returned on crutches to continue fighting. It was just above Monfalcone that the Austrians had broken into the Italian trenches in the first sweep of the Tolmein Breakthrough. Toti had hit the enemy with one of his crutches, and then he had been killed.

Who killed Toti? Was it Herr Krauss? Or somebody else too busy or frightened to notice that he had only one leg? Or perhaps it had happened in the night, under my very eyes, as I stared aghast from San Gabriele, and the slayer hadn't seen Toti at all, just got angry when somebody hit him with a crutch.

Whoever killed Toti did not know that he had killed a hero, just as the Italian soldiers who killed Herr Krauss couldn't know that he was Herr Krauss. But the people of Monfalcone found them both and buried them together. Toti got roses, carnations, lilies, and gladioli. Herr Krauss got clover: just as good.

Toti was removed in 1923 from Monfalcone and reburied with pomp in Rome. Herr Krauss was left in Monfalcone and he will remain there forever if he does not fall victim to one of those gruesome time limits cemeteries have for nobodies who do not renew their leases. Enrico Toti lost a leg, lost his life, won fame; Herr Krauss lost his life, lost his first name, and his last will be forgotten. In final balance, on the hills of Monfalcone two mothers lost their sons.

It was blue twilight when I arrived in Gorizia, and there was a chill in the mountains. I ran across the road at the railway station, dumped my bags in the Hotel Città di Trieste, and ran out again to hail a taxi in front of the station.

"Do you know where the Geschütz Kaverne is on Monte San Gabriele?"

The driver gave me a puzzled look.

"There's a cavern on the mountainside," I insisted.

He shook his head, unbelieving.

"Just drive me up the Gabriele," I said, "and drop me at Dol, where the road turns to the right."

We drove through the peaceful village I'd known only by its ruins, though its name cuts me so deep. Angry dogs snapped at our wheels, children with dirty faces and huge eyes stared at the stranger in a car. The trains were running again in the Isonzo Valley, the iron bridge that had fallen into the river was up again. We drove along the serpentine road, past the dreadful humps of Sabotino and the cone of Monte Santo, where once Toscanini had played military marches; they traced a silent ultramarine outline against the sky, edged still with blue and gold. It seemed to me I recognized the hillside where eighteen years before I had seen the beautiful Italian with his hand across his chest in saintly death.

"Stop!" I shouted to the driver. And as a horse feels his way in the night, I set foot on the path that led to the entrance to the cavern. I walked a hundred steps. It was my road indeed, but it was getting dark; I was afraid. I walked down again to the taxi, and we drove back to the hotel. On the way I looked down into the valley, saw the lights of Gorizia flickering as I had seen them before, when I was not permitted to enter.

Trembling fear seized me. Eighteen years earlier my mind had lost its moorings in this place. Now it did so again: I would have to leave the hotel. If the Slovenian farmers and truck drivers drinking wine and *slivovitz* in the bar would know me for an enemy, they'd murder me in the night. I leapt from the taxi, telling the driver to wait, grabbed my luggage in haste, put down ten lire for the night in front of the owner, ran out. "This is a clean hotel!" he shouted indignantly, but I got back into the taxi. "Take me to the biggest hotel in town," I said, and the driver took me to the Hotel Quarnero in the center of town.

This was more like home. The Austro-Hungarian Empire had failed to unite its people, but it certainly succeeded in co-ordinating the drabness of every hotel dining room in the territory of the dual monarchy. The high ceiling without hope, the bare walls without warmth, the potted palms without life, the bobtailed red plush curtains hanging in dusty misery around high baroque

windows could have been those of the dining room of the White
Ship Hotel in Györ, or of the Hotel Saint Nepomuc in Leitmeritz
in Bohemia. I began to feel safe, and ordered some spaghetti; but
not for long. Gorizia was a garrison town, and a table at the
Hotel Quarnero was reserved for officers. They strutted into the
dining room in high cocked kepis and flowing cloaks. I huddled
at my corner table, afraid that they might recognize me as a
fugitive from the cavern, a spy from the San Gabriele. Dizzy
and scared, I sneaked upstairs to my room, pulled the bedcovers
over my head, and settled down, not to sleep but to shudder.

In the darkness I saw the cavern, the inferno where damned
souls squirmed, the zombies with stone faces under steel helmets,
hands frozen to their grenades, standing petrified vigil. I saw the
wounded around the puddle again, again the bloody mud I'd
have to use for walls. It was a silent movie, badly edited, so
dead, so horrifyingly alive.

Eighteen years had passed since I left that cavern. I had lost
my father, my mother, a sister, a brother, but that night they
came back to life. All that evening I had been living in an emotional flashback; I felt as I had felt in 1917. Somewhere in the
distance I had a home, a nest of warm feeling, a mother sitting
at the window as she used to do, gentians in the garden shy
under evergreens, a home where people gently trembled for me,
not suspecting where I was. Never since I had lost that home had
I belonged to it so firmly as that night in the Hotel Quarnero.
I paced the room, alert for the Italian lynching mob, looked
under the bed to be certain no Italian general was hiding there,
and in the end lay down and slept.

When I woke, all this seemed as foolish as it does on paper; and
it was foolish. In 1936 Mussolini was the patron saint of Hungary.
I had only to walk into the local tourist agency and tell them I
was Hungarian, and they'd give me an honor guard. I did so, and
indeed the director himself, Cavaliere Capitano Bramo, a stout
man in Fascist uniform and a pince-nez, took me in charge. I
asked him about the cavern. He'd never heard of it, but he said

that the San Gabriele was now a hunting ground of the Count
of Udine, and that he would call upon the game warden, who
knew the mountain better than anyone else, and ask him to
assist me.

The game warden was a husky, middle-aged Slovenian who
seemed not to have heard of the cavern. But when I explained
that it had to be above the place where the road at Dol turned
sharply to the right, his eyes lit up. "Capitano!" he exclaimed.
"That's the cavern that was so full of foxes. That must be it!"

That was it. The Inferno was now a haven of little foxes.

The game warden said that a few months before, while he was
making his rounds on the San Gabriele, the ground had given
way under him and he had sunk up to his knees in a hole that
turned out to be an old dugout. They found sixteen skeletons
there in Hungarian uniform, clinging to their guns: they must
have been buried alive, he said. One of them had ten kreutzers
on him. He told me, too, about the five Balillas, Mussolini's boy
scouts, who had built a campfire on the Gabriele, but just over a
grenade buried in the ground. It had exploded and torn them
to bits.

Capitano Bramo placed a black limousine with a chauffeur at
my disposal; then he decided to come along himself. In such
state, in broad daylight, I completed my pilgrimage. A little
forest had already grown on the mountainside, nothing of importance, just like a teen-ager's beard, but enough for a rabbit
to hide from the gun of the Count of Udine. On the road we
met men and women carrying heavy sacks on their backs. The
capitano explained that they made a living by collecting scrap
iron on the mountains and selling it at four lire per kilo, a
couple of cents. It was a dangerous profession because there were
still live grenades there. I walked up the steep pathway that led
to the cavern with Capitano Bramo behind me, and there I saw
the entrance I had once prepared to have blown up. It had
collapsed. I could have climbed in but didn't dare: it looked as
if it might have buried a man alive. After eighteen years, it seemed

the San Gabriele was still hungry for the lives of men and women and boys. So I stood in front of it in the bright calm day, on the path of sorrows.

The ground around it was still a waste yard of glory. I saw a broken spoon, the fragment of a skull, a dehydrated shoe, a pile of empty cans. I thought it curious that it was not metal, but leather, old belts and shoe heels, that resisted best the ravages of time and weather. I found an enamel cup such as we used to carry, stamped Austria 1917. I picked up a broken teaspoon, a piece of bone, a grenade splinter, and put them in my pocket.

The mountain smelled like a cemetery. All cemeteries smell alike. Is it the bodies? I don't know. But in our country cemeteries around Györ, sometimes on hot summer nights an emanation arose which flamed into a will-o'-the-wisp and drove our peasants insane with fear.

When summer dies, the grass turns to standing hay. Some flowers remain, but the berries are ripe. "Do you see that thorny shrub with red berries?" said Cavaliere Capitano Bramo. "People around here say they didn't grow before the war, and they think that shrub grows only where human blood has been spilled."

I'd heard similar tales, and put them down to superstition. But casting my eye around, I saw clearly that the crimson shrub crept in arteries exactly where our trenches used to be.

We left Gabriele and moved to Sabotino. The Italian government had declared this region a *zona sacra*; the battle lines had been left untouched, heaps of empty ration cans littered the hillside, there were machine guns in position, a field telephone and telegraph in the dugout, and, in a hidden canyon, a soup kitchen.

At the top of Sabotino there was a row of white tombstones, at least twenty of them, and on each was the name of a regiment that had fought there.

It was a sacred morning in the sacred zone. Buses were arriving with men and women, pilgrims like me, with cameras in holsters.

But the women climbed to the top of Sabotino, fell on their knees before the regimental tombstones, prayed and wept.

Under the crisp white sun in the soft breeze of the silent mountain, my conversation with Capitano Bramo turned to the politics of the day. Without any special provocation, he suddenly stiffened, clenched his fist, straddled his legs; the breath of anger stretched his nostrils, and he brutishly bared his canine teeth toward the left as he spoke of France grabbing the African colonies.

Angry little Fascist, Capitano Bramo! What an odd figure you cut against the silhouette of Monte San Gabriele, where the new shrubs had hardly begun to take root!

XII

Désarroi de l'Esprit

Two MONTHS after Cavaliere Capitano Bramo had cried out his fury amid the mourning women of Monte Sabotino, Mussolini attacked Ethiopia. To Geneva came the former press officer of the Italian delegation at the Versailles Peace Conference, Baron Pompeo Aloisi. He wore a monocle. I never saw this monocle other than as a one-eyed pirate's patch. With a knife in his mouth, he would have made a good press officer for Captain Kidd.

It was the job of this toothless, yoghurt-eyed Yul Brynner to muddle the League into believing that it was not the Capitoline Wolf who had attacked the Lion of Judah, but the reverse. Once Yoshizawa had sent up a similar smoke screen with his long-barrelled cigar. Aloisi did it with cigarettes. Bemused, the League sought the aggressor the way a jealous husband in a French farce seeks the seducer of his wife: He looks under the bed and says: "He isn't there." He looks behind the curtain and says: "He isn't there." Then he opens the closet and, finding a hefty

Zouave with a drawn gun, slams the door, saying: "He isn't there!" Eyes swivelled around the council table like the eyes of Pharisees, and in Ethiopia the war rolled on against a people unarmed, unskilled in war, primitive.

We prepared a menu-card for that year in which we attempted to express the idea that Ethiopians are important, that morality is indivisible. Our drawing depicted a tent in the desert in which Pierre Laval, Anthony Eden, Eduard Beneš, Colonel Beck of Poland, and other members of the Council deliberated. Outside, by the flap of the tent, sat pint-sized Ethiopian delegate, Teclé Hawariate, hanging on to an ass burdened with bundles of treaties and pacts. In the sky were inscribed the proverbs of Solomon: *Blessed is the man that heareth me, watching daily at my gates, waiting at the posts of my doors.* One proverb was aimed at the members of the Security Council: *He that walketh uprightly walketh surely, but he that perverteth truth, his ways shall be known.* Another was for the appeasers: *He that winketh with the eye causeth sorrow, but a prating fool shall fall.*

Only by hiding behind King Solomon could Derso and I have gotten away with that much wisdom.

We hoped that the League of Nations would use the measures at their disposal against Mussolini: that they would close the Suez Canal or cut off the sale of oil. This would have been a lesson not only to Il Duce but to the Fuehrer. Unfortunately, Pierre Laval of France, and Britain's foreign secretary, Sir Samuel Hoare, were also students of the Bible. *A gift in secret pacifieth anger, and a reward in the bosom, strong wrath:* this was the expedient proverb they followed when they threw Ethiopia to the Duce.

By May 1936 Ethiopia was conquered. Mussolini proclaimed the Italian king Emperor of Abyssinia, and the Negus, Haile Selassie, fled to Palestine. Soon after, he requested permission to come to Geneva to put his case before the League's Assembly, of which his country was a sovereign member.

In reply, the credentials committee of the League, which was made up mostly of representatives of the Great Powers, brought to bear on the situation the most cynical axiom of international politics: a *fait accompli* has precedence over treaties. They stated that as there was no longer such a thing as the "sovereign state of Ethiopia," the Negus did not represent anybody and therefore could not be permitted to speak before the Assembly.

The Negus then telephoned his former American adviser,

COUNT CIANO AND KING VICTOR EMMANUEL III

Everitt Colson, who lay gravely ill of a heart ailment in Évian. Colson left his bed and hurried to Geneva. He succeeded in mobilizing small nations against this infamous decision. When the recommendation of the credentials committee was placed before the Assembly, therefore, it was rejected. The Emperor and his delegation were permitted to come to the League.

The day the Negus arrived, two Neguses were to be seen in Geneva. One of them, a dark, bearded, sad-eyed figure in a limousine, drove ceremoniously through the streets to the market place. Here he bought a bunch of flowers while peddlers and squatting market women cheered. He then proceeded to the Monument of the Reformation and gravely deposited the bouquet at the foot of Calvin's statue. Afterwards he drove to the Palais des Nations, but here the guards turned him back. For he

was a bogus Negus with his face charcoaled and a false beard.
The police had countenanced his mockery because, in a free
country, you cannot arrest a practical joker.

In 1923 I had seen the Ethiopian delegation enter the League
like a ghost. Now he came, the King of Kings, but he was a
Ghost of Ghosts. Not only the ghost of Ethiopia came with him,
but that of China, and the ghost of Dr. Yen's warning to the

Assembly: If you let one aggressor get away with murder, others
will follow.

I have always seen the funny side of majesty. But there is a
drawing the artist David made as he stood in a crowd watching
Marie Antoinette ride for the last time through the Paris streets
with straight back and bent head; majesty on a tumbril is majestic indeed. And I thought of this as I watched the Negus
mount the rostrum and confront us, great-eyed, bearded, his
face like that of a shadowy Christ. He wore a black cape held
together with golden clasps, and a white silk scarf edged his
violet velvet collar. In the dimness of the hall, only a gooseneck
lamp spotlighted the paper he held in his hand and reflected
on his face, and where his cape opened in front, the ends of the
white silk scarf blazed like a piercing sword.

He made his address in a language nobody understood, and

yet everybody understood it. In its very unintelligibility it told his story with eloquence, and it was heard in dead silence and funereal gloom. Once before a man had attempted to defend himself in a related tongue; but there were those who interrupted and cried out: "Crucify him!"

Then, to the right of the balcony opposite where I was sitting, pandemonium broke out. A group of Italian journalists began to whistle, shout, roar, rattle. The Negus faltered. From either side of the balcony husky figures darted, took the journalists by their coats, and wrestled them toward the door.

The Negus continued his enigmatic address. Then his nephew translated the Amharic into French. The delegates listened. But they washed their hands of him all the same.

As for the Italian journalists, they played cards in prison for a day and then were asked to leave the country. The demonstration had been ordered by the Duce.

In July, civil war broke out in Spain. Hitler and Mussolini seized the opportunity for a dress rehearsal of World War II. Goering testified in Nuremberg that he was glad to try out "my young Luftwaffe . . . under combat conditions." Seven hundred thousand Spaniards died in that test-tube war.

The Leftist government of Spain had been duly elected; therefore the case came up before the League of Nations, with Juan Negrín and Álvarez del Vayo pleading the government's case. Again the League looked in the closet and, finding General Franco armed with a German gun, shut the door. Hitler and Mussolini proceeded with their dress rehearsal. The Russians put their oar in briefly, then pulled it out. But liberal elements formed an international brigade named after that famous Bolshevik, Abraham Lincoln, while Britain and France agreed on strict nonintervention in Spain.

A communiqué from the Franco headquarters stays in my mind: "We captured a Czechoslovak munitions ship bringing grenades to our enemy which we ourselves badly needed. By a miracle these grenades fitted our guns, proof that God is on our side."

Constitutional psychologists, in their studies of individuals of predominantly muscular body build, have noted how consistently this sort of man identifies his purposes, however aggressive and ruthless, with God. It seems such men can explain their overpowering determination only by a sense of "divine mission." And generals too readily name God an aide-de-camp.

The Spaniards did not subscribe to Hitler's race theories. Once the Jews had streamed out of Spain to all parts of medieval Europe, fleeing the Inquisition. Now they flowed back from the modern countries they had helped to fashion, in a great confluence toward the Pyrenees and thence in a tragic river across Spain and Portugal on their way to anywhere. They were not allowed to remain in Spain, but they were given harbor and food and human kindness. I know an elderly Munich art dealer named Tannhäuser who was held up for months in the Pyrenees on the Spanish border. Finally he plucked up courage to walk up to a Spanish officer and ask permission to enter Spain. "What is your name?" asked the guard.

"Tannhäuser!"

"Tannhäuser! The great composer!" And he was permitted to cross the border.

There is one explanation for the perfidious politics in Europe in the thirties: *désarroi de l'esprit*, confusion of the mind, a condition that darkened judgment and dissolved ordinary knowledge of right and wrong. It was a spiritual failure induced by fear of iniquitous men: Hitler, Mussolini, and Stalin. People who were not Communists supported Stalin because they feared Hitler; others who were not Nazis or Fascists supported Hitler and Mussolini out of fear of Communism. On both sides they cheered the devil because they feared the deep blue sea.

I am not surprised at those who became Communists or fellow travelers because they had convinced themselves that

Communism had an altruistic aim. But to this day I am dumfounded that rational and religious people lined up with the Nazis, whose philosophy was frankly selfish and who threatened not only sitting ducks like Jews and gypsies, but every non-Nordic contrivance from Christian doctrine to the stock exchange.

Franz Shoenberner, editor of *Simplicissimus,* was one of the few non-Jewish Germans who very early in the game walked out of his job to live as best he could abroad. Years later, in New York, he told me: "I thought I'd be only one of a long line of Germans who would go into exile rather than adopt Nazi *Kultur* as German culture. But when I looked behind me, there was scarcely anyone there."

In Geneva the schism in the Secretariat and in the press was quite open. Everyone knew who was who's agent and who sympathized with whom. Journalists quarreled vociferously in public. Members of the Secretariat kept kicking one another out of their offices. Secretary General Sir Eric Drummond suddenly abandoned his sinking rats, changed his name to Lord Perth, and went off to Rome as Britain's ambassador to Mussolini.

In Paris, Otto Abetz, Hitler's briber-plenipotentiary, was feeding a howling Fascist press. In London, Lord Rothermere opened his influential *Daily Mail* to Hitler, and he endorsed Horthy's revisionism so ably that when I went home to Hungary for my vacation I found his bulldog face framed like an ikon in every peasant home, and innocent people were calling him "Our Lord." Less innocent ones were seriously considering crowning him or his son, Harmsworth, King of Hungary. If this was not *désarroi de l'esprit,* I don't know what is.

Heaviest of all memories of those times is that of the youngsters, of the small boys taught to goosestep in German and Italian towns, of the healthy German youths in the Bavaria spouting Hitler's incredible philosophies over their sauerkraut; and at the next table, weedier specimens masticating Marx. In Paris there were Sorbonne students who boycotted the lectures of Pro-

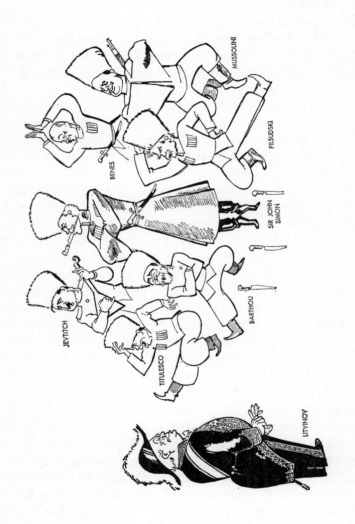

fessor Gaston Jèze because he championed the cause of the Emperor of Ethiopia.

These youths had grown up amid the schism. They had made up their minds where they stood, and they knew that they were right. No one had a voice loud enough to suggest to them that only the spirit is for knowing; the mind is for questioning.

In the streets of Geneva, *désarroi de l'esprit* showed itself in popular acclaim for the Duce. Who was the Lion of Judah anyway, and what was the League but a collection of foreigners drawing fat salaries and paying no taxes? By night the local Fascists organized torch-lit demonstrations. Students at the university set up a Fascist-minded society called *Les Petits-fils de Toepffer*, the grandsons of Toepffer. This Toepffer was a predecessor of mine, a caricaturist and writer of the nineteenth century, and his grandsons honored him by playing practical jokes on the League. One night they stretched chains across the road leading to the Palais des Nations: this was meant to indicate that the Ethiopians were a nation of slavers. They stuffed a dummy of John Bull and floated him out onto the lake opposite the Quai Wilson with a British flag stuck in his belly. They had invitations to a cocktail party made up in the name of local Socialist leaders and sent them to Socialist delegates such as Léon Blum. Those who accepted drove sprucely to the given address and found themselves in a cow pasture.

In spite of the crawling mayhem, the prosperous landlady of our family pension, Mme Tonetti, took over the management of a hotel close to the new Palais des Nations, and she decided that what this hotel needed more than anything else was a mural by Derso and Kelen. She did not offer us cash; just freedom from bills. So generous was she that if the League had not collapsed we would now be the oldest nonpaying guests of the pension Mon Chez Moi, and valuable tourist attractions in ourselves.

All my furniture except for a couch on which I slept was now thrown out of my room, and a six by ten foot canvas affixed to the wall. It was long enough so that Derso, who is lefthanded, and I, who am righthanded, could both stand in front of it and work simultaneously. We had no trouble finding an appropriate subject. Geneva has in its history an episode called L'Escalade. In 1602, on the night of December 11, the Savoyards, bad Frenchmen led by the Duc de Savoie, sneaked up to the walls of Geneva with ladders, intending to take the city by surprise. The guard was not prepared to repulse them. But the housewives of Geneva were cooking *pot au feu*, and these brave women carried their caldrons to the top of the city wall and poured the scalding contents on the heads of the men of Savoy, who retired very red in the face. This victory is celebrated annually in Geneva; everybody runs into the streets yodeling, the children dressed as Pierrots, fathers as wolves, mothers as shepherdesses in powdered wigs, and throughout the night fancy-dress balls are held in the casino and the dance halls. In the stores you can buy miniature caldrons of peerless Swiss chocolate filled with carrots, turnips, and parsley made of marzipan, reminders of that splendid dish that saved the city.

We took L'Escalade as the subject of our painting, calling it *Assault on the Rostrum*. We dressed our delegates in the costumes of three hundred years ago, and had them attacking the rostrum of the League Assembly with ladders, while Mlle Vacarescu played the lyre in one corner and Stalin and Hitler growled at each other over a dice game. Like our other large compositions, we made it a panorama of the political situation of the times: on a rope above the abyss hung Titulescu, Laval, and Spain's del Vayo; Professor Gaston Jèze, legal adviser to Haile Selassie, was carrying a kicking Negus to the microphone.

I worked on the mural for three months, eating and sleeping with it. I was so saturated with the subject that one day, riding on a streetcar, I suddenly saw everyone in the garb of a Landsknecht, and the most astonishing part of it was that I perceived that the human face had not evolved in the last three hundred

years. The faces of modern-day burghers fitted just as well into
the fearsome helmets of the past, and if by chance some face
seemed more sensitive, it fitted into the five-foot-long, upcurled
hat of an old Jesuit. I suspect, reading Plato and the Bible, that
the human mind has not progressed either, and that those who
were right two thousand or five thousand years ago are still
right.

At our pension lived a photographer named Ralph Crane, now
a *Life* man. He took a picture of the mural, gave it an American-
style caption, "The World's Biggest Cartoon," and sent it to his
agency. *La Tribune de Genève* got it via London and published
it on the front page.

The next day a snarling article appeared in another Geneva
paper, denouncing us for having "desecrated a glorious page of
our history," and warning us that if the mural should ever see a
wall there'd be, as it were, a *pot au feu* out of sliced brisket of
Derso and Kelen, with the mural shredded up for flavor.

We were surprised. We had not suspected that an event which
had taken few lives and three hundred years later was celebrated
with false noses could provoke such high feelings. When a rumor spread abroad that the grandsons of Toepffer were planning
to assault the mural with ink bottles, I called up an insurance
company to insure it against damage.

"Is that the mural mentioned in the paper?" the agent asked.

"Yes."

"No!" said the agent and hung up.

I called the president of *Action Civique* (who was behind
the *brouhaha*), and invited him to come and look at our drawing. He arrived flanked by two well-dressed discus-throwing types,
sat on my unmade bed, and with an air of a connoisseur con-
templated the picture.

"You see," he said, "these uniforms are real Landsknecht uniforms."

It was quite early in the afternoon, but Derso had risen from
his bed for the occasion and stood by, uncombed, unshaved, in

a checked robe, with his naked, hairy legs showing below. Always annoyed when awakened early, he now lost his temper.

"For two francs," he shouted, "I can rent a Landsknecht uniform and lie in the gutter in it drunk!"

I, more conciliatory and better attired, made the following suggestion: "Suppose we add a necktie to the Landsknecht uniforms to distinguish them from real ones?" The President of *Action Civique* agreed that this would be an improvement. He then pointed to Giuseppe Motta, the Swiss delegate, who had a Red Cross on his Chest. "You see," he said mournfully, "that looks like the Swiss flag."

"But sir," I objected, "the Swiss flag is a white cross on a red field and this is a red cross on a white field."

"Yes," he said, "just the same, it looks like the Swiss flag."

We agreed that the red cross would be replaced by a bouquet of edelweiss. The president looked satisfied, and so did the discus-throwers.

"Please understand our vigilance," he said. "Since the Russians entered the League, we have subversive forces within our walls."

The next day he published a statement in the local papers that Derso and Kelen had given full satisfaction to the people of Geneva.

Indeed, we had not meant to offend the people of Geneva, whose hospitality and friendship we had enjoyed for so long, with whom from youth to middle age we had put on false noses and danced through the night of December 11 Chez Maxim. I can ascribe this incident only to the *désarroi de l'esprit* that prevailed in those days wherever the shadows of Hitler, Mussolini, and Stalin fell.

One morning in the Assembly Hall there was a crack like a whip, and on the floor, in an enclosure reserved for photographers, commotion. The president of the Assembly, Van Zeeland of Belgium, forgot to turn off his microphone, and I overheard the following conversation.

"What happened?"

"Somebody committed suicide."

"What! Are people coming here now to commit suicide? The hall must be poorly guarded."

"We can't search everybody who enters. Anyone with a press card is entitled to come here and commit suicide."

Then Van Zeeland's voice replied: "This is a showplace of fatal events. We are bound to witness fatalities."

What had happened was that a journalist from Prague, a Jewish refugee by the name of Lux, had deliberately walked onto the floor and shot himself. After his body had been removed, President Van Zeeland did what Emil Combes of France had done in the French parliament when someone threw a bomb from the gallery. He uttered the classic words: "*La séance continue. . . .*"

Lux left a testament in three copies: one for his wife, one for Secretary General Avenol, and one for a journalist friend, Paul du Bochet. This last was the one I saw. It read: "I wanted to attract the world's attention to the fact that Hitler is preparing the most horrible war of history, and that international diplomacy is doing nothing to prevent it." I recall this particular sentence: *Dieses Glacéhandschuh Idyll muss endlich einmal aufhören!*—This kid-glove idyll must cease, once and for all!

I'm not a funeral bluff, and if I could avoid going to my own funeral I would do so. But I went to the funeral of Lux because I felt he had died for nothing. The strange thing was, there were so few others: just his widow and a six-year-old son; a delegate from the Geneva Jewish Community; the German, Max Beer; the American, Clarence Streit; the Englishman, Robert Dell; The Swiss, du Bochet; and a Hungarian caricaturist.

Few attended Lux's funeral because few were left who thought it remarkable or sad that a man should stand in the temple of the last best hope for peace and take his life.

The Umbrella Age

By JANUARY 1936 the stage was set for the Second World War. Three more years passed before the shooting started, because certain rough edges remained to be ironed out. One of them was the remilitarization of the Rhineland. Hitler undertook this job on March 7, 1936.

I heard the news over the radio in my studio in Paris. "We'll not tolerate that Strasbourg should be within range of German cannon!" cried Prime Minister Albert Sarraut.

"This is the end of Hitler," said I and made haste to London, where the League of Nations Council had called an emergency session. On the train I met my Bolshevik friend, Rothstein, correspondent of TASS, and asked him: "If there's a war, will Stalin honor his mutual assistance pact with France?"

"I don't know what Stalin will do," replied Rothstein. "The beauty of that pact is that Hitler doesn't know either."

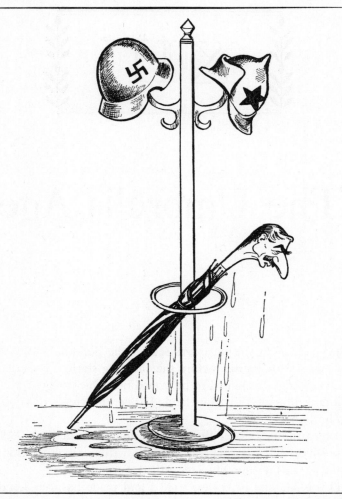

Here's a good definition of a pact: something to confuse both enemies and friends. And, indeed, what was France's surprise when Stalin signed a nonaggression pact with Hitler! And what was Stalin's surprise when Hitler attacked him anyway! It goes to show that politics is like the heart, which has its reasons that reason cannot fathom.

The Council met at my old hunting grounds, St. James's Palace, in the Queen Anne's Room, a royal salon Frenchified with complicated window drapes and three-tiered candelabra. Ancestors in skirts and on horseback watched from the walls.

Into it, with a posture like a winged horse, moved Joachim von Ribbentrop, Hitler's Special Envoy. There were those who called him, contemptuously, "the champagne salesman," but they were unjust. When you marry the daughter of a champagne manufacturer, you can hardly refuse to push papa's product. Mussolini was more judicious: he said Ribbentrop was a truly sinister man, because he was both an imbecile and presumptuous. Goering despised him and warned Hitler against naming him ambassador to the Court of St. James. When Hitler insisted that Ribbentrop knew people, Goering remarked: "Yes. The difficulty is, they know Ribbentrop."[1]

I have always thought Ribbentrop was Hitler's ego-ideal; he spoke various languages, was a member of the *Herrenklub*, and had everything Hitler admired and had not: a high, vertical forehead, a straight nose, real teeth, a defiant chin, and a small claim to squeeze the noble prefix *von* in front of his name. Years before, in Munich, he had been similarly impressed by the clotheshorse, Rosenberg. Half-man Hitler was no judge of men, as was a whole man like Churchill.

Hitler had sent von Ribbentrop to London in those windy days in March to sell a heady bottle to the mugwumps in Queen Anne's Room: a Twenty-five Year Peace Plan. And the mugwumps bought it! Before long the whole horseshoe table became embroiled in a dramatic discussion of the proper translation of the word *alsbald* in Hitler's proposal. Some wanted it to be interpreted as *in due course*, others as *immediately*. The best linguists of Britain were called upon, but they could not agree. The German Foreign Office was asked to settle the matter. Back came the reply that *alsbald* had one meaning in southern

[1] William L. Shirer: *The Rise and Fall of the Third Reich* (New York: Simon and Schuster; 1960), p. 298.

Germany and another in northern Germany. Jules Sauerwein, dean of French journalists, said that for a Frenchman it meant immediately; for an Englishman, *after the marriage*. The Council adjourned for two days.

If they had concerned themselves with Hitler's preposterous

face instead of with his invidious words, they would have known that it made no difference whether the proposed peace was to go into effect immediately or in due course, because he was preparing to go to war.

Queen Anne had thirteen stillborn children, and after I had listened for a while to the speeches in Queen Anne's Room I remarked that we were witnessing the stillbirth of the fourteenth. This quip turned up in the *Daily Telegraph* under the heading, *Acid Drop*, but I scarcely knew how acid it really was. For France and England allowed themselves to be so bamboozled by the peace plan proposed by the greatest liar since Ananias that his presence in the Rhineland seemed unimportant. "After all," said Lord Lothian, "the Germans are only going into their own back yard."[2]

When Mussolini moved into Ethiopia, the British might have gone to war; but the French were reluctant. When Hitler moved into the Rhineland, the French might have gone to war; but the British were reluctant. This was the dilemma of those years.

Hitler, *alsbald*, immediately, gave the *coup de grâce* to the dying Versailles Treaty; and to the Treaty of Locarno; and he abused the League; and he disposed of France's security system in Eastern Europe, which for fifteen years she had laboriously built around Poland, Czechoslovakia, Rumania, and Yugoslavia.

Was the Queen Anne's Room Conference really a "turning point in history"? Can we even fathom "what would have happened *if* . . ." the Locarnists had held together?

Hitler had hardly three divisions in the Rhineland, and the French alone had thirteen along the Maginot Line. General Jodl testified at Nuremberg: "The French covering army could have blown us all to pieces." Hitler called these days ". . . the most nervewracking days of my life . . . we would have had to withdraw with our tails between our legs."[3]

My drawing of the horseshoe table shows at one end Herr von Ribbentrop with a conqueror's mouth and folded arms; at the other end, William Strang of the Foreign Office. Neither the *chef de protocole* who seated them there, nor the caricaturist, could have foreseen that these two men would in 1939 simultaneously negotiate with Stalin; that Strang would fail, that Ribbentrop would succeed and bring on the war and eventually be hanged for it.

Napoleon I, in 1803, coined the phrase: "perfidious Albion." It's curious that whereas England's citizens are famed for probity,

---

[2] Ibid., p. 393.
[3] Ibid.

Albion's politics are famed for perfidy. In the thirties, this phrase went into all the languages of the world, and much of the perfidy was laid at the door of a certain cloak-and-dagger society known as the Cliveden set, after the sumptuous country estate of the Astors.

Viscount Waldorf Astor owned Britain's two most influential newspapers, the *Times* and the *Observer*, but his American wife, Nancy, had a wider circulation than both papers put together. She was the first woman to sit in the British Parliament, where her nuisance value—as she admitted—was enormous. One M.P. called her "the cheekiest little sparrow that ever sat on a doorstep."[4] Churchill noted: "She combines a kindly heart with a sharp and wagging tongue."[5] Bernard Shaw, a friend, remarked: "Her interruptions are better than her regular speeches."[6]

Cliveden is a mid-Victorian edifice designed by Sir Charles Barry, architect of the Houses of Parliament. It is surrounded by a romantic park which descends gently to the river Thames near Maidenhead Bridge; and it put a roof over the heads of six housemaids, two pantry maids, a chef with four scullery maids, a butler, a groom of the chambers, a valet, three footmen, and an odd-jobs man for the fire and coal. The money for it came from the Astors, who, as Nancy precisely told Grace Vanderbilt, "had skinned skunks a hundred years before the Vanderbilts ran ferryboats."[7]

King Gustaf V of Sweden had been a guest at Cliveden; Archduke Franz Ferdinand and his wife had stayed there two years before they were murdered at Sarajevo; the Prince of Wales had drunk its famous 1828 brandy. Colonel Charles Lindbergh slept there; F.D.R. also slept there; Mr. and Mrs. Henry Ford were entertained there, and when they left, Mr. Ford gave each of the Astor children a Ford motorcar; Bernard Shaw was invited there

[4] Collis: *Nancy Astor*, p. 110.
[5] Ibid., p. 171.
[6] Ibid., p. 179.
[7] Ibid., p. 222.

for three days and stayed three weeks, dressing up as Santa Claus for the children of the staff.

As for Derso and Kelen, they were honored with an invitation to a garden party at Cliveden. We lined up with the other guests in front of a little doorway that opened onto the park. Just inside it we could see Lady Astor dressed in a fluffy pink gown and a tiny hat, dispensing handshakes by the score. Ahead of us in the line was a bosomy lady of about two hundred pounds in a summer dress abloom with giant rhododendrons, cypripediums, and petunias. Stoutly bound in a corset, she resembled a camouflaged battleship, and as we waited, I heard a subdued sound out of the depths of her, like the whimper of a puppy in distress. As we approached the magic door step by step, this whimper became louder and louder, so that when she entered the gate and found herself face to face with Lady Astor, it had turned into a hysterical lament, and she began to swivel around on her heels in solemn majesty. Then the expeditive, quick-witted, managerial soul of Lady Astor was revealed. Swiftly she stepped forward, took Derso and me by the arm, propped the lady firmly between us, and giving us a motherly shove onto the precincts of Cliveden, snapped: "You two take care of her!"

We dared not desert our distressed flagship until we got her on an even keel again, a good three quarters of an hour later.

Spread around us was a scene from *Tatler*, with two thousand gray top hats, black and gray morning coats, and floating English garden-party dresses in soft sunrise colors, all milling in slow motion up and down the terrace steps. On the velvet lawn, under red and white striped tents, footmen much better dressed than I served champagne and canapés wrought of anchovies, caviar, and eyes of olive and egg, each one a little masterpiece of abstract art. At the bottom of the garden, where the Thames flowed bluish in the midsummer mist, by the awful whim of the rich, there were fairies: kids gotten up in muslin nightshirts with dragonfly wings on their shoulders, tripping in continuous hide-and-seek in and out of the bushes. So irrelevant was this sideshow to the top-hatted crowd that for a moment I thought I'd had too much champagne.

I made my way through the dunes of marquesses and footmen until I spotted what I was looking for: a countryman. He was Zsiga Strobl, the Hungarian Jo Davidson, a sculptor and businessman of considerable talent. I'd known him long before, in Budapest, when he was preparing the busts of Bela Kun and his friends for posterity. After they cleared out, he just wetted some more clay and sculpted Horthy and his crowd.

He was up to his old tricks in 1936 when he visited the Olympic Games in Berlin, and Hitler wrote him a letter inviting him to do his bust. In those days there was a shortage of coffee cream in Berlin. Zsiga carried Hitler's letter around in his pocket, and whenever he ordered coffee in a restaurant he'd take it out and wave it about. He was always given cream.

In due course he made busts of those who ran Horthy out of Hungary, among them Premier Imredy and his foreign minister, Bardossy. After they were captured by the Russians and publicly hanged, the time was ripe for Zsiga to get to work on Marshal Voroshilov, Rakosi, and the Commissars.

We don't call Zsiga Praxiteles. We call him Practical-es.

Yet I have no word of blame for an artist who separates art from politics: as long as his art is as good as Zsiga's, it stands as its own explanation. We would never see a Velasquez, a Van Dyke, or a Gainsborough if there were no such thing as l'art pour l'argent.

At Cliveden, Zsiga told me that he was Lady Astor's guest because he was busily busting London society. He invited me to the opening of his exhibition in Bond Street. I recall particularly a delightful bust of little Princess Elizabeth, the present Queen, and another of her uncle, the Duke of Kent, who was to die in the war. There were busts of Lord Rothermere and of his son, almost-Apostolic King Harmsworth; and a diabolical bust of Bernard Shaw, who had written a preface to Zsiga's catalogue. The late Dowager Queen Mary, who was then simply "the Queen," came to grace the opening day with her sovereign eye and to disclose a secret treasured by my countrymen, that through her grandmother, the Countess Rhedey, the British royal family are only watered-down Hungarians, God save them, every one!

Maurice Collis, biographer of Nancy Astor, wrote of her relationship with Lawrence of Arabia: "He (Lawrence) was a type of man who leans on strong women and finds refuge in them, as also was Bernard Shaw. There are people who would account for both Lawrence's and Shaw's feeling for her by their fundamental need of a mother to go to."[8]

I drew the members of the Cliveden set repeatedly, Lord Londonderry, Lord Lothian, Viscount Astor, and many others. I have no doubt that Collis's remarks may apply to most of these influential gentlemen.

I never drew Londonderry in Geneva other than as a yawning, weedy man holding his ebony cane as if it were a lily in his medieval hand. An aristocrat who appeared to suffer from a deficiency of iron in his blood, he had a natural admiration for Hermann Goering's high blood pressure.

Lord Lothian (who was known in Versailles as Philip Kerr) was one of my models at the Indian Round Table Conference, and I came to know him as an erudite man, a fine writer, soft-talking, soft-walking; he had a bashful smile and a soft curl that fell on his forehead. It is said that when he was ambassador to Washington he dined alone, in a kilt, with a Scottish bagpiper in gala uniform playing and walking around the Embassy's immense dining table.

Men like these feel an inevitable need to have a horsewoman with strong hands about. Lady Astor was a regular Boadicea with a stubborn forehead, a Roman nose, a solid, jutting jaw, and a large mouth. The minute I walked in the door to the Cliveden garden and saw, framed by a welcoming smile, those strong, solid teeth, I said to myself: "There's the Cliveden set!"

[8] Ibid., p. 152.

I have never decried her. She was an amateur politician and an *enfant terrible*; that is, she was completely equipped to be a political caricaturist. To accuse her or the Clivedens of conspiring with Hitler was a symptom of *désarroi de l'esprit*.

Yet I believe that the policy which came to be called appeasement was hatched at Cliveden, and that with a nest of highly placed weekend cronies, six members of the Astor family in Parliament, two great newspapers, and Lady Astor's sharp and wagging tongue, the Cliveden set was successful in putting that policy over on the nation.

A policy is a many-splendored thing, and only a politician will try to convince you that his policy has a single clear aim. There is always a cluster of aims, as in any move in a chess game, and aims change as the game progresses. The Cliveden set wanted peace. They also wanted to gain time in order to arm. They wanted to right the wrong done to Germany at Versailles, even over the dead body of Czechoslovakia; this would have had the desirable side effect of weakening France's influence on the Continent. As the highest good of all, they wanted Hitler to move closer to Stalin's throat.

The Clivedens abhorred Hitler's inhumanities; nevertheless, they condoned them for the sake of the higher good. They erred because they disregarded the fact (as did millions of people) that you cannot buy a mad Muscleman piecemeal, you've got to buy him on the hoof: not just the filet mignon, but the tripe as well. Hitler proved to be mostly tripe.

As an instrument of policy the Lord placed in the hands of the Cliveden set a tightly-rolled umbrella of a man, Neville Chamberlain. He was the younger half-brother of Sir Austen Chamberlain, whom I had drawn when he helped raise the Spirit of Locarno, and I saw him first in London when that triumphant treaty was signed. He turned up also as a member of the British delegation to the Lausanne Reparations Conference in 1932, and at the

World Economic and Monetary Conference held in London in 1933, where he negotiated with Cordell Hull.

His most striking feature was his small occiput. Lloyd George, who believed in phrenology, called his head "the wrong shape." Phrenologists are so intoxicated by head bumps that they overlook the fact that skulls belong to people and that every bump is part of an ensemble involving other developments of the head and ultimately of the body. Chamberlain got his small brain case in a package deal, along with coarse hair, bushy eyebrows, a thick mustache, a beaky nose, and close, deep-set, vigilant, timorous eyes. Herbert Morrison said he had a "death's head,"[9] but in the caricaturist's typology he was a fine specimen of the "bird-faced man." The Secretary Bird, which you may watch at the zoo walking back and forth on stiff legs with an expression of honest purpose on its face, is nature's parallel creation to men like Neville Chamberlain.

Chamberlain could not laugh, and if he smiled, the smile ran down the tips of his wilted mustache like the juice of a bitter melon. He had a neck of concrete, and liquid lime flowed in his veins. For me, it was written all over him that he was a domineering, unrelaxed, immovable man full of misplaced self-confidence.

The "bird-faced man" has, generally speaking, what the psychologists call the "autistic personality." He is introspective and irresponsive to the world around him. In 1936, the very year Hitler occupied the Rhineland and Nazi bestiality was already apparent, Chamberlain rented his London house in Eaton Square to the Ribbentrops. He wrote: "I think it is very amusing, considering my affection for Germans in generals, and Ribbentrop in particular."[1]

It is amusing, if crippled judgment is funny. Here was a man sensitive enough to perceive that Hitler was a "lunatic," and "half mad." Yet he collected rent from Hitler's ambassador at a

[9] Iain Macleod: *Neville Chamberlain* (New York: Atheneum; 1962), p. 184.
[1] Ibid., p. 17.

time when he not only was a cabinet minister but, because of Baldwin's illness, was marked out to be prime minister.

The Chamberlain family fortune was built on shoemaking and screwmaking, and was founded by Neville's grandfather, Joseph Chamberlain, the manager of whose company described him in these words: "He was reserved, sincere, zealous, rigid, pleasant, and quiet in his manner, but not to be moved from what he had said by anybody—you could see it in his face."[2]

O wise manager! if only there were more like you to look sharply at the boss and read his mind's complexion! It would not have escaped you that this straight-laced Neville, so like his grandfather, had too much character to face Hitler, who had none.

The umbrella will go down in history as a symbol of perfidious appeasement, and its owner as a high-minded sucker. He has my sympathy. I am a fisherman, and I know how it feels to be the wrong man at the wrong time at the wrong place with the wrong bait.

There was a man in England more callous than Chamberlain or any of the gentlemen of the Cliveden set, but more apt to look squarely at events and recognize their gruesome reality. Winston Churchill held himself aloof from the Cliveden set and heartily disapproved of Lady Astor. "A woman's intrusion into the House of Commons," he said to her, "is as embarrassing as if she burst into my bathroom when I had nothing to defend myself with but a sponge." Said she: "You are not handsome enough to have worries of that kind."[3]

"If I were your wife," said Lady Astor to the man of destiny, "I'd put poison in your coffee."

"If I were your husband," said Churchill, "I'd drink it."[4]

Churchill never came to Geneva; note that he has never come to the United Nations either. But from the early twenties his

[2] Ibid., p. 206.
[3] Collis: *Nancy Astor*, p. 204.
[4] Ibid., p. 77.

righthand man, Anthony Eden, the Beau Brummel of the world, was a habitué at the Quai Wilson. A long, skinny man, he shared with my colleague Derso the talent for looking wonderful no matter what he wore, so that women and haberdashers swooned as he passed. His profile was straight, cut with sharp scissors. He had auburn hair, long, black eyelashes, and a mustache of a forthright red, as if in acquiescence to Darwin's

observation that men and simians have their gaudiest colors on the face.

I suppose it takes a caricaturist with his unabashed eye to step in here and remark that Eden had buck teeth. But I do not do so in malice, only to say that I believe this feature has reference to the personality. Whenever I observe it in a politician, I suspect that despite a certain stubbornness and tenacity, he might turn out, in the long run, to be too vulnerable a soul for political doings. I hold this flattering opinion of Sir Anthony Eden. He was not a born politician, but a shy man who had learned (as did his caricaturist) to be a pacifist in World War I, in which he lost two brothers. His success was to rest chiefly on his career as a fat man's lean man.

A fat millionaire in ideas like Sir Winston is in dire need of a systematic, introverted, departmentalized mind like that of lean

Anthony Eden. But in the thirties, when Eden stood alone as foreign minister, this man of good will was powerless to halt the lowering tread of war; and as prime minister in the fifties, he slipped and fell into the Suez Canal.

There was a fashion in early Victorian England that a person of exquisite cultivation "spoke Persian like a gentlemen." To it we owe FitzGerald's translations of Omar Khayyam. That Sir Anthony Eden, a student of Persian language and letters, still practices this escapist pleasure is far more a key to his real character, I think, than any of his public actions, political or sartorial.

By 1938 the law of *fait accompli* was working so smoothly in Europe that Hitler was able to achieve the abduction of Austria almost without ruffling a hair in Geneva. The only disturbance was caused by Austria, which had presented a Gobelin tapestry to the League and now asked to have it back.

The man who held the ladder during Austria's abduction was Baron Franz von Papen.

If there had ever been a Mr. Diplomat Contest, the Germans might well have run their Franz against Britain's Anthony. Though born a Prussian, to the naked eye he was the very picture of a Viennese gentleman of the old school, with sideburns, kid gloves, and a Malacca cane hung on his arm. He could raise his eyebrows and click his heels with amiability and suavity.

For my purposes I have to look beyond governess-induced demeanor, past the façade erected by tailors and barbers; I have to look at the king naked. Throughout the years, I had built up a network of friendly cookie-pushers of all races, creeds, and nations by whose good graces I could meet important people face to face and get them to sit still long enough to permit their portraits to be drawn. My German accomplice was a young diplomat of the Wilhelmstrasse, Hans Thomsen, a well-pressed son of a good family, discreet, urbane, measured in speech. I must admit that my raking eye failed me in his case: nothing about him pre-

pared me for the day he showed up in Washington as Nazi
chargé d'affaires.

Thomsen had introduced me to Stresemann and Chancellor
Hans Luther. In the summer of 1932, at the Reparations Conference in Lausanne, he made an appointment for me at the
Hôtel Splendide with Herr von Papen. Von Papen received me
with a martial, at-your-service posture proper to a former captain
of the Uhlans, and I noted at once Point Number One in his
favor over Anthony Eden: there was nothing whatsoever wrong
with his dentition. The entire biting area was strong and prog-
nathous; with his deep-set, fast-blinking eyes, beetling brow,
spasmodic grin, abrupt locomotion, and barking voice, he was next
best thing to a chacma baboon. Ruthless aggressiveness was boldly
marked on him, but he was careful to underplay it with urbane
manners.

When a baboon is happy, his lower jaw quivers, and so did
that of Baron von Papen throughout our interview. I showed him
some of our albums. Paging through, he said: "You draw so many
great statesmen." Then he smiled with fraudulent humility and
added: "I am only an *Übergangspolitiker*"—an interim-politician.

This hasty robber baron, cold, cunning, unscrupulous, was as
conceited as a lifeguard at the height of the season, impudent as
a market fly, self-confident as a strutting wrestler. His record
with the diplomatic switchblade was unparalleled in our time. I
stood in a group of journalists at the Reparations Conference on
the evening of the very day Germany had agreed to pay, when
feasible, a final balance of three billion marks. Von Papen told
us: "France imagines she will get money. Not a red penny, I'm
telling you . . . never a red penny!"

It was von Papen who in the beginning had put the Austrian
corporal over on reluctant old von Hindenburg and boosted him
into the chancellorship. He hoped, as vice chancellor, to lead
Hitler by the nose. Failing that, he became Hitler's unscrupulous
tool. With a speech at Marburg he started the blood purge of
1934, to which his own close collaborators fell victim. He himself,

in his villa on the Tiergartenstrasse, received a visit from SS men, who beat him and knocked out all those beautiful teeth I had drawn with such joy. His life was barely saved by Goering.

Incredible as it seems, directly after this beating, he accepted from Hitler the appointment of minister to Austria, in which office he was to engineer the German occupation of that country. But Austria had some respite for a little time, while von Papen's dentist in Berlin constructed for him a set of new, flashy dental plates.

For all his cunning, von Papen was too hasty a man, too much of a hustler to think his plans clean through. He was one of the group imprisoned at Nuremberg after the war. They were all given intelligence tests. At the head of the class was Dr. Hjalmar Schacht. Von Papen came out fifth. Ribbentrop was tenth, and at the tail end of the list was Julius Streicher, the Jew-baiter.

In the courtroom an atrocity film about the concentration camps was shown to these men. Minister of Economics Walter Funk, whose bank had collected gold fillings from the teeth of the victims, wept all the way through. Deputy Fuehrer Rudolf Hess said: "I don't believe it," Economic wizard Schacht was indignant: "How dare they make me sit here with these criminals and watch a film on concentration camp atrocities?" Ribbentrop repeated: "I don't understand." Baldur von Schirach, the handsome leader of the Hitler Youth, said: "I don't know how Germans could do such things." Field Marshal Goering complained: "It was such a good afternoon until they showed that film."[5]

Von Papen sat with his hand on his brow, looking down. He did not watch the screen. Was this devoutly religious man, this believer in God, trying to reconcile his deeds with his religion?

Politicians feel entitled to operate on a different plane of morality from that taught by religion. But when the results of their actions are clear to the sight, it is the "religious" politician who cannot raise his eyes.

[5] G.M. Gilbert: *Nuremberg Diary* (New York: Farrar, Straus & Co.; 1947), p. 147.

Symptomatic of the ferocity that was brewing in the Nazi Party was the episode of the visit to Geneva in 1936 of Herr Greiser, president of the Danzig senate. He had succeeded Hermann Rauschning, who recognized early that Hitler must be mad and bowed out of politics in time to save himself the trouble of being shot out of it.

Herr Greiser had been invited to Geneva to appear before the League Council in connection with some disagreement with the League's high commissioner in the free city of Danzig. On his way, he stopped in Berlin for an interview with Hitler. From that point on, his every word and deed reflected Hitler's intentions toward the League.

On an afternoon in July he appeared at the door of the Disarmament Building accompanied by an apple-cheeked wife in apple green. As was the custom, the guards at the gate asked for

his credentials. Herr Greiser's blue eyes slitted and flashed like ice under a winter sun. "I didn't fly two thousand kilometers to walk another three thousand for a ticket," he snapped. Then he made a sign to his wife: *"Komm, Püppchen!"*—Come, little doll!—and dashed up the steps like a furious polar bear, followed, a little behind, by *Püppchen*.

I was standing at the top of the steps with a group of journalists,

watching his swift approach, and I saw the black pupils of his
ice-blue eyes vibrating with murderous gleam. His cheekbones
were immense, primitive. Pausing at the top of the steps, he said
to us with a saber-toothed growl: *"Höchste Zeit dass ein deutsches
Bombengeschwader hier darüberfliegt!"*—High time a German
bomber squadron flew over this place.

He sat down at the council table and pulled out of his pocket a
speech Goebbels had given him. I watched his motions, as I always watch the gestures of politicians, because they are revealing: Kennedy jabbing downward, Truman chopping with two
hands held straight, Khrushchev waving his little fists. Greiser
balled his fists like clubs and with every word he shook them close
to his clenched teeth. He spoke in German, and I made these
notes:

> I am authorized to speak in the name of the entire Ger-
> man people. This is *the "erster Vorstoss auf dem Wege der
> Revision"*—the first attack toward revision. What has the
> League done to alleviate the economic crisis in Danzig?
> Nothing. She had gone about the business with characteristic
> sluggishness. In the next three months the German people
> expect the League to do something "that I may be spared
> the trouble of appearing before this . . . this . . ." and he
> added, with profound disdain, "this League of Nations."

He then arranged his papers into a pile, slammed it on the
council table with a bang, leaned back in his chair, threw up his
chin, and bawled: "And now I feel better!" He lit a cigarette
and blew clouds of smoke under the nose of Titulescu.

During Greiser's speech, Anthony Eden, who was presiding,
massaged his face and fingered his mustache. He now said: "It
was only a polite act that the Council requested the visit of Mr.
Greiser. Now the Council unanimously regrets Mr. Greiser's
manner."

The Australian member, used to dealing with kangaroos, added
with somewhat greater acerbity: "The League of Nations is not

accustomed to this tone of voice. The behavior of Mr. Greiser will not enhance the prestige of the Danzig Senate."

Greiser heard this with subdued rage. The Council then thanked him for his appearance. He rose from his place, strutted up to Eden, and for the first time in history the Hitler salute was thrust under the nose of the president of the League Council. Then he turned to Secretary General Avenol and again gave the Hitler salute. A rustle of amusement was heard. As Herr Greiser walked by the press gallery, where I sat in the front row, he stopped directly in front of me, put out his tongue, and thumbed his nose at all of us. There were shouts: "Disgrace! . . . Shame! . . . Mr. President!" Robert Dell, the mustached old musketeer of the *Manchester Guardian*, jumped to his feet and, in his emotion quite forgetting that he and Mr. Eden were both Englishmen, burst out in French: "*Monsieur le Président . . . Monsieur le Président . . . cet homme a fait à la presse. . . .*" Not knowing the French expression for thumbing the nose, he stumbled ahead: "*Il a fait . . . il a fait . . . comme ça . . .*" and he thumbed his nose in the direction of Anthony Eden.

In the electric atmosphere, no one laughed. Eden, who had seen only Greiser's retreating back, said: "I have seen no incident. If there was such a thing, we had better disregard it."

Herr Greiser left the chamber and plump *Püppchen* rose from the side rows reserved for admirers of delegates and followed him. Everyone supposed that after such an incident he had left the building. Not at all. After the meeting adjourned, we found him sitting in the corridor with two secretaries and *Püppchen*, having tea. A hundred journalists surrounded him. There were shouts: "Nazi swine! This isn't the Council! We do as we like here! Get out!" A fist fight was in the making when Mr. Stencek, a high official of the League, saved the situation by advising Greiser to leave at once. As he left the building, a journalist called after him: "*Auf Wiedersehen!*"

Indeed, the press was to see Mr. Greiser again. On April 5, 1945, *The New York Times* reported: "Arthur Greiser, overlord of the Posen district of Poland, one of the most detested of all Nazis, high on the list of war criminals, has been captured by the Red Army . . . at the mass execution for which he was best known he compelled the victims to dig a mass grave. They were then chained together in groups. Germans fired into their backs. As the first group fell into the prepared grave, those in the second group were forced to cover the bodies with straw. Then they were shot . . . Greiser had selected as the execution field the ground behind a church . . . young Nazis acted as though they were at a circus, shouting with glee as the victims fell."

And one year later, in July, exactly ten years after he had called the Nazi curse down on the family of nations, *The New York Times* reported: "Weak-kneed and solemnly mumbling prayers, one-time Nazi Gauleiter Arthur Greiser . . . was hanged from a newly-erected scaffold in Citadel Place early today before a crowd of 15,000 . . . the black-garbed white-gloved hangman quickly slung the noose around Greiser's neck and the trap was sprung.

"Although his neck was broken, Greiser continued to squirm for seven minutes before the physicians pronounced him dead."

This monstrous man, who, even as I saw him in 1936, was shaped in such wickedness that I shuddered as he passed me on the steps of the Disarmament Building, contended throughout his trial that he was innocent, that he had been forced to obey orders given by Hitler and Himmler. And he promised that if his life were spared, he would serve Comrade Stalin faithfully for the rest of his life.

Diplomatic bon ton, its language and manners, is not accidental. It was painstakingly constructed by *chefs de protocole* through the centuries during which Europe was divided into touchy little states. These courtiers were anxious to spare feelings and broken heads among ambassadors and facilitate civilized communication in a savage profession. In the nineteen thirties, as the Musclemen came to power, the historic structure fell to ruin.

My friend Ladislas Farago, strictly from Hungary, was in those
days a reporter for *The New York Times'* Wide World photo
agency in Berlin. Every Friday his company called the Chancellery to inform themselves of the Fuehrer's weekend plans so that
they could send a photographer to cover any noteworthy events.
One day Farago made the call and it was answered by Hitler's
adjutant, Lieutenant Brueckner.

"Would you be good enough, sir, to inform us of the Fuehrer's
weekend plans?"

"It's none of your damned business!" shouted Brueckner.

Farago's Hussar blood boiled up and he spluttered: "How dare
you . . . how dare you . . . talk like that to *The New York Times?*"

"Leck' mich am Arsch!"—You can kiss my ass—snarled Brueckner and hung up.

Diplomatic language never quite recovered from the shaking it
had in the thirties.

As the decade wore on, its ghastliest secret was disclosed: that
in order to appease the rage of Hitler and buy his services against
Bolshevism, an entire people was to be delivered into his hands.

There was an ancient people, the Carthaginians, who paid
homage to the abominable god Moloch. When their prosperity
was threatened, they were called upon to place their children,
alive, in the god's bronze hands, whence they were dropped into
a fiery furnace. The leading families of Carthage, not wishing to
dispose of their own children in this way, bought other people's
babes and substituted them for their own.

In the twentieth century after Christ, the leading families of
Western Europe would have sworn to you that their cultural
roots lay with noble Romans and wise Greeks. But when nobility
and wisdom were asked of them, they took their cue from the
Carthaginians. They used the children of Israel as currency to
buy peace.

Once Deskaheh, Chief of the Cayuga Nation, had come to
Geneva to show the world how helpless the League was to aid

an Indian against a real-estate man. Now we saw that the League
was also unable to save scientists, university professors, musicians,
doctors, old rabbis, women, and little children from a depraved
government.

Early in March 1938, Derso and I made a huge, sad painting: a
sea of refugees fleeing before trampling, bloody boots, but halted
by a huge hand clad in the white kid glove of diplomacy.

That was the plight of the Jews as we saw it then, and it continued, relentlessly, to be their fate until six million of them, along
with millions of youths of all races, creeds, and nations, and a
handful of madmen, were dead.

For some time an American phenomenon—dollars—had been
interfering with my life. In the early thirties, the magazine *Vanity
Fair* published some of my sketches. Its editor, Clare Boothe
(whom I saw in my mind's eye as a motherly editorial type),
offered me a guarantee if I would come to the United States for
a visit. I reasoned in this way: Americans, when they make money,
come to Europe to have a good time. I was making money and
already having a good time.

Prentiss Gilbert, the American consul, told me there was something wrong with my reasoning.

Prentiss Gilbert was one of the most colorful habitués of the
Brasserie Bavaria. A tall, sad-eyed man who moved in slow motion,
who never wore a hat and never took his hand out of his trousers
pocket, he had about him a specifically transatlantic aura suggestive of Ambrose Bierce and Teddy Roosevelt—the intellectual
cum adventurer. At the age of sixteen he had fought in the
Spanish-American War; afterwards he became a world traveler and
writer, and then a teacher of dramatics at the University of
Rochester and at Columbia. During World War I he was an
Intelligence officer and had gravitated finally into the State Department.

He was the American consul by title, but was in fact much
more than that: he was his country's watchdog on the Geneva

scene, the first and only American diplomat to be invited to sit at the horseshoe table of the League's Council. This happened during the Manchurian crisis.

His consulate was extravagantly overstaffed. I learned that only two of its members were occupied with filling out forms in triplicate. The others were there to learn about international politics and the art of diplomacy under Gilbert's tutelage. He ran a veritable school for ambassadors, with the events in Geneva providing field study for his pupils.

In 1937 Gilbert realized that his school would have to disband, and he commissioned Derso and myself to make a drawing in lieu of a graduation photo. We showed him in Napoleonic uniform, reviewing his troop of six young men and saying, as Napoleon once said: "Every man in my army has a Marshal's *baton* in his knapsack."

I wish he had lived to see young Llewellyn E. (Tommy) Thompson become United States ambassador to Moscow; James W. Riddleberger, ambassador to Athens; and Jacob Beam, as ambassador to Warsaw, riding a better car than the one he tried to unload on me for five dollars.

Diplomats, by training, are lonely men. The "top secret," the "highly confidential," the "classified" enter their bloodstream; they develop a professional distrust, like pawnshop owners, and in everyone suspect a traitor or a secret agent. It is only the odd career diplomat who dares to form a friendship with a Hungarian caricaturist!

But a man like Gilbert, who had a full life outside diplomacy and time to build up a body of personal—rather than official— wisdom, does not shed the habit of placing confidence in people. Once when like a good diplomat I said what good I could about a very distinguished visiting American, he made a melancholy face and replied, like a good caricaturist: "I don't like men with small mouths."

He became our valued friend, whose curious ambition it was to make American citizens out of us. When finally we arrived in

America and sent him a Christmas card to Nazi Berlin, where he had become *chargé d'affaires,* he replied with a long, nostalgic letter recalling the good years we had spent together. Only a week after, he died of a heart attack.

One day, at the Bavaria, another American friend, Jay Allen, correspondent of the *Chicago Tribune,* told us that he was about to become editor of a new magazine that was to be published in the United States and wanted to use our drawings. He named prices, which, like all things in America, are bigger than anywhere else. We gave him a number of prints, which he carried across the Atlantic several times and on to the Spanish battle front before he finally deposited them on the proper desk. He then admonished us: "If you ever hear from the guy, don't let on you know me. I've quit." Plush jobs come and go in America quicker than anywhere else.

In the winter of 1938 we were ice-skating in Mégève when a pageboy on skates delivered a cable from Chicago: PREPARE DOUBLE IN COLOR, GINGRICH. We had never heard that name, and Derso, who is not a man to leap at the sound of a work whistle, was all for forgetting it at once. But I felt Fate banging on the door, and I talked him into returning to Geneva with me to check on this peremptory Gingrich in the files of the League library. We did so and found that he was seventy years old, the editor of a magazine—no doubt a venerable sheet—called *Esquire.* We prepared for him, therefore, a colored double spread.

Shortly afterward, in Paris, we met an Arnold Gingrich, about thirty-five years of age, and we asked him how his father was. When we finally got untangled, we learned that this youthful editorial genius and squire of *Esquire* was embarking on a new enterprise: he was going to create a magazine devoted to politics, which would tell the American people the unvarnished TRUTH; and we were to be among its regular contributors. It was to be called *Ken,* after the Scottish verb meaning *know.*

Ken was born. It declared that there would be a Second World

War; that Japanese fishermen the length and breadth of the Pacific carried little cameras with them and were spies; that the Nazis had a Brown House in Paris whence a certain Otto Abetz distributed money to the press. A batty French general, through my persuasion, gave *Ken* an article in which he daringly predicted that the war would be fought in Africa.

But in that happy land where no red-berry bushes delineated the path of trenches, whose cruelest history had recently become a romantic chapter in *Gone with the Wind*, *Ken* was damned. Of the first issue, *The New Yorker* critic wrote that he had counted so many gallons of blood, so many dozens of dead rats, and so many corpses, that his suggestion to the publisher was to get the memoirs of Shirley Temple. Ernest Hemingway, a contributor, tore his first issue in two; only a strong man could have done it since the first issue contained forty-six pages of advertising. Such opinions were a mere buzzing of flies compared to the wrath of the advertisers. They informed the publisher that if *Ken* persisted in its warmongering and lack of confidence in the American way of life, they would take out their revenge on *Esquire*. They did. *Esquire*, in one issue, lost $50,000 worth of advertising, and in order to keep the Petty and Varga girls bulging, *Ken* bought Shirley Temple's memoirs posthaste.

Ken, indeed, might well have been edited by the ghost of Lux: it walked onto the world stage and committed suicide. But while it lasted, Derso and I forsook diplomatic niceties and drew the world as we saw it shaping up around us: there were the refugees; and Jews shot dead; and cannon factories very much alive; and there was Hitler, as Gulliver, sprawled across the great field of Europe, twiddling with his fingers such Lilliputians as Neville Chamberlain, Lord Halifax, and Daladier.

Hitler in Austria, Mussolini in Ethiopia, Matsuoka in Manchukuo, Franco with his Moors and Nazis and Fascists in Spain— those who had once believed in the League of Nations wandered its corridors like sick flies. My last good memory of Geneva is of

Ferenc Molnar, who came after the Lido season was over in 1938 and sat in a little sidewalk café of the kind he liked. When I heard he was there, I hurried to him, and he opened his arms and sang out: "Kelen! Where have you been? This we'll celebrate. *Garçon! Une fine.*" And for himself he ordered cognac.

He showered so generously on us Hungarians the jewels of his wit and his wisdom, hard-hitting and yet caressing, like the slap Liliom gave his daughter; but he never bought us so much as an apple. We called him parsimonious, but I rather think he was just afraid that if he bought somebody a *fine* he would one day die of starvation. A great playwright, but no hero, he had bought a house in Budapest, in the Zsigmond Utca, opposite the fire station, in case his house should burn down; and now, with the world about to burst into flame, he came to Geneva because the League of Nations was still the nearest thing to a fire station the world had.

Day after day, Derso and I dined with him and watched his strange ritual: after dinner he would wipe his monocle with his napkin; then, under the table, he would wipe his dental plate with the same napkin. This practice horrified and worried Derso. "One day he'll make a mistake," he said. "He'll put his monocle into his mouth and his false teeth into his eye."

And now the season's pilgrimage began. Just as nowadays anybody who is anybody visits the Kremlin, in those years the great of the world—Lloyd George, Sir John Simon, Anthony Eden, Lord Halifax, Lord Londonderry, Charles Lindbergh, Neville Chamberlain—visited Berchtesgaden; and as the decade drew to a close, they tended to do so in a mood of appeasement, like Henry IV going to the Pope at Canossa.

Our menu card for the year 1938 was done. It represented a druidic feast, with Eamon de Valera, president of the Nineteenth Assembly of the League of Nations, dressed as a bard, singing a Celtic lament. De Valera was a tall, hungry, bird-faced man, thin of nose and lips, and taciturn. In Hungary, before the printing press became popular, whenever a man died, the news was carried from house to house by a professional messenger clothed in black, with a stovepipe hat on his head from which long mourning weeds floated. He carried a long stick with a lemon affixed on the top. Eamon de Valera would have graced this profession. He was well cast to sing from the Ballad of Oisin: *Oh, how lamentable the news thou tellest me, O Cleric.*

Our wretched maiden, Miss Geneva, had donned wings and

contorted herself into the shape of a harp to accompany the last melody that would ever be sung in her honor.

This girl of ours had changed since first we drew her in her skinny innocence, and then in her full-blown beauty as she danced with those who courted her. It was but a year since she had been installed in the sumptuous new Palais des Nations, and His Highness the Aga Khan, always generous to poor girls, had thrown her a magnificent party in which three thousand bottles of champagne had been pushed to and fro on the go-carts that usually served to carry documents.

But after this hour of glory, she had gone to seed. She had grown short-sighted and had to wear thick glasses; she had developed a taste for silly hats—one I recall was made out of the shell of a snail, snail and all; and her nose was red from weeping, for

MUNICH MINUET

she was a maid betrayed. She had been abandoned by her be-
gettors, jilted by her suitors, and raped; but more devastating than
all of this, she had lost the love of those whose guardian angel she
was born to be. The people turned against the League of Nations,
and our girl was doomed.

When in the Brasserie Bavaria, that tumultuous market place
of bad news, I learned that Chamberlain had taken his umbrella to Munich, that the press luncheon was cancelled, that the
delegates to the Nineteenth, and last, Assembly of the League of
Nations were fleeing like rabbits, I rolled up the latest pencil
sketch we had made of Miss Geneva and walked over to the office
of Prentiss Gilbert to ask for a visa.

Early
Pioneering Days

For a long time I lingered in Paris with an American visa in my pocket, unable to tear myself away from the artist's life I lived, between assemblies and conferences, in Montparnasse, where the wise French tolerate a concentration camp for harmless lunatics. Just as in cartoon films the laws of physics are suspended, in Montparnasse the laws of ordinary behavior are suspended. It was an island paradise for me. After the mannered behavior of the diplomatic world, I could live there like a beachcomber, among the wits and half-wits of the cafés, those with rings in their ears and those with rings in their noses.

It was still 1938, Christmas was in the offing, and the world was at peace. Yet I felt, as so many years before I had felt when I left Hungary, that I had come to another break; and that whatever I should leave behind me, I'd never find again. Going to America seemed to me like falling off the edge of the world.

In December, nine months before war broke out, Herr von Ribbentrop came to Paris to sign—as you might have guessed—a friendship pact with France. A reception was held in the Hôtel de Ville, which leading French politicians refused to attend. But this is just the sort of affair caricaturists do not miss.

Sad to relate, throughout my career my merits as a caricaturist had gone unnoticed in royal circles. Derso, an the other hand, had been honored by King Peter of Yugoslavia, who bestowed on him the Order of the Holy Sava, a golden crown to be worn around the neck on a blue, white, and blue ribbon attached to the back collar button. On the gala occasion when Derso had stood before the king in the royal palace in Belgrade, and the chamberlain had attempted to hang this decoration around his neck, a difficulty arose: the chamberlain couldn't locate the collar button. Indeed, there was none; Derso had attached his collar to his shirt with a paper clip. After some fruitless fumbling, both gentlemen excused themselves and repaired to the men's room, where the chamberlain somehow managed to decorate Derso with the Order of the Holy Sava.

On the evening of the Ribbentrop reception, Derso asked me: "Shall I wear my decoration?" Knowing that I should have the privilege of standing next to him, I replied with an unqualified "Yes!"

We entered the Hôtel de Ville, where a flunky dressed in the manner of an eighteenth-century field marshal announced our arrival in resonant tones. Derso entered like a papal ambassador who has left all his decorations at home save the one with a blue, white, and blue ribbon which suits his pale complexion. But when he came face to face with the guest of honor, Herr von Ribbentrop, surrounded by a galaxy of Nazi generals in field-gray uniforms crisscrossed by rainbows and pockmarked from larynx to pancreas with moons, suns, stars, and crosses, he stopped dead in his tracks. A feeling of inferiority gripped him. He retired briefly, then reappeared shorn of the Holy Sava. The decoration he had received in a room marked *Za Gospodu* he relinquished in a room marked *Messieurs*.

He never wore it again. But one day, in his travels, the Holy Sava disappeared from his hotel room as old socks and handkerchiefs do, and as finally the royal family of Yugoslavia did.

In those days I belonged to a society of artists and writers who called themselves the Trente et Quarante. Our only common bond was that we worshipped food and were between thirty and forty years of age. We met once a month for a seven-course dinner at the Auberge de la Belle Aurore, on the rue Gomboust. We were dining there on the evening of the day the friendship pact was signed, when the owner came to our table to tell us that some Nazi journalists from Ribbentrop's entourage had just entered the premises. "Let's invite them over," we said.

Two Teutonic piano-movers came to our table. One of them, the editor of the *Westdeutscher Beobachter*, sat down next to me. Wine flowed, and patriotic ardor ran over. A French journalist put his foot on the table and, rolling his trousers to the knee, revealed a deep scar and proclaimed: "That's what I got at Verdun!" Like a jack rabbit the Nazi next to me jumped up, unbuttoned his trousers, pulled out his shirt, and displayed a bullet hole in his naked belly. "That's what I got in the Ardennes!" he shouted.

If patriotism had run its course, it would have stripped us all naked, because most of us in that age group had bullet holes in some part of our anatomies. Somehow pacifism prevailed, and the editor of the *Westdeutscher Beobachter* told us about the last *Parteitag*, when the Fuehrer had received the editors of Nazi papers and complained that the Third Reich had a sad lack of caricaturists. "We need caricaturists," said the Fuehrer, "like those two fellows in Geneva—what are their names?"

"Derso and Kelen," somebody said.

"Yes," said Hitler, "they are the ones."

When he was told that Kelen was sitting at his side, the bullet almost fell out of the editor's stomach, and he turned on me a gaze full of admiration.

When the Germans occupied Paris, the Gestapo paid several visits to my studio and repeatedly questioned the maid about my health. They finally convinced themselves that I had left for America: two large trucks drove up to the house and took away everything I owned. It's nice that the Fuehrer admired my work, but did he have to admire my Persian carpets too?

About the same time that von Ribbentrop came to Paris, from the opposite direction came Albin (Jack) Johnson, commissioner for European participation in the New York World's Fair. This gentleman knew how to deal with governments, and also caricaturists. He grabbed Derso and me by the ears and took us to a travel bureau, where he reserved passage to New York for us. If there was any chance of giving destiny the slip, Derso ruined it. He went to a dinner of the Anglo-American press and, finding himself seated next to a hungry-looking bald-pated gentleman, he confided to him his lifelong hatred of all official forms that are filled out in quintuplicate, holding that all such forms are basically unnecessary. "Look at me," he said. "I have lived in Paris for fifteen years without a residence permit!"

"I don't believe we've met," said the bald gentleman. "My name is Monsieur Langeron, and I am the chief of police of the city of Paris."

On December 13, 1938, we embarked on the S.S. *Champlain* bound for New York. We arrived there on December 21, at 7 p.m. At 8 p.m. I tasted for the first time *le hot dog*. American friends met us and asked: "How do you like America?" They should have asked how I liked the hot dog. I was to learn that Americans never inquire, as the French do, how you have enjoyed your last meal. They seem to know that this is an explosive question.

It takes a while to discover a country. You see the nonsense first and only afterwards the sense. There are miracles that wear off and miracles you never get used to. After twenty-five years I have learned to believe that $3.95 is not $4.00. I know that anything that comes "free" is expensive. I am aware that if I don't rush into the subway, the turnstile will thwack me in the hind quarters.

But the sight of the New York skyline, that mutiny of earth against sky, majestic in its barbarism as a gargantuan Stonehenge, and the women on Fifth Avenue wearing slacks, these took my breath away when I first saw them, and they still do, because the New York skyline has a thousand aspects, and so do women's slacks.

Those concrete mastodons of New York, so gray and grave on cloudy days, so light and airy on a creamy morning, and through the misty rain as unsubstantial as a child's breath on a cold windowpane, have some pleasant surprises between their feet. I could not have imagined finding under the stern stare of Rockefeller Center a skating rink with a kaleidoscope of little children whirling on it; or at the bottom of these oppressive piles of steel and stone, windows like aquariums filled with technicolor wonders; or upon entering a hole in a concrete block, a warm, cozy lobby lighted dimly with dainty lamps on gilded tables, a pretty place utterly unlike the vestibules of European apartment houses, which are stark and cold as crypts.

I have a mind like a puppy: I imagine everything human is my concern. When I saw two men quarreling in the street, I stood and listened. Street quarrels are not typically an American pastime; they happen far more frequently in Paris than in New York. But this transatlantic quarrel baffled me because when one of the parties ran out of arguments he shouted angrily at the other: "I am an American citizen and I pay my taxes!"

Now here was something new. No fighting Frenchman would think of calling attention to his citizenship, still less publicly admit that he had paid his taxes. But among Americans there is a pervading sense of gratitude for their citizenship; and they wear

the receipt from the Collector of Internal Revenue like the
Légion d'honneur.

A Hungarian who wants to gain a proper understanding of his
new country naturally seeks out another Hungarian to give it to
him. I found Iles Brody, with whom years before in Budapest I
had been attacked by a Lenin-boy with a gun. Since Hungary exports horses, food, and girls, Brody had hired out to *Esquire* as an
expert on horses and food; he now wished to show me that he
was well ahead in the girl department. "What you must see," he
said, "is a burlesque show." I agreed.

We sat in the Eltinge Theater, on Forty-second Street, in a
twilight hotter than ashes, and around us was a congregation of
awestruck males, who, though seemingly a uniform mass, har-
bored individual thoughts regarding the redhead onstage who
was peeling off in bits whatever the prop man had put on her.
Fresh out of Paris, I found these activities more provocative in
their primitive simplicity than any device of the French. But just
when the redhead had got herself good and naked and ought to
have stayed awhile, she dodged into the wings, giving us a last
wink with half a haunch. There followed a hootchy-kootchy dance
performed by blasé blondes who kicked up more dust than a herd
of buffalo. Suddenly my friend Brody exclaimed: "Suzy! That
blonde on the right! That's Suzy, a girl friend of mine."

He proceeded to light one match after another, holding them
close to his face until his fingers sizzled, in the hope that Suzy
would notice him in the darkened orchestra. But Suzy waved not
and neither did she wink with any part of her anatomy. "We'd
better wait for her after the show at the stage door," said Brody.

We waited for some time, but Suzy did not emerge. We
sneaked back into the darkened theater, where on the lighted
stage we saw that romantic rehearsal scene, so familiar in Hollywood movies, in which girls in panties and pullovers kick up their
heels to a tinny tune from an upright piano, while a hoarse
gymnast barks at them. As we came down the shadowy aisles, a

shrimp scuttered up and blocked our path. "What do you want?" he asked.

"We want to see Suzy," said Brody.

"Sam!" shouted the little man. "These gentlemen wish to see Suzy."

A huge slab of a stagehand in overalls moved in from the side, towering over us.

"So you want to see Suzy?"

"Yes."

"Giddout!" thundered Sam.

"Oh no," said Brody, pulling out his wallet. "I am from *Esquire*. Here is my press card."

"Gi-i-i-DOUT!" hollered Sam. The "gid" was long, the "out" was short, and we got out. They say the pen is mightier than the sword, but on Forty-second Street, Sam is bigger than both of them.

In a Hungarian restaurant on Seventy-ninth Street I asked the waiter if he was married. "What, me marry!" he exclaimed indignantly. "And have American children? Never!"

He explained to me that American children are noisy. In time I tested his statement by becoming an American father, and it is the truth.

But it remains a riddle to me why these noisy children grow up to be such quiet adults. Quiet French children, on the other hand, grow up to be noisy adults.

The average American keeps calm and speaks in level tones on a low key. I have never seen an American audience hoot even the worst performer off a stage, as the French do. To make a noise the American adult needs a special pretext such as a convention, or a fire engine, or a police car.

One day I entered a drugstore and asked for a glass of luke-warm milk. The soda jerk, whose routine it is to push a button and splash out ice-cold milk, looked at me aghast.

"What did you want?"

"A glass of lukewarm milk."

He called the manager. "This man," he said, "wants lukewarm milk."

The manager took my measure with a side glance, then instructed his lieutenant: "Take a pan, fill it with cold milk, put the pan on the burner. When the milk begins to steam, pour the contents of the pan into a glass and hand it to the customer."

The young man listened earnestly. He learned to make lukewarm milk that day. I learned to like my milk ice-cold.

Soon I'd take my plunge into the melting pot and be rendered into an American like the rest of the Hungarians, Czechs, Poles, Irish, Swedes, and what not. My children would not speak the sweet private language of their father, and the best I could hope was that they would know how to appreciate a *puszta*-educated chicken paprika.

The melting pot operates not by coercion, but by osmosis. This gives rise to certain phenomena: you can dine in a restaurant called the Chinese Rathskeller; you can buy kosher pickles bottled by S.S. Pierce of Boston, or Buitoni Chinese egg roll, or Mother's Gefillte Fish d'Oeuvres, an etymological monstrosity, but a tasty dish.

The tribalism of our old Austro-Hungarian Empire did not survive the melting pot. In a Czech or Austrian restaurant I am likely to be treated like a fellow Central European, slightly more on the human side than an Irishman or a Swede. One hears nothing like "Lithuania for the Lithuanians," or "Germany for the Aryans." America is a framework built to embrace many, even with stress and strain. The framework is under strain today as America seeks to "integrate."

For me, coming from Europe, where chauvinism and intolerance were girding for the most bloody ordeal in history, the miracle of America was not so much the melting pot itself as those myriad national groups in New York which still speak their native language, dance their national dances, sing their old songs, parade in national costume, pray as they choose, with nobody to bother them.

I am always deeply touched when governments let people be.

I met my first American politicians at the New York World's Fair, where Derso and I were put to work by Jack Johnson and

greeted by Grover Whalen, who would have deserved his position as Official Greeter of New York City if only for his enormous hand.

I met and drew the Little Flower, Fiorello H. La Guardia, the balloon-shaped mayor of New York, who spoke enough Hungarian to have a fractured conversation with me. He told me that his sister, Gamma, had married a Hungarian and lived in Budapest. This brother-in-law, a Jew, was later to be deported by the Nazis to Mauthausen, and there beaten so severely that he died in the arms of another inmate, Zoltan Klar, who today edits the Hungarian weekly *Az Ember* in New York.

La Guardia was a pocket edition of the type of man I call the human dynamo: a Round Man with plenty of hard muscle under the fat. Thus has nature shaped countless mayors, *Bürgermeister*, and headmen of countless towns, cities, and tribes the world over. Such men are born showmen with a natural

yearning for the limelight. La Guardia loved to lead the band; he would not have missed an important fire; with his own hands he smashed slot machines; and during a newspaper-delivery strike, who read the comics to the kiddies over the radio? The Little Flower himself, with a voice like a bagpipe. He succeeded in making the New York multitudes feel that they were all citizens of a small town with a brother-in-law for mayor.

Like everyone in my human-dynamo pigeonhole, he was a hypomanic man with a well-lubricated mind and body, who did what came naturally. He lost his temper easily and showered insults on all around him. Once he had let off steam, he would give anything to cheer up the needy—except perhaps his fireman's hat.

La Guardia was an amateur of everything, and a professional in just one thing: politics. He knew all the low blows, the high blows, the kidney punches, the rabbit punches, and the knee drops. He knew how to stay in power and at the same time serve New Yorkers, for whom he felt genuine affection. He was himself a meatball from the melting pot, with an Italian father and a Jewish mother.

La Guardia relied heavily in his election campaigns on the ethnic groups of New York City. In a campaign which took place shortly after my arrival, he appointed a certain Hungarian, whom I'll call Mr. Z before I think of something worse, to be his public-relations manager among the national minorities. This Mr. Z had the meritorious idea of organizing a La Guardia poster contest among artists of exotic extraction, and he invited me to participate.

I'd rather buy a bogus sweepstake ticket than enter a poster contest, and I told him so. But Mr. Z knew how to catch a Hungarian bird by the beak. Most of the contestants, he told me, would be schoolchildren. It was tremendously important to the prestige of La Guardia that an artist of my standing should participate, and after all, *somebody* had to draw a decent poster for the Little Flower. Naturally, I'd win first prize.

I drew a spectacular black-eyed Susan growing out of the New York skyline. The center of the daisy was Fiorello's head, and each petal bore the name of something he had built or accomplished: the Triborough Bridge, La Guardia Airport, and so forth. I sent the poster to the exhibition, which was held in City Hall.

The first prize went to an eleven-year-old Negro girl. The second prize went to a thirteen-year-old Jewish girl. I got nothing. I took a carving knife and went down to City Hall to kill Mr. Z. I found the lobby boiling with Hungarian artists, Henry Major, Marcel Vertès, André Dugo, all with carving knives and all howling for the first prize Mr. Z had promised them. The culprit, naturally, was not to be found, for he had gone underground. He remained incommunicado for two full weeks before I finally got him on the telephone by giving a false name. After I had let him have a shampoo in our native language, he replied in the most natural tone of voice: "Mr. Kelen, you didn't really think it was a poster contest, did you? It was politics."

On the day the World's Fair opened, I saw Franklin Delano Roosevelt for the first time.

The feature of a man's face that strikes you first always has a significant reference to his personality. In the case of FDR it

was, of course, his jaw, massive and challenging, and he used it as men use hands and elephants use trunks, for meaningful gesticulation. In time I was to study many photos of the president, and I made a singular discovery about this jaw: it wasn't really there!

FDR's childhood photos show clearly a little boy with a voluminous brain case and small, pointed chin—the triangular face of childhood. In adulthood, and especially after his illness, the lower part of the face began to accumulate fat and muscle, and by middle age he had even developed a round, hard, chin-eminence like his mother's. This was the defiant Roosevelt jaw we remember. But in his last photo, taken shortly before his death, the weight around the jaw had gone, and the triangular face of childhood had reappeared.

The body build of each man consists of a mixture of three basic types; and at different periods in his life different types might become prominent. It is my belief that these changes correspond to similar changes in temperament. In some people these changes are extraordinary; among famous people—such as Florence Nightingale—they become a puzzle to biographers.

FDR needed to fight. His fighting jaw assisted him through all his fighting years. But when, with all the battles won, he slipped into illness and death, the jaw left him.

What did not change in Roosevelt from childhood to death were the tight-set eyes, alert to the world within and without; and the long, delicate midface. These are the trademark of the soul-searcher, sensitive and idealistic. In FDR, they showed an introvert in an extrovert business.

Derso visited President Roosevelt in his office shortly after our arrival and was the first to tell me about the ornaments and toys that densely populated his desk. He was an all-round collector; he collected stamps, birds, books. Like all collectors, he must have been vulnerable and in need of firm friendship, for the love one invests in inanimate objects is safe from deception.

"Cactus" Jack Garner and Jim Farley—these were the friends of political expediency. Roosevelt's lasting friends, his wife Eleanor, Frances Perkins, Harry Hopkins, Robert Sherwood, Cordell Hull, were every one of them sensitive people, yet made of iron.

Roosevelt was a fox grafted onto a lion, which was what Niccolo Machiavelli recommended the prince be. When the prince is also endowed with humanity and compassion, he nears greatness, in spite of any offenses committed by a false fighting jaw.

Derso and I had camped at the Savoy Plaza Hotel pending the time we should make our first million dollars. One morning, about four o'clock, while we were working on a drawing, we heard a feminine voice behind us: "What are you doing, little boys?"

We turned and saw a baby-faced blonde in a wall-to-wall mink coat and a diamond ring the size of a plum on her finger. It seemed she lived next door to us, and following a friendly American custom, she had come to pay us a neighborly visit.

Her name was Peggy Hopkins Joyce; she was a barber's daughter who had become a Ziegfeld Follies girl; and in the land of unlimited opportunity she had collected an unlimited number of husbands and diamonds. She offered to introduce me to New York night life, of which she appeared to be the crowned queen.

Night after night I started out with this lady, tête-à-tête in a taxi, but no sooner did we set foot in a public place than hordes of people gathered around her. By dawn we were an expedition; led by reliable Sherpas, we would assault the heights of strange penthouses to plunder forsaken iceboxes full of pumpernickel, caviar, and champagne. I cannot remember the names of my companions in these early pioneer days in America; they are lost in the sands of the society columns. But one historic phrase I do recall: ". . . and don't you remember, dear, he slapped your face and the tiara fell off your head and cut your nose?"

What impressed me greatly about New York night life were those night-club owners who ruled like feudal lords and were buddies with presidents. Whenever they said anything fit to print in the morning papers, it was taken down by scribes; and though they commanded armies of bouncers whose tuxedos were knobby with firearms, they had the democratic habit of cracking the jaws of favored customers with their own fists. Quiet, taxpaying Americans lined up in evening dress along the street on winter nights, waiting for a magnanimous sign from a bouncer-de-luxe that they would be permitted to enter the inner sanctum. Snobbery flourishes everywhere. The French would express theirs by refusing to line up in a blizzard. I had no painful choice to make, because Peggy's mobile diamond collection was welcomed everywhere.

I acted as a sort of Brink's guard to this collection. Once, at seven o'clock in the evening, I was in a taxi with Peggy navigating toward a dinner party three blocks away. She happened to glance through the back window and immediately began to scream hysterically: "We're being followed. Four men in a black car are following us! Driver! Quick! Drive to the nearest police station!"

I couldn't understand then what she was screaming about. But Peggy knew better than I that wild and woolly ways die hard in America. The phantom outlines of the Great Train Robbery are still limned on the landscape. The office girl who hands out pay-envelopes is guarded by a policeman with a drawn revolver; and when an armored car stops in front of a bank on Fifth Avenue, a wall of security men, guns in hand, blocks the sidewalk until the moneybags are safely carried in.

When Peggy Hopkins Joyce clasped her hands to her throat in loyal concern for her best friends and wailed at the dinner hour on Madison Avenue, only a tenderfoot would think there was something odd about it.

Shortly after I arrived in New York, on New Year's Eve, having graduated from several parties in a daze, I wandered in the streets at dawn among the dandified drunks. There was just enough snow in Central Park to make it piebald like an old gypsy's head, and in front of the Plaza Hotel was a giant Christmas tree with decorations that sparkled against the night like colored mica in anthracite. The siren of a fire engine shrieked through the barren streets of the strange city, leaving nerveless silence behind. Suddenly my heart crumbled. I knew that there would be a war.

I had come to this side of the Atlantic to realize with such crushing suddenness the impending catastrophe. The Japanese have a saying: "He who lives beneath the lighthouse doesn't see the light." But entering the year 1939, I understood that the American reporters we considered babes in our political woods had, in fact, seen events in Europe better than we.

The French press in those days was split down the middle. German, Japanese, and Italian money was greasing palms at such a rate that one journalist confused the other, and together they confused public opinion. The British press had no bribery problem—as Robert Dell, of the *Manchester Guardian*, told me: "In order to bribe a British newspaperman, you've got to have a *lot* of money." But both press and public in Britain were hoodwinked by the policy called appeasement.

American journalists did not wear blinkers. Public opinion at home was unanimous: to hell with Europe. American reporters, therefore, could afford the luxury of being objective, and Bill Shirer, Erwin Canham, John Gunther, Bill Hillman, Clarence Streit, Leland Stowe, Dorothy Thompson, and all those who came to the Bavaria had seen clearly what was in store for us.

In the fall of 1939 war broke out, and soon, of Poland, Finland, Norway, and the others, nothing was left but pavilions in Flushing Meadows.

The day the Germans blitzed Poland, I dined at Arpenik's, an Armenian restaurant, on Twenty-seventh Street, with a bearded story-teller named Matchakadzian, and a giant Armenian painter whose name I never knew, but I remember what he said: "This country will be at war in no time. And once we begin to arm, we'll outarm everybody."

Now, how is it that this Armenian painter who didn't even own a necktie knew what my well-pressed friend, Hans Thomsen, Hitler's *Gauleiter* in Washington, did not?

The answer, I believe, lies partly in the textbooks on constitutional psychology. It has been noted that men of predominantly muscular body build tend to overweening self-confidence. Their boundless egotism impairs their most careful calculations. Power-grabbers, dictators, tend to be men of predominant muscularity. That is why Hitler and Mussolini were not aware of the potential of the United States and that of the Soviet Union. That is why Hitler laughed when Roosevelt de-

THAT'S WHAT I GET FOR MARRYING YOU

clared that the United States would build fifty thousand aircraft a year.

This type of man admires and understands only one thing: brute force. Thus, Mussolini was led to make incredible statements about his adversaries. Of Neville Chamberlain, he said: ". . . a tired son of a long line of rich men, not at all of the same stuff as that magnificent adventurer, Francis Drake."

In his totalitarian head he ignored the fact that in a democracy a prime minister can be toppled by a vote. He ought rather to have taken the measure of Winston Churchill.

Of Roosevelt, Mussolini said: "There have been bald kings, fat kings, handsome, and even stupid kings, but never kings who, in order to go to the bathroom and the dinner table, have to be supported by other men."

It escaped him utterly that it is not necessary for an elected leader to drive a hot rod and fence naked. A brain and human compassion are what is needed to lead a democratic population to surpass itself.

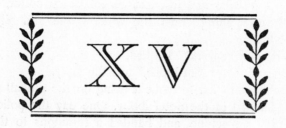

The
Home of the Brave

Just before the war started, *Ken* magazine ceased publication. Night life had impoverished me. I was stranded in a strange country with two trunks to my name, no income, and a partner with the same horoscope. We moved out of the Savoy Plaza straight to the Albert Hotel in Greenwich Village, which was already overflowing with other shipwrecked Hungarians.

When an American is broke, it means he has no money. When a Hungarian is broke, he is a mental case. An American without a job turns his hand to anything; a Hungarian waits until another Hungarian gives him a job. The American knows that he must make a living, the Hungarian feels the world owes him a living.

George May, who had just lost his job as an editor, watched the raindrops running down the windowpane and sighed: "I don't like loafing without pay."

"Why don't you work?" I asked.

"I can't work when I'm broke," was the reply.

For a while we tried to make a living on the pinball machine a newsdealer had in the hotel lobby. One day the police came, confiscated the machine, and handed a summons to the newsdealer for gambling. But he wasn't gambling. We were. The newsdealer was running a perfectly sound enterprise.

Three months after I had gone around with half a million dollars worth of diamonds, I did not have a dime to buy myself baked beans. How short is the road, for an artist, between a luxury hotel and the corridor of the Albert Hotel leading to a door which is locked because he has not paid his bill! To be sure, a warmhearted management opens another room for the night; but where is his toothbrush, his clean socks and shaving cream, his pencil sharpener?

This was a horrifying experience that had not happened to me before, to turn in one week from beau to bum, in seven days to shed all human dignity. I had not realized that human dignity begins only after one's hotel bill is paid.

Yet it is a mistake to think that poverty is dull and riches are glamorous. To be poor, you have to be inventive, brave, crafty, fatalistic, and a dreamer. To be rich, all you need is money. The poor man's life is full of sudden splendors. The rich man's life is nature imitating advertising art.

There had been a time during the inflation in Germany when I'd longed to have an uncle who was a beggar in America. Now that I was in that enviable position myself, I made friends with a brother beggar on Broadway and asked him how to get rich overnight. He fed me the story of the man who wrote the Coca-Cola Company: "Bottle it!" For these two words and an exclamation point he collected $25,000. Within minutes I thought up an equally dazzling scheme which I tried to present to a buyer at Macy's—the owner of whose soul, Mrs. Straus, had not so long ago invited me to dine to meet the director of the Metropolitan Museum of Art—but I discovered that in a democracy it was easier to see the president, whose office is elective, than a buyer at Macy's, whose office is not. I gave my idea to my beggar friend, and he is still a beggar.

I then became associated with a Hungarian publisher of art books who had the bright idea of publishing the Bible in the form of a comic strip to be sold to Sunday Schools in weekly leaflets. He scraped together a bevy of bishops and other learned men and women to form an advisory committee for this enterprise. They decided that Jesus needed a new public image: the longhair favored by Leonardo and El Greco would not do. They directed me to create a modern Christ for modern kids who would be a good deal blonder than usual, and muscular—a Flash Gordon in a short chiton, a trim beard, and no sticky ringlets. A coiffure suggestive of a crew cut was found appropriate. Revealed Gospel was put through the mangle: instead of saying that young Jesus astonished the rabbis by his understanding, we wrote: "Jesus stumps the experts."

In one week we got 75,000 subscriptions. One Sunday School teacher wrote: "This is what I have been praying for all my life."

Far from wishing to revolutionize religious art, my Hungarian publisher milked every penny from his comic strip to feed his regular publication of the works of Leonardo and El Greco. Very soon our printers became ugly, as unpaid printers will—not to speak of unpaid artists. Besides, as the war progressed, it was increasingly difficult to get paper. Subscribers were receiving their Christmas issue for Easter and the Easter issue for Epiphany, and Sunday School teachers everywhere complained they were not getting what they were praying, or paying for.

My publisher decided to unload his burden onto American shoulders. He actually succeeded in finding a printer in Philadelphia who was willing to take over the comic strip. All contracts were ready for signing when the printer changed his mind. "Why?" asked the publisher.

"I've been talking to my lawyer," replied the man from Philadelphia. "He advised me that you can't sue priests."

People who are subject only to heavenly justice have a very poor credit rating, it seems.

After a lifetime spent around my mother's sacred kitchen, and in France, where *Bon Appetit!* stands next to *Vive la France!* as a national slogan, my greatest suffering in being a poor new American was having to accustom myself to the American drugstore cuisine: ham sandwiches flavored with Chanel No. 5, and bread baked with baby powder.

One night I joined forces with a penniless American couple, residents of the Albert Hotel who kept a stove in their room. Having a dollar in my pocket, I offered to buy us all a dozen eggs for an omelette, which, as an ex-*Parisien*, I naturally supposed I would be entreated to cook. Instead, the young American wife arranged the eggs on a pretty Mexican plate and began to pull out of a bottom drawer ketchup, relish, and an ominous can of peas. In answer to my anxious question, she outlined a wicked plot against eggs, on which I placed my seal of disapproval. A heated argument ensued which ended with my seizing the Mexican plate of eggs and heaving it up to the ceiling. The young woman began to cry, while the quiet American husband, eyeing the mess dripping down on his bed, said: "You can't do a thing like that!"

"Why not?" I shouted. "I'm a guest!"

In our distress, Providence sent to Derso and Kelen a Yankee and a Pole. The Pole had a plan and the Yankee a medium-sized advertising agency. The Polish plan was to launch a Derso and Kelen cartoon syndicate dealing with foreign policy. Newspapers would buy our cartoons while the advertising agency, in one easy operation, would buy space. You might call it a reciprocal trade agreement, but in Hungary the idiom was: "Hand washes hand."

"Now gentlemen," said the Yankee, "we'll run this business as *friends*."

The trouble was that the Pole was bossy. It wasn't only that he tried to tell us how to draw editorial cartoons; but when the money came flowing in, he refused to split it then and there, pirate-fashion, as you would do with friends. "That's bad business practice," said he. "The proper way is to render an accounting once a month."

Derso, as we know, has no faith in paper work, and I had none in the Pole. The syndicate was located in the Pole's bedroom; the art department was next door, in Derso's bedroom. One night Derso, in bare feet and striped pyjamas, charged into the Pole's room like a wild zebra and furiously began to destroy all bills, letters, books, every piece of paper he could lay his hands on, shouting hysterically: "There goes your syndicate! There goes your syndicate!" When he caught sight of the Pole watching this horrifying scene from a dark corner, he leapt through the paper blizzard straight at the Pole's throat, still screaming: "There goes your syndicate!"

There went our syndicate, indeed. The next day, when the Yankee partner came to inspect the disaster area, he drawled disapprovingly: "Gentlemen, gentlemen. This isn't friendship any more. This is business."

It can be seen that in the melting pot much of the diplomatic manner was being boiled out of Derso and Kelen.

The Yankee-Pole episode nevertheless had a significance in our lives: it got us back into harness as political caricaturists, and we commenced a collection of American faces. Our Yankee took us to see Jim Farley, a gentleman with a very hard brain case who at the time was seriously considering assuming the office of president in the next election. Farley explained how very simple this would be, because, like a feudal liege, he commanded the "Catholic vote." He seemed to me to be an expeditive man; but I was relieved when in the end he consented to stick to expediting Coca-Cola.

Our Yankee chaperoned us to a dinner at the Republican Club, and over a before-dinner cocktail he said: "I'm going to bring a man to meet you, you ought to take a good look at. He might be the next president of the United States." He brought to our table a bear of a man, soft and untidy. His name was Wendell Willkie, and his political assets seemed to consist of dimples, pugnacity, and a shrewd intellect. Over a Martini he told us that he wouldn't dream of getting mixed up in politics. After dinner, he made a speech in which he elaborated on this theme. Six months later I saw him accept the nomination for president at

JIM FARLEY AND SENATOR WAGNER

the Republican Convention in Philadelphia, where we had been sent to draw pictures for the New York *Post*.

I was immensely curious about those periodic political shindigs in which the Americans temporarily give their country back to the Indians. As a caricaturist, I can't be expected to look down my nose at conventions, as some people do. I went to Philadelphia expecting to have fun, and I found it—good country fun: a gigantic picnic organized by the mayor's entertainment committee in honor of a new fire engine to be presented to the local Voluntary Fire Brigade, with everybody sweating in shirtsleeves and grinning happily. In the background, a brass band beats the gizzard out of a popular tune, while a nightingale with political connections tests her mettle against the tuba. Joe Martin of Massachusetts, chairman of the entertainment committee, beats time with a gavel big enough to fell a buffalo, while intoning that great bipartisan battle cry: *"Clear the aisles!"*

Round about the picnic grounds is the Ladies' Auxiliary bazaar, where you can buy campaign buttons, flags, frankfurters,

"TIELESS" JOE TOLBERT

crackerjacks, and root beer, and throw the soggy paper cups and crumpled straws beside an overflowing wastebasket. Celebrities abound: Jeff Davis, a hobo who said he was the duly-elected Emperor of the League of Hobos of the World; "Tieless" Joe of South Carolina, who told me that in 1888 he had voted for Benjamin Harrison and had never missed a convention since, and had never owned a necktie; an Indian Chief on the warpath selling post cards; General Coxey, a little man with a frog mouth and squinting eyes who carried his shrunken head in the chalice of a winged collar. Before I was born, he had led his army to Washington to force Congress to legislate a relief program for four million unemployed. He was arrested for walking on the White House lawn.

"GENERAL" COXEY

Europeans who believe that Americans tend to overblow their horns find no disillusionment at conventions. I have wondered if this national habit is not rooted in pioneer times, when American forefathers were so obsessed with notions of greatness and achievements against fearful odds that they used to hold boasting contests. Van Wyck Brooks, in *The World of Washington Irving*, speaks of ". . . a harmless showing off, as if their unbounded freedom had gone to men's heads, and they leaped on stumps and flapped their arms, crowing in spread-eagle fashion, while they challenged every comer to a fight." He quotes some typical language: "I'm a ring-tailed squealer. . . . I'm a gentleman, and my name's *Fight*. Foot and hand, tooth and nail, claw and mud-scraper, knife, gun and tomahawk, or any other way you choose to take me, I'm your man! Cock-a-doodle-doo!"

This was the language of Paul Bunyan and Mike Fink, and it survives to this day on Madison Avenue, and at political rallies. Thus we hear the familiar chant: "The Garden State of New Jersey . . . the home of giant tomatoes . . . PASSES!"

Any alternate who accomplishes the hazardous climb to the rostrum is presented as ". . . that grrrreat Amerrrrican!"

I have only one objection to tall talk: nobody believes it. And when a really great American comes along, he is not recognized. A Jefferson, a Lincoln, a Wilson, or a Roosevelt has so much mud thrown at him in his lifetime that it takes centuries to wash him clean.

I stared at everyone, famous and funny. Whenever a committeeman, a senator, a congressman, a governor saw me gazing with indiscreet eyes, he rushed up to me and enveloped my hand in a hospitable fist; for all he knew, I might have been an alternate delegate whose half-vote he needed. Thus I got my hand shaken by a boy who looked like the president of the Hasty Pudding Club, but he was the United States Senator from Massachusetts, Henry Cabot Lodge. His grandfather, Cabot Lodge, had been the first betrayer of my Geneva maid. Yet ten years later, Lodge Jr., looking not a day older, played a starring role in my United Nations television programs as ambassador to the UN.

I also drew Senator Arthur H. Vandenberg of Michigan, a staunch isolationist in Philadelphia, but during the next five years of war he was to help Roosevelt formulate a bipartisan foreign policy, and to urge his country on the first difficult step to internationalism. He was a diehard only in the matter of caricature: he wrote a letter to the New York *Post* protesting against the innocent portrait I had made of him.

Robert Taft was careful to get his hand back before I should put it in my pocket. The senator from Ohio, a perennial candidate, who at every convention was *almost* nominated, walked on eggs with mechanical grace. His laughter lacked sunshine. It was a mere spasm, baring his teeth. Once I saw a girl photographer touch him on the forearm; he jumped away like a goat from an electric fence. Rarely have I met a mimosa-natured politician, but Robert Taft was one. I took note that the campaigning of this introvert man was done by Mrs. Taft, an extrovert woman with dash and common sense. In the following years I came to the opinion that Mr. Taft had a mind like a shoe store: a lot of boxes containing different shoes and no communication between the boxes.

In Philadelphia, I studied the senator's bald pate and the desperate means he took to camouflage it, allowing side hairs to grow long and plastering these across his head. Men who have recourse to this artifice are, from my observation, a different kettle of fish from, let's say, Winston Churchill or Paul-Henri Spaak, who permit their pates to shine in the naked light of day. The former I consider vain, apprehensive, pedantic, and irrational.

They are vain, as they want to have hair where there is none; apprehensive, as they don't want others to notice a capillary de-

ficiency; pedantic, as it is not an easy trick to place the hairs just
so; irrational, as the entire exercise is futile—those hairs will
slip and baldness will shine through.

Despite all this, I think Taft was a great American of noble
spirit and integrity, who throughout his career made an effort to
translate noble abstractions, with pedantic exactitude, into reality.
But his was a rigidly exclusive nature without the gift of com-

promise or a concern with popularity, so that the huge pile of
votes he built up in 1940, 1944, and 1948 jumped away from him
on second ballots with the same alacrity as he jumped away from
the girl photographer.

It was Wendell Willkie whom the Republicans chose in 1940
to send into the arena and "meet the champ," Roosevelt. As his
bandwagon began to roll, it was like a hot rod bearing Elijah
to heaven, with everybody wanting to jump on. The stampede was
reminiscent of a pagan sausage festival. Men and women in paper
hats leapt to their feet brandishing posters, tooting tooters, rattling
rattles, hooting battlecries, chanting, screaming, stomping, forming a great caterpillar which ran in circles like an overheated
steam engine gone mad, while a storm of balloons rose to the
ceiling, and wherever you turned, an oversized ikon of Willkie

collided with your glance. Peter Brueghel should have seen it through my eyes.

There are Americans who are self-conscious about our unconventional conventions and the nonsense of our campaigns and want to change them. But I am not among them. A caricaturist is in his element in pandemonium; but there's more to it than that.

In an autocratic government, it is the Muscleman who grabs power. In a democracy, too, only individuals of strength climb to the top. But in order to get through the filter of campaigns and conventions, he must possess more flexible human qualities than the outright Muscleman. He must satisfy labor, management, ethnic groups, women; he must slap backs and kiss babies with a certain amount of conviction. In a country of huge size, all forces come to a boil at a convention, and, somehow or other, utter confusion serves to throw to the top the best kind of man either party has to offer as president.

I prefer funny hats to steel helmets, bandwagons to armored cars, and smoke-filled rooms to smoke-filled skies. I beg those hell-bent on making order out of chaos to recall the flawless order of the display put on by the *Standartenfuehrers* of the SA on

Hitler's *Parteitag* in 1933 at Nuremberg. That's the recollection
that came to me in Philadelphia, and that is when I took off
my coat and sweated happily.

Like "Tieless" Joe, I became a convention addict, and I have
attended six of them on behalf of various papers and magazines.
In the end, some of the people who shook my hand actually
knew who I was.

I learned to tell a Texan from a New Englander, a Midwest-
erner from a Southerner, not only by their hats, but by their looks.

Professor Franz Boas, who is sometimes called "the father of
American anthropology," was the first to note with calipers that
certain physical changes are taking place in Americans, who are
diverging from the European parent stock. The eye, too, can discern these changes, and others, some of them unmeasurable.
Americans appear to me to be taller and stronger than Europeans;
their heads are bigger, their skin is looser, and their bones are
heavier. They are strikingly longer in the rump and narrower
in the hips.

Closest to the Europeans in looks, I think, are the New Eng-
landers; the farthest, therefore the most American in looks, are
the Midwesterners. Midwesterners seem to produce not only
surplus wheat but also surplus skin. In old age it grows a full-
size larger than necessary, and empty turkey wattles hang from
the chin.

There is a glandular condition, in its acute form called acromegaly, in which the bones of the facial skeleton and those of
the hands and feet grow disproportionately to the rest of the body.
According to my observation, old age, with its glandular changes,
produces some slight degree of acromegaly in everyone, but this
is especially noticeable among aged Midwesterners, whose heads
become heavy, and whose locomotion grows sluggish as the bones
of the extremities actually increase in weight.

Texans are tighter and narrower in build and their locomotion
is gangling.

SENATOR BANKHEAD

SENATOR GUFFEY

SENATOR HIRAM JOHNSON

SENATOR CLARK

JACK GARNER

SENATOR CARTER GLASS

When Boas made his startling discovery at the turn of the century, it was suggested that better nutrition and health habits in America are responsible for changes in stature and head form. This idea has since gained the standing of a popular belief and is immortalized in my daughter's schoolbooks.

The fact is that anthropologists know very little about the

causes of racial differentiation. They do not even know for sure why a Negro is black or a Mongoloid yellow, let alone agree on the mysterious sculpturings of bone, or what sets glands to work on body and mind.

And so, while these fellows with the calipers are for once in too shaky a position to talk back, I'll let my eye have its say, which is this: the American environment produces physical and personality changes—regardless of racial origins—reminiscent of the aboriginal population of North America.

Here is a description by Earnest Hooton, of Harvard, of the Plains Indians: "The face is of great size, both in breadth and length. The eyes are deep set and brilliant with narrow lid openings. The nose hawk-like, the mouth a steel trap. The characteristic expression of these Indians is one of sombre strength . . . unrelieved by any softness. Nowhere has nature moulded the lineaments of the human countenance with such a bold, firm hand. Dignified, taciturn, courageous, and unrelenting in warfare . . . intelligent, even spiritual, too proud to be adaptable."

Now this is a very good description, not only of the noble redskin; if I were to write for foreigners my impression of the typical quiet American, I would copy it word for word. Any board-of-directors meeting, any television show involving a panel of politicians, yields a crop of such great stone faces.

This American type caught my eye first at conventions. Many senators, among them Tom Connally of Texas, Pat McCarran of Nevada, Claude Pepper of Florida, Robinson of Arkansas, Jimmy Byrnes of South Carolina, could figure, with feathers, on a buffalo nickel. And in place of feathers they becomingly wear fluffy hairdos.

It is quite possible that forces exist, unknown or unrecognized, which influence us physically and mentally. When the strange, wild, semi-religious stomp of the conventions gets underway, I sometimes wonder if it is pure accident, or if it rises from the ineluctable heart of a continent.

On December 7, 1941, sponsored by Tojo, Matsuoka, and Admiral Nagano, the United States of America entered, through fiery portals, the family of nations. Pearl Harbor was attacked, and hundreds of thousands of American boys set out on the road to their San Gabriele.

Technically I was now an "enemy alien" and was visited by numerous young Irishmen in the employ of Edgar Hoover who wanted to make sure that I was a friendly enemy alien. I presented no problem to them; but Derso was a puzzle. To one of them he said: "I am not interested in everyday politics. I am a dreamer."

A few days later, the same FBI man came to see me and said in genuine commiseration: "You know, Mr. Kelen, your partner, Mr. Derso, is a dreamer. Every time I go to see him, he is in bed."

Apart from these amiable check-ups, I was allowed to live, work, and travel as I pleased. My fellow refugees in England and France were put in internment camps.

Derso and I were engaged by the Royal Yugoslav Information Center to prepare editorial cartoons about the Yugloslav war effort for release to the press. Our hero was Draja Mikhailovitch, commander of a guerilla force called the Chetniks, who were fighting the Nazis in the mountains of Yugoslavia. Together with Mr. Yevtich, a former Yugoslav foreign minister whose face was like a hot cross bun with a false mustache, we dreamed of the day we would enter Belgrade in triumphal procession for the opening, at the National Museum, of an exhibition of the originals of our drawings.

But there was in Yugoslavia another dedicated band of guerillas called Partisans, under one Josip Broz, called Tito. In time, the clash between these rivals, the Partisans and the Chetniks, was heard on Fifth Avenue, where doors slammed, fists banged, and explosive words flew. It came to our ears in veiled hints that the voice of Radio Free Yugoslavia now originated in southern Russia. One day, hero Tito captured hero Mikhailovitch and executed him as a war criminal, and thereby another batch of

Derso and Kelen drawings found their way into the rogues'
gallery.

With the war in full swing, I was informed by a book publisher that, in addition to America's other troubles, her youth
was in a state of crisis. Cotton cloth was no longer available
to make ragbooks for children. Here was my chance to aid the
war effort while becoming a millionaire. I got hold of a rich Yugoslav businessman and talked him into increasing his fortune by
printing such books on plastic. He bit; he'd provide the money.
I was hooked; I'd do the work.

I made up several picture books, all highly educational; but, of
course, the overwhelming advantage our product had over the
old, outmoded ragbooks was that baby could read them underwater. Because no one had ever tried to print books on plastic
before, I experienced all the hardships of a pioneer. In the first
place, plastic is alive, and if you put fifty yards of it on a table, it
walks off by itself, especially when it is not paid for. Furthermore,
the colored lacquers with which we printed the pictures had a
frightful stench. I might have come to grief over that problem,
but American know-how rescued me. I found that Americans
manufacture various kinds of artificial smells, which they put,
presumably, into their artificially flavored foods. Chemicals smelling of chocolate, mint, and fresh strawberry shortcake were available to mix with our colors in order to make them more palatable
to baby.

Then the tenants in the building where our printing was done
began to raise cain. They had accustomed themselves to the stink
of plastic colors; now they complained that the smell of chocolate
and strawberries gave them headaches and threatened to call in
the housing inspectors if we did not desist. Next to leap on our
necks was the Pure Food and Drug Administration. Our books
smelled good; but were they good to eat? A laboratory test was
arranged. A baby book was cut up julienne and fed to a rabbit.
All night we sat in anguish, my Yugoslav and I, worrying about
that rabbit, which happily survived.

Our books were printed, approved, and scattered abroad. One day, a printer presented me with an invoice covered with numbers I had never heard of before, but years of experience in publishing our albums had taught me that printers know arithmetic and I do not; therefore I signed it. Closer examination revealed that a decimal point had been cleverly misplaced, so that my unfortunate Yugoslav was obliged to unpocket ten times the amount agreed upon. He now decided to relinquish one fortune rather than lose another, and thus the Yugoslav period of my life came to an end. I didn't get the Holy Sava for it, either.

When I was young, I thought that the average American was a millionaire. When I came to America I saw a stranger thing: that the millionaire is an average American. In countenance, demeanor, and outlook on life he does not differ from other citizens; he eats the same hot dogs, sees the same movies, wears the same howling neckties. And if he wants better hot dogs or better movies, he can't get them.

When Henry Ford was greeted by one of his factory workers with: "Good morning, Mr. Ford!" he replied: "Henry, to you."

The American millionaire does not want to be different.

Many of the great European fortunes had their foundation in the feudal system. Five hundred years of gracious living, removed from the common crush, have left their mark on the body and behavior of the European millionaire so that his nose is on a different joint, his head has another shape, and he carries it differently. The expression on his face is different, and so is his manner; what's more, he wants to be different.

A caricaturist feels bereaved when a type dies out, and from this point of view I mourn the passing of the aristocrat, that delicate product of education and idleness, gone forever, eliminated by direct violence and indirect taxation. What was good in those counts and barons of my youth—their etiquette, their command of languages, their way of dodging creditors—we bourgeois boys acquired if we could; and what was bad in them, we couldn't afford.

While working for the office of the Co-ordinator of Inter-American Affairs, headed by Nelson Rockefeller, I was invited to a small party held in the Rockefeller home on Fifth Avenue. Nelson walked with hasty steps among his guests, hugging shoulders, dispensing tart smiles, and he had a high-pitched good word for everybody. Mrs. Rockefeller, who has since added an "ex-" to her name, was a tall, elegant woman, vivacious in motion and talk.

For the caricaturist, the really engrossing Rockefeller was, of course, old John D., the founder of the family fortune. As a young man he looked like a desert fox, and in old age like the mummy of Rameses II. Whenever I see a sharp, angular profile like his, I suspect that its owner is a strict, cold disciplinarian. Frederick the Great of Prussia was a man of this stamp, and so was Field Marshal von Moltke. John D. Rockefeller III, whom I met when he handed to Trygve Lie a check for eight and a half million dollars to buy the United Nations plot, has inherited his grandfather's magpie nose, small receding chin, and stiff eyes. That is why he directs the vast Rockefeller interests from a wood-paneled eyrie atop Rockefeller Plaza, while his brother Nelson lives, comparatively, in the basement, making political speeches.

Nelson Rockefeller does not resemble the old oil-pharaoh. He is his grandmother's boy, with her square face and cold twinkle in the eye; and she was a woman of iron determination and strong religious convictions. Governor Rockefeller has been shaped in a baby-kissing, back-slapping democracy. At election time he is to be found in Brooklyn, eating corned beef and cabbage with the McGillicuddys; or gefillte fish with the Bernsteins in the Bronx. Possibly he likes it. But it is my impression that while Mr. Rockefeller wants to be like everybody else, he is not. His arm does not really belong around other people's shoulders. Whatever chummy things he says seem to turn back on him like a yo-yo.

He is one of the ablest politicians we have, liberal, honest, conscientious, and more tactful than most. But "Rocky" is a singularly fitting name for him.

After a while in the Rockefeller apartment, I said to myself: "Here's bad news: Americans like abstract painting." There were many pictures on the walls, but an abstract panel attracted my attention because it seemed to fit my judgment of Mr. Rockefeller's personality with its geometric correctness, cold, contrasting colors, its grandiose and humorless style.

Two giant nonobjective Léger murals decorate the United Nations General Assembly Hall, facing each other angrily. One looks like a grasshopper somebody stepped on, the other like a pizza pie somebody sat on. Jealous rumor among artists has it that Léger was paid sixty thousand dollars for these murals by an anonymous donor. I have always suspected a Rockefeller.

When I was in high school, a dyspeptic teacher of philosophy tried to teach me the definition of art. "Art," he said, "is the deployment of surplus energy." Since then, I have come to feel that everything is art, the pebble in the brook, the driftwood on the sand, the leaf on the fern, the horseshoe crab, everything that has shape, color, and composition, and evokes a feeling and a thought.

People who are not artists often ask me what I think about modern art, by which they usually mean abstract, or nonobjective, art.

I can only reply that art is a private affair of the artist and to like it is the private affair of the one who looks at it. From this point of view, I defend to the death the right of Léger, Paul

Klee, and everyone who owns a box of paints to use them, including chimpanzees and angle worms.

But the scope of art is long; it reaches from the most primitive expression of emotions to the highest message to the intellect: that is, from the last segment of the tailbone to the top cell in the gray matter.

The message to the intellect can be anything: the beauty of the human body, a scene in history, the character of a man, a philosophical opinion expressed by three prunes and a banana arranged around a water jug; or simply, JOIN THE NAVY.

Nonobjective art does not reach the level of reasoning. It roams in the subconscious, and through its color, composition, and symbolic squiggles evokes an emotion. People complain: "I don't understand it." Well, you don't have to understand it, you just feel whether your tail is wagging at it, or not.

I don't see what is "modern" about nonobjective art; it is merely fashionable. Primitive art is full of abstractions; there are Africans who paint masterpieces daily on their bellies. I am sure that Neanderthal man splashed paints around him as he discovered them, and perhaps in some instances splashed them gloriously. But he also chipped the little artifacts archaeologists label Mousterian flint implements, and these move me more because they have style, form, development. They contain the marvel of reason.

It seems to me that there is one main nuisance in the vogue for abstract art: it invites the charlatan, the faddist, the snob with a jargon who wishes to be thought a connoisseur. Forty years ago, the art schools I attended were well padded with nonobjective artists. They were mostly the sons of rich parents who had enough money to refuse to learn to paint things as they appear to be.

Far be it from me to decry anyone who finds joy in wielding a brush; but, for myself, I think that art does not become "superior," or "advanced," when it gets bogged down below the level of reason. I don't see why artists of worth should have to face the competition of apes and angle worms.

In the spring of 1943, we knew the days of Hitler's Thousand-Year Reich were numbered. Peace was in sight, but it would be a tremendous burden on the victors, who would have the task of feeding the millions of needy on the scorched earth. A conference to deal with this problem was called in Hot Springs, Virginia.

"LIVING SPACE"

The Hot Springs Food Conference was the first sign that peace-making would be inspired by a different spirit than that of Versailles. There was to be no deliberate chopping up of the corpses of defeated countries; no demand for impossible reparations nor deliberate crippling of a nation's economy; no starving and humiliation of peoples. Peace was to be organized in a spirit of reconciliation and rehabilitation.

The Hot Springs Conference was followed by another at Bretton Woods, to fashion the postwar world's financial structure; by another at Dumbarton Oaks, which outlined plans for a United Nations Organization; by a meeting of a committee of jurists in

Washington to revamp the International Court of Justice; and, finally, by the San Francisco Conference, which framed the United Nations Charter, a most impressive manifesto of man's ultimate humanity to man.

The spirit that inspired the Food Conference later inspired the Marshall Plan, the Point Four Program, Technical Assistance, and the European Common Market. The Conference itself was the forerunner of the United Nations Food and Agricultural Organization.

There was no sign at Hot Springs that the Soviet Union would one day become a lone wolf and that peace would have to be strengthened, not with the Russians, but against them.

The delegates to the conference, with the exception of Mr. Dean Acheson, were not especially glamorous. They all seemed to be experts of the digestive tract: doctors, nutritionists, hybridizers, dehydrizers, fletcherizers, and people who attached great hopes to soybeans, seaweed, and ground nuts.

Fortune magazine called Derso and me to a powwow to discuss the advisability of drawing these people in color.

The offices of *Fortune* were at that time on the forty-first floor of the Time and Life Building in Rockefeller Plaza. An elevator man tried to squeeze us into his elevator, but succeeded in absorbing me only, leaving Derso to follow in another elevator.

By mistake I got out on the fortieth floor. I decided to walk up one floor. I found a stairway and mounted to the forty-first floor, but discovered that the door leading into the hall was locked. I banged, but nobody came. I walked back to the fortieth floor, only to find that that door had now automatically locked. I went down to the thirty-ninth floor, the thirty-eighth floor, the thirty-seventh floor, banging, rattling, and shouting all the way. I had to walk down forty floors and into the cellar before I came to a door with a little window through which I could see the blessed daylight, but a contraption fixed to the top of it with wires, which might have been a burglar alarm or a fire alarm, worried me. I finally decided that it would be better to be arrested than to have my skeleton found in the cellar of the Time and Life Building, so I commended myself to heaven, opened the door, and found myself on a ramp that led up to the street. I didn't wait to find out whether the police or the firemen were racing to the scene; I whipped back into the building by the front entrance and took an elevator to the forty-first floor, where I found Derso trying to convince a large crowd that, a half hour before, he had seen me entering an elevator going up.

It isn't every foreigner who can walk in and baffle an army of Luce-men.

Fortune comforted us with a commission to prepare eight pages about the Hot Springs Food Conference. On our way to Virginia, we stopped in Washington to do some preliminary sketches in the State Department and the Department of Agriculture. I also telephoned the Soviet Embassy to set up an appointment with Mr. Alexey D. Krutikov, the head of the Soviet delegation. Somebody picked up the receiver, listened to me, then uttered a short word which was soon to become the best-known Russian word in the world next to vodka, and hung up.

This one-sided conversation repeated itself four times. Years ago I'd had a similar experience with the Ethiopians and I did what I had done then: I went in person to the Soviet Embassy and rang the bell. I was turned away from the doorstep.

The Iron Curtain had not then been invented. I did not know that this would be the face the Russians would turn to the world for years to come. But Mr. Krutikov knew, and at the conference he earned a nickname: Inskrutikov.

The delegates to the conference were housed at the Homestead Hotel in Hot Springs, where a remarkable Southern cuisine flourishes amid glorious mountains so gently sculpted with pathways that the fattest stockbroker can stroll to the top with no increase in blood pressure. We journalists were stabled off the grounds, and we needed a special pass to enter the Homestead park, which resembled an armed camp. Two military police were stationed at every door, and they scanned credentials with short but sensitive noses, jealously guarding the sight of Mr. Dean Acheson in shorts, with long, bare legs, chasing a ball in the tennis court. He was a most un-American-looking American; more of a captain of the Coldstream Guards with a marmalade-colored mustache brushed upwards, tomcat style. He had come to Hot Springs, for one thing, to smooth the ruffled feelings of us newsmen who were wondering what had happened to the principle of open covenants, openly arrived at.

The reason for these precautions was, of course, the continuing war. It was just after the victory of Stalingrad, and the Russians had brought with them the first film report of that battle. The South African ambassador, Andrew Brennan, invited Derso and me to the hotel for dinner on the night the film was to be shown. All titles were in Cyrillic script, which I cannot read, but the pictures told eloquently of the defeat of Hitler's supermen; and the years rolled back to the time I'd seen them drinking beer and yodeling at the *Oktoberfest*, their arms around the shoulders of girls, proud, young, and duped. After the show our host offered us a nightcap at the bar, and we spent some time talking about war and peace.

The next day we were called on the carpet by Michael McDermott, press chief of the State Department. "Gentlemen," he said solemnly, "I am advised that last night you entered the premises of the Homestead Hotel at 7:30 p.m. and left at 1:38 a.m. You were not supposed to stay so late. Promise me that you will never do it again."

We promised. But the incident reminded us that this was no ordinary conference; it was an appendage to the war. Walls had ears, bottles had eyes, and there were hidden microphones in the hominy grits.

No security measures deterred two brave congressmen on the warpath from Washington. Representative Frederick C. Smith of Ohio and Fred Bradley of Michigan, both Republicans, descended on the Homestead, hoping to be bounced. Election time was but a year away and it would have been glorious to report to the rationed voters about all those foreigners at the Homestead stuffing themselves with buttered hush-puppies at the taxpayer's expense, while duly elected representatives of the people were excluded. However, they were welcomed—if not heartily—and permitted to see for themselves what picky eaters soybean experts usually are.

I was standing in the garden of the Homestead sketching Mr. Bradley when a bee happened along and buzzed around his head. He broke into a wild Indian dance, waving his arm in circles, trying to bat away the bee, and shouted: "Go away, you! There's no honey in me!"

Right he was. But he was stung nevertheless by the publicity bug that compels fan dancers to walk naked down Park Avenue. Americans take such infantile doings on the part of their leaders with a smile, as an inevitable side show of the political circus. Friends and allies despair. They cannot understand that holders of public trust should embarrass their government in the midst of delicate negotiations in order to get their names in the papers.

As for the taxpayer's money, that goes down the drain anyway.

A year before the Hot Springs Conference, I had gone to an American magazine publisher to try to sell him some drawings. After listening silently to my list of publications, qualifications, and exhibitions, he raised his voice so that it could be heard in the adjoining office: "Hey, Sam! Do you want to see a European refugee artist? Come in here!"

Sam came in, and together they stared at me as if I were an Egyptian gecko.

On the way home from the Hot Springs Conference, I stopped in Washington again, and took some shirts to be shredded by a Chinese laundryman just off Massachusetts Avenue. As I explained to him in my goulash English how he might best accomplish this mission, he gave me a shrewd look.

"You are not from here," he said.

"No."

"You are from New York."

"Well—yes."

"I can always tell a New Yorker," he said with satisfaction, "by his accent."

That's how it is in America. One year you are a homeless wanderer. The next year you are received into the melting pot.

Revival in
the San Francisco
Opera House

LORD BALFOUR once said that if the League of Nations should collapse, it would have to be reconstructed.

The League collapsed. On April 25, 1945, the United Nations Conference met in San Francisco. On March 1, reporting to Congress on the Yalta Conference, Franklin D. Roosevelt had said: "We shall have to take the responsibility for a world collaboration, or we shall have to bear the responsibility for another world conflict."[1]

[1] Stefan Lorant: *F.D.R.: A pictorial biography* (New York: Simon and Schuster; 1950), p. 149.

Thirteen days before the conference was to open, on April 12, 1945, President Roosevelt died in Warm Springs.

When we talk about "balance of power," we think we mean "balance of military potentialities." It is generally overlooked that the personality of leaders is an important factor in power. Through Roosevelt's death, the United States lost not one cannon nor one bomber; yet the balance of power changed. Just as twenty years before, the Briand-Chamberlain-Stresemann complex had a different significance from the Briand-Chamberlain-Curtius combination, so Churchill-Stalin-Roosevelt did not add up the same as Churchill-Stalin-Truman. I do not mean that Curtius or Truman were not good men, only that they were different men, so that the balance of the group changed.

For a while there was talk of postponing the conference, but in the end it was decided to proceed. Two special trains headed for the Golden Gate, one from New York, the other from Washington. Together they carried two thousand American journalists and five hundred foreign correspondents. If the two trains converging on Chicago had collided, a good part of the diplomatic press of the world would have been wiped out.

Derso and I were on the New York train. At home, my wife, with the aid of a map and a compass, had calculated where I would have arrived had I traveled the same distance from Györ: Murmansk, Akmolinsk, Samarkand, Togoland. For three days and three nights we rolled across the vast continent, but the legal tender for the U. S. hot dog was still the U. S. dollar. The Pennsylvania Railroad unrolled across my coach windows hundreds of factories, steaming and glowing in the night. Factories are magnificent art, fashioned with the divine harmony imposed by utility. In Cheyenne I saw a cowboy on the hurricane deck of a pinto pony, pistol at his hip, lasso on his saddle, exactly like a print from one of my boyhood books; but there was something in this living picture that I could not have imagined: the cowboy was riding past a factory!

In North Platte, Nebraska, the U.S.O., with sure instinct, forti-

TRUMAN AS LOHENGRIN

fied us with exactly the same fare with which our boys were sent off to the war in the Pacific: ham sandwiches and orange pop.

So far this trip was, for Derso and me, purely a sentimental journey. Prince Charming in shining armor made in Detroit, Michigan, was about to awaken our maiden with a kiss, and we intended to be there. But on the train I met Erwin D. Canham, a familiar figure from my Geneva days, where I had known him as an abstemious young correspondent who shied away from the journalistic honky-tonk at the Brasserie Bavaria. Now he was editor of the *Christian Science Monitor*. He said he would like to buy our San Francisco caricatures, but added: "I'm ashamed to tell you, Mr. Kelen, how little we can pay."

"Just tell me," I said, "I'll blush and accept it." And so it was.

The station at San Francisco was bedecked with flags and flowers, and we were welcomed by Mayor Lapham. The presence of white-helmeted military police reminded us that in the far corners of the world the fighting was continuing. The delegates did not come from warm, well-valeted chancelleries. Some of them had jumped over Nazi prison walls or had crawled from holes underground; or had lived in exile in shabby hotels. Their waistcoats did not match their trousers, and they came with such apologies as: "That's all I had on when I jumped through the window."

In Lausanne, soldiers had come straight from the battlefields to talk about peace. But many of the delegates to San Francisco were neither generals nor diplomats. They were ordinary people wrenched from ordinary lives by war. General Carlos P. Romulo of the Philippines had been a playwright and journalist. Now there was a Japanese price tag on his head. Yugoslav Finance Minister Dedijer was a Partisan leader whose wife had fought by his side and had been killed in action. French Foreign Minister Georges Bidault was a history teacher who had become a leader of the French resistance.

After the First World War, poor nations had pretended to be rich. I had long noted that the best food and wines were offered at the diplomatic receptions of poor countries. The rich ones were more apt to offer fleet demonstrations. After the Second World War, poor countries made sure you knew how poor they were. Greek Foreign Minister John Sofianopulos, who had recently escaped from a Nazi jail, shed tears on my shoulder as he described the starved earth and privations of Greece.

In the next few years it was to become a badge of honor for a country to be poor, just as today being underdeveloped is like money in the bank.

Sometimes the Heavenly Producer who moves us on our stage plots a rare stroke of drama. One of the first familiar faces I saw in San Francisco was that of Makonnen Endalkatau, whom I had drawn when as a young man he was delegate to the League of

LORD HALIFAX   LORD CRANBORNE

Nations from the country the League betrayed, Ethiopia. Now he was prime minister, a tall man, erect as a poplar, with the straight profile of a Carthaginian proconsul. He wore a black cape with golden buckles very like the one the Negus had worn on the tragic afternoon that marked the true end of the League.

I saw Paul Boncour of France, who was thought to resemble Robespierre by those who had never looked at a portrait of Robespierre. The resemblance was limited to the fact that Boncour was short, eloquent, and incorruptible.

Then with real joy I came face to face with Anthony Eden. "How nice to see you, *Monsieur le Ministre*, you haven't changed at all." "Nor you, *cher ami*."

But these were lies; all of us old Geneva hands had changed —by twenty million dead.

When Americans organize a conference, they do so with grass-roots common sense: they install a cafeteria. This seems normal to them, but in diplomatic history the cafeteria at San Francisco was a staggering novelty. The fact that food was also a novelty to most of the delegates no doubt silenced criticism.

It brought me up short to see, standing in a line of workers

in overalls and chirping secretaries, holding jello on their trays like coronets on cushions, Edward Frederick Lindley Wood, First Earl of Halifax, First Baron Irwin, British ambassador to Washington; and Robert Arthur James Gascoyne-Cecil, the Right Honorable Viscount Cranborne, Secretary of State for Dominion Affairs, Leader of the House of Lords.

I am a child of Napoleon's century—though he died at the beginning of it and I was born at the end. But I am old enough to think of lords bearing names that make my tail curl as men who live in castles and dine alone by candlelight with braided livery plying them with grouse, *petits-pois Lucullus,* and champagne, while from the wombs of the castle vaults the ghostly sounds of old battles won by their ancestors rumble and echo.

Lord Halifax was six feet four inches tall, a tower of bones topped by a bowler hat, and he had the saddest horse-face I ever drew, with eyebrows that slanted down over anguish-flecked eyes; his jaw hung so heavy that it left his incisors uncovered. He was a scholarly man of great integrity, deeply religious, and a collector of ghost stories. He shared Lord Curzon's mystic belief that imperialism was a mission delegated by Providence to the British. It was certainly not the worst sort of imperialism to have been inflicted on our world, this British effort to marry humanism to exploitation.

As Viceroy of India, Halifax had not only put Gandhi behind bars with tender loving care; he had also coaxed him into a reasonable mood so that he could be released and allowed to attend the Second Indian Round Table Conference. When, during these negotiations, Gandhi stalked out of the room, forgetting his shawl, the Viceroy snatched it up and ran after him, saying: "You haven't so much on, sir, that you can afford to leave this."

Lord Cranborne was a scion of the Salisbury line and a relative of that Lord Cecil who so long ago had been my favorite prophet in the service of the League. He was an aristocrat made out of sheet iron, with a long, thin nose, a delicate facial skeleton, and skin so tight that it failed to cover his teeth, which were like a picket fence. When I see such a fragile face with such strong teeth, I know I am looking at a man who, once he gets those teeth into a matter of principle, will hold on to what he has bitten.

The sight of these two lords waiting in line with trays in their hands and composing their menus in reverse from jello to tomato soup was a symbol in itself that diplomatic manners had suddenly been turned inside out. But seeing them together reminded me what agitations had brought the new era to birth. For Lord Halifax had been an appeaser in Neville Chamberlain's cabinet, while Lord Cranborne had resigned from that cabinet in protest against the appeasement policy. In the war that followed, both men lost a son.

In San Francisco they stuck together; I hardly ever saw them apart. They walked through the streets and corridors with long, stiff, identical steps.

The committees of the conference met in the Veterans Building. Plenary meetings were held in the adjacent War Memorial Opera House, and it was here that the star performers were on display. Certainly, one of the most spectacular members of the cast at the Opera House was the old Boer, the perennial prime minister of South Africa, Field Marshal Jan Christiaan Smuts. He had fought against the British; then he fought on their side in two world wars. He had put Gandhi in jail; then he became his friend. He had stood at the cradle of the League; then for twenty years he ignored her. Now here he was again, at the birth of the United Nations, in his uniform, with a pair of stiff, blue falcon's eyes staring from under the red rocks of his brow, close set at the root of a chunky nose: a man of deep sensitivities imprisoned in a fortress of bones, muscles, and sinews.

Very much in evidence was the beaming face of Paul-Henri Spaak, Belgian foreign minister, who already bore the nickname, "Baby Churchill." I had known him in Geneva, where he first appeared bobbing in the wake of the Socialist leader, Emile Vandervelde, wearing the black, wide-brimmed hat of the Second International—as did Vandervelde himself, as well as Léon Jouhaux, Salomon Grumbach, and Léon Blum. This had contrasted with the cap of the Third International worn by Lenin, Rykov, Kamenev, and Molotov.

Perhaps it is an organic fault in a caricaturist to attach significance to sartorial foibles; but I insist that the fact that Khrushchev wears the cosmopolitan homburg, while Mao Tse-tung sticks to his ideologically orthodox cap, is important.

The composition of the American delegation clearly reflected that a lesson had been learned from the old battle between Woodrow Wilson and Henry Cabot Lodge, Sr.

There were 150 members, perhaps reflecting the notion that there is safety in numbers. Close inspection revealed that the delegation was not merely bipartisan, it was bifocal. One eye was on international obligations, the other on moderate entanglement. Isolationism is not a policy that can be changed by presidential decision; it is a state of a nation's soul. There was baptismal value in the prominent place assigned to Senator Vandenberg, who had undergone a sudden conversion from isolationist Saul to internationalist Paul. But one could not expect men like Senator Tom Connally of Texas, or Sol Bloom, congressman from New York, to become internationalists overnight.

Once a Jewish grocer was urged by the abbot of a local mon-

"HOW COLD YOUR LITTLE HAND IS . . ."

astery to have himself baptized, because it was not seemly for the monastery to buy groceries at a Jewish store. The grocer placed a crucifix above his counter. "There!" he told the abbot. "The store is Christian. But I will remain a Jew."

Such was the case of Connally and Bloom. Such is the case today, I think, of many men in American politics whose business is internationalism—but they remain isolationists.

Tom Connally was a monumental Texan built like a railway-station water tank and dressed like a cartoon senator, in shoestring bow tie, frock coat, and wide-brimmed hat. His long, white hair was as painstakingly worked and whorled as the beard of a Sikh maharaja. A fleshy proboscis overhung a thin-lipped, be-it-resolved, jowl-to-jowl mouth, and a mischievous twinkle played at the corners of his eyes. He was a wonderful old ham, a master of the thunderous style of oratory left over from the days before the microphone was invented. He sounded like a traveling salesman selling horse liniment behind the church.

Sol Bloom was a "chin-up" little man with a huge grin and a big cigar, dressed with the flashy elegance of a Broadway theatrical agent at Lindy's in the gaslight era. He wore a polka-dot bow tie, a fancy vest, striped starched shirt, and an owlish pince-nez on a black shoelace. He was a star-spangled Jew for whom the Fourth of July was more awesome than Yom Kippur.

For such men it was both an honor and an obligation to be members of the United States delegation. The honor was that they would be taken for statesmen of stature. The obligation was to go back to Washington and report to their colleagues in Congress that to the best of their knowledge no American babies are roasted and eaten at international conferences; and moreover, to sell Congress the United Nations Charter.

Commander Harold E. Stassen was a farm boy, tall and heavy-boned, yet doughy. He had been owner of a pigeon-and-rabbit business and had once run a roadside vegetable stand: one would have expected to find him up to his ears in food and agriculture. Instead, he helped to set up the Trusteeship Council, which would assist the peoples of dependent territories to achieve independence—in due course, of course.

There were seven selected banner carriers in the delegation. Besides Connally, Bloom, Stassen, and Vandenberg, Virginia

Gildersleeve, dean of Barnard College, was there to see that the interests of half the world—the female half—were not glossed over in the charter. The head of the delegation was Edward R. Stettinius, Jr., one of those who reinforce my belief that in their looks Americans are going back to the Indians. Last, there was Representative Charles A. Eaton. Stettinius and Eaton were graduates of the steel industry. Stettinius had wanted to be a minister of the Gospel when he was young; Eaton had been trained for the ministry and actually had held pastorates. I dare say it comes in handy for a couple of steel men, when they have to frame a charter, to have a bit of an inspirational background.

Behind the banner carriers stood a phalanx of advisers. Among them were John Foster Dulles, Adlai Stevenson, Nelson Rockefeller, John J. McCloy, "Chip" Bohlen, and my old model from Geneva, Llewellyn (Tommy) Thompson. There were names I had not heard before, but I was to hear of them later: Ralph Bunche, Philip C. Jessup, and Andrew Cordier.

This American practice of sending a double-barreled delegation to the UN survives to this day. The people you see in the front row of a United States delegation are the public darlings and the party tenors; but the men in the background have at least as much influence. The voice may be the voice of Marian Anderson, but the hand is the hand of the State Department.

The gray eminences of San Francisco were to become banner carriers in the years following. I was more than curious to draw John Foster Dulles, the Republican Party's legendary wizard of foreign policy who had thrown his tremendous influence behind Roosevelt's internationalism. He sat for me immobile as a stone owl, smoking a straight-stemmed pipe. It is my habit while I draw to strike up a conversation in order to see my model's face in motion—no luck with Mr. Dulles. I believe I made him the more impatient to be off. When I finished, I showed him my sketch. Without a smile or the slightest sign of pleasure or displeasure, he walked away, somewhat stooped, with his left hand in his trousers pocket.

Naturally, I bloom when statesmen have kind words for my work; but I don't insist on them. For me it is more interesting to see the reaction of a man to his own caricature. I have explained my deep suspicions of the statesman who lacks a sense of self-mockery.

Dulles was dead serious about himself. This was advertised by

his physique. He was massive, with all his strength expressed in the upper part of his body: broad shoulders, heavy jaw, doorpost neck, and square head, which he carried bent resolutely forward. He was a man of obviously muscular intent.

He had a facial tic. I checked up on this tic and was told that it was a relic of malaria, but the explanation did not convince me. Dulles had many tics: his eyes blinked intermittently like an electric bulb loose in its socket, and he made sucking motions with his mouth as if chewing thumbtacks.

Tics, in my view, are a sign of aggressiveness out of control, and they go with habits of runaway self-assertion.

Dulles's famous expressions reveal the sort of man he was. Only a Muscleman who thinks monolithically coins such phrases as "massive retaliation." His "agonizing reappraisal" was that sudden reversal of point of view which in the deep nature of the Muscleman replaces flexibility. His "brinkmanship" revealed the intoxicating effect that risk and danger had on him. By temperament, such a man cannot co-exist. He can only fight.

Dulles was a man of brilliant conceptions. A United States of Europe was one of his pet ideas, and as a first step he helped found the European Common Market, though he knew that it would compete with United States trade. A champion of the freedom of the individual, nevertheless he had not the sensitivity and warmth to deal with human beings—he himself admitted that he had no talent for public relations. With other statesmen, as with the millions of *fellahin* to whom he denied the benefits of the Aswan Dam, he dealt no more successfully than he did with me. So that when he died, and those who had harassed him called him a Pillar of Strength, a Soldier of Peace, a Builder of Security, a Defender of Freedom, I was reminded of Voltaire's remark at the funeral of a nobleman: "He was a great patriot, a humanitarian, a loyal friend—provided, of course, that he is really dead."

I met Adlai Stevenson in the offices of the American delegation and made a vain effort to draw him. It is not a simple thing to draw a man who laughs easily while his eyes remain staring and rotating like a couple of Andromeda nebulae.

When Stevenson became a nationally known figure, the word "egghead" entered the American language as a term synonymous with "intellectual." Actually it is an old word, containing an astute folk observation that heads shaped like eggs are likely to contain thoughts of a theoretical, dialectical, hypothetical nature. Bertrand Russell, Kant, Herbert Spencer had true eggheads.

Stevenson has a mixed egghead. The top of it is the round head of a plump, warmhearted, paternal grandpa; then it tapers down to the triangular face of a rocky, composed, inward-looking maternal grandpa. Put them together, and you have the familiar Stevenson, cheerful, fluid, and warmhearted, yet prone to excited self-analysis and subtle abstractions.

Thousands of Stevenson's admirers are convinced that he lost two elections because he was too superior to the electorate. It is true that the positive-thinking Americans view Stevenson's skepticism with distrust. They like their politicians to be hard-hitting, finger-waving, and pious. But deeper than this, I think, the public sensed a flaw in him, the flaw of a highly sensitive and introspective man whose physical strength is not sufficient to provide firm

anchorage for a restless, inquisitive, abstract mind. This is so well expressed in Stevenson's tense, apprehensive, rotating eyes, which made him difficult to draw, for they are in contradiction to his smiling face, fluent speech, urbane manner, and solid handshake.

When Stevenson was appointed permanent delegate to the United Nations by the Kennedy administration, I reminded him of our meeting fifteen years back in San Francisco and of the poor drawing I had made. He gave me a thousand-wrinkle smile and with quick grace pretended it had all happened yesterday. Here is the ideal man to juggle those touchy foreigners at the United Nations.

When I was a boy, all I knew about China was that when a mishap occurred, such as a flood or the sinking of a ferry boat that in Hungary would have cost the lives of five people, in China it killed masses. In Geneva, as we know, Sir John Simon put China in her place. "What is China," he said, "but a geographical expression?"

Except for their brief agony during the Manchurian affair, I had noticed Chinese delegates mainly because, of all my models, they had the smallest hands and feet, voices of highest pitch, and the most diminutive chins.

Nothing could have taught me how wildly the world had swung in a half dozen years than to come to San Francisco and find China a great power, a sponsor of the United Nations, whose silver-bell language was one of the official languages of the world. Her delegation was composed of Nationalists and Communists, both parties having fought the Japanese together. Thus, Chinese Reds who are today not permitted to sit at the United Nations helped to frame the United Nations Charter.

The head of the delegation was Foreign Minister Dr. T. V. Soong. He is a sort of brother-in-law to the Chinese Republic, one if his sisters having married Sun Yat-sen, the founder of the Republic, and another sister having married Chiang Kai-shek. Today, Mme Sun is a Communist in China while Mme Chiang is a capitalist in Taiwan. A third sister, Mme Kung, is a capitalist on Long Island. The father of these fabulous people was a barefoot boy who peddled hammocks in America and Bibles in China.

A familiar face from my Geneva days was that of Dr. Wellington Koo, a prize specimen in my collection of ageless Mongoloids. At twenty-seven, he had been ambassador to Washington, the youngest man (in modern times) ever to hold an ambassadorial post. At thirty, he was his country's delegate to the Versailles Peace Conference. Today, at seventy-four, he has retired to that haven of superannuated diplomats, the International Court of Justice. But in all the years since I first drew him, he has changed very little in appearance.

He was thin and stiff as a skewer, and even among Chinese he was champion of the diminutive chin. He walked with a curious gait, throwing his legs stiffly outwards like a Chinese woman with bound feet. I have noticed this particular walk only among very lean Chinese diplomats and in the classic Chinese theater; and I have wondered whether it is caused by some special structure of the body, or whether it is a deliberate imitation of a style of loco-motion fashionable long ago—a sort of Thin Man's hobby, like Anthony Eden's Persian poetry.

A story too good to be new, which I suspect has been attached to every Chinese ambassador, was resuscitated in San Francisco and pinned on Wellington Koo. At a banquet, they say, he was seated next to a senator who did not trouble himself overmuch with his neighbor; but from time to time, for the sake of bon ton, he would turn to him and inquire: "Likee soupee?" or "Likee meatee?"

When the time came for the speeches, Dr. Koo arose and in exquisite English addressed the gathering. After sitting down, he turned to the senator and asked: "Likee speechee?"

No one could have rejoiced more than a caricaturist at the in-dependence of the new Arab nations. It was a fine sight to see the proud-nosed Syrians, Lebanese, and Iraqis marching in a line like a bas-relief of Assyrian kings. There was Dr. Charles H. Malik of Lebanon, a philosopher and snail expert, built like the coach of a Sumerian football team; the bowlegged fiery rebel, Fadhil Jamali, who was sentenced to life imprisonment by Karim Kassem; and, dressed in a creamy cloak and golden headgear with black pompoms, Allah's own gift to an artist, His Royal Highness Faisal Ibn Abdul Aziz, Viceroy of Hedjaz, Viceroy of Mecca, sec-ond son of King Ibn Saud, and owner of a face of Arabian Nights sophistication—a warning in itself of the quasi-occult forces which in the new world of diplomacy we have to learn to deal with.

I looked in vain for a familiar face among the members of the Soviet delegation; but the few years of war had swept away the old chess players of the cafés. They had been replaced by new men, hatched in the Soviet chicken coop, who arrived in bombers flown by Soviet pilots and brought Soviet stalwarts to guard them.

Only the mother hen was old. Vyacheslav Mikhailovich Molotov; and even he was a man who had not tasted the sweet ennui of the political émigré. There were no more dinner invitations for caricaturists or clangorous arguments between the old ways and the new. The Iron Curtain had not yet a name, but it came down anyway with a bang and cut all arguments in two. The Soviet men lived in unquestioning submission to a new, strange discipline.

At a press conference held by Molotov I found myself quite close to a Russian admiral who was surrounded by a group of young Russians. I can always find good use for a Russian admiral, and so I made a sketch of him. When I had finished I asked one of the young Russians to tell me his name. He did not reply, so I asked another, who stared at me with a face as forbidding as the Kremlin walls. I approached four or five; they let me talk and pretended to be dead. In the end, the admiral himself became aware of my distress and told me his name, Rodionov. It seems that nobody but the admiral dared to be responsible for his name.

All attempts to get one of my usual appointments with the Soviet delegation failed. Then Mr. Molotov gave a reception at the St. Francis Hotel in honor of the delegations. But he forgot to invite me.

I had not traveled the distance from Györ to Togoland in order to go home without a parcel of Russian scalps, so I decided to crash the gates. In Stresa, I had quite easily followed Mussolini to a party. But what had worked with a cordon of flighty Italians did not work with earnest Slavs. I was nabbed at the door by a husky Russian. I pulled out of my pocket my press card, my alien-registration card, my meat-ration stamps, and my half-price ticket on the Swiss railways, explaining with hands and feet that I was an artist and that I desired to draw Comrade Molotov. He listened bleakly and said: "Не ПОНИМАЮ," which, as you rightly think, means: "I don't understand." He then called a portly Russian, to whom I explained my mission and showed my bits of paper. He allowed his eyes to bulge at me, then retired and came back with a skinny Russian who wore eyeglasses and spoke a little English. This fellow had the grace to be embarrassed by my bad manners. He explained to me sternly what I knew, that I needed an invitation. I explained to him what he knew, that I had none. Now we were even. For a while the trio of mesomorphic, endomorphic, and ectomorphic Slavs glowered at me. The ectomorph withdrew and returned directly with an efficient Russian who seemed to be some kind of press attaché. In quite a good humor he rang up the Iron Curtain and allowed me to enter. It seemed to me that I'd had a whiff of organized Russian "nyetism" and that it was a brew of fatalism, obedience, laziness, fear, and good will; and it brought about a working order unfathomable to the Western mind.

In a few minutes I was drawing Molotov. He had a face like a bulldog: the midface bashed in and flanked by salient cheekbones, an extraordinarily bulging brow, and a sledgehammer jaw. He had small, cinder eyes, like a raccoon. An old-fashioned pince-nez was attached to the root of a saddle nose rather precariously, for there was little nose to pinch.

The bulldog face in Molotov—and also in a bulldog—is caused by a dwarfed upper jaw. Such localized dwarfism is often accompanied by dwarfism of the extremities—that's why Molotov—and bulldogs—stand on stumpy legs.

The familiar names of many statesmen are not the names they were born with; they are pseudonyms, and I have often thought that the name a leader selects reveals his image of himself. Joseph Dzhugashvili called himself Stalin, the "Man of Steel." The pseudonym Ben Gurion means "Son of the Lion." Molotov's name means "Hammer"; and indeed he looked and behaved like a steam-driven pile driver which goes thump! thump! thump! Characteristic of Soviet diplomatic negotiation is the stubborn, forceful repetition of the same argument; thus Molotov, in name, looks, and manner, was a very model of Soviet diplomacy.

There is no question in my mind that in such an unusually

muscular matrix the dwarfism evident in Molotov's midface and legs introduces tension, and it explains why Molotov the Hammer was a stutterer in his youth. Once, when rebuked by Trotsky at a Party Congress, he stood up and said: "Not everybody can be as perfect as T-T-T-T-Tovarish T-T-T-T-T-Trotsky."

Among the early revolutionists, many of whom were brilliant men, Mr. Molotov did not shine. Lenin, a good judge of men, called him the best file clerk in Russia. But as another non-intellectual, Stalin (whom Lenin despised), rose to power, Molotov rose with him. Nevertheless, remembering those close-set, vigilant raccoon eyes, I can well believe Dulles's remark that Molotov was one of the most observant and quick-minded statesmen in the business.

Molotov is not popular among his colleagues because he is a bully. Khrushchev very sensibly gave him a job in Outer Mongolia; and then, presumably in a spirit of compromise, brought him back to represent Russia for a while at the International Atomic Energy Agency in Vienna. But as I see him, with that chopping-block head and snubbing-post body, I cannot believe that Molotov is capable of compromise. Whatever Khrushchev does—short of shooting him—he will always have, in Molotov, Stalin's hammer banging down upon his hands.

Near Molotov at the Russian reception stood a young man who, with bulbous nose, dolorous eyes, and tight lips, looked like a

punchinello whose feelings have been wounded: Andrey Gromyko. He was to become Molotov's successor, the first of the new Russian diplomats who, too young to remember the tsar or the Revolution, are made-to-measure Marxists, wearers of the fat iron mask. They grew up under Communism and have an induced outlook altogether different from such old-timers as Chicherin, Litvinov, Molotov, Vishinsky, or Khrushchev, all of whom have lived under two flags.

Just as diplomats follow firm protocol in the order in which they arrive at a party—a prime minister first, then his foreign minister and other cabinet members, senior advisers, junior advisers, and first, second, and third secretaries—so do they follow an unwritten protocol in the order in which they sneak out. Prime ministers sneak out first, then foreign ministers, and so on. Second and third secretaries are apt to sneak out last, having done their bit to prevent a needless waste of spirituous liquors.

As a member of a starveling caste, the artists, I follow no protocol. I arrive early for the buffet and stay late for the conversation, which is most engrossing when the captains and the kings have departed.

I stayed late at Molotov's party, which ended like a gangster's funeral when, after the family members have gone, only the FBI agents are left standing beside the grave. Thus I found myself in the company of spies, counterspies, secret agents, Washington hawkshaws, and Moscow bodyguards, all happily poking at the lacerated buffet table, and warmed by vodka, chatting gaily in every fractured tongue while eying one another with friendly curiosity. It was an odd moment of international benevolence among the unlikeliest people.

Once a farmer's son who was a student in the city sent his father a telegram: DEAR FATHER SEND ME TEN DOLLARS I AM IN NEED.

The farmer, who was illiterate, asked a husky blacksmith to

read it for him. The blacksmith read in a booming voice: DEAR FATHER SEND ME TEN DOLLARS I AM IN NEED.

"How dare he talk to his father like that!" exclaimed the farmer. "I won't send him a penny!"

Two days later another telegram arrived with the same request. Again the farmer took it to the blacksmith, but he was not there; only his eighty-year-old mother was home, and she read it in a quavering, weak voice: "Dear Father . . . Send me ten dollars . . . I am in need."

"That's different," said the father, wiping a tear from his eye. And he sent the money.

In my years in the world of diplomacy, I have become convinced that this is a very serious tale which ought to be memorized by all statesmen who have to deal through interpreters. The personality of interpreters has a bearing on world events.

At a critical time in history, Neville Chamberlain went to Berchtesgaden for a three-hour tête-à-tête with Hitler at which the only other person present was Hitler's mild-mannered, dough-faced interpreter, Dr. Paul Schmidt. After the interview, Chamberlain wrote to his sister, in effect, that "here was a man who could be relied upon when he has given his word." Obviously, he must have meant the word of Dr. Schmidt.

Molotov was a bulldog. But his interpreter, Pavlov, was a pussycat. When the bulldog growled, the pussy translated the growl into a miaow. Pavlov had been Stalin's interpreter at Yalta, and long before.

I do not claim to have been the only gate crasher in San Francisco. There was a following of uninvited guests consisting of a storm troop of young Indians (led by Madame Pandit), Spanish Republicans, Koreans, Zionists, London Poles, Lithuanians, Estonians, and Latvians, all hoping to pick up a country they could call their own out of the broken bits of the world. There was even a delegate from heaven who protested violently that God's name was not mentioned at meetings. The police arrested him, not because they doubted the authenticity of his credentials, but because he attempted to penetrate the premises of the American delegation by force.

What could they do in San Francisco, these Poles who had been invited but had no delegation, the Hindus who had a delegation but no independence, the Koreans who had neither independence nor a delegation? Like seagulls following fishing boats, they trailed in the wake of accredited delegates to swoop on them at every opportunity. They gave argumentative cocktail parties, distributed recriminatory tracts, and asked disagreeable questions at press conferences.

We had an old joke in Geneva: A publisher offered a prize for the best book about the elephant. The Englishman submitted a book entitled *Hunting Elephants in India*. The Frenchman's book was called *The Love Life of Elephants*. The Pole submitted *The Elephant and the Polish Question*.

Naturally, the San Francisco Conference had a Polish Question. I can't remember a conference that did not. In my lifetime, Poland had been partitioned first by Germany, Russia, and Austria; then by Hitler and Stalin; and now, in 1945, it had been partitioned by Stalin alone.

Poland was one of the twenty-six nations that had signed the United Nations Declaration in 1942 and, as such, was a charter member. But she was not represented in San Francisco because there was no Polish government. Throughout the war there had been two separate governments-in-exile: London Poles friendly to the Western Allies; and Lublin Poles friendly to the Soviets. The Allies had urged them to form a coalition government; but the London Poles refused to breathe the same air as the Lubliners, as did the Lubliners with the Londoners.

To complicate matters, Stalin had jailed sixteen leaders of non-Communist political parties in Poland. Britain had asked for full explanations; but the fullest explanations cannot get Poles out of Russian prisons.

The London Poles had sent to San Francisco a propaganda

brigade, boiling with indignation, whose mission it was to rub in at every press conference the plight of the Poles in the poky. At Anthony Eden's press conference, a Pole lay in wait to spring an awkward question about it. Eden replied in the grand tradition: "The jailing of the sixteen Polish leaders makes the solution of the Polish question difficult." This brought a young Hindu leaping to his feet to inquire whether the jailing of Indian leaders did not make the solution of the Indian question difficult.

In the end it was left to Molotov at his press conference to say the last word on the Polish Question of 1945: he hoped, he said, "that it would find the same satisfactory solution as the Yugoslav question."

And indeed it did.

An unofficial Jewish delegation was divided into Zionist, and just plain Jews; but they had a united argument: if the Russian provinces of Byelorussia and the Ukraine were each to have separate votes in world affairs, on the grounds that they had suffered in the war, why not the Jews? Had they not suffered? This claim was the more convincing when presented by a pretty blond actress, Stella Adler.

The Spanish Republicans, headed by Juan Negrín and Álvarez del Vayo, who had defended the cause of the Republic before the League with no success, had come to San Francisco to prevent the admission of Franco's Spain to the United Nations—with no greater success in the long run.

Certainly, the loveliest specimen of an agitator at the conference was Vijaya Lakshmi Pandit, sister of Jawaharlal Nehru. I met her at a cocktail party, where she had harsh words to say about the official Indian delegation led by three tame knighted Indians. She quickly gained the sympathetic ear of Molotov, who was always eager to liberate anybody from anybody else. But when she turned to Wellington Koo to enlist China's support, he gave her a remarkable reply: "We never support lost causes." The lost cause turned out to be, not that of India, but that of the Kuomintang.

BEVIN AND BEN GURION

Madame Pandit had a soft grace, but she carried her chin high and to the side, like a woman who does not intend to listen to back talk. Like her brother, Jawaharlal, she is reputed to have a quick temper. This is perhaps a legacy from their father, Motilal, who once gave his son such a thorough thrashing that the Prime Minister of India still remembers it.

Krishna Menon, a man who can find two obstacles to every solution, rubs her the wrong way. Once she complained to her brother: "Krishna can be charming and irritating, but it's about a quarter of one and three quarters of the other."[2]

Speaking of uninvited guests, Henry J. Kaiser, the shipbuilder, called a press conference in which he presented his ideas for a better postwar world. Mr. Kaiser entered the auditorium at the head of a squadron of press agents and blank-faced engineers who toted rolled-up blueprints on their shoulders like bazookas. The fireworks of flashbulbs turned his entry into something of a Fourth of July celebration.

Mr. Kaiser was a burly man with a stiff back and a soft belly, the picture of a thumping good businessman, who wore his baldness proudly; he even shaved his whole head clean like an Outer Mongolian khan. He related to us his fantastic dream of the city of the future, complete with bathtubs, gas station, town hall, butcher shop, all stamped out of a single piece of material, which could be wrapped, crated, and delivered C.O.D., to be set up overnight, if necessary, in the middle of the Gobi Desert.

A Hungarian journalist, Lucien Aigner, actually found his voice to pick a fault: "Don't you think, Mr. Kaiser, that something more than material comfort is needed for the happiness of peoples?"

Mr. Kaiser looked puzzled: "I don't get the question."

"Spiritual values."

"You mean religion?"

"Yes."

"I don't deal in religion," snapped Mr. Kaiser.

So far as I know, one cannot yet buy a one-piece city at Sears Roebuck; nor did any of the other spectacular schemes which were part of the atmosphere of the postwar days come to fruition. We continued to put our energy and money, and our faith too, into grandiose new weapons of war.

I remember those dreams affectionately. They seem to indicate

[2] *Time*, February 2, 1962.

that with the use of man's imagination the world's economy could, after all, survive disarmament.

Among all who came to San Francisco to be a nuisance, my fondest memories are of the Korean Independence Movement, whose members pinned visiting cards to their coat lapels in order that they should not be taken for Japanese. On one of these cards I read the name of Syngman Rhee, future president of South Korea. Somehow, in a conversation I had with his secretary, Colonel Limb, the notion emerged that Hungarians and Koreans are second cousins. We even found a word, *szilva*, plum, common to both languages. This discovery made us exceedingly happy. We felt that indeed the world is just one big happy family, though regional differences must always exist. We Hungarians, for example, let our sauerkraut rot in a barrel, while the Koreans let theirs rot in the ground. Possibly, in point of stinking sauerkraut, we Hungarians must bow gracefully to our second cousins.

Korea at that time was still under Japanese occupation; but with victory in sight, my Koreans were beginning to feel anxious, not to say suspicious, about their future status as an independent nation. To be sure, the Big Four had promised that their country would be granted full independence "in due course." But, as we have observed before, this is one of the most villainous expressions in diplomatic phraseology, because it can mean anything: one year, five years, ten years, or, in Khrushchev's words, "when the crayfish learns to whistle in the cornfields."

Hitler in 1936 had offered us twenty-five years of peace *alsbald*, in due course, and the whole Queen Anne's Room Conference had hung on the meaning of that expression. By this time, of course, the proper translation was all too clear. It meant, "after a Nazi victory."

There was still another "in due course" that troubled the San Francisco Conference—and it has troubled the United Nations ever since. This phrase had wormed its way into the Dumbarton Oaks proposals which had laid the foundation of the world organization: it said that France should be recognized as one of the Big

Five "in due course." France had not been invited to participate in the talks at Yalta, where the San Francisco Conference had been officially proposed. Therefore, when she was invited to be one of the sponsors of the Conference, France declined the honor.

President de Gaulle has a memory as long as his nose. He developed an allergy to the United Nations that did not improve when the UN meddled in his African affairs.

My Koreans had good reason to run around the Opera House with visiting cards pinned to their lapels and anguish to their faces.

Let us look at the dénouement of this swirl of interests that lapped at the edges of the conference.

Korea escaped a Four Power Trusteeship and was liberated; but "in due course" she was divided at the 38th parallel. India became independent in 1947, and the pretty agitator, Lakshmi Pandit, became ambassador to Moscow and then to Washington. Generalissimo Franco got into the UN.

The Jews got their homeland. Israel was received into the United Nations on May 11, 1949, at Flushing Meadows, and the day was marked by a speech by Moshe Sharett, foreign minister and head of the Israeli delegation, a quiet and most touching speech which Mr. Sharett ended by pointing out how fitting it was that there should be a place in a peace organization for a people that had voiced man's ancient hope: "They shall beat their swords into plowshares and their spears into pruning hooks. Nation shall not lift up sword against nation, neither shall they learn war any more."

Were these words not already engraved in the minds of most men, they might have been hardly heard, because Mr. Sharett's voice became choked with tears. There were sobs from the visitors' gallery, where sat the old Jewish mothers from the Bronx. There were shouts from the huge, bearded Israeli warriors, who jumped over the barriers onto the floor and converged upon their little, weeping delegate. As you might guess, the British, whose good manners survive every calamity, were the first to reach Mr. Sharett's hand. Most of the world's representatives seemed deeply moved as they congratulated him. Only the Arab delegations did not respond, because, at the beginning of Mr. Sharett's speech, they had walked out.

It is my business to notice small things. Outside in the corridor, I saw Moslems shaking Moshe Sharett's hand.

Poland did not get a delegation admitted to the San Francisco Conference, and when the Charter was signed, the space for Poland was left blank. It was filled in four months later, when Stanislaw Mikolajczyk, chief of the London Poles, agreed to return to Warsaw and become deputy premier in a coalition government. Very soon he found himself in the salami-slicing machine; but before the knife could touch him, he fled with nothing but his life.

Today Mr. Mikolajczyk lives in the United States, and is a crony of former Hungarian premier, Ferenc Nagy—another slice of salami.

Besides Poland, there is another phantom of the San Francisco Opera House: Czechoslovakia. In 1945, Czechoslovakia was a Western-oriented sovereign nation and was represented by debonair Jan Masaryk, son of Tomáš Masaryk, founder of the Czechoslovak Republic. Today, Czechoslovakia is a Communist country. Some say Valerian Zorin engineered the coup. Whatever happened, Valerian Zorin became the permanent delegate of the Soviet Union to the United Nations. Jan Masaryk, however, jumped out of a window.

From the window of my office at the United Nations, I can see a poster with a giant cartoon representing Premier Khrushchev in an unflattering position. The "captive nations" set it up. Above it I see nine flags at half mast, and one—that of the United States—flying high. One of the flags is Poland's; another, Czechoslovakia's; and, of course, my native flag of Hungary is there.

Sometimes people ask me: do you think Hungary will ever get its freedom back?

Everybody will get his freedom back. Freedom is not man-made. It is an instinct, a biological necessity of life, which no state or manifesto can suppress. Sooner or later a dictator is bound to come up against the Supreme Dictator, life itself. It is a long and tortuous process, but inevitably everyone must get his freedom back.

I lived at the Palace Hotel, where the gurus of the press, the thunderbolts of the radio, and the mother superiors of Hollywood were housed. Here dwelt Walter Lippmann, with a face as neatly laid out as the garden of the Louvre, whose big brown eyes, so well and widely set, seem astounded, penetrating, and timid all at once. James Reston looks like a sleepy pussycat which would never miss a mouse. There was Westbrook Pegler, erect as the Washington Monument, and shrill Walter Winchell, delegate from Mr. and Mrs. America.

Bob Considine looked at the world with the direct gaze of a watchdog; he struck me as a man who believes in miracles but just doesn't think they are going to happen. Delicate Alice Hughes walked through the motley crowd like an Easter lily in a flea market. Roundish Earl Wilson covered himself with glory by asking Molotov at a press conference how to spell vodka. After the question had been translated by meek Pavlov, Molotov replied: "I like your pronunciation," and scooted out of the room.

Lawrence Spivak of the television program, *Meet the Press*, looked quick and sharp as a chicken hawk. Edgar Mowrer's face bore an expression of delicate dismay. Kingsley Martin of the *New Statesman* had dark shadows around his eyes like a man who never sleeps at night and rinses his eyes with black coffee in the morning. Geneviève Tabouis, who will live to be the Grandma Moses of journalism, flitted like a butterfly from journalist to journalist; her earlobes were always so transparent that for forty years I have feared she would not live to see the morning.

The stars of Hollywood had come running to see the celebrities of politics. Here was Hedda Hopper with a hat like a vegetable stand and sandy eyes. Possibly she regretted the absence of the Cecil B. DeMille touch at the conference, for I heard her exclaiming in the hotel bar: "This is the most boring clambake I ever went to." Louella Parsons navigated the crowds with some difficulty, like a Mother Goose pregnant with human-interest stories. Ebullient Orson Welles temporarily sported a Van Dyke beard, and was temporarily married to Rita Hayworth. Bedroom-eyed Charles Boyer lived down the corridor from me. This male sex symbol of his time seemed to me to be a man handcuffed to rehearsed elegance. I noted in his favor that he had left his toupé at home.

The Hollywood Hungarians were represented by Peter Lorre, on-screen a poisoned jello, but off-screen a blancmange so mild that you could cure your ulcers with it.

The strangest bird in San Francisco was the Armenian-Canadian photographer, Yousuf Karsh, who looked like the little top man on a pyramid of acrobats from Tiflis; and he had curly locks at the back of his head. He took me to the famous restaurant, Omar Khayyam's, headquarters of George Mardikian's shish-kebab empire. Mardikian has an endearing habit of wandering from table to table among his guests and deciding whether they deserve to be presented with a bill or not.

In some ways, artists and photographers are antipodal. The camera is a machine. It has no opinion about its model. It registers but a single moment in time, whereas the pencil is free to compile in one drawing various dynamic aspects of a face which cannot be seen simultaneously.

But when the camera is in the hands of a photographer of Karsh's caliber, it becomes, like the pencil or the brush, just another tool of art. I am sure that before he takes a picture, Karsh studies his model; he evolves an opinion about him. He is a patient man. He moves lights and waits until his model has naturally assumed a position that brings into relief the essential shapes of his face—those that will express a synthesis of the model's personality as Karsh sees it.

In a world that has no time to stand and stare, and in which so many artists are up to their tails in abstractions, it would not dumfound me to know that camera portraits like those by Karsh would be looked back upon in the future as the great master-pieces of our time.

The main battle fought at San Francisco was that of the small powers against the veto-privilege of the great powers. This battle

was lost before it began. The method of voting in the Security Council had been agreed upon two months earlier in Yalta, and that was the end of that. Churchill had expressed perfectly the point of view of great powers with regard to small ones: "The eagle should permit small birds to sing and care not whereof they sing."[3]

The fight against the eagles was led by a plump bird, Herbert Vere Evatt, foreign minister of Australia, and he waged it twenty-four hours a day, causing ambassadors to run around with diplomatic pouches under their eyes. I drew Bert Evatt sitting on

[3] *Time*, March 29, 1958, p. 28.

the side of his unmade bed, and I would never have caught him sitting at all except that his personal secretary, Sam Atyeo, held him down for me.

Australian politicians, whether of the Conservative or Labor parties, are a species apart. They tend to burst with common sense and do what comes naturally. They call a spade a "spoid." Sam Atyeo had a streak of Bohemianism, having spent some time in Montparnasse, where he studied painting. Once at dinner with him and other members of the Australian delegation, a lady tossed into the conversation a remark that she had heard that Australians are mostly descendants of deported convicts. It is true that Australia was first colonized by the inhabitants of England's overflowing prisons, including the notorious Newgate; but somehow this lady's remark did not contain a smile. An icy silence ensued, which was broken by Sam Atyeo. "When I was a little boy we had a cabbage patch surrounded by a wire fence. One morning I heard my grandfather shouting; 'Sam! Come to the window!' I saw my grandfather standing in the cabbage patch holding a shotgun. He fired into the air and at that moment one hundred kangaroos jumped over the fence. My grandfather said to me: 'And they deported me for stealing just one rabbit in Liverpool.'"

Sam now lives in Sète, in southern France, where he raises roses and sells them to the perfume industry, living proof that diplomacy leads to everything, provided one quits in time.

There were plenty of reminders that the San Francisco Conference was not a peace conference. It could not be, for there were no victors yet to dictate terms. Many of the delegates wore military uniforms, and there were wounded soldiers in the audience with crutches beside them.

While the delegates in the committee rooms struggled with the twelve hundred amendments submitted to the Charter, while journalists struggled to report everything in plain language, while conference followers of every kind ran around in search of a future, I found a window on the war. It was a little movie house reserved for delegates and the press where films were shown that were sent to the delegations straight from the battle fronts, and they arrived just as they had been processed in makeshift laboratories in foreign fields. There was no time to translate captions; these were in Russian, French, Italian, or there were none at all —but the images were explicit enough.

Generally this theater was empty. The conference was bogged down in procedure. But here was the substance.

I saw the first films of a liberated concentration camp. It was Maidenek in Poland, and there were gold teeth and children's shoes and women's shorn hair, all the pathetic bits of himself a human being may leave behind to be discovered when the crematorium yawns. I did not believe what I saw. I thought they must have been atrocity films manufactured for the occasion. After all, a hole in the wall is no proof that cyanide gas ever came out of it; a crematorium was not proof that children had been thrown in alive. When fifty thousand people live in a concentration camp, many die.

But then there was the evidence of Auschwitz, Belsen, Buchenwald, Ravensbruck. I saw the lawyer, the doctor, the bookkeeper, the grocer, the adolescent lad in striped rags, clinging to chicken wire with eyes aghast in black sockets, reduced to the common denominator of their skeletons; and bulldozers shoveling great mounds of naked corpses into mass graves. How was it possible? And how is it possible that today there are some who applaud this sort of thing and ask for an encore?

It seems to me that anti-Semitism on the lips of my generation, which saw these films, is contemptible. But anti-Semitism on the lips of the young is a warning that part of our moral selves which we pass on to other generations is still lagging in the middle ages. We must identify that part and change it. The Freedoms we seek are indivisible. If they don't exist for everybody, they don't exist at all.

Here in the UN theater I saw the hanging of Mussolini. Bodies lay helter-skelter on the ground, and on the top of the heap was Il Duce, his face kicked to a pulp. An old woman bent down and spat on him. A wire was attached to his boots, and slowly his body was raised to an iron crossbeam on a garage. From it they dangled the Duce upside down, his arms flung stiffly apart like a pig at market, his shirt fallen over his face, leaving his belly naked. Next to him they strung up another man whose face I recognized with horror as one I had drawn in Pallanza: Achille Starace. Mussolini had been annoyed with him for wearing a distinguished-service medal without having earned it. He had earned it now.

Then they hanged Mussolini's mistress, Clara Petacci, by her pretty legs. In that indecent scene there was a queer touch of decency. Some charitable soul had pinned her skirt between her legs to keep it from falling away from her body.

That afternoon, in the foyer of the San Francisco Opera House, I met Paul Boncour, who in the tragic thirties was France's delegate to the League. Once he had made a speech in the Chamber of Deputies in which he called Mussolini "Caesar of the Carnival." Mussolini was furious, and this remark earned Boncour lasting enemies in France.

Now he was old and deaf. Like Ismet Inonu, he had developed an all-purpose response to whatever was said to him: *"Merci beaucoup, merci beaucoup."*

We shook hands, and I told him the news. *"Monsieur le Président,* do you remember when in the Chamber you called Mussolini 'Caesar of the Carnival'? An hour ago I saw Caesar hanging by his feet."

Paul Boncour pumped my hand and said: *"Merci beaucoup, merci beaucoup."*

I saw another film from the Russian front, on the battle of Budapest.

The siege of a city is, as the saying goes, a dull affair. When you have seen one, you have seen them all. Walls crumble; howitzers, set up in apple orchards, bark; and tanks crawl through deserted streets with huddled soldiers on either side. Someone throws a hand grenade into a cellar, and like cigarettes out of a machine, out comes the enemy, hands up.

War is a movie badly produced and repetitious, played by underpaid ham actors. But when you know the setting, when you might imminently recognize one of the extras, it is a terror to watch. Somewhere in the tumbling rubble of Budapest there were people close to me, my sisters and their families. When an apartment house crumbled like an almond cookie, I wondered if they were hiding in the cellar, or even if any single explosion I saw before my eyes might be the last for them.

The captions of the film were in Cyrillic letters. To compound confusion, a commentator explained in Russian what I could plainly see: Marshal Malinovsky, looking like his own Neanderthal ancestor, barking orders; the Hungarian high brass signing surrender papers; a Russian soldier setting to rights a sign post that had been shot down. The word BUDAPEST was written on the sign post. But then the soldier took a piece of chalk out of his pocket, and slowly, in clear letters, he wrote: БУДАПЕШТ.

I recalled a story told to me by Lipot Herman, a Hungarian painter who in 1914, in the early months of World War I, was an artillery officer in Poland. Two peasants appeared at the edge of a forest and made signs that they wished to talk to him. "Herr Lieutenant," they asked, "how does the war go?"

"We have captured ten thousand Russians."

"How many generals?"

"Four generals."

"What are you going to do now?"

"I guess we'll bombard Lemberg."

"The main street too?"

"Yes."

The two men became pensive. One said: "What a pity for those nice people."

This is the phrase that came to my mind as I saw the familiar

THE VOLGA BOATMEN

squares and streets of Budapest mauled and lost in the billowing dust and smoke—it was a pity for those nice people.

The most tragic details of a cataclysm are little things. Photographers know this and do not fail to focus on a child's toy in a gutter, or a cat wandering aimlessly in the ruins of a bombed city:

humble reminders of lost love in the immensity of God-willed or man-made devastation. Some unknown Russian photographer sent a picture arrowing to my heart. It was a wooden store sign hanging from half a wall, on which was written: Rigler Jozsef, Ede. This was the name of the man who manufactured the ink with which I learned to draw.

In time the mails opened up and letters began to arrive from Budapest telling me what had been left out of the Russian films. In the thick of battle, the officers of the Red Army had not desisted in their efforts to impose elegant hygiene upon the simple sons of the steppes. The Russian soldiers, by regulation, washed and shaved daily. Even as they bayoneted Nazis, their hair was impeccably groomed and their fingernails were manicured. But the water they needed for these embellishments, they obtained from the men's rooms by pulling the chain.

Man can be disciplined long before he can be civilized.

These soldiers developed a special fascination for the miraculous gadgets that go tick-tock on people's wrists, and they harvested them by the thousands. One met soldiers with wrist watches all over their forearms, hand to elbow. A friend of mine was stopped by a Russian officer who indicated by signs that he wished to exchange his gold wrist watch for my friend's cheap metal one. The swap consummated, my friend found himself in possession of an expensive watch that simply needed winding. The Russian officer had not known how to do it.

They were farm boys from the heart of a barren land, and they liked babies. One soldier broke into an apartment and shouted: "Let's have those watches!" The noise woke the baby, who began to cry in its cradle. The Russian looked dumfounded. He shouldered his tommygun, picked up the baby with care, gently patting it on the back, and paced the room murmuring: "Babushka . . . babushka." When the baby finally went back to sleep and he put it back into the crib, he turned to the family and whispered: "Now let's have those watches."

Armies rape. Victorious armies rape more than defeated ones, and the Russians were victorious. They raped even in Yugoslavia, a friendly country. Hungary was an enemy country. The Russian boys, fundamentally good natured, had an ideologically impeccable argument: I have liberated you; you are a woman; I need a woman; if you refuse me what I need, you are an enemy of the people. Because soldiers are predominantly muscular, callous to the feelings of others, they could not understand that mothers and husbands did not share this reasoning. Paul Lukas, the actor, told how his old grandmother handled one of these aborigines who was intent on raping a young girl in her kitchen. "What do you think you're doing, you big ox? Look at the girl! She's only a child. Sit down and have a bite with us instead!"

The soldier not only sat down and had a bite with them, but during the rest of the days of terror he patrolled the street in front of the house to make sure that none of his comrades succeeded where he had failed.

Marshal Voroshilov visited the studio of my practical friend, the sculptor, Zsiga Strobl, and saw a statue Zsiga had prepared in memory of Istvan Horthy, son of the Regent, who had been killed in action. Zsiga was able to sell it to him to be set up on Mount Gellert as a monument to the memory of the liberating Russian soldier. Bitter about the rapes, the people of Budapest call this the "Monument to the Unknown Father."

The Russians did not disturb the statue of St. Gellert the Martyr, who had introduced Christianity to Hungary before being packed in a nail-lined barrel and rolled down the side of the mountain that bears his name. Today, St. Gellert and the Monument to the Unknown Father stand in peaceful co-existence on the slopes overlooking Pest.

The first news that my family in Budapest were safe reached me by way of England. A British soldier, W. S. Davison, had escaped from a prison camp and gone into hiding in Budapest, where he spoke to them. I asked the soldier what I could send him in return for this wonderful news. What does an Englishman need most in a country which for six years has been drained of all good things, whose schoolmates have been cut down, who has survived his San Gabriele?

My boon was once a lemon. His were three tennis balls. "It is great to know," he wrote, "that once again we (wife and I) can play!"

What does a Hungarian want whose house is smashed and his land scorched? Fearing that my family were starving, I sent them a great box of surplus C-rations. I got back an indignant letter.

"What kind of a package is that? We broke our teeth on the dog biscuit, the soap doesn't make suds, and it smelled like chocolate. But the worst was the stuff you call pemmican. We gave it to a gypsy, who uses it for resin for the bow of his fiddle."

Well, it was good to know Hitler had left a gypsy alive in Hungary and that he was playing his fiddle.

It was May 8, 1945, the day of victory in Europe. Hitler was defeated and half the world took a long step from war to peace.

In the Veterans' Building the committees observed a minute of silence. On the stage of the War Memorial Opera House the representatives of the Big Four addressed the world on the radio.

Secretary of State Stettinius said: "May God give us the strength of wisdom and of purpose to keep faith with the living and the dead."

Anthony Eden said: "We greet the dawn of our deliverance."

Bidault of France said: "In another theater, another equally tragic act is taking place."

Wellington Koo of China said: "Only on the surrender of Japan can we of the United Nations say that victory is complete."

Looking down from the press gallery, I saw many delegates with their noses buried in the local newspapers. After the meeting, I went down to the floor and picked up a copy of the San Francisco *Call-Bulletin* which had been left on one of the plush seats. I still have it. After two decades, it makes exhilarating reading.

On the front page, at the top in blue, is a heading: CEASE FIRING TODAY. Underneath, in a flame of red four inches

high: V-E DAY. Then in black: TRUMAN AND CHURCHILL
ANNOUNCE SURRENDER.

Then:

HAPPY BIRTHDAY: "V-E Day—Victory in Europe—that was the
present President Truman received from the Allies today on his
sixty-first birthday."

Inside we read:

U.S. LIBERTY BELL RINGS OUT STORY OF GERMAN DEFEAT: "Once
again the cracked chime in the cradle of liberty was called to
service to tell the world of a freedom-loving nation's victory over
an aggressor . . . the bell croaked out in dull tones the joyous
news."

REPORT BODY BELIEVED HITLER FOUND IN BERLIN: "A Russian
General said the body of a man identified as Adolf Hitler was
found in the ruins of Berlin." [And I first saw him through a hole
in a ruined wall.]

The Fuehrer had designated Admiral Karl Doenitz as his successor.

TEXT OF DOENITZ SWAN SONG: ". . . We must face facts squarely.
The unity of state and party does not exist any more. The party
has left the scene of its activities . . . the power has been transferred to the occupying authorities. It is up to them to confirm
me in my function." [They confirmed him for ten years for war
crimes.]

LEAVES TOMORROW: "Russia's Foreign Commissar [Mr. Molotov]
will leave San Francisco tomorrow for Moscow." [This was the
very moment when Yalta began to fade.]

NAZI WAR COST U.S. 732,270 CASUALTIES

PRUSSIAN GENERAL SIGNS, BEGS MERCY FOR GERMAN PEOPLE [The
name of the general was Gustaf Jodl. He was hanged at Nuremberg. But the German people were granted mercy.]

STERN WARNING TO JAPAN: "Mr. Truman . . . pledged that the Japanese face 'utter destruction' . . . unless they too lay down their arms in unconditional surrender." [This was before Hiroshima. The president must have known something we did not know.]

FIRST V-E BABY IN SAN FRANCISCO: "Born 5:37 a.m., St. John's hospital, 1055 Pine Street, to Mr. and Mrs. McKinley Hall, 659-A Natoma Street. The name, *Victoria Elizabeth*."

SAYS HORSERACING BAN OFF TOMORROW [The fellow who rang out this glad news was one William Hornblower.]

Yes, May 8, 1945 was a great day for Mr. and Mrs. McKinley Hall, for the bookmakers, and for the world.

After each world war, man looked into the mirror and saw a fool.

It was evident at San Francisco, as it had been at Versailles, that world order could not be had without concessions to national sovereignty; also, that world order cannot operate without concessions from national sovereignty.

We have fought two world wars. Millions are dead, and a new generation of children is growing up in the prospect of imminent death. Yet we are still unable to make the equation: how much national sovereignty is worth how much world order?

When, therefore, on June 26, 1945, a round table was set up on the stage of the San Francisco Opera House and the flags of nations were placed in a semicircle around it, with the emblem of the United Nations rising like a sun behind them, and one by one the heads of delegations were invited to step on the stage and set their signatures to the United Nations Charter, they signed a lame document. They remind me of the man who broke his glasses and continued to wear the frames without lenses, saying: "It's better than nothing!"

When Mr. Stettinius walked onto the stage, the entire United States delegation trooped in with him. A little apart from them and to the side stood the former vice president who had become the new president of the United States, Harry S. Truman. While the Charter was being signed, Mr. Truman waved and smiled happily into the camera. Afterwards he went fishing.

Five years later, almost to the day, on June 25, 1950, there fell on Mr. Truman the burden of the first hard decision to risk flesh against an aggressor. The Korean War was called "Truman's War," but I think it was one of the most important wars of modern times. It was the war the League failed to fight when Japan invaded Manchuria, or when Mussolini went into Ethiopia, or when Hitler occupied the Rhineland. The Tass correspondent, Rothstein, had once told me that the beauty of the Franco-Soviet Pact was that in case of war Hitler would not know what Stalin would do.

Since Truman's war, the beauty of the United Nations Charter is that a would-be aggressor does not know what the United Nations will do. In the case of the League he knew that the League would do nothing.

Ever since the Charter was signed, we have had wars—little wars. If the United Nations can do nothing else for us but keep little wars little, it seems to me that the candle is worth the flame.

But who wants these wars? Do you want them? Do I? Does your wife want them, or the children of Yuri Gagarin or those of Colonel Glenn?

Somebody must want them badly because we get them.

In the forty years that have passed since the late Azmi Bey touched my shoulder and baptized me a political caricaturist, I have noticed with dismay that a switch of types has occurred among diplomats, politicians, and statesmen. The rocky face of the Muscleman has taken over. The more delicate face of the cerebral man shows up with increasing frequency among the military. In consequence, while diplomatic behavior has deteriorated, military behavior has improved. It is a historic curiosity, surely, that the Marshall Plan bears the name of a conquering hero!

Recently, in the delegates' lounge of the United Nations, a soldier-diplomat was asked: "Your Excellency, shall I call you general or ambassador?" He replied: "Call me general. There are too many cheap ambassadors around here."

Since World War II alone, we have seen the ruthless competition of strong men for power in the Soviet Union; the conniving of the salami slicers in Central Europe; angry Arab nationalism; the contest for the driver's seat in the newly liberated African and Asian countries. It is not possible that all this should have happened without bringing to the surface individuals of predominant muscularity in physique and intent. They emphasize their aggressive beliefs by growing beards, wearing fatigue uniforms, carrying riding whips to the United Nations rostrum, using arrogant and brazen language. These are the International Musclemen. They can be found on both sides of the Iron Curtain, wherever people feel that their lives depend on the virtues of such Musclemen: their courage, perseverance, yearning for action, love of discipline and unity, and their heroic readiness to kill and to be killed.

There's no doubt in my mind that it is the International Muscleman who always finds good reasons for starting—in the words of Frederick the Great—a "crisp and joyous war." It is this fellow me must examine to find out what primitive impulses underpin his reasoning, because it is here, in the temperament of the Muscleman, that we find the germ of war.

By nature the Muscleman is predatory, self-righteous, self-centered. Convinced of his superiority, he is incapable of self-criticism. Insight and reflection do not delay his actions, and in an adverse situation the first thing that comes into his mind is to solve the problem by force. His intellect and impulses form a solid block. If he changes his mind, he reverses himself totally, with epileptic suddenness.

He seeks the friendship of others of his kind, but he often turns on his cronies. He can harbor vengeance for a long time. His cunning is that of the tiger: a prelude to violence. He forgives himself any excess of violence because he believes himself to be an instrument of providence. A mystic fog envelopes his brain.

The highest aspiration in his life is power. He uses power to stay in power.

After a young peer had made his maiden speech in the House of Lords, he approached an older member for criticism. "Excellent, young man, excellent," said the elder peer. "You make your points clearly and forcefully. But if I may—with your permission—make a suggestion? Sometimes *hesitate*."

The trouble with the Muscleman is that he never hesitates. Whatever he does in the economic, social, or cultural fields, he is convinced that he is right, and he sees it as his mission to shape our environment to his notions. The society described by George Orwell in 1984 is nothing but the absolute Muscleman-society.

I believe that one of the chief problems of our time is the taming of the International Muscleman. We must learn to recognize him by his looks, words, and deeds. Ultimately, we must outgrow our need and our admiration for his reckless leadership. We have come to a stage in history when the whole world has to pay too tragic a price for the blunders of such men. Somehow, we must accept a framework, such as a strong United Nations with in-built shock-absorbers, which can protect us from the aggression of rapacious men, whose muscular notions are as anachronistic in the atomic age as are those of a knight in armor.

"Until philosophers bear rule, states and individuals will have no rest from evil." Plato said this five hundred years before Christ.[4]

For six decades I have been drawing my fellow man and poking fun at his face. The truth is that the human face expresses for me the essence and the drama of life. It fills me with awe, worship, and compassion, because if man is God's most perfect creation, it is in his face that you can see it.

It is so accomplished in its details, so quick and eager to laugh. Why must some ogre always come and impress on it the mask of grief?

[4] Plato's *Republic*, Book IV, Classic Club edition, p. 387.

Index

Abd-el-Krim, 110
Abetz, Otto, 318, 349
Acheson, Dean, 395, 397
Addis, Sir Charles, 173
Adenauer, Konrad, 77
Adler, Stella, 423
Aga Khan, 125, 243, 246, 351
Ahrens, Russian press officer, 112
Aigner, Lucien, 425
Alexander I, King of Yugoslavia, 184, 189
Alexander, First Lord of the Admiralty, 191
Alexandra, Queen, 106
Alfieri, Dino, 288, 301, 302
Ali Hassan, 117
Allen, Jay, 348
Aloisi, Baron Pompeo, 312
Alvar, Maharaja of, 243
Ambedkar, Bhimrao Ramji, 242
Amundsen, Roald, 185
Anderson, Marian, 411
Anne, Queen, 328
Apponyi, Count Albert, 140, 144, 185
Arco, Count Anton, 204–5
Aristotle, 199
Arnold, Karl, 203
Astor, Nancy, 259, 262, 330–4, 336
Astor, Waldorf, 330, 333
Ataturk, Kemal, 101

Atyeo, Sam, 432
Avenol, Joseph, 324, 343
Azmi Bey, 91, 110, 442

Baker, Josephine, 300
Balbo, Italo, 292
Baldwin, Stanley, 107, 162, 336
Balfour, Lord Arthur, 128, 162, 400
Bankhead, Senator John Hollis, 386
Barde, Henry, 157, 158, 287
Bardossy, Artur, 332
Barnum, Phineas T., 71
Baroda, Gaekwar of, 243, 246, 248–50
Baroda, Maharani of, 246–7, 250
Barry, Sir Charles, 330
Barthou, Louis, 184, 319
Bartlett, Vernon, 177
Beam, Jacob, 347
Beck, Jozef, 313
Beer, Max, 116, 190, 324
Beerbohm, Max, 194, 195
Beneš, Eduard, 137–8, 144, 188, 313, 319
Beneš, Madame, 137
Ben Gurion, David, 418, 424
Berchtold, Count Leopold, 61
Bernard, Tristan, 192
Bernhardt, Georg, 190
Bernstorff, Count Johann Heinrich, 252

Berthelot, Philip, 175
Bevin, Ernest, 424
Bhopal, Nawab of, 245
Bidault, Georges, 439
Bierce, Ambrose, 346
Bikaner, Maharaja of, 244
Bleuler, Eugen, Dr., 186, 292
Blomberg, Werner von, 233–5
Bloom, Sol, 408, 410
Blum, Léon, 320, 408
Boas, Franz, 385, 386
Bohlen, "Chip," 411
Bompard, Maurice, 120
Bompard, Madame, 120
Bonnet, George, 352
Bordonaro, Italian admiral, 191
Boris, Ladislas, 65, 69
Bormann, Martin Ludwig, 211
Bose, Chandra, 262
Bourgeois, Léon, 142, 150
Bradley, Fred, 397, 398
Bramo, Capitano, 308–12
Branco, Rio, 128
Branting, Hjalmar, 127, 150, 151
Brennan, Andrew, 397
Briand, Aristide, 153, 154, 155, 160,
    162, 163–4, 167, 168, 169, 170,
    171, 172–7, 188, 191, 202, 212,
    214, 265, 401
Brinon, Count Fernand de, 110
Brody, Iles, 56, 360, 361
Bromfield, Louis, 246, 250
Brooks, Van Wyck, 380
Brouckère, Louis de, 106
Broun, Heywood, 80
Broz, Josip (Tito), 388
Brueckner, Wilhelm, 345
Brüning, Heinrich, 228, 233
Bulganin, Nikolay, 106
Bunche, Ralph, 411
Byrnes, James F., 387

Cadbury, Edward, 279
Cadorna, Luigi, 289, 290, 291
Caesar, Julius, 157
Cambronne, Pierre, 103
Campione, director of CIGA, 293,
    294, 301, 302
Canham, Erwin D., 370, 402
Carron, Jeanne-Andrée, 246

Catherine II (the Great), Empress,
    113
Cavallero, Ugo, 235
Cecil, Viscount Robert, 127, 132,
    142–4, 150, 151, 265, 406
Cecil, Lady, 143
Chamberlain, Sir Austen, 106, 138,
    143, 153, 154, 155, 159, 160, 161,
    162, 164, 170, 172, 188, 334, 401
Chamberlain, Lady Austen, 154, 159
Chamberlain, Joseph, 106, 336
Chamberlain, Neville, 153, 162, 326,
    334–6, 349, 350, 353, 371, 407,
    421
Charles I, Emperor, 11, 12, 22, 23,
    26, 43, 268, 299
Chiang Kai-shek, 415
Chiang Kai-shek, Madame, 415
Chicherin, Boris Nikolayevich, 106,
    113–16, 420
Chichibu, Prince, 221
Churchill, Sir Winston, 162, 164,
    172, 259, 327, 330, 336, 337, 372,
    382, 401, 431, 440
Ciano, Costanzo, 301
Ciano, Count Galeazzo, 59, 153, 289,
    292, 301–3, 314
Clark, Mark, 220
Clark, Senator James Beauchamp,
    386
Clausewitz, Karl von, 93
Clemenceau, Georges, 50, 64, 128,
    190, 192
Clive, Robert, 270
Collis, Maurice, 333
Colonna, Jerry 156
Colson, Everitt, 314
Combes, Emil, 324
Comert, Pierre, 188
Confucius, quoted, 232
Connally, Senator Tom, 387, 408,
    410
Conradi, Russian émigré, 94, 116
Considine, Bob, 429
Cooch Behar, Maharani of, 249
Coolidge, Calvin, 168
Cordier, Andrew, 411
Cosgrave, William Thomas, 131, 166
Coubertin, Baron Pierre de, 94, 95,
    96
Coudenhove-Kalergi, Count, 186

Coxey, "General," 379, 380
Cranborne, Lord, 404, 405, 406–7
Crane, Ralph, 322
Cromwell, Oliver, 157
Curtius, Julius, 401
Curzon, Lord, 88, 89, 91, 92, 96, 97–103, 107–8, 109, 118, 120, 121, 124, 264, 405

Da Costa, Vasco, 182
Daladier, Edouard, 349, 353
Dali, Salvador, 156
Dandurand, Hon. Raoul, 138
Daranyi, Bela, 297, 298, 303
Daranyi, Kalman, 297
Darbhanga, Maharajiraja of, 245
Darling, Lord, judge, 271
Darwin, Charles, 199, 201, 337
Dashill, Sam, 213
Dass, Jarmani, 244, 246, 269, 275
Daudet, Léon, 171
Daumier, Honoré, 48, 235
David, Jacques Louis, 315
Davidson, Jo, 109, 332
Da Vinci, Leonardo, 194, 195, 199, 375
Davis, Jeff, 379
Davis, Norman H., 219
Davison, W. S., 438
Dawes, Charles G., 173, 191
Dedijer, Vladimir, 403
De Gaulle, Charles, 220, 427
Dell, Robert, 324, 343, 370
Del Piombo, Sebastiano, 44
Del Vayo, Alvarez, 316, 321, 423
Demaître, Edmond, 190, 192
DeMille, Cecil B., 430
Derso, Alois, 47, 111, 112, 117, 118, 124, 130, 135, 136, 159, 161, 165, 176, 178, 183, 188, 189, 195, 214, 216, 220, 225, 277, 279–82, 293, 295, 297, 313, 320, 321, 322, 323, 331, 337, 346, 347, 349, 350, 353, 356, 357, 363, 367, 376, 377, 388, 389, 395, 396, 397, 402
Deskaheh, Chief of Cayuga Nation, 147–9, 345
de Valera, Eamon, 166, 350–1
Dewall, Wolf von, 205
Dholpur, Maharaja of, 244, 269
Díaz de Olivera, Horacio, 186

Dietrich, Sepp, 211
Dingman, Mary A., 238
Diogenes, 129
Disraeli, Benjamin, 264
Doenitz Admiral Karl, 440
Dollfuss, Engelbert, 284
Doré, Gustave, 18
Dozsa, Gyorgy, 4, 5
Drake, Sir Francis, 371
Drummond, Sir Eric, 128, 129, 135, 318
Du Bochet, Paul, 324
Dugo, André, 64, 76, 79, 365
Dulles, John Foster, 411, 412, 413, 419
Dyson, Will, 280
Dzerzhinsky, Felix, 106

Eaton, Charles A., 411
Ebert, Friedrich, 207
Eden, Sir Anthony, 143, 313, 337–8, 342, 343, 350, 404, 416, 423, 439
Eichmann, Adolf, 230
Einstein, Albert, 265
Eisenhower, Dwight D., 158
Eisner, Kurt, 106, 204, 205
Elizabeth II, Queen, 332
Engels, Friedrich, 51
Epp, Ritter von, 71, 84, 85, 205, 298
Erzberger, Matthias, 170
Eszterhazy, Prince Miklos Jozsef, 44
Eszterhazy, Prince Paul, 44
Evatt, Vere, 431

Farago, Ladislas, 345
Farinacci, Roberto, 302
Farley, James, 367, 377, 378
Faulhaber, Cardinal, 67
Feuchtwanger, Lion, 76
Fischer, Louis, 263
Fitzgerald, D., 166, 168
Fitzpatrick, Daniel Robert, 157
Flandin, Pierre-Etienne, 173, 284, 285, 286, 290
Ford, Henry, 330, 390
Ford, Mrs. Henry, 330
Forrest, Wilbur, 109
Franchet d'Esperey, Marshal, 46, 50
Franco, Francisco, 316, 349, 427
Franqui, Belgian financier, 173
Franz Ferdinand, Archduke, 61, 330

Franz Josef, I, Emperor, 8, 36, 59, 106
Fraser, Leon, 173
Freddi, Luigi, 301, 302
Frederick the Great, 443
Frick, Wilhelm, 64, 65, 86, 207, 209
Friedheim, Ernst, 195, 196, 260
Fry, C. B., 240
Funk, Walter, 340

Gabor, Zsa Zsa, 63
Gagarin, Yuri, 442
Gamelin, Marie-Gustave, 235
Gandhi, Devadas, 262
Gandhi, Mahatma, 240, 242, 243, 248, 250, 253–68, 271, 276, 277, 283, 406, 407
García-Palacios, Carlos, 217, 218
Garner, Jack, 367, 386
Garroni, Marquis de, 96
Garu, Sir Annepu Patro, 252
George III, King of England, 153
George V, King of England, 243, 264
Gellert, Saint, 4, 438
Gellhorn, Martha, 15
Gershwin, George, 126
Gibbon, Edward, 124
Gibson, Hugh, 191, 218
Gilbert, Prentiss, 346–7, 354
Gildersleeve, Virginia, 411
Gingrich, Arnold, 348
Glass, Senator Carter, 386
Glendower, Owen, 264
Glenn, John H., 442
Goebbels, Josef, 86, 153, 207, 211, 231–3, 288, 352, 436
Goering, Hermann, 73, 83, 84, 86, 207, 208, 234, 316, 327, 333, 340, 352, 436
Goya, Francisco, 194
Grandi, Count Dino, 191, 235, 280
Greco, El, 64, 182, 220, 375
Greiser, Arthur, 211, 341–4
Greiser, Frau, 341
Grew, Joseph C., 122, 216, 223
Gromyko, Andrey, 409, 420
Gross, Ernest, 194
Grumbach, Salomon, 408
Guffey, Senator Joseph F., 386
Gunther, John, 189, 370

Gustaf V, King of Sweden, 330
Gutt, Camille, 173

Hadik, Janos, 24
Hahn, Emily, 136
Haig, Earl, 220
Haile Selassie, 313–16, 320, 321, 404
Hailsham, Lord (Douglas McGarel), 162
Halifax, Lord, 46, 253, 349, 350, 352, 404–7
Hammarskjold, Dag, 146
Hammurabi, 199
Hanfstaengl, Ernst, 79–82, 87
Hankey, Sir Maurice, 191
Hapsburg, Otto von, 11
Hard, Bill, 189
Harding, Warren G., 125, 218
Hawariate, Teclé, 313
Hayashi, Baron Gonzuke, 120, 223
Haydn, Joseph, 44
Hayworth, Rita, 430
Heine, Thomas Theodore, 227
Heines, Edmund, 86, 209, 210, 211, 298
Heltai, Eugen, 53
Hemingway, Ernest, 15, 349
Henderson, Arthur, 187, 191, 237
Henie, Sonja, 87
Henry IV, King of France, 350
Henry VIII, King of England, 268
Hepburn, Arthur J., 219
Herczeg, Geza, 47, 111
Herman, Lipot, 435
Hess, Rudolf, 39, 68, 69, 71, 340
Heydrich, Reinhard, 229, 230
Hillman, William, 189, 370
Himmler, Heinrich, 64, 227, 229, 230, 344
Hindenburg, Paul von, 231, 234, 339
Hitler, Adolf, 59, 60, 64, 69–74, 78–81, 84, 85–6, 89, 110, 128, 138, 153, 156, 157, 161, 202, 205–7, 209, 211, 227, 228, 229, 230, 231, 233, 234, 235, 262, 265, 283, 285, 288, 299, 303, 313, 316, 317, 318, 321, 323, 325, 326, 327, 328, 329, 332, 334, 335, 338, 339, 341, 343, 344, 345, 349, 353, 357, 358, 370, 371, 385, 394, 421, 422, 426, 436, 439, 440, 442

Hoare, Sir Samuel, 313
Hofmann, Hans, 75
Hoffmann, Heinrich, 74
Hooton, Earnest, 387
Hoover, Edgar, 388
Hopkins, Harry, 367
Hopper, Hedda, 429
Horthy, Nicolas, 46, 58, 59, 61, 63,
    193, 332
Hughes, Alice, 429
Hull, Cordell, 228, 335, 367
Hunyadi, Janos, 5
Hutton, Barbara, 113, 299
Hydari, Sir Muhammed, 252, 253
Hyderabad, Nizam of, 253
Hymans, Paul, 151, 228

Imredy, Bela, 332
Inonu, Ismet, 101–7, 119

Jacob, Hans, 229
Jaipur, Maharani of, 249
Jamali, Fadhil, 416
James, Edwin L., 109
Jaszi, Oskar, 59
Jaurès, Jean Léon, 106
Jefferson, Thomas, 139, 381
Jessup, Philip C., 411
Jevtitch, Yugoslav foreign minister,
    319, 388
Jèze, Gaston, 320, 321
Jinnah, Ali, 266–8
Jodl, Gustav, 329, 440
John XXIII, Pope, 15
Johnson, Albin, 358, 363
Johnson, Senator Hiram, 386
Joseph, Archduke, 43
Jouhaux, Léon, 408
Joyce, Peggy Hopkins, 368–9
Jung, Kushru, 269

Kahr, Gustav von, 207
Kaiser, Henry J., 425
Kalinin, Mikhail Ivanovich, 106
Kaltenborn, H. V., 189
Kamenev, Leo, 106
Kant, Immanuel, 413
Kapurthala, Maharaja, 125, 244, 293
Karan Singh, 275
Karolyi, Count Michael, 42–6, 48,
    50, 51, 56, 61, 111

Karsh, Yousuf, 430–1
Kashmir, Maharaja of, 241, 269–72,
    275–6
Kassem, Karim, 416
Kelen, Margit, 247
Kellogg, Frank B., 168–71, 214
Kennedy, Hugh, 131
Kennedy, John F., 166, 342, 414
Kent, Duke of, 332
Khan, Zafrullah, 251
Khrushchev, Nikita, 53, 54, 136, 157,
    158, 210, 236, 342, 408, 419, 420,
    426, 428
King, Alexander, 111
King, Thomas, 238
Kinizsi, Paul, 4, 5
Kinkaid, Thomas C., 219, 235
Kipling, Rudyard, 270
Kirby, Rollin, 157
Kisch, Egon Erwin, 192, 193
Kitchener, Lord, 220
Kiss, Kasimir von, 34, 35, 40
Klar, Zoltan, 363
Klee, Paul, 393
Koestler, Arthur, 63
Koo, Wellington, 415–16, 423, 439
Kossuth, Lajos, 6, 54, 166
Kretschmer, Ernst, 196–8, 210, 260
Krutikov, Alexey D., 396
Kun, Bela, 46, 49, 51, 53, 56, 58,
    112, 193, 332
Kung, Mme., 415

Lagarde, Comte, 133, 134
La Guardia, Fiorello H., 363–5
Landowsky, Paul, 147
Landru, 31
Lange, Christian L., 150
Lemarr, Hedy, 297–8, 303
Lambrino, Zizi, 134
Lamont, Thomas, 173
Lassalle, Ferdinand, 51
Laughton, Charles, 268
Laval, Pierre, 284–6, 290, 313, 321
Lawrence of Arabia, 333
Léger, Alexis, 175
Léger, Fernand, 392
Lehmann, Baron, 134
Lenin, Nicolay, 52, 56, 106, 116,
    145, 180, 408, 419
Leroy, Amé, 175

Leygues, Georges, 191
Liddell Hart, Basil Henry, 189
Lie Trygve, 391
Lifar, Serge, 300
Lincoln, Abraham, 85, 203, 316
Lincoln, Mary, 85
Lindbergh, Charles, 330, 350
Linder, Bela, 43, 46
Limb, Colonel, 426
Lippmann, Walter, 429
Liszt, Franz, 126
Litvinov, Maxim, 180, 188, 319, 353, 420
Lloyd George, David, 64, 78, 263, 278, 335, 350
Lodge, Henry Cabot, Jr., 382
Lodge, Henry Cabot, Sr., 382, 408
Londonderry, Lord, 350
Lorant, Stefan, 202–4
Lorre, Peter, 63, 430
Lothian, Lord, 262, 329, 333
Loucheur, Louis, 175
Low, David, 157, 225, 279
Luce, Clare Boothe, 346
Luce, Henry, 396
Ludendorff, Erich, 171
Lugosi, Bela, 63
Lukas, Paul, 438
Lukasich, Baron Geza von, 25
Lunacharsky, Anatoly, 106
Lupescu, Magda, 134
Luther, Hans, 155, 173, 339
Luther, Martin, quoted, 249
Lux, journalist, 324, 349
Lytton, Lord, 216, 224–6, 228

MacArthur, Douglas, 219
McCarran, Senator Pat, 387
McCloy, John J., 411
McDermott, Michael, 397
MacDonald, Ramsay, 188, 191, 242, 290
Machiavelli, Niccolo, 201, 367
McGarrah, Gates W., 173
MacSweeny, Marquis, 131
Madariaga, Salvador de, 236
Maisky, Ivan Mikhailovich, 106
Major, Henry, 7, 195, 365
Makonnen, Endalkatau, 403
Malavya, Pandit, 262
Malik, Charles H., 416

Malinovsky, Rodion, 435
Mandl, Fritz, 297, 299
Mann, Heinrich, 76
Mann, Thomas, 76
Mao Tse-tung, 157, 408
Mardikian, George, 430
Marie Antoinette, 315
Marie, Queen of Rumania, 134
Marshall, George C., 442
Martin, Joseph W., 378
Martin, Kingsley, 429
Martin, William, 214
Marx, Karl, 51, 106, 145, 318
Mary, Queen of England, 332
Masaryk, Jan, 428
Masaryk, Tomáš, 261, 428
Massigli, René, 175
Massip, Jean, 191
Mathieu, George, 237
Matsudaira, Viscount Tsumeo, 221, 223, 236
Matsui, Iwane, 222
Matsuoka, Yosuke, 227, 228, 349, 388
Matthias Corvinus Rex, 5
May, George, 374
Maxwell, Elsa, 293
Mdivani, Prince, 112–14, 116
Mellon, Andrew, 173
Menaka, dancer, 246, 247
Menemencioglu, Numan, 106
Menon, Krishna, 251, 425
Mikhailovitch, Draja, 388
Mikolajczyk, Stanislaw, 428
Miliukov, Pavel, 180
Molnar, Ferenc, 63, 225, 294–7, 350
Molotov, Vyacheslav, 408, 417–21, 423, 429, 440
Moltke, Helmuth von, 391
Montez, Lola, 270
Montgomery of Alamein, Viscount, 220
Morgan, J. P., Jr., 173
Morrison, Herbert, 335
Morrow, Dwight, 173, 191
Motta, Giuseppe, 323
Mowrer, Edgar, 429
Mudaliar, Sir Ramaswami, 251
Mueller, Adolf, 66–8, 69–74, 202
Mussolini, Benito, 59, 88–92, 97, 108, 118, 121, 130, 140, 150, 151, 153,

155–8, 205, 227, 235, 236, 284–
92, 298, 301, 302, 303, 308, 309,
312, 313, 316, 318, 319, 323, 329,
349, 353, 370–2, 417, 434, 442
Mussolini, Edda, Countess Ciano,
302, 303

Nadolny, Rudolf, 229
Nagano, Osami, 222–3, 235, 388
Nagy, Ferenc, 428
Naidu, Sarojini, 243, 247–8, 258,
261, 262
Nansen, Fridtjof, 96–7, 150
Navanagar, Jam Saheb, Maharaja of
("Ranji"), 239–41
Negrín, Juan, 316, 423
Nehru, Jawaharlal, 249, 269, 275,
423, 424
Nehru, Motilal, 424
Neiger, restaurateur, 188, 189
Neiger, Madame, 193–4
Nelson, Lord, 220
Nemanov, journalist, 180
Nemes, Marcel von, 64
Neurath, Baron von, 231
Nicolson, Sir Harold, 99, 101, 109
Nietzsche, Friedrich, 69
Nightingale, Florence, 367
Noailles, Anne, Comtesse de, 126,
136, 248
Noel-Baker, Philip, 15, 128
Norman, Montague, 173
Norstad, Lauris, 220
Noue, Jehan de, 125
Nur, Riza, 94
Nypels, George, 157–8, 287

Orczy, Baroness, 95, 282
Ord, James B., 219
Orwell, George, 444

Paderewski, Ignace, 126
Pandit, Madame, 421, 423–4, 427
Pankhurst, Sylvia, 190
Papen, Franz von, 228, 338–40
Parker, Gilbert, 173
Parsons, Louella, 430
Patiala, Maharaja of, 241, 243, 245,
269
Pattani, Sir Prabhasankar, 241
Paul-Boncour, Joseph, 213, 214, 404,
434

Pavlov, interpreter, 421
Pegler, Westbrook, 429
Pellé, Maurice, 122
Pepper, Claude, 387
Perkins, Frances, 367
Pertinax, 190
Petacci, Clara, 434
Peter, King of Yugoslavia, 356
Pilsudski, Joseph, 135, 319
Plato, quoted, 444
Poincaré, Raymond, 8, 64, 88, 89,
91–92, 108, 121, 124, 168, 169
Politis, Nicolas, 151
Polya, Tibor, 25, 52
Porta, Giambattista della, 199
Pospischil, Oberstabsarzt, 36, 40, 41
Price, Ward, 205
Princip, Gavrilo, 7

Quesnay, Pierre, 173

Rakosi, Matthias, 53, 54
Rakovsky, Christian, 112–15
Randolph, John, of Roanoke, 139,
141
Rathenau, Walter, 113, 170
Rauschning, Hermann, 341
René de Bourbon Parme, Prince, 299
Reston, James, 429
Reventlow, Count Ernst, 208
Rhee, Syngman, 426
Rheinbaben, Baron von, 231
Ribbentrop, Joachim von, 151, 153,
327, 329, 335, 352, 356–7, 436
Richthofen, Baron Manfred von, 83
Rickover, Hyman, 220
Riddleberger, James W., 347
Robinson, Senator Joseph Taylor, 387
Rockefeller, John D. III, 391
Rockefeller, John D., Sr., 391
Rockefeller, Mrs. Mary Todhunter,
391
Rockefeller, Nelson, 391–2, 411
Roda Roda, 76, 77
Rodionov, Russian admiral, 417
Roehm, Ernst, 68, 71, 84–6, 211,
234, 298
Rogers, Will, 189, 225–6, 252
Romulo, Carlos P., 403
Roosevelt, Franklin Delano, 172, 228,

330, 366–7, 370, 372, 381–4, 400, 401
Roosevelt, Theodore, 346
Rosenberg, Alfred, 71, 78–9, 327
Rothermere, Lord Harold Sydney, 318, 332
Rothschild, Maurice de, 125
Rothstein, Tass correspondent, 325, 442
Rumbold, Sir Horace, 107, 119, 121
Runciman, Lord Walter, 162
Russell, Bertrand, 413
Rykov, Alexey, 408

Saito, Jiro, 223
Saito, Hiroshi, 221, 223
Salandra, Antonio, 127, 151
Saracco, Maurice, 33, 41
Sarraut, Albert, 325
Sato, Naotake, 119, 120, 213, 214, 216
Saud, Prince Abdul Aziz ibn, 416
Saud, King ibn, 416
Sauerwein, Jules, 109, 328
Savonarola, 143
Schacht, Hjalmar, 173, 340
Scheonberner, Franz, 318
Schirach, Baldur von, 340
Schmidt, Paul, 161, 229, 421
Schnabel, Fritz, 235
Schuschnigg, Kurt, 298
Scialoja, Vittorio, 158
Sennep, Jehan, 157
Sethna, Sir Pheroze, 252
Seybold, Eugen, 65, 67, 69, 70, 72, 74, 202
Sharett, Moshe, 427, 428
Shaw, G. B., 190, 192, 225, 265, 277, 330, 332, 333
Sheean, Vincent, 110
Sheldon, W. H., 197, 200, 201
Shirer, William, 189, 370
Simon, Sir John, 143, 213, 277–81, 319, 350, 415
Simonds, Frank, 225
Simonds, George S., 219
Slade, Madeleine, 255, 263, 264
Slocombe, George, 157, 158
Smith, Frederick C., 397
Smuts, Jan Christiaan, 142, 265, 408
Snowden, Sir Philip, 173

Sobani, Umar, 259
Sofianopulos, John, 403
Soong, T. V., 415
Spaak, Paul-Henri, 382, 408
Spencer, Herbert, 413
Spivak, Lawrence, 429
Staempfli, Father, 78
Stalin, Joseph, 52, 69, 116, 138, 153, 172, 265, 321, 323, 325, 326, 329, 334, 344, 371, 401, 418, 421, 422, 436
Stambulisky, Alexander, 180
Starace, Achille, 290, 434
Starhemberg, Princess Fanny, 299
Starhemberg, Prince Ernst Rudiger von, 298–9
Stassen, Harold E., 410
Steed, Wickham, 109
Steffens, Lincoln, 56, 109
Stettinius, Edward R., Jr., 411, 439
Stevenson, Adlai, 413, 414
Steward, George, 159, 161, 191
Stimson, Henry, 218
Stockard, Charles R., 96, 199
Stowe, Leland, 370
Strang, William, 329
Strasser, Gregor, 86, 209
Streicher, Julius, 86, 340
Streit, Clarence, 324, 370
Stresemann, Gustave, 153, 154, 155, 160, 161, 164, 167, 168, 171, 172, 188, 229, 401
Stresemann, Frau, 163
Strobl, Stefan, 201
Strobl, Zsiga, 332, 438
Strong, George V., 219
Sun, Madame, 415
Sun Yat-sen, 415
Suvich, F., 290
Swanson, Senator Claude A., 218
Sweetser, Arthur, 225
Szechenyi, Count Istvan, 281
Szechenyi, Count Laszlo, 281–2
Szvatopluk, King, 4

Tabouis, Geneviève, 189, 429
Taft, Robert A., 382–3
Taft, Mrs. Robert A., 382
Tagore, Rabindranath, 133
Takahashi, Korekiyo, 223
Tannhäuser, art dealer, 317

Tardieu, André, 191
Temperley, Harold William Vazeille, 229
Thomas, Albert, 106, 144–7
Thomsen, Hans, 338, 339, 370
Thompson, Dorothy, 370
Thompson, Llewellyn E., 347, 411
Tihanyi, Lajos, 50–1
Titulescu, Nicolas, 137, 138–42, 234, 319, 321, 342
Toepffer, Adolphe, 320, 322
Tojo, Hideki, 219, 265, 388
Tolbert, "Tieless" Joe, 379, 385
Toscanini, Arturo, 15, 22
Toti, Enrico, 305, 306
Trotsky, Leon, 84, 106, 116, 145, 180
Truman, Harry S., 342, 401, 440–2
Twain, Mark, 294
Tyrrell, William, 101, 109, 119

Udet, Ernst, 83–4
Unden, Osten, 127

Vacarescu, Elena, 135, 248
Vago, Joseph, 193
Vandenberg, Arthur H., 382, 408–10
Vanderbilt, Gladys, 282
Vanderbilt, Grace, 330
Vandervelde, Emile, 408
Van Zeeland, Paul, 323, 324
Venizelos, Eleutherios, 94
Ventzoff, Simon, 235
Verdi, Giuseppe, 126
Vertès, Marcel, 47, 52, 365
Victor Emmanuel III, King of Italy, 314
Vishinsky, Andrey, 420

Volpi, Count Giuseppe, 301
Voltaire, quoted, 413
Voroshilov, Klimenty, 332, 438
Vorovsky, Russian diplomat, 113–14, 116–17

Wagner, Adolf, 84
Wagner, Richard, 126
Wagner, Robert F., 378
Wakatsuki, Reijiro, 191
Wallace, Edgar, 254
Weber, Tibor, 258
Weiss, Bernhard, 210, 211
Weizsäcker, Baron von, 231
Welles, Orson, 430
Whalen, Grover, 363
Wilde, Oscar, 193, 195
Wilhelm II, Emperor, 8
Willert, Sir Arthur, 191
Willkie, Wendell, 378, 383–4
Wilson, Earl, 429
Wilson, Woodrow, 45, 46, 50, 64, 78, 126, 127, 129, 130, 142, 151, 381, 408
Wilson, Mrs. Woodrow, 126, 163
Winchell, Walter, 429

Yen, W. W., 212, 315
Yoshizawa, Japanese diplomat, 212, 312
Young, Owen D., 173, 220, 221

Zetland, Lord Lawrence John Lumley, 99, 101, 108
Zimmern, Sir Alfred, 194
Zita, Queen, 11
Zorin, Valerian, 428

A Note about the Author

EMERY KELEN was born in Hungary in 1896 and was educated at art schools in Budapest, Munich, and Paris. His brilliant career as a political cartoonist began in 1922, when he emerged from three and a half years in World War I to find himself in Lausanne, sketching Poincaré, Venizelos, Mussolini, Ismet Pasha, and Lord Curzon from close up. Mr. Kelen's caricatures, often done in collaboration with his friend Derso, decorate the walls of the Palais des Nations, the League of Nations Museum in Geneva, and many other government buildings and libraries throughout the world. His limited editions, containing portraits of statesmen of our time, are collector's items and are considered to be documents of contemporary history. His exhibition in London was opened by the Foreign Minister in the presence of ambassadors to the Court of St. James. Much of his work was done at the League of Nations and at international conferences elsewhere. From 1948 to 1957 he was television director and producer at the United Nations, where he continues to broadcast weekly. Productions he directed for the United Nations have won many awards, including the Emmy, Peabody, Ohio state awards. Mr. Kelen is now a syndicated writer, artist, and consultant for television. His work has appeared in leading newspapers and magazines in this country, incuding *The New York Times*, The New York *Herald Tribune*, *Fortune*, *Esquire*, *The Christian Science Monitor*.

June 1963

A Note on the Type

THIS BOOK is set in ELECTRA, a linotype face designed by W. A. Dwiggins (1880-1956). This face cannot be classified as either modern or old-style. It is not based on any historical model, nor does it echo any particular period or style. It avoids the extreme contrasts between thick and thin elements that mark most modern faces, and attempts to give a feeling of fluidity, power, and speed.

Composed, printed, and bound by
The Haddon Craftsmen, Inc., Scranton, Pa.
Typography and binding design by
VINCENT TORRE